Overcoming the Saving Slump

Overcoming the Saving Slump

How to Increase the Effectiveness of Financial Education and Saving Programs

EDITED BY ANNAMARIA LUSARDI

THE UNIVERSITY OF CHICAGO PRESS   CHICAGO AND LONDON

ANNAMARIA LUSARDI is professor of economics at Dartmouth College and a research associate at the National Bureau of Economic Research. She is a member of the Advisory Board for the Pension Research Council at the Wharton School, a member of the Scientific Committee of the Center for Research on Pensions and Welfare Policies, Turin, Italy, and a recipient of the Fidelity Pyramid Prize.

The University of Chicago Press, Chicago 60637
The University of Chicago Press, Ltd., London
© 2008 by The University of Chicago
All rights reserved. Published 2008
Printed in the United States of America
17 16 15 14 13 12 11 10 09 08   1 2 3 4 5

ISBN-13: 978-0-226-49709-9 (cloth)
ISBN-10: 0-226-49709-7 (cloth)

Library of Congress Cataloging-in-Publication Data
Overcoming the saving slump : how to increase the effectiveness of financial education and saving programs / edited by Annamaria Lusardi.
    p. cm.
Includes index.
ISBN-13: 978-0-226-49709-9 (cloth : alk. paper)
ISBN-10: 0-226-49709-7 (cloth : alk. paper)
    1. Saving and investment. 2. Finance, Personal—Study and teaching. I. Lusardi, Annamaria.
HC79.S3094 2009
332.6—dc22

                    2008016093

⊗ The paper used in this publication meets the minimum requirements of the American National Standard for Information Sciences—Permanence of Paper for Printed Library Materials, ANSI Z39.48–1992.

Contents

IV. Learning from the United States and Other Countries

Preface

This volume is the result of a project that started several years ago and that culminated in two conferences held at the Rockefeller Center at Dartmouth College in October 2005 and at the National Bureau of Economic Research (NBER) and the Royal Sonesta Hotel in May 2007. I would like to thank the participants of the first conference, "How to Increase the Effectiveness of Financial Education: Lessons from Economics and Psychology," and the participants of the second conference, "Improving the Effectiveness of Financial Education and Saving Programs," for many suggestions and comments. I would like to thank in particular John Ameriks, Nava Ashraf, Andrew Biggs, Kathleen Camilli, Shawn Cole, Gary Engelhardt, Peter Fisher, Benjamin Friedman, Robert Ganem, Sarah Holden, Jeffrey Kling, André Laboul, Brigitte Madrian, Olivia Mitchell, Shaun Mundy, Karen Pence, Pamela Perun, Michael Pompian, James Poterba, John Tatom, Maarten van Rooij, Kent Womack, and David Wray for their discussions of and comments on the chapters in the book. Special thanks go also to Ted Beck, John Campbell, John Gannon, Dan Iannicola, Joseph Peri, and Peter Tufano. I am especially grateful to Martin Feldstein for hosting one of the conferences at the NBER and to George Daly for guiding my research. This book could not have been written without the support of Dartmouth College, and I am very grateful to Dean Carol Folt and Dean Michael Mastanduno for supporting this project, Andrew Samwick for financing the first conference held at Dartmouth College, and to all of my colleagues in the Economics Department for their encouragement and collaboration. Punam Keller at the Tuck School of Business and Adam Keller at the Finance and Administration Division at Dartmouth College have been invaluable collaborators, and this book has benefited a lot from our joint work. I am grateful to my editor, David Pervin, for many suggestions and comments. I am also grateful to Audrey Brown and Kate Flaim for editorial help and to Mark Christman and Kory Hirak for helping me organize the conferences. I would like to dedicate this book to my parents who, while in Italy, have followed each step of the process and know everything about *il libro*.

Introduction

Annamaria Lusardi

The saving rate has fallen precipitously in the United States in the past two decades. From a level of about 8 percent in the mid-1980s, the personal saving rate has dropped to zero and has remained at that level for several years. While the aggregate statistics only describe a specific measure of saving, there is additional evidence at the microlevel that the slump in saving is for real. Many Americans are doing little or no saving and get close to retirement with no wealth apart from their homes. There is research that shows that many households are not preparing adequately for retirement and will have to cut back spending when they stop working.

This situation is worrisome because, more than ever before, individuals are in charge of their own financial security after retirement. With the shift from defined benefit to defined contribution pension plans that has occurred over the past twenty years, individuals increasingly have to decide how much to save and how to allocate their pension wealth. The necessary decisions are daunting and are made more difficult by the increased complexity of financial instruments: investors have to deal with a vast array of new and sophisticated financial products. Saving decisions now require not only that individuals be informed about their pensions but also that they be knowledgeable about finance and economics.

This book explores the many challenges that have arisen in the transition to a pension system that requires more individual responsibility, focusing on microbehavior as it relates to saving and pensions and illustrating the impediments and barriers to saving. The issues at hand have not gone unnoticed. The financial industry, employers, and the government have taken initiatives to promote saving and financial education programs. The financial industry has developed and provided products that can better suit the needs of investors. In addition, financial education programs have been offered in different forms and from different institutions. This book tries to evaluate whether and how these developments are helping to effectively bridge the way to a new system. The authors who have contributed to this book have analyzed programs that are in place, examined available investment products, and taken a close look at the experiences of countries that have privatized their pension systems or experienced changes in their social security systems. From these contributions emerge what is perhaps the most important objective of this book: to provide suggestions on how to improve the effectiveness of these programs and products, thereby enabling the United States to make the transition to this new system more smoothly.

As many of the chapters in the book show, the problems are many and the challenges are daunting, but programs can be designed to change saving behavior and overcome the saving slump now facing so many individuals. We have a wealth of information to rely on, as we are increasingly understanding the variables at play in providing and promoting effective saving and financial education programs. That information should make effective financial education and improved saving increasingly possible as we move further into a very different pension landscape.

Transitioning to a New System

The economic changes that are occurring in the pension landscape in the United States are well documented in the first chapter of this book, which traces the increase in individual retirement accounts (IRAs) that has occurred in recent decades. Workers retiring before the 1980s relied mainly on Social Security and employer-sponsored defined benefit pension plans for their retirement income. The situation is very different for current workers, who will reach retirement with a different mix of funds—not only Social Security and defined benefit plans, but also personal retirement accounts, including IRAs and defined contribution pension plans. And future retirees' pension funds will be even more different, as defined benefit plan coverage continues to decline and the prevalence of personal accounts continues to grow. One characteristic of these accounts is that individuals are in charge of deciding how much to contribute and how to allocate their retirement savings. The increase in the number of individuals with their own retirement accounts means that personal finances will be more directly affected by the fluctuations in financial markets, by the new instruments that these markets offer, and by individuals' financial decisions. Low contribution rates or allocation in conservative assets can quickly translate into inadequate accumulation for retirement.

In addition to deciding how much to save and how to allocate pension wealth, individuals must decide how to decumulate their wealth when they reach retirement. A comprehensive retirement-planning strategy requires consideration not only of how to save but also how to spend down wealth. Individuals have to make sure that retirement wealth lasts a lifetime. With the shift that has taken place from defined benefit to defined contribution plans, how to spend down is becoming an increasingly important part of retirement planning.

The risk of individuals making costly mistakes in their saving and retirement planning is real. Throughout the book, evidence is presented of widespread financial illiteracy in the United States. Chapter 9 documents that high school students are sorely in need of financial knowledge. Data from five surveys conducted by the Jump$tart Coalition for Personal Financial Literacy from 1997 to 2006 show that only a small minority of students score above a passing grade in financial literacy. Low scores are not only pervasive among high school students but have changed little over time. Older individuals are also unfamiliar with basic concepts of economics and finance, such as the power of interest compounding, the effects of inflation, and the workings of risk diversification. Many individuals in custom-made surveys (chapter 7) report that not having enough knowledge about finance/investing represents one of the most difficult elements of their saving decisions. Consistent with this fact, many individuals consider themselves simple investors, reporting they know little about bonds and stocks.

Findings discussed in chapter 2 point to the same concern about a lack of information about critical components of retirement savings. This chapter documents widespread lack of information about pensions. Using data from 1983, when pensions were still dominated by defined benefit plans, the authors find a mismatch of 40 percent between respondents' and employers' reports of pension plan information. Data from 1992, when defined contribution plans became more prevalent, show a similar finding, with the mismatch between employers' reports and workers' reports at close to 50 percent. Looking closely at a more recent time period, in which defined contribution pension plans have become even more prevalent, does not change the main finding. As recently as 2004, data show systematic differences in the plan type reported by workers versus the plan type reported by employers. Thus, irrespective of the change in the pension landscape in recent decades and the increase in individual responsibility, the level of knowledge about pensions has not improved much, if at all.

Workers misreport their pension plan type because they do not understand their pension well, and today's workers need—at minimum—an adequate level of understanding of pensions in order to be sure of funding them properly. As chapter 2 notes, as defined benefit plans take on more features of defined contribution plans, morphing through cash balances or related plans, and as defined contribution plans take on more characteristics of defined benefit plans, offering opportunities for annuitizing benefits and imposing defaults and participation requirements, it will be much harder to clearly determine pension plan types, making it even less likely that workers will be able to understand, correctly identify, and adequately fund their plans.

Lack of information and lack of financial literacy provide fertile ground for financial errors. Left to their own devices, employees may choose to invest their pension wealth in either too conservative or too aggressive assets. An analysis of portfolio allocation from a large sample of Vanguard investors offers compelling evidence that portfolio allocation can be improved upon. Chapter 4 examines data from over 2,000 defined contribution plans and nearly 2.9 million 401(k) participants and uses a simple stoplight color scheme—green, yellow, and red—to classify participants' portfolio selection. Only about 45 percent of investors are determined to be doing fine, constructing "green" portfolios with equity allocation consistent with expert advice. More than a quarter of participants hold "yellow" portfolios that are either too aggressively invested in stocks or too conservative. The remainder hold "red" portfolios with more serious errors, including zero participation in the stock market and overexposure to single-stock risk.

Another potential error individuals make is the failure to annuitize. As mentioned earlier, in addition to deciding how much to save and how to allocate pension wealth, workers today must decide how to decumulate their wealth when they reach retirement. One of the difficulties in deciding how to spend down is uncertainty about the length of life. Life annuities are designed to eliminate longevity risk by allowing an individual to exchange a lump sum of wealth for a stream of payments that continue as long as the individual (and spouse) is alive. Economic theory suggests that life annuities can substantially increase welfare by eliminating the risk associated with uncertain life expectancies and providing consumers with a higher level of lifetime consumption. Yet, as described in chapter 6, most individuals do not annuitize as often as the theory predicts, if they annuitize at all.

There are a number of reasons why it may be optimal not to annuitize. While many are plausible, they can hardly explain why the annuity market is so small and why so many individuals do not annuitize at all or buy specific annuity contracts, nor can these behaviors be explained by classical economic theory. In fact, researchers have recently resorted to explanations more grounded in behavioral economics to explain lack of annuitization. For one, annuities are rather complex products and those who lack financial sophistication may not fully appreciate the benefits of annuities. Moreover, annuities may be viewed as a gamble. Without the annuity, investors have some money for certain, but in buying an annuity, they face the possibility of not receiving much from it if they die too soon. Other explanations are offered in chapter 6 as to why individuals are reluctant to buy annuities. But to increase the size of the annuity market, we need to do a better job in understanding the barriers that prevent people from buying annuities.

Note that financial products are often sold via intermediaries. In principle, this could facilitate financial transactions and overcome some of the challenges that investors face. However, relying on recommendations of financial service industry professionals creates a number of potential problems for individuals. For example, a financial advisor may steer an individual's decision in a direction that serves the interest of the advisor and not the client. This practice may be accentuated by the presence of a collateral benefit for the advisor—a side payment or the provision of some ancillary service.

This problem—yet another of the issues surrounding the saving slump—is labeled "the trilateral dilemma in financial regulation" and is rather pervasive, as discussed in detail in chapter 3. Trilateral dilemmas appear in multiple areas of the financial service industry and are particularly important in regard to pension plans. An example of a trilateral dilemma is the practice of pension consultants advising employer sponsors on the selection of investment options and then receiving compensatory payments from the financial services firms that offer 401(k) programs. These arrangements pose risks to participants in 401(k) programs because consultants may be tempted to guide plan sponsors to less than optimal service providers. Compensatory payments may also increase the cost of 401(k) programs, resulting in higher fees and expenses for participants.

It is still unclear whether side payments are necessary or if they simply prey on individuals' lack of sophistication and general confusion about financial matters. Moreover, because side payments are often associated with ancillary services, it may be easy for individuals to overlook them. For example, workers focused on making a decision about how much to save and how to best invest those savings may spend little time in checking the fees of the funds offered by their plan. Furthermore, costs from side payments can be blended into pricing arrangements that cover many services and may be hard for individuals to identify and disentangle.

Putting concerns about issues such as the trilateral dilemma aside for the moment, it is important to point out that the financial industry has developed several products that can overcome problems of widespread financial illiteracy as well as limit portfolio mistakes. While there are now many such products, this book highlights a few important examples, such as managed accounts, life-cycle funds, and specific types of annuities.

As proposed in chapter 4, rather than investing on their own, investors could turn funds over to managed accounts. These types of accounts can substantially limit the magnitude of portfolio mistakes. For the small group of investors followed by the authors who shifted to managed accounts, changes in portfolio allocation are staggering. Prior to the adoption of an advisory service, nearly half of the group's participants were at three focal points in their investment allocations: zero equities, 100 percent equities, and 50 percent equities. After the advisory service took control of participant accounts, the distribution changed dramatically; extreme equity holdings were entirely eliminated and equity holdings became more normally distributed, with a mean equity exposure at a healthy 76 percent.

Portfolio errors of the sort made by individuals followed in chapter 4 can be costly, causing investors to potentially forfeit over 350 basis points in expected return. Studies have shown that these errors are most prevalent in specific groups of participants, often those with lower income, lower wealth, and less financial sophistication.

Another of the financial products that investors can resort to for better saving outcomes are life-cycle funds. These funds change asset allocation based on the age of the investor. As investors approach retirement, the life-cycle fund shifts from riskier assets, such as stocks, to more conservative assets, such as bonds. As noted in chapter 5, there are several reasons "age-based investing" is appropriate. First, stock returns are much less volatile when they are measured over long holding periods, evidence that has been used to promote a strategy of buying and holding equities for the long term. Second, one of the significant elements of total wealth is human capital, or the present discounted value of expected future earnings. This has important implications for asset allocation. As illustrated in chapter 5, for an investor who knows his income in advance with perfect certainty, human capital is equivalent to an implicit investment in bonds. When the investor is young and has many years of labor income ahead of him, but little wealth saved, human capital represents a large share of total wealth. This investor should tilt his financial portfolio toward equities. However, as the investor ages, the value of human capital declines, while financial wealth grows. Thus, the investor will want to attenuate the tilt toward risky assets in his financial portfolio. Life-cycle funds can be particularly well suited for personal retirement accounts, which are investments for the long run. Moreover, life-cycle funds greatly simplify investment decisions and help investors to decrease exposure to risk as they approach retirement.

In the annuity market as well, new products have been developed to overcome some of the barriers to investing in these contracts. For example, several insurance companies have begun to offer products that are designed to provide life annuity payments that start at some future date (deferred payout). This may overcome the psychological barrier that people face in converting a large stock of wealth into income at the time of retirement. Other contracts offer guaranteed minimum withdrawals. Typically, they guarantee that the individual will receive a fixed percentage of the account balance at a specific point in time. These guaranteed withdrawals may help overcome investors' desire to avoid regret or the perception of annuities as a gamble. There are also annuities that offer some liquidity, providing an option to withdraw, on a one-time-only basis, up to 30 percent of the expected value of the remaining annuity payments based on mortality rates at the time of purchase.

While the development of products to help investors make better decisions is important, it cannot offset the importance of investors' abilities to understand how to use the products to effectively save and invest. Such understanding requires a certain level of financial knowledge and grasp of information, yet both have been shown to be lacking in the U.S. population. In this environment, it is clear that financial education can play a critical role in overcoming the saving slump. Both employers and the government have promoted financial education programs to help workers in their saving and investment decisions. Programs have taken many different forms. In the United States, many firms—particularly large ones—have begun to offer retirement seminars to workers. Moreover, financial education programs have been implemented into many high school curricula.

There exists, however, a debate about the effectiveness of financial education programs. Certain issues that arise in the evaluation of these programs can be seen in chapter 8, which discusses a well-crafted financial education program implemented by Teachers Insurance and Annuity Association–College Retirement Equities Fund (TIAA-CREF). One of the problems in evaluating such a program is that those attending seminars are not necessarily a random group of employees. Thus, it is hard to determine whether it is the seminar that affects behavior or whether seminar participants display specific characteristics that are already conducive to that behavior. Moreover, seminars result in improved financial planning for only a small fraction of participants. In the TIAA-CREF program, for example, only about 12 percent of seminar participants reported that they planned to change the age at which they would retire, and close to 30 percent planned to change their retirement income goal. Furthermore, intentions may not necessarily lead to actions. When surveyed several months later, many participants reported failing to follow through on their plans. Another feature highlighted in the study was that the effect of the seminar was rather different among demographic groups. For example, rather pronounced gender differences in saving behavior were seen. Before attending the seminars, women displayed less confidence in their abilities to attain their retirement goals than men. But women were substantially more likely than men to increase their expected retirement age and to alter their retirement goals. Thus, evaluating the effects of seminars on the whole population of participants may understate the impacts on specific groups.

More disappointing results are provided by financial education programs in high schools. As reported in chapter 9, students who took courses in financial management or personal finance did not do any better on financial literacy tests than students who did not take any such course, a finding that does not seem to be explained by the caliber of the students who enroll in such courses, the training of the teachers, or the quality of the courses.

The mixed evidence of the effectiveness of financial education programs has led some to question whether it is worth trying to improve financial literacy. However, the evidence gathered in this book—while highlighting the challenges we are currently facing in the saving arena—shows that financial education programs can be effective and that increased literacy does result in better saving habits. Given the complexity of current financial instruments and the financial decisions required in everyday life, individuals need to know how to read and write financially. Just as it is impossible to live well and operate effectively without being literate, that is, without knowing how to read and write, so it is becoming very hard to live well and operate effectively without being financially literate. However, increasing financial literacy and promoting saving behavior is clearly a challenge, and it is important to highlight ways to increase the effectiveness of programs designed to address these problems.

How to Increase the Effectiveness of Financial Education and Saving Programs

One of the key objectives of this book is to provide suggestions on how to increase the effectiveness of financial education programs. Effectively designing education and saving programs needs to take into account a number of factors: identification of barriers to effective saving, differences among demographic groups, and flexible program design.

It is critical to identify the barriers individuals are facing when trying to make saving decisions. A variety of barriers are described throughout the book, from lack of literacy to lack of information to behavioral biases. However, this hardly exhausts the list of things that can affect individual behavior. The research that deals with increasing the effectiveness of financial education and saving programs, discussed in chapters 7, 8, 10, and 13, points to a variety of factors that need to be considered. Because individuals differ widely in their barriers to saving, it is important to develop methods to uncover those barriers. In designing effective programs, approaches such as in-depth interviews, focus groups, and ethnographic studies may need to be employed.

The many differences among individuals must also be taken into account for successful implementation of financial education programs. Targeted education programs may better serve the needs of specific groups of the population, such as women, younger and older individuals, and those with low income. Chapters throughout the book document the many differences that exist among these groups.

One-time financial education seminars—typical of the programs offered by many large companies—may simply be insufficient to address widespread illiteracy and lack of information. Chapter 10, specifically, provides evidence that financial education proves to be effective when several hours and sessions of financial education are offered. Moreover, financial education should not be limited to information about financial products. As described in chapter 3, individuals also need to be educated about the intermediaries who influence their selection of financial products and the incentives those intermediaries may face.

When these broader influences on saving education and behavior are considered, more effective outcomes may be seen. Chapter 7 documents improved saving behavior resulting from a customized planning aid designed to stimulate contributions to supplementary pensions for individuals who displayed low levels of information about saving options and reported not knowing where to start in regards to saving. The planning aid has several interesting features. First, it breaks down the process of enrollment in a supplementary pension plan into several small steps, describing to participants exactly what they need to do at each step. Then the aid provides several pieces of information to help overcome barriers to saving, such as describing the low minimum amount of income employees can contribute (in addition to the maximum) and indicating the default fund that the employer has chosen for them (a life-cycle fund). Finally, it contains pictures and messages designed to motivate participants to save. Initiatives such as this indicate that there are innovative and potentially more cost-effective ways to stimulate saving than, for example, relying on tax incentives and employer matches. The chapter also shows that, to both understand and exploit differences in individual behavior, it is important to incorporate concepts of marketing and psychology into economics.

Fundamentally, to overcome the saving slump, as is discussed in chapter 10, it is important to create an infrastructure that promotes saving and asset accumulation. Such an infrastructure would include not only effectively designed financial education and saving programs but also a variety of policies and initiatives to stimulate saving. For example, access to saving opportunities can be fundamental. About half of private sector workers have jobs that do not offer pensions, making it particularly difficult for those workers to accumulate retirement wealth, and it is important to find ways to facilitate saving among those individuals. Low-income households also display little or no saving. However, specific programs targeted to the poor, such as individual development accounts, which are matched savings accounts, seem effective in stimulating saving among this group of the population. Automatic enrollment in pensions also greatly facilitates plan participation and accumulation of retirement wealth. Another important policy demand, given the findings reported in chapter 9, is to prepare young people for financial life. This is a challenging task, and a lot more has to be done to find effective ways to teach financial education in schools. As discussed in more detail in chapter 10, such an infrastructure should pay attention to program design. For example, centralized and efficient accounting, low-cost investment options, and outreach can play important roles in stimulating saving.

Another key point that is illustrated throughout the chapters is that individuals often lack information necessary to make sound saving and investment decisions; thus it is critical to find effective ways to deliver information to consumers. One example of effective delivery is point-of-sale education, which is offered as consumers obtain products. Moreover, we should explore opportunities to provide education at teachable moments. As the program described in chapter 7 shows, new hires are particularly malleable to change, and the start of a new job may provide a good opportunity to implement education programs.

The experiences of other countries offer important lessons for the United States. While the increase in individual responsibility that is required in the system we are transitioning to provides incentives for individuals to become knowledgeable and informed, one has to be cautious about relying simply on individual initiative. For example, lack of understanding of critical components of pensions is a persistent feature, even in economies in which personal retirement accounts have been in place for many years. For example, in Chile, which adopted personal retirement accounts more than twenty-five years ago, there is a remarkably low level of knowledge about pensions. As reported in chapter 11, only 69 percent of participants in the Chilean system indicate that they receive an annual statement summarizing past contributions and projecting future benefit amounts while, in fact, every participant is sent a statement. Less than half of the participants know how much they contribute to the system, even though the contribution rate has been set at 10 percent of pay since the system's inception. Understanding of what workers have accumulated and how their assets are invested is also scanty. For example, just one-third of respondents stated knowing how their own money is invested, and only 16 percent can correctly identify which funds they hold (compared with administrative records).

In Sweden, which implemented comprehensive pension reform during the 1990s, transforming the old public defined benefit plan into a defined contribution plan and implementing a broad public information campaign, the level of knowledge is also not high. The cornerstone of communication of information to plan participants in Sweden is the Orange Envelope. The envelope is sent out annually and contains account information and a projection of benefits. Overall, three-fourths of all participants say they have opened the envelope, although only half report reading at least some of its content. Relying on self-reports of participants, chapter 12 documents that half of participants rate their knowledge of pensions as poor. Moreover, the share of respondents who report having a good understanding of the pension system has decreased over time. Measuring actual knowledge of the pension system from surveys that ask respondents about components of the system confirms the evidence provided by self-reports. Many participants are still unaware of the key principles regarding how benefits are determined, and many overstate the importance of individual accounts.

Another problematic area for U.S. investors, which is validated in looking at the experiences of other countries, is knowledge of commissions and fees. High fees can prevent investors from accumulating adequately for retirement. However, as discussed in chapter 3, fees can be easily overlooked. The experience of Chile provides compelling evidence that this is the case; only a minuscule fraction of pension participants (around 2 percent) seem to know the fees that are charged on their accounts.

The experience of Sweden further shows that when individuals are confronted with a very broad range of funds in which to invest—as many as eight hundred—there can be a substantial increase in information and search costs. In fact, fewer than 10 percent of new participants in Sweden make an "active choice" and choose their portfolios. The large majority invests in a default fund. Thus, it is critically important to design defaults in a way that promotes wise portfolio allocation.

Moreover, widespread evidence of illiteracy is not unique to the United States but is present throughout Organisation for Economic Co-operation and Development countries. Importantly, illiteracy in all countries is particularly severe among certain groups, such as women, those with low income and education, and the elderly. This suggests that these groups are particularly vulnerable to many of the changes that are occurring in modern economies. It also suggests that it is possible to share programs across countries and develop international cooperation in efforts to develop effective financial education programs.

A wealth of information is presented in the thirteen chapters of this book. While some of the contents are technical in nature, the book is intended for a wide audience. Chapters 10 and 13 are particularly suited to readers interested in public policy issues. Readers interested in the legal aspects of financial education and financial advice should refer to chapter 3. Chapters 1 and 2 provide a richness of information, and a number of important statistics, about pensions and the new pension landscape and are particularly suited for an academic audience. Applications of behavioral economics and psychology to saving and financial education programs are discussed in chapters 6, 7, and 13, with specific financial education programs discussed in chapters 7, 8, and 13. Readers interested in managed accounts, life-cycle funds, and annuities should read chapters 4, 5, and 6, and those interested in the outcome of pension privatization and reliance on IRAs should read chapters 11 and 12. Finally, readers with an interest in financial literacy among young adults and in high school financial education programs should read chapter 9.

My aim in editing this book is to illuminate the issues facing so many Americans in regards to saving and retirement planning and to evaluate the existing programs and products that have been designed to facilitate saving. My hope is that such a close look at the situation that individuals, businesses, and policy makers face today will help to provide a foundation to continue to devise effective financial education and saving programs, which can contribute to overcoming America's saving slump.

PART I

The Shift from Defined Benefit to Defined Contribution Pensions and Financial Regulation

CHAPTER ONE

The Changing Landscape of Pensions in the United States

James M. Poterba, Steven F. Venti, and David A. Wise

Introduction

The leading edge of the baby boom generation will reach retirement age in the next few years. Younger members of this generation will continue to retire through about 2030. These retirees will face a very different pension landscape than their parents faced. Workers who retired before the early 1980s relied heavily on Social Security and employer-sponsored defined benefit (DB) pension plans for support in retirement. Those retiring since then have accumulated a mix of wealth in Social Security, DB plans, and various personal retirement accounts, including 401(k)s, individual retirement accounts (IRAs), and similar plans. Balances in these personal account plans for recent retirees are often modest because the retirees were only able to avail themselves of these plans late in their careers.

Future retirees will reach retirement with a very different mix of assets, as DB plan coverage continues to decline and personal account plan coverage continues to grow. This chapter considers the effect of the changing pension landscape on the wealth of future retirees. It reports three key findings. First, the total value of assets in retirement accounts has increased substantially since 1980. Assets in all retirement accounts increased from about 71 percent of National Income and Product Account (NIPA) wage and salary earnings in 1980 to 261 percent in 2005. Thus there has already been a very large increase in the accumulation of savings for retirement.

Although the demographic structure of the population today is different from that in 1980, and this means it is not possible to simply compare the aggregate ratio of retirement wealth to labor income, the increase in the wealth-to-income ratio suggests an increase in the capacity to replace pre-retirement income over this period.

Second, the proportion of employees covered by at least one pension plan has remained about the same over the past twenty-five years, but the proportion covered by more than one plan has increased substantially. The future spread of 401(k) plans and the participation rate of eligible employees will likely depend primarily on the adoption of plans by small firms that currently do not offer pension plans and by employers' adoption of plan features such as automatic enrollment and default options that encourage participation.

Third, our projections show that 401(k) assets will increase enormously over the next three decades. The sum of Social Security wealth and 401(k) assets held by households that reach retirement age in 2040 will be at least twice as large (in real dollars) as the sum of these assets in 2000. Moreover, retirement assets are projected to grow for households all along the distribution of Social Security wealth.

The chapter is divided into six sections. The first section describes the changing pattern of contributions to pension plans over the past twenty-five years. The second section tracks the enormous increase in pension assets over this time period. The third section considers changing participation behavior in pension plans. We emphasize in these three sections the growth of personal retirement accounts and the decline in DB plans. In the fourth section, we discuss the evolving features of 401(k)-like plans and how they compare with DB plans. We also consider some of the more subtle changes within the 401(k) sector that have occurred since the inception of 401(k) plans in the early 1980s. The fifth section summarizes our recent work on projecting the wealth of future retirees. We project the 401(k) assets of future retirees and consider how the evolution of the 401(k) system is likely to affect the retirement wealth of future retirees with different levels of lifetime earnings. There is a brief conclusion.

The Growth and Changing Mix of Pension Contributions

We first show the growth and changing mix of dollar contributions to pension plans and then consider contributions as a percentage of wage and sal-

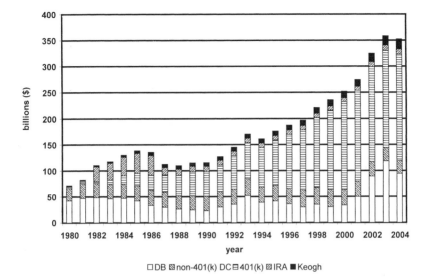

FIGURE 1.1 Growth of private sector pension contributions, 1980–2004, by plan type.

ary earnings. We also distinguish contributions to private plans, to federal government plans, and to state and local government plans. Contributions to private sector plans between 1980 and 2004, measured in nominal dollars, are shown in figure 1.1. The appendix describes the data sources used to construct this figure and all subsequent figures and tables. The figure distinguishes contributions to DB plans and to personal account savings plans including traditional defined contribution (DC) plans, 401(k) plans, IRAs, and Keogh plans. The most noticeable feature of the figure is the increase in contributions to 401(k) plans, which now account for the bulk of contributions to all personal retirement plans. In 1980, only 40 percent of private contributions were to personal accounts, and most of these contributions were accounted for by traditional employer-provided DC plans. Contributions to IRA and 401(k) plans began in 1982. By 2000, about 87 percent of contributions were to personal accounts, primarily to 401(k) plans. Contributions to 401(k) plans have grown since 2000, attaining $204 billion in 2004, but the proportion of total contributions accounted for by personal accounts has declined from 87 percent in 2000 to 73 percent in 2004. This decline is attributable to an increase in contributions to DB plans, largely driven by catch-up contributions following the fall in the stock market in 2000.

Figure 1.2 shows total contributions to all pension plans, including

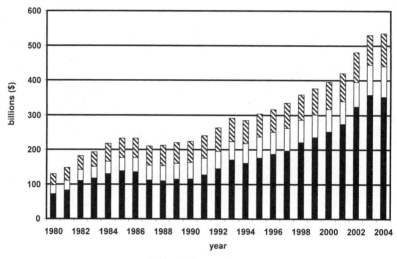

FIGURE 1.2 Growth of pension contributions, 1980–2004, by sector.

private, federal government, and state and local government plans over
time. The nominal dollar amount of contributions increased from about
$130 billion in 1980 to about $535 billion in 2004. Between 1980 and 2004,
total contributions increased by 488 percent in the private sector, by 337
percent in the state and local sector, and by 295 percent in the federal
sector. In real dollars, converting 1980 dollars to 2004 dollars using the
Consumer Price Index, total contributions rose from $298 billion to $535
billion, or by 80 percent. In both figures 1.1 and 1.2, there is a clear rise
in total contributions between 1982 and 1986—the years when the fully
deductible IRA was available.

Total pension contributions have increased because of economic growth
in general and in particular because of growth in wage and salary earnings.
It is therefore natural to consider contributions as a percentage of NIPA
wage and salary earnings. We begin with the aggregate pension contribution rates and then show detail by sector. Figure 1.3 shows total pension
contributions as a percentage of total NIPA wage and salary earnings and
private pension contributions as a percentage of private sector NIPA wage
and salary earnings for the 1980–2004 interval. The total contribution rate
was about 10 percent in 1980 and again in 2004, but it ranged widely in
the interim. The highest rate was almost 12 percent in 1984, while the low
was just over 8 percent in 1990. As will be discussed in more detail, this

fluctuation is due largely to changes in IRA contributions and contributions to DB plans.

The private contribution rate was about 2 percentage points higher at
the end than it was at the beginning of the period, but it also fluctuated
substantially. The pension contribution rate was about 8.6 percent between
1982 and 1985 but declined to 5.2 percent by 1990. Again, this decline was
largely accounted for by reductions in IRA contributions.

The contribution rate differs greatly by sector and, within the private
sector, by plan type. Figure 1.4 shows contribution rates in the private sector by plan type, all as a percentage of NIPA private wage and salary earnings. There are several noticeable features of this figure. First, the growth
in 401(k) plan contributions stands out. Contributions increased from 0.3
percent of wage and salary earnings in 1982 to 4.6 percent in 2004.

Second, contributions to all personal retirement accounts increased
from 2.6 percent of wage and salary earnings in 1980 to 5.8 percent in
2004. Conversely, contributions to DB plans were 3.8 percent in 1980 and
fell to 2.1 percent by 2004. Third, the figure suggests that curtailing the
IRA program after 1986 affected the pension saving rate in the ensuing
years. Tax-deductible contributions to IRAs were 2.6 percent of wage and
salary earnings in 1986 but dropped to 1.1 percent in 1987 and to only 0.7

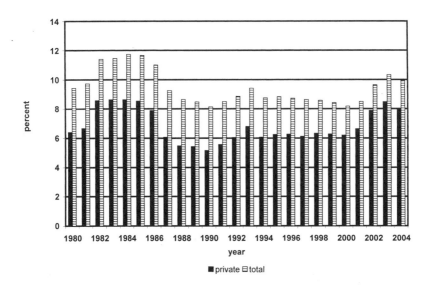

FIGURE 1.3 Total (private) pension contributions as percentage of total (private) NIPA wage
and salary.

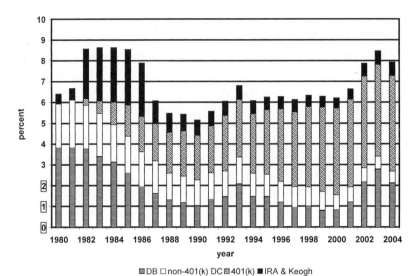

FIGURE 1.4 Private sector pension contributions as a percentage of private NIPA wage and salary, 1980–2004, by plan type.

percent by 1990. It seems likely that if the IRA program had not been curtailed, the total private pension contribution rate today would be higher than it is.

Fourth, the total private pension contribution rate reached a low of 5.2 percent in 1990 and then grew to nearly 8 percent in 2004. As a percentage of wage and salary earnings, DB contributions fell more than non-IRA personal account contributions increased between 1980 and 2000. DB contributions declined from 3.1 percent to 0.8 percent, and personal account contributions increased from 2.9 percent to 4.9 percent. The depressing effect of changes in DB funding rules, which Schieber and Shoven (1997), Ippolitto (2001), and Poterba, Venti, and Wise (2004) discuss, swamped the positive effect of increasing personal account contributions. Fifth, aside from changes due to the curtailment of the IRA program, the fluctuation in the total private pension saving rate is due almost exclusively to fluctuation in the DB plan contribution rate.

The contribution rate in the federal sector is much higher than the contribution rate in the private sector. Figure 1.5 shows federal DB and DC pension contributions as a percentage of federal NIPA wage and salary earnings. Over the 1980–2004 period, the total federal contribution rate was around 40 percent in most years, compared with an average of around

6.5 percent in the private sector. The data for figure 1.5 include both military and civilian pension contributions. Figure 1.6 shows the contribution rate for civilian employees as a percentage of NIPA wage and salary earnings for federal civilian employees. The total pension contribution rate for federal civilian employees was around 35 percent, roughly four times greater than the contribution rate in the private sector.

Figure 1.7 shows the pension contribution rate of state and local government employees as a percentage of NIPA wage and salary earnings of these employees. The data on state and local pensions do not allow us to distinguish between DB and DC contributions. The state and local rate shows a substantial decline, from about 16 percent in the early 1980s to around 12 percent by 2004. The state and local contribution rate is about twice as high as the private rate.

The difference between the contribution rates in the private and public sectors is likely explained in large part by differences in coverage and in plan generosity. Coverage is nearly universal in the federal sector and is over 90 percent in the state and local sector but is less than 50 percent in the private sector. Thus, all else constant, the ratio of contributions to earnings should be twice as high in the public sector as in the private

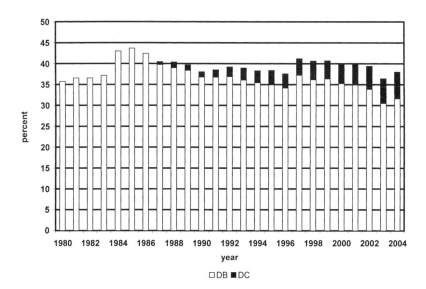

FIGURE 1.5 Federal sector pension contributions as a percentage of federal NIPA wage and salary, 1980–2004, by plan type (note that contributions include military retirement and wage and salary includes military pay).

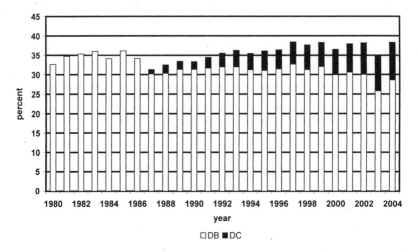

FIGURE 1.6 Federal civilian pension contributions as a percentage of federal civilian NIPA wage and salary, 1980–2004, by plan type.

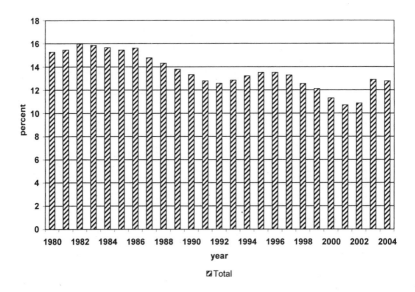

FIGURE 1.7 State and local sector pension contributions as a percentage of state and local NIPA wage and salary, 1980–2004.

TABLE 1.1 **Mean pension benefits for persons with pension, by age and source, 2003**

Source	55–60	60–65	65–70	70–75	75–80	80+	All
	Age						
Pension from company or union	1,294	1,191	860	717	656	566	830
Local government pensions	1,863	1,932	1,586	1,117	1,038	810	1,410
State government pensions	2,015	1,704	1,473	1,242	1,232	875	1,416
U.S. military retirement pay	1,852	1,980	1,578	1,559	1,509	1,656	1,714
Federal civilian retirement pension	2,161	2,567	2,009	1,664	1,523	1,468	1,836

Source: Authors' calculations from wave 7 of the 2001 Survey of Income and Program Participation.

sector. Moreover, the generosity of employer plans is much greater in the public sector.

Table 1.1 shows monthly pension benefits by age in 2003, based on data from the Survey of Income and Program Participation (SIPP). Over all ages, state and local government pension benefits were about 1.7 times larger than benefits from private sector union or company pensions. Military retirement benefits were almost 2.1 times larger than private sector benefits, and federal civilian benefits were over 2.2 times as large. These differences in generosity may, in part, stem from differences in job turnover. Employee turnover is higher in the private than in the public sector. Therefore, given the back loading of DB pension accruals, many private sector workers may receive reduced benefits on account of changing jobs. Differences in the number of years over which benefits are collected will also affect employer contributions. DB pensions are more prevalent in the public sector and are typically associated with earlier retirement dates than private sector DC plans.

Another factor that affects contributions in a particular year is whether employers are required to or choose to pay down unfunded liabilities. A spike in contributions to private DB plans is clearly evident in figure 1.4 for 2002 and 2003, when firms were legally obligated to increase contributions to offset the decline in equity prices. Purcell (2003) explains that in the federal sector current contributions must not only fund the "new" (fully funded) Federal Employee Retirement System program but must also pay off obligations of the "old" Civil Service Retirement System program, which has substantial unfunded liabilities.

The pension contribution rates in the private sector reveal the transition from a pension system dominated by employer-provided DB plans to a system composed primarily of personal retirement accounts of which the

401(k) plan is the most important. The contribution rates also highlight the much greater generosity of government plans compared with private sector plans. The pension contribution rate for federal plans is perhaps four times as large, and that for state and local governments is twice as large, as that for private plans.

The Growth in Pension Assets

The foregoing evidence suggests that aside from the years of fully deductible IRAs, total pension contributions as a percentage of wage and salary earnings remained between 8 and 10 percent between 1980 and 2004. However, private sector contributions as a percentage of wage and salary earnings increased from about 5 percent in 1990 to about 8 percent in 2004, and assets in pension plans grew dramatically over this period. Figure 1.8 shows pension assets by sector. Total pension assets, measured in nominal dollars, grew from $464 billion in 1980 to $14,185 billion in 2005. In constant 2005 dollars, the 1980 pension assets would be valued at $1,100 billion. The drop in assets after 2000, as well as the sharp increase after 2002, is directly related to fluctuating stock market values.

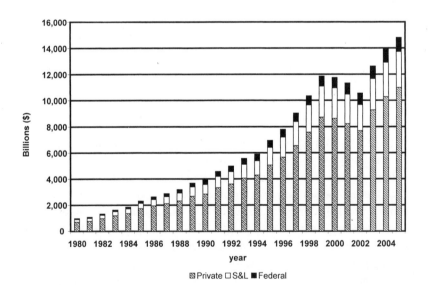

FIGURE 1.8 Growth of pension assets, 1980–2005, by sector.

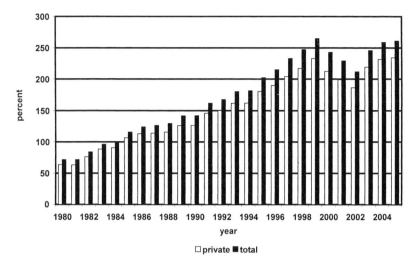

FIGURE 1.9 Total (private) pension assets as percentage of total (private) NIPA wage and salary.

Figure 1.9 shows assets as a percent of NIPA wage and salary earnings. Total pension assets grew from 71.5 percent of wage and salary earnings in 1980 to 261.1 percent in 2005, a 3.65-fold increase. Assets in private pension plans grew from 63.7 percent of private NIPA wage and salary earnings in 1980 to 234 percent in 2005. This increase in the wealth-to-income ratio describes the rise in retirement asset accumulation over this period.

Demographic changes between 1980 and 2005 complicate comparison of the pension assets-to-earnings ratios in the two years. The U.S. population was older in 2005 than in 1980, so even if the age profile of pension wealth was the same in the two years, there would still be a higher aggregate pension wealth-to-earnings ratio in 2005. Yet demographic changes do not seem large enough to explain the observed differences. The share of the population over the age of 55 rose from 20.9 percent in 1980 to 22.7 percent in 2005. The share between ages 45 and 54 rose from 10.1 percent to 14.3 percent, reflecting the presence of many members of the baby boom cohort in this age range in 2005. Even this increase of nearly 40 percent in the population share in key preretirement age groups is more modest than the increase in pension assets relative to earnings. The increase in pension assets relative to earnings suggests that, on average, the capacity to replace preretirement income has increased rather substantially over the past twenty-five years, although it does not mean that all current or future retirees have sufficient retirement assets. Workers retiring in 2005 retire earlier and live longer than workers who retired in 1980, so the wealth-to-income ratio required to replace preretirement earnings should be higher in 2005 than in 1980.

This increase in retirement assets can also be seen in the micro data. Tabulations for all households ages 63–67 in the Health and Retirement Study (HRS) in 2000 show that the mean of DB pension assets, defined as the present value of expected benefits, is $92,228; 401(k) assets in this year are $26,098; and IRA and Keogh assets, which include rollovers from 401(k) plans, are $77,716. Poterba, Venti, and Wise (2007b) show that the real value of DB assets at age 65 was higher in 2000 than in 1980. Similarly 401(k) and IRA assets were much higher in 2000 than in 1980, indicating that the accumulation of assets dedicated to retirement increased substantially between 1980 and 2000. For comparison, mean household Social Security wealth was $181,373 in 2000. On average, the sum of DB, 401(k), IRA, and Keogh assets exceeds the present value of future Social Security benefits in 2000.

Pension Participation

While assets in pension plans have grown dramatically since 1980, the proportion of private sector employees participating in a pension plan has remained roughly constant, according to estimates from the Current Population Survey (CPS) described in Munnell and Perun (2006) and Purcell (2006). Other surveys—summarized, for example, by Sanzenbacher (2006)—yield similar profiles, although some report slightly rising participation and others report slightly falling participation. The percentage of public sector workers participating in a pension plan has remained constant at nearly 100 percent between 1980 and 2004.

The data from the Form 5500 reports that we have used to track contributions and assets are not helpful for studying overall trends in participation. They report the number of active participants in each pension plan offered by each employer. Since many employers offer more than one pension plan to their employees, most commonly a DB and a 401(k), the total number of active participants in the Form 5500 may reflect a double count of many employees. Buessing and Soto (2006) have carefully attempted to adjust for double counting by making a number of assumptions to distinguish between primary and supplemental plans. By eliminating supple-

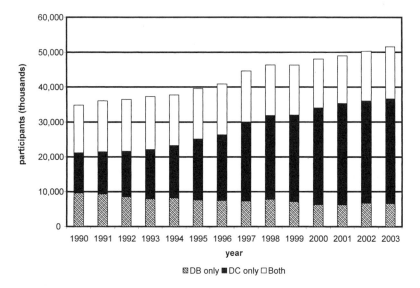

FIGURE 1.10 Growth of private sector participants, 1990–2003.

mental plans they derive an estimate of pension plan participants for each year between 1990 and 2003 for private firms with at least one hundred employees. Figure 1.10 shows their estimates. Over this period the number of employees covered by a DB plan declined by about one-third, while the number covered by only a DC plan (primarily 401[k]s) increased almost three-fold. The number of employees participating in both a DB and a DC plan remained roughly constant. Overall, participation increased from about 35 million in 1990 to nearly 52 million in 2003.

To place these changes in perspective, we graph participation as a percentage of private sector employment in figure 1.11. In contrast to the results obtained from the CPS, these results show an upward trend in the overall number of private sector pension participants, from 38.2 percent in 1990 to 47.6 percent in 2003. The overall participation rate is slightly lower than the level found in the CPS, probably because Buessing and Soto (2006) exclude small firms. Because much of the recent growth in the coverage of 401(k)s is in small firms, these results are likely to understate the growth in 401(k) participation.

The double-counting problem does not prevent the use of the Form 5500 data to study trends in participation in each type of pension since employers typically offer each worker at most one DB plan and one personal account plan. Figure 1.12 shows the change in the number of active participants by plan type in the private sector between 1980 and 2004. Unlike in the previous two figures, IRA and Keogh participants (many of whom also have employer-sponsored pensions) are included here. Without any adjustment for double counting, the total number of participants was seen to increase from just over 50 million in 1980 to almost 80 million in 2004. The figure shows the large increase in the number of 401(k) participants and the much smaller decline in the number of DB participants. Between 1982 and 2004, while the number of 401(k) participants grew by over 44 million, the number of DB participants declined by about 10 million. Poterba, Venti, and Wise (2004) show very little replacement of DB plans by 401(k) plans between 1984 and 1997. The majority of new 401(k) plans during this period supplemented existing DB plans.

Figure 1.12 also shows the decline in the number of traditional employer-provided DC plans. It is likely that some of the growth in 401(k) plans is due to the conversion of traditional employer-provided DC plans to 401(k) plans. Benjamin (2003) estimates that about 30 percent of 401(k) assets in 1991 were originally contributed to traditional DC plans. Gale, Papke, and VanDerhei (2005) estimate that between 23 and 41 percent of

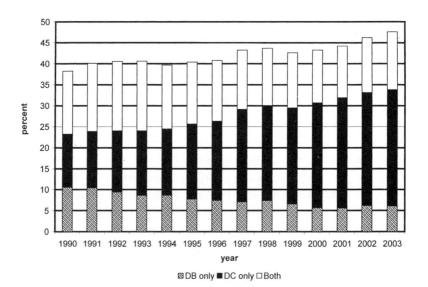

FIGURE 1.11 Private sector participants as a percentage of private sector employment, 1990–2003.

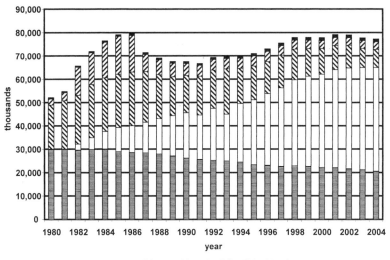

FIGURE 1.12 Active participants in the private sector, 1980–2004.

existing 401(k) plans in 1989 had been converted from previously existing DC plans.

Figure 1.13 shows the average contribution per participant in the private sector. The estimate for DB plans is total contributions to DB plans divided by Buessing and Soto's (2006) estimate of the number of participants in these plans. The estimate for 401(k) and traditional DC plans is the sum of all contributions to 401(k) plans and to traditional DC plans divided by the estimate of participants in these plans. Contributions per participant to 401(k)-like plans increased from $3,000 in 1980 to almost $5,000 by 1990. Between 1990 and 2000, 401(k)-like plan contributions were between two and three times as large as DB contributions per participant in most years. Contributions per participant to DB plans exceed $3,000 only in the last two years when plan sponsors had to catch up as a result of the sharp decline in equity prices.

The federal sector estimates, shown in figure 1.14, are total DB contributions divided by the number of federal DB participants and total contributions to 401(k)-like plans also divided by the number of DB participants. This calculation assumes that all federal sector 401(k)-like plans are supplementary. The relationship between DB and 401(k)-like contributions per participant in the federal sector is the opposite of that observed

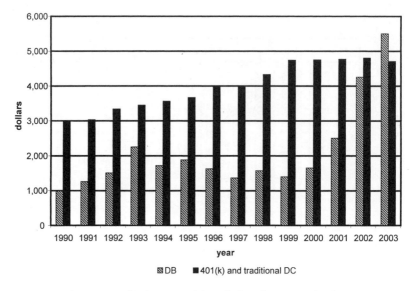

FIGURE I.13 Average contribution per participant in the private sector, by plan type.

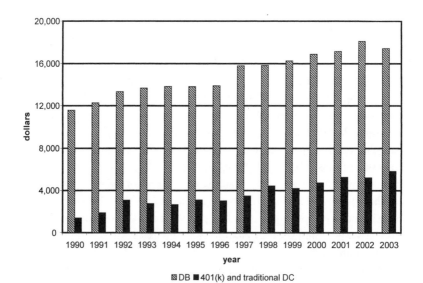

FIGURE I.14 Average contribution per participant in the federal sector, by plan type.

in the private sector. The level of 401(k)-like contributions per participant in the federal sector is very similar to the level of 401(k)-like contributions per participant in the private sector. However, federal sector DB contributions are much larger than federal sector 401(k)-like contributions. We do not present comparable estimates for the state and local sector because we are unable to distinguish between DB and 401(k)-like plans in this sector and thus cannot correct for double counting.

The Evolving Features of Personal Retirement Plans

There has been a transition from employer-provided DB plans to personal retirement accounts in the private sector. The proportion of personal accounts has also grown in the federal and in the state and local sectors. We now consider several other evolving dimensions of the transition and their implications. The next section considers how the transition will affect the retirement wealth of future retirees.

There has been a great deal of concern in the press and elsewhere that the rise of 401(k) plans exposes workers to financial market risks that they would not face in a traditional DB system. Indeed, the perceived risk of 401(k) portfolios has been increasing in recent years. Data from the Federal Reserve's Flow of Funds Accounts show that the proportion of 401(k) assets allocated to equities increased substantially between 1985 and 2005, from 42 percent to 63 percent. The percentage of DB assets invested in equities displays the same level and trend over this period.

While the financial market risk of 401(k) plans has been widely emphasized, the job change risk of DB plans has received little, if any, attention. DB plans effectively penalize employees who change jobs; DC plans do not. This job change or turnover risk of DB plans is emphasized by Kotlikoff and Wise (1989). Whether the transition from DB plans to DC-like plans increases risk exposure depends on the relative magnitudes of job change risk and market risk. Several recent studies have directly addressed this question.

Samwick and Skinner (2004) use a sample of pension plans from the Survey of Consumer Finances to compare the risks associated with DB and DC plans. They consider risks associated with both job change and financial market returns. They conclude that the distribution of expected retirement income provided by 401(k) plans is preferred to the distribution provided by DB plans for all but the most risk-averse investors.

Schrager (2005) uses the Panel Study of Income Dynamics to estimate a life-cycle model of wealth accumulation that also incorporates both asset market risk and job turnover risk. She finds that because of rising job turnover in the 1990s, DC plans provide a more desirable source of retirement income for many workers. Her findings suggest that industries with the highest job risk have experienced the largest increases in DC participation over the last 15 years.

Aaronson and Coronado (2005) also suggest that the transition to DC plans has been stimulated by increasing rates of worker mobility. Poterba et al. (2006b) analyze pension risk using actual earnings histories that incorporate job changes. They conclude that the job change risk inherent in DB plans outweighs the financial market risk of 401(k) plans. Thus the evidence indicates that the transition to DC-like plans has not increased the overall level of risk faced by workers and indeed may have reduced it. There is, of course, substantial heterogeneity in the circumstances of different workers. For some workers with very little risk of job turnover, for example, the transition from a DB plan to a DC plan with significant equity exposure may increase overall risk.

The role of DC plans *within* the DC sector has also changed over the past two decades. Early adopters tended to be large firms with preexisting DB plans. The data in table 1.2 show that in the early years, over three-quarters of 401(k) participants also had a DB plan. As 401(k) plans spread to smaller firms, fewer new participants were also covered by a DB plan; the 401(k) plan was the sole plan. Perhaps the most important question about future 401(k) plan growth is the extent to which 401(k) plans will continue to be adopted by small firms. The projections discussed in the next section incorporate assumptions about the future spread of 401(k) plans. The realized diffusion of these plans, however, will depend importantly on government legislation and institutional arrangements that might facilitate the adoption of plans by small firms.

Future participation in 401(k) plans, given plan eligibility, may be aided by recent legislation that makes it easier for firms to offer 401(k) plans containing participation-enhancing features. The Pension Protection Act (PPA) of 2006, for example, makes it easier for employers to implement automatic enrollment, set default contribution rates, and set default asset allocations in 401(k) plans. The enormous influence that changes in these plan features may have on participation and the accumulation of assets has been extensively studied by Choi, Laibson, and Madrian (2004), Beshears et al. (2006), and Holden and VanDerhei (2005).

TABLE 1.2 **Percentage of 401(k) participants also covered by a defined benefit plan**

Year	All 401(k) plans	Preexisting 401(k) plans	First-year 401(k) plans
1984	82.4		
1985	78.0		
1986	75.3		
1987	69.7		
1988	67.8	69.3	47.5
1989	65.3	66.8	46.0
1990	61.8	63.5	32.8
1991	58.2	60.2	26.1
1992	55.7	58.3	19.0
1993	52.9	54.4	22.9
1994	51.0	51.6	32.9
1995	46.9	47.6	28.0
1996	45.8	46.0	39.4
1997	42.4	43.2	22.5
1998	40.1	41.1	16.7
1999	37.3	37.5	33.6
2000	36.6	36.6	38.0
2001	35.2	34.9	41.4
2002	36.0	36.2	29.0
2003	34.3	34.4	29.3

Note: The number of active participants used in these calculations includes noncontributors.
Source: Authors' calculations from Form 5500 filings.

Finally, the investment options available to 401(k) participants are evolving rapidly. Recent legislation has greatly reduced the role of employer stock as an investment option and encouraged plan sponsors to diversify investment offerings. More and more plans are offering life-cycle or target-retirement funds that maintain a well-diversified investment mix that is intended to be appropriate for the participant's age or retirement date, as discussed in the chapter by Viceira (chapter 5 in this volume). Poterba et al. (2006a) suggest that these plans have the potential to either reduce risk or increase returns for some participants, depending on the investment options that otherwise would have been available. The PPA of 2006 enables plan sponsors to offer such funds as "defaults" for participants.

Projections of Future 401(k) Wealth

We now consider how the future spread of 401(k)-like plans will affect the retirement wealth of future retirees. The results are drawn from Poterba, Venti, and Wise (2007a, 2007b, 2007c, 2007d), which explain our method

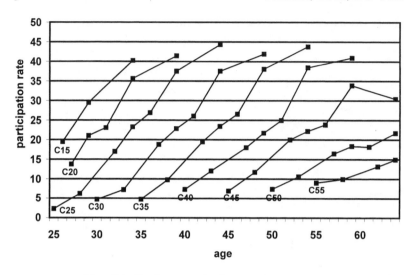

FIGURE 1.15 401(k) participation for persons in nine age cohorts.

and underlying assumptions in detail. We project future 401(k) participation rates based on historical data from the SIPP. These data, organized into cohort format, are shown for persons in selected cohorts in figure 1.15, where the cohort age "XX" in 1984 is identified as "CXX." Such data cannot be directly extrapolated to project participation rates for a given cohort in subsequent years. We assume that participation continues to grow in the future but more slowly than in the past. The maximum participation rate attained is under 60 percent for all but the five cohorts that retire between 2035 and 2040. For those cohorts the projected participation rate attains 75 percent in some instances.

We have projected the average 401(k) retirement assets of families who will attain age 65 between now and 2040. We have also considered how the advance of 401(k) plans will affect future wealth for families with different levels of Social Security wealth. We group families by Social Security wealth because a large fraction of households now rely primarily on Social Security benefits for support in retirement, and we want to understand how these families in particular will be affected by the spread of 401(k) plans. The results reported here are taken for the most part from Poterba, Venti, and Wise (2007c).

For comparison, we tabulate the composition of household wealth for households between ages 63 and 67 in 2000 in the HRS. We do not show the detail here, but a striking feature of these data is the relationship of assets at retirement to lifetime earnings. Figure 1.16 shows the ratio of dedicated retirement assets (the sum of DB, 401(k), SS, IRA, and Keogh assets) to lifetime earnings for households in each Social Security wealth decile. It also shows the ratio of total wealth to lifetime earnings. There is little variation across deciles and no systematic increase in total wealth with rising Social Security wealth.

Over the next thirty-five years 'our projections show an enormous increase in the 401(k)-like assets of future retirees. Figure 1.17 shows the average 401(k) assets of all persons reaching age 65 in each decade between 2000 and 2040, assuming that historical rates of return on equities persist into the future. By 2040, the projections suggest that the average 65-year-old will have over $450,000 (in year 2000 dollars) in personal retirement accounts. Figure 1.18 shows that if future equity returns fall three hundred basis points below the historical average, average 401(k)-like wealth at retirement will be almost $270,000.

These projections are roughly in line with projections contained in other studies that have modeled aspects of the retirement accumulation process. Holden and VanDerhei (2002a, 2002b) project 401(k) at retirement for persons who are ages 26–35 in 2000. They base their projections of future participation rates on the 2000 cross section by age and thus

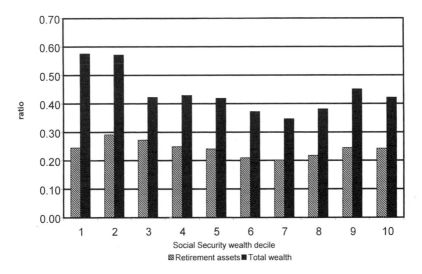

FIGURE 1.16 Ratio of retirement assets to lifetime earnings and ratio of total wealth to lifetime earnings, by Social Security wealth decile.

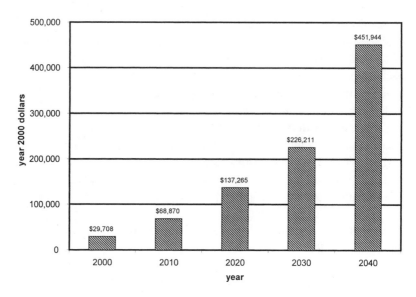

FIGURE 1.17 Growth of 401(k) assets at retirement (all persons) assuming historical returns on equity.

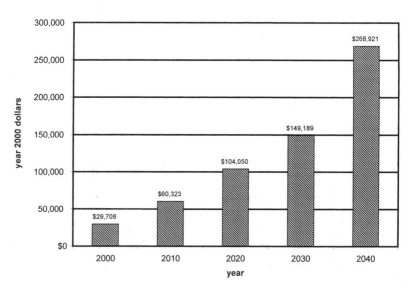

FIGURE 1.18 Growth of 401(k) assets at retirement (all persons) assuming historical returns on equity less three hundred basis points.

do not allow for younger cohorts to have higher participation rates than older cohorts had at the same age. Their results are presented in terms of the proportion of preretirement income that will be replaced by 401(k) income after retirement. Although it is difficult to directly compare their estimates to ours, their baseline estimates suggest that 401(k) income will replace between 50 and 70 percent of preretirement income. Purcell (2007) calculates 401(k) accumulations for young households in 2004 under the assumption of 100 percent participation. He projects a median 401(k) balance at age 65 of $844,000 in year 2004 dollars.

To put these data in a broader economic context, we show projected total 401(k) assets and projected DB assets relative to projected gross domestic product (GDP). The projected DB assets are from Poterba, Venti, and Wise (2007b), and the GDP projections are the "intermediate" forecasts from the Social Security Administration. Ratios assuming historical equity returns are shown in figure 1.19, while ratios calculated under the assumption that equity returns average three hundred basis points below the historical average are shown in figure 1.20. Under both of the equity return assumptions, the sum of DB and DC assets continues to grow as a percentage of GDP, and the increase in 401(k) assets far outweighs the decrease in DB assets.

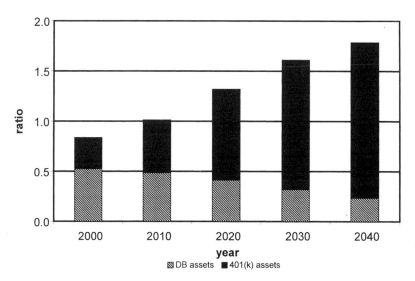

FIGURE 1.19 Ratio of projected 401(k) and DB assets to projected GDP for selected years (historical equity returns).

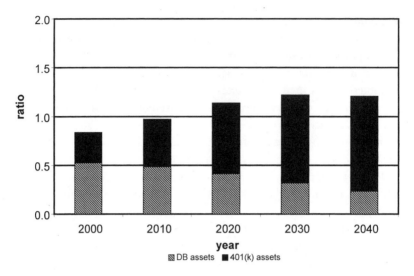

FIGURE 1.20 Ratio of projected 401(k) and DB assets to projected GDP for selected years (historical returns less three hundred basis points).

The projections show a very large increase in aggregate 401(k)-like retirement assets and in total retirement assets including both 401(k) and DB pensions. Because 401(k) assets appear to be the dominant form of retirement assets for most future retirees, we consider how these assets will affect the wealth of future retirees. We first show our projections of 401(k) assets for households in each decile of the Social Security wealth distribution and then show projections of the sum of Social Security wealth and 401(k) assets.

Figure 1.21 shows the ratio of projected 401(k) assets in 2040 (in year 2000 dollars) to 401(k) assets in 2000, by deciles of the Social Security wealth distribution, for both of our rate-of-return assumptions. In both cases, the increase for the second decile is greater than expected because of the Social Security coverage issues discussed by Poterba, Venti, and Wise (2007b). The first decile includes many households that worked at least part of their careers outside the Social Security system and thus accumulated substantial assets but little Social Security wealth. Ratios for the first two deciles are expected to be high because these households held very little 401(k) wealth in 2000. For both equity return assumptions, there is a large relative increase for all Social Security wealth deciles. If historical returns continue, the projections suggest that households in 2040 will have more than eight times the 401(k) assets held by households in

2000. Households in 2000 only had at most eighteen years to contribute to a 401(k), and most contributed for fewer than ten years. In 2040, however, 401(k) assets will be based on as many as forty years of contributions. A similar pattern arises if equity returns are three hundred basis points lower in the future. In this case, the ratio of assets in 2040 to assets in 2000 exceeds 5 for all Social Security wealth deciles.

Finally, for each Social Security wealth decile, figure 1.22 shows the ratio of the sum of Social Security wealth and 401(k) assets in 2040 (in year 2000 dollars) to the same sum in 2000. The figure shows the ratios assuming the historical rate of return on equity and the ratios assuming that the return on equity is three hundred basis points lower than the historical return. With the exception of the lowest decile, retirees will have combined Social Security and 401(k) asset balances in 2040 that are 2.2–3.8 times as great as those in 2000 if historical rates of return prevail. If future returns on equity are three hundred basis points lower than historical returns, the ratio ranges from 1.7 to 2.6 for all but the lowest decile of the Social Security wealth distribution. There is no systematic pattern across the Social Security wealth deciles, although the very low level of 401(k)

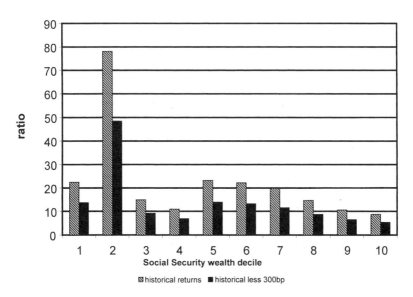

FIGURE 1.21 Ratio of 401(k) assets in 2040 to 401(k) assets in 2000 by Social Security wealth decile assuming historical equity returns and historical returns less three hundred basis points (bp).

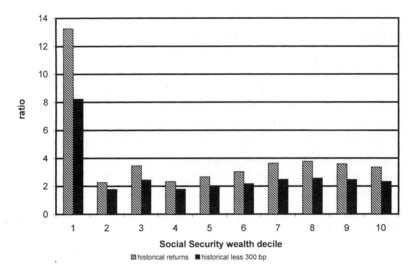

FIGURE 1.22 Ratio of the sum of Social Security wealth (SSW) and 401(k) assets in 2040 to the sum of SSW and 401(k) assets in 2000 by SSW decile assuming historical equity returns and historical returns less three hundred basis points (bp).

assets in 2000 for persons in the lowest decile makes the ratio very high. Thus our projections suggest that the spread of 401(k) assets will result in a substantial increase in the retirement assets of households with the lowest Social Security wealth and will result in a doubling or tripling of retirement assets for households in the rest of the Social Security wealth distribution. Because Social Security wealth is determined in large part by lifetime earnings, the ratios are similar if households are grouped by lifetime earnings rather than by Social Security wealth.

Concluding Remarks

Over the past twenty-five years, personal retirement accounts have become the principal form of retirement saving in the United States, especially for people who have entered the labor force during this period. While today most contributions to pension plans are to personal retirement accounts, three decades ago most contributions were to employer-provided DB plans. We have described these past changes in the pension landscape, projected future changes, and considered how these changes will affect the well-being of future retirees. We conclude that the advent of personal account saving is projected to yield very large increases in the financial assets of future retirees across the lifetime earnings spectrum.

Appendix

Data Sources for Figures

Table 1.1. Authors' calculations from wave 7 of the 2001 SIPP.
Table 1.2. Authors' calculations from the Form 5500 filings.
Figure 1.1. DB and DC contributions are from Form 5500 (published in the Private Pension Plan Bulletin, various years). IRA and Keogh contributions are from the Internal Revenue Service (IRS) Statistics of Income. The figure includes IRA contributions from both private and public sector employees (the data do not distinguish one from the other). The IRA amount includes tax-deductible contributions only.
Figure 1.2. Private sector contributions are from the Form 5500. Federal, state, and local contributions are from the NIPA, table 6–11, and the Employee Benefit Research Institute (EBRI) *Databook.*
Figures 1.3 and 1.4. Pension contributions are from Form 5500. Wage and salary data are from the NIPA.
Figure 1.5–1.7. Contributions are from the NIPA and EBRI *Databook.* Wage and salary data are from the NIPA.
Figure 1.8. Pension assets are from the Federal Reserve's Flow of Funds Accounts. IRA and Keogh assets are included in the private sector totals. IRA assets include assets originating as deductible IRAs, Roth IRAs, and rollovers from other pensions.
Figure 1.9. Pension assets as described for figure 1.8. Wage and salary data are from the NIPA.
Figure 1.10. The number of active participants in the private sector is from Buessing and Soto (2006), table A11.
Figure 1.11. The number of participants is from Buessing and Soto (2006). Private sector employment is from U.S. Bureau of Labor Statistics, Employment and Earnings.
Figure 1.12. Data for DB and DC participants are from Form 5500. No adjustment is made for double counting of participants. Data for IRA and Keogh participants are from the IRS Statistics of Income.
Figure 1.13. The dollar value of contributions is obtained from Form 5500. The number of participants is from Buessing and Soto (2006).
Figure 1.14. The dollar value of contributions and the number of participants are from the NIPA and the EBRI *Databook.*

Figure 1.15. Authors' calculations are from various panels of the SIPP.
Figure 1.16–1.22. Authors' calculations are based on projection model described by Poterba, Venti, and Wise (2007a, 2007c).

Note

We thank Sarah Holden for her comments. The research reported here was pursuant to grants from the National Institute on Aging, grant no. P01 AG005842 to the National Bureau of Economic Research (NBER), and the U.S. Social Security Administration (SSA) funded as part of the Retirement Research Consortium. The findings and conclusions expressed are solely those of the authors and do not represent the views of any agency of the U.S. Federal Government, the NBER, or the SSA.

References

Aaronson, Stephanie, and Julia Coronado. 2005. Are Firms or Workers behind the Shift away from DB Plans. FEDS Paper 2005–17, Federal Reserve Board.

Benjamin, Daniel. 2003. Does 401(k) Eligibility Increase Saving: Evidence from Propensity Score Subclassification. *Journal of Public Economics* 87: 1259–90.

Beshears, John, James Choi, David Laibson, and Brigitte Madrian. 2006. The Importance of Default Options for Retirement Saving Outcomes: Evidence from the United States. NBER Working Paper No. 12009. National Bureau of Economic Research, Cambridge, MA.

Buessing, Marric, and Mauricio Soto. 2006. The State of Private Pensions: Current Form 5500 Data. Issue Brief 42, Center for Retirement Research at Boston College, Boston, MA.

Choi, James, David Laibson, and Brigitte C. Madrian. 2004. Plan Design and 401(k) Savings Outcomes. *National Tax Journal* 57: 275–98.

Employee Benefit Research Institute (EBRI). 2007. *EBRI Databook on Employee Benefits.* Washington, DC: EBRI.

Gale, William, Leslie Papke, and Jack VanDerhei. 2005. The Shifting Structure of Private Pensions. In *The Evolving Pension System,* edited by W. Gale, J. Shoven, and M. Warshawsky, 51–76. Washington, DC: Brookings Institution Press.

Holden, Sarah, and Jack VanDerhei. 2002a. Can 401(k) Accumulations Generate Significant Income for Future Retirees? In *Perspective* 8(3). Washington, DC: Investment Company Institute.

———. 2002b. Appendix: EBRI/ICI 401(k) Accumulation Projection Model. In *Perspective* 8(3a). Washington, DC: Investment Company Institute.

————. 2005. The Influence of Automatic Enrollment, Catch-Up, and IRA Contributions on 401(k) Accumulations at Retirement. Issue Brief 283, EBRI.

Ippolito, Richard. 2001. Reversion Taxes, Contingent Benefits, and the Decline in Pension Funding. *Journal of Law and Economics* 44: 199–232.

Kotlikoff, Laurence, and David Wise. 1989. *The Wage Carrot and the Pension Stick.* Kalamazoo, MI: Upjohn Institute.

Munnell, Alicia, and Pamela Perun. 2006. An Update on Private Pensions. Issue Brief 50, Center for Retirement Research at Boston College, Boston, MA.

Poterba, James, Joshua Rauh, Steven Venti, and David A. Wise. 2006a. Lifecycle Asset Allocation Strategies and the Distribution of 401(k) Retirement Wealth. NBER Working Paper No. 11974. National Bureau of Economic Research, Cambridge, MA.

————. 2006b. Defined Contribution Plans, Defined Benefit Plans, and the Accumulation of Retirement Wealth. NBER Working Paper No. 12597. National Bureau of Economic Research, Cambridge, MA.

Poterba, James, Steven Venti, and David A. Wise. 2004. The Transition to Personal Accounts and Increasing Retirement Wealth: Macro and Micro Evidence. In *Perspectives on the Economics of Aging,* edited by David A. Wise, 17–79. Chicago: University of Chicago Press.

————. 2007a. New Estimates of the Future Path of 401(k) Assets. NBER Working Paper No. 13083. National Bureau of Economic Research, Cambridge, MA.

————. 2007b. The Decline of Defined Benefit Retirement Plans and Asset Flows. NBER Working Paper No. 12834. National Bureau of Economic Research, Cambridge, MA.

————. 2007c. The Rise of 401(k) Plans, Lifetime Earnings, and Wealth at Retirement. NBER Working Paper No. 13091. National Bureau of Economic Research, Cambridge, MA.

————. 2007d. The Shift from Defined Benefit Pensions to 401(k) Plans and the Pension Assets of the Baby Boom Cohort. *Proceedings of the National Academy of Sciences* 104: 13,238–43.

Purcell, Patrick. 2003. Federal Employees' Retirement System: Benefits and Financing. Congressional Research Service Report for Congress, June.

————. 2006. Pension Sponsorship and Participation: Summary of Recent Trends. Congressional Research Service Report for Congress, August.

————. 2007. Retirement Savings: How Much Will Workers Have When They Retire? Congressional Research Service Report for Congress, January.

Samwick, Andrew, and Jonathan Skinner. 2004. How Will 401(k) Plans Affect Retirement Income. *American Economic Review* 94: 329–43.

Sanzenbacher, Geoffrey. 2006. Estimating Pension Coverage Using Different Data Sets. Issue Brief 51, Center for Retirement Research at Boston College, Boston, MA.

Schrager, Allison. 2005. A Life-Cycle Analysis of the Decline of Defined Benefit Plans and Job Tenure. Mimeo. Yale University, New Haven, CT.

Schieber, Sylvester, and John Shoven. 1997. The Consequences of Population Aging on Private Pension Fund Saving and Asset Markets. In *The Economic Effects of Aging in the United States and Japan,* edited by Michael Hurd and Naohiro Yashiro, 111–30. Chicago: University of Chicago Press.

Viceira, Luis. 2008. Life-Cycle Funds. This volume.

CHAPTER TWO

Do Workers Know about Their Pension Plan Type? Comparing Workers' and Employers' Pension Information

Alan L. Gustman, Thomas L. Steinmeier, and Nahid Tabatabai

1. Introduction

This chapter shows that many people approaching retirement do not understand what type of pension plan they have. We analyze a number of surveys. In all of them, reports by a third or more of respondents disagree with their employers' reports as to what type of pension they hold. Discrepancies between respondent and firm reports are found in cross-sectional data, over time, and in panel data and are confirmed to be present in other surveys.

Discrepancies between respondent and firm reports might arise from errors in the firm reports. However, the evidence presented here suggests that while the process of matching employer-produced pension plan descriptions to survey respondents is not error free, the employer-provided data are a much more accurate indicator of pension plan type than respondent-provided data are.

Most of our results are based on data from the Health and Retirement Study (HRS), a longitudinal survey of the older population that was first fielded in 1992. As in other data sources, in a significant minority of cases, the pension plan type reported by respondents to the HRS disagrees with the plan type obtained from pension plan descriptions produced by their employers, which are called summary plan descriptions (SPDs). Findings for respondents who report that their plans have not changed run counter to the well-known trend toward defined contribution (DC) plans and well-documented evidence that firms have not been adopting defined benefit (DB) plans. For example, 22 percent of respondents who reported having a DC plan only in 1992, and who reported in each wave through 1998 that their plan had not changed, reported having a DB plan only in 1998, with another 14 percent gaining a DB plan between 1992 and 1998. Similar changes were reported between 1998 and 2004 and between 1992 and 2004. Not only are these purported gains in DB plan coverage inconsistent with known trends, but they are also inconsistent with trends in the plan type reported in matched employer data.

Various types of other evidence are explored. Data from the Survey of Consumer Finances are used together with HRS data to document changes in the relationship between employer and respondent reports about pensions. We also introduce information from a number of experimental questions in the HRS pertaining to plan characteristics and plan type.

Watson Wyatt Company has made a sample available that includes employer payroll data as well as respondent reports of their pensions. Differences between employer and respondent pension reports are sometimes attributed to the failure to match an employee with the appropriate pension offered by the firm. Plan descriptions from payroll data are perfectly matched to the respondents so that all discrepancies are due to errors in information provided by the respondent.

The data produced by the Watson Wyatt Company support the view that discrepancies between respondent reports of plan type and reports obtained from employers are mainly due to errors in respondent reports. These data show the same types of discrepancies between respondent and firm reports of plan type as are seen when SPDs obtained from employers of HRS respondents are compared with the plan types reported by the respondents themselves. The analysis with the Watson Wyatt data is inconsistent with a view that discrepancies between respondent and firm reports of plan type in the HRS are due to mismatching employer plan descriptions with respondents.

Taking all of this evidence together, it appears that discrepancies between respondent and firm reports of plan type are mainly due to errors in respondent data. If misreporting by respondents is at the heart of these discrepancies and, more generally, if misreporting results because respondents are misinformed about their pensions, then models of retirement and saving behavior should allow for imperfect knowledge of pensions by decision makers.

Together with other evidence from the HRS, our findings suggest a number of changes in survey design that can help to reduce reporting error. Our findings also suggest what not to do. To avoid asking the wrong questions of a respondent who may have misreported a plan type and to avoid skipping over questions that are relevant, one possibility is to ask all respondents all possible questions about pensions, whether the questions are suitable for those with DB plans or for those with DC plans. However, our findings suggest that respondents will provide answers to questions that are most appropriate for those who hold a different plan type than their own. The problem is that these answers will be highly misleading. For example, those with a DB plan will respond to a question about how much is in their account, but their answer will pertain to another plan rather than the plan in question or will deviate widely from the implied value of the pension given the reported payment stream.

The chapter is organized as follows: section 2 provides an overview of the main topics. Reasons why firm and respondent reports may contain errors are considered in section 3. Section 4 compares reports of pension plan type from respondent data with reports from employer-produced plan descriptions. Consistencies and inconsistencies over time in firm and respondent reports of plan type are documented for those reporting that their plans have not changed in section 5. Section 6 explores survey and matched payroll data from Watson Wyatt. In section 7, we analyze variation in self-reported plan type in seven waves of the HRS panel for those members of the original HRS cohort who reported that they were covered by a pension and who also reported that their pension plans were unchanged over time. Section 8 reports the results of an experiment in which those who reported a DB plan were asked questions relevant to a DC plan and vice versa. This suggests the nature of errors that would arise should the HRS be redesigned so that questions are not conditioned on plan type. Under that approach, some people with one type of pension would be asked about pension characteristics for a plan type they do not have. A brief summary is presented and implications are discussed in section 9.

2. Overview

To understand the role of pensions in retirement and saving, surveys have
gathered data from respondents as well as from their employers. In the
case of the HRS, the SPDs are collected from employers, from Department of Labor files, from the Web, and from respondents themselves who
request the plan descriptions from their employers.

Our focus here is on plan type, whether the plan is DB, DC, or some
other type. With a DB plan, a formula determines the benefit based on
past earnings, experience, and age of retirement. DB plans typically pay
a stream of benefits beginning at retirement and lasting for as long as the
covered worker (or the worker and/or spouse) lives. There may be a bonus
for retiring early and other differences in the total value of the pension
that depend on when a person retires.[1] A DC plan is essentially an account
that will be turned over to the covered worker upon separation (assuming
the worker has stayed long enough for the pension to be vested) or upon
retirement. Contributions by the employer and/or the employee are accumulated and invested, and the employee is entitled to the contributions
plus the returns. Unless the DC plan is one of the few that offer benefits
in the form of an annuity, the pace and size of withdrawals from the plan
are determined by the retiree. Hybrid plans combine features of DB and
DC plans. For example, a common type of hybrid plan called a cash balance plan creates a notional account with a prespecified return, with the
firm funding the implied liability from these accounts as it would fund the
liabilities from a DB plan.

Plan type is a key piece of the information that is required to understand a pension plan. It is a major determinant of the value and incentives
created by a pension. Thus, surveys asking respondents about their pensions often begin by asking about plan type. For example, the HRS asks
about their pension plan as follows: "In some retirement plans, call them
Type A, benefits are usually based on a formula involving age, years of
service and salary. In other plans, call them Type B, money is accumulated
in an account for you." The respondent is then asked whether their plan is
type A, type B, or both.

Once plan type is determined, the HRS asks other detailed questions
about the benefits and features of a worker's pension. Which question is
asked often depends on what plan type was reported. For example, those
with a DB plan are typically asked when they expect to retire and what

their yearly benefit will be. Holders of DC plans are often asked to report the current balance in their plan account.

If plan type is incorrectly reported, questions may be asked that are not appropriate for the plan that is held. Moreover, respondents who misreport plan type may not be asked questions that are important for determining the value and properties of their pension.

Yet evidence continues to accumulate that there are substantial differences between pension outcomes reported by some pension-covered workers and the same outcomes gleaned from employer-produced data.[2] If respondent errors are common and are the main cause of discrepancies between respondent-reported pension outcomes and outcomes obtained from employer plan descriptions, then there are important implications for analyses of retirement and saving behavior. Respondent errors would call into question the assumption in standard models that retirement and saving decisions are always made by well-informed agents.[3] For example, questions would be raised about how well people do in determining the adequacy of their retirement saving; whether covered workers understand the choice set created by the complex rules governing retirement plans, in particular various discontinuities in the reward structure that affect the incentive to retire; and whether people appropriately value the pension plans their employers provide as part of their compensation packages.

3. Reasons for Differences between Firm and Respondent Reports

As we will document extensively, there are wide differences between workers' and employers' reports of their pension plan types. One can think of a number of reasons why respondent reports of plan type differ from the reports submitted by their employers. There are several reasons offered here as to why respondent reports may differ from employer reports.

The fault may lie with the respondent or the respondent's knowledge (see Gustman and Steinmeier 2005).

1. Some respondents may be badly informed about their pensions because their plans are too complex for them to understand. Other respondents may be able to understand their pensions after some effort but may choose not to exert the effort because the benefits are not worth the costs (Lusardi 1999). Either the

costs may be high because of the difficulty of the calculation or the benefits may be low. Low benefits may reflect a low dollar value of the pension, or they may reflect a good pension that, together with Social Security, will provide a good replacement rate so that further investigation will not affect either retirement or saving decisions.

2. When there is more than one plan, respondents may be confused when asked in the HRS and other surveys to talk about their most important plan. In most cases, the DB plan is the most important plan. Nevertheless, some respondents may think the DC plan is the most important of their plans. Even worse, the respondent may report that one plan is more important in some waves and that the other is more important in other waves. This confusion as to which plan is most important may be the result of the complexity of the pension calculation.

3. If some respondents do not participate in a plan and do not report being eligible for the plan, they consequently may report being covered by fewer plans than are listed by the firm. This could be a particular problem for those with a DC plan who do not contribute each year and who consider themselves not to be covered by the plan in years they do not contribute.

4. Respondents may misreport whether their plan has changed over time, which affects the plan type that is reported in different waves.

The fault may lie with the survey questions and design.

5. Survey questions that attempt to distinguish plan type may be poorly crafted. For example, the survey may present definitions of DB and DC plans and describe the properties of different plans, noting that a DB plan provides a benefit that is determined by salary and years of service, while a DC plan provides an account. These descriptions may be unclear to the respondent.

The fault may lie with the process of collecting and matching employer-provided plan descriptions to a particular respondent (Rohwedder 2003).

6. A firm may offer a large number of plans of different types and may have submitted many plan descriptions. SPDs list the characteristics of those workers who are covered by the particular plan being described, for example, union, full time, hired in a specified window, say from 1990 to 2000. Still, the characteristics of the respondent and of the covered workers may not be stated precisely enough. As a result, the wrong plan description may be selected from the group of plans submitted by the firm to the HRS.

7. In some cases, the firm may not have sent in all the available plan descriptions for its employees, or the full set of plan descriptions may not have been available from the supplementary sources used by the HRS when collecting plan documents.[4]

8. There may be some matching problems based on the date of the SPD, whether received from the firm or from other sources.[5]

Public pension plans may be a particular source of confusion as to plan type. First, DB plans offered by government entities commonly require a contribution by the covered worker, while most private sector DB plans do not. Second, there is a separate accounting in the public sector for the employee's contribution. Third, at the time of job termination, instead of waiting for a payment from the DB plan, government employees are often given the opportunity to cash out or roll over an account that holds only the employee's contribution. About 43 percent (1,000/2,325) of all respondents to the HRS with matched plan documents are government employees. Those respondents usually have a DB plan or both a DB and a DC plan. Only about 3 percent of them have a DC plan only.

We will examine the importance of these explanations in the remainder of the chapter.

4. Consistency between Employer and Respondent Reports

The period we consider to examine the consistency between respondent and firm reports spans from the early 1980s through 2004. The early data are from the 1983 Survey of Consumer Finances (SCF); the later data are from the HRS. The intervening period is characterized by a sharp trend in pension plan type, with the share of respondents reporting a DB plan falling from 91.6 percent in the 1983 SCF to 38 percent in the 2004 HRS. Each of the two surveys provides information both from respondents and from employers, and both sets of data are consistent with other data highlighting the trend to DC plans. Note that all tables in this section include only observations where respondent reports have been matched to employer reports. Although the trend in plan type will have a major effect on the changing distributions among years, and is clearly reflected in the tables presented in this section, in dealing only with matched data, we are analyzing a selected sample that should not be used to measure the overall size of the trend to DC plans.[6] Readers who are interested only in the summary of the comparison between employer and respondent reports can move to table 2.4.

The SCF affords an opportunity to document for the period of the 1980s the extent of agreement between respondent reports of pension plan type and reports from firms indicating the type of pension covering the workers in the sample. It is based on a representative sample of all households and obtains detailed pension plan descriptions for those respondents who report they are covered by a pension.

Despite the overwhelming dominance of DB plans in the early 1980s, 40.3 percent of SCF respondents report either that they do not know the plan type or report a plan type that does not correspond to the plan type reported by the employer. One way of illustrating the extent of agreement and difference between the reports of respondents and firms is to contrast the column totals with the row totals in table 2.1A. Although 88.1 percent of firm reports in the 1983 SCF indicate coverage by a DB plan only, 58.9 percent of respondent reports indicate coverage by a DB plan only. Even adjusting for the "do not knows" (DKs), dividing 58.9 by .836, the fraction with a DB plan only is lower in the respondent data at 70.5 percent than in the firms' reports. Moreover, the fraction with both types of plans is also much higher in the respondent data, with 17.3 percent of respondents (20.7 percent of respondents who identified a plan type) suggesting they are covered by both types of plans, but only 3.5 percent of firm documents indicating coverage by both types of plans.

The number of respondents who thought they had a DC plan only corresponds rather well with firm reports of DC plan only. Adjusting the 7.4 percent figure in column 2, row 4 of table 2.1A for the fraction who answered DK, 8.9 percent of respondents who answered said they had a DC plan only. According to matched employer reports, as seen in row 2, column 5, 8.5 percent had a DC plan only. Moreover, by adding the total number of respondents who said they had a DB plan, either because they had a DB plan only or both types, the fraction of respondents who report a plan type who have a DB plan $[(58.9 + 17.3)/.836 = 91.1]$ is very close to the fraction whose employers reported they had a DB plan (91.6). The major difference is that the number of respondents who report any DC plan $[(7.4 + 17.3)/.836 = 29.5]$ greatly exceeds the 12 percent with a DC plan as reported in the firm data. The source of the discrepancy is the very high number with both types of plans in the respondent data compared with the firm reports.

TABLE 2.1 **Pension plan type as reported by the respondent and the firm, for current job held in 1983, including only those respondents with a matched pension plan**

A. Percentages with self-reported versus firm-provided plan types (Survey of Consumer Finances 1983)

	Self-reported in 1983, %				
	DB	DC	Both	DK	Total
Provider report in 1983	(1)	(2)	(3)	(4)	(5)
1. DB	55.2	4.0	15.1	13.8	88.1
2. DC	2.4	3.1	0.9	2.1	8.5
3. Both	1.2	0.3	1.4	0.5	3.5
4. Total	58.9	7.4	17.3	16.4	100.0
5. Number of observations	341.0	43.0	100.0	95.0	579.0

B. Percentages with self-reported plan type conditional on firm report of plan type (percentage of row total; Survey of Consumer Finances 1983)

1. DB	62.7	4.5	17.1	15.7	100
2. DC	28.6	36.7	10.2	24.5	100
3. Both	35.0	10.0	40.0	15.0	100
4. Total	58.9	7.4	17.3	16.4	100

Note: In panel A, agreements between firm and respondent reports are along the main diagonal. Disagreements between reports are reflected in the cells from rows 1, 2, and 3 and columns 1, 2, and 3 that are off the main diagonal. DB = defined benefit; DC = defined contribution; DK = do not know.
Source: Panel B: Gustman and Steinmeier (1989, table 6).

The diagonal of table 2.1A includes those cases in which the respondent and firm both report the same plan type. Along the diagonal, plan type reported in respondent data matches plan type in firm data for 59.7 percent of observations. The response is DK for 16.4 percent of respondents (row 4, column 4, of table 2.1A). Numbers that are off the diagonal are associated with some type of disagreement between the two indicators of plan type. Summing the remaining off-diagonal elements of the table and excluding DKs, 23.9 percent of the cases have misidentified their plan type.[7]

As seen in table 2.1B, at a time when most people had a DB plan, most people who could answer questions about plan type told interviewers they had a DB plan when their employer said they had one and told interviewers they had a DC plan when employer data suggested they had one. Thus in table 2.1B, only 4.5 percent of those whose employers' documents said they had a DB plan only reported they had a DC plan only. Of the 8.5 percent of respondents whose employer documents said they had a DC plan only, as seen in column 2, row 2, 36.7 percent of them agreed, with another 10.2 percent suggesting they had both a DB and a DC plan. Although 28.6 percent (column 1, row 2) of those whose employers reported they had a DC plan only reported having a DB plan only, that difference represents only 2.4 percent of all those with a pension.

Now consider more recent data from the HRS. We begin with HRS data from 1992, covering a population born in 1931–41 during a period in which there has been an obvious decline in the prevalence of DC plans. Comparing tables 2.1A and 2.2A, the growth in DC plans is obvious. According to the employer data from 1992, 52 percent (column 5 of table 2.2A, sum of rows 2 and 3) of all respondents reported a DC plan, either held alone or in combination with a DB plan. This compares with 12 percent with a DC plan (table 2.1A, column 5, sum of rows 2 and 3) in 1983. Note that the respondents who are older than 50 with greater union and manufacturing employment would be expected to have a larger fraction of a population with a DB plan and a smaller fraction of a population with a DC plan. Nevertheless, the strong trend to DC plans is obvious even given a comparison with the earlier SCF data covering the full age range of pension-covered workers.

TABLE 2.2 **Pension plan type as reported by the respondent and the firm, for current job held in 1992, including only those respondents with a matched pension plan**

A. Percentages with self-reported versus firm-provided plan types (Health and Retirement Study 1992)

	Self-reported in 1992, %				
	DB	DC	Both	DK	Total
Provider report in 1992	(1)	(2)	(3)	(4)	(5)
1. DB	27	7	13	1	48
2. DC	6	11	4	0	21
3. Both	14	6	11	1	31
4. Total	46	24	28	2	100
5. Number of observations	1,342	699	806	60	2,907

B. Percentages with self-reported plan type conditional on firm report of plan type (percentage of row total; Health and Retirement Study 1992)

1. DB	56	15	27	2	100
2. DC	26	54	18	2	100
3. Both	45	18	35	2	100
4. Total	46	24	28	2	100

Note: DB = defined benefit; DC = defined contribution; DK = do not know.
Source: Panel B: Gustman and Steinmeier (2004, table 6).

In 1992 the fraction of DK responses in the HRS was only 2 percent. This compares with a DK level of 16.4 percent recorded in the SCF survey from nine years earlier. One reason for the higher DK frequency in the SCF data may be the younger population of the SCF.

Comparing row totals with column totals, first in table 2.1A and then in table 2.2A, while in 1983 there were systematic discrepancies between the frequencies of reports of different plan types by respondents and employers, in 1992 there are no such discrepancies. In 1983, self-reports of DB plans fell below firm reports, and self-reports of coverage by both types of plans exceeded firm reports. In the 1992 HRS data, the overall distributions of plan type—DB only, DC only, and both—are similar whether reported by respondents or firms.[8]

Turning to the question of how often the respondent and employer reports of plan type agree for a given respondent, a larger number of responses fall in off-diagonal elements in 1992 than in 1983, signaling less agreement in each matched pair of reports in the latter year. Thus from table 2.2A, only 49 percent of responses lie along the main diagonal in 1992, versus 60 percent in 1983.

The extent of overall disagreement in 1992 between employers and respondents appears larger when we condition on provider (employer) responses and ask how well respondents' answers agree. From table 2.2B (row 1, column 2), among those whose firm report indicates a DB plan only, 15 percent of respondents report a DC plan only. Among those with a firm report of a DC plan only, 26 percent report a DB plan only (row 2, column 1). In row 3, column 2, 18 percent of respondents whose employer documents report both types of plans instead report having a DC plan only. Most of the rest reported a DB plan only, with only 35 percent of those respondents whose firms reported both a DB and a DC plan reporting having both a DB and a DC plan (row 3, column 3).

Moving to a more recent date when DC pensions have become even more prevalent, table 2.3 shows the distribution of plan type reported in 2004 by respondents in the core of the HRS and gleaned from firm documents. By 2004, employer-provided plan descriptions, which as of this writing are only available for 790 cases working in the private sector, reflect the very strong trend toward DC plans.[9] Only 38 percent of the private sector cases with at least one plan description and/or a statement from respondents' current pension plan(s) are DB, either held as DB plans alone (17 percent, from row 1, column 5) or in combination with a DC plan (21 percent, from row 3, column 5).[10]

TABLE 2.3 **Pension plan type as reported by the respondent and the firm, for current job held in 2004, including only private sector respondents with a matched pension plan**

A. Percentage of total responses (Health and Retirement Study 2004)

	Self-reported in 2004, %				
	DB	DC	Both	DK	Total
Provider report in 2004	(1)	(2)	(3)	(4)	(5)
1. DB	11	2	3	0	17
2. DC	9	43	8	2	62
3. Both	6	7	8	0	21
4. Total	25	52	20	3	100
5. Number of observations	201	412	155	22	790

B. Percentage of row total (Health and Retirement Study 2004)

1. DB	65	13	20	2	100
2. DC	14	70	14	3	100
3. Both	28	32	37	2	100
4. Total	25	52	20	3	100

Note: Employer data include plans processed as of May 2006. DB = defined benefit; DC = defined contribution; DK = do not know.

From table 2.3A, in 2004, as in 1983, we observe systematic differences in the average plan type reported between respondents and their employers. In total, from column 5, row 1, 17 percent of provider reports indicate a DB plan only, while 25 percent of respondent reports (column 1, row 4) indicate coverage by a DB plan only. Although 62 percent of provider reports (row 2, column 5) suggest coverage by a DC plan only, 52 percent of respondents (row 4, column 2) indicate coverage by a DC plan only. Since 20 percent of the respondent reports (row 4, column 3) and 21 percent of the firm reports (row 3, column 5) indicate coverage by both types of plans, the difference between respondent and firm reports lies in the overstatement of those with a DB plan and the corresponding understatement by respondents of the fraction with a DC plan. Altogether, 38 percent of firm reports indicate coverage by a DB plan, either exclusively (row 1, column 5) or in combination with a DC plan (row 3, column 5), while 45 percent of respondent reports indicate coverage by a DB plan (row 4, column 1 plus row 4, column 3).

In 2004, almost two-thirds (62 percent) of the observations lie along the main diagonal, indicating a higher number of cases in which respondents and their employers agree as to the plan type. This is somewhat better than the situation in 1983 and much better than the situation with the HRS data in the first year of the survey, 1992. Only 3 percent of respondents report they do not know their plan type.

Other discrepancies are reported in table 2.3B. Of those whose firm reports coverage by a DC plan only, 14 percent of respondents report coverage by a DB plan only, and 14 percent report coverage by both a DB and a DC plan (row 2, sum of columns 1 and 3). Among those whose firm reports a DB plan only, 13 percent report coverage by a DC plan only (row 1, column 2), while 20 percent report coverage by both types of plans (row 1, column 3).

Table 2.4 summarizes a number of the key findings over the three surveys, highlighted here as follows:

- The trend from DB to DC plans is reflected in the values from employer-produced plan descriptions seen for those respondents who report having a pension and who have matched employer pension plan descriptions. Row 1 indicates the decline in the proportion of respondents with matched plan descriptions holding DB plans only, from 88.1 percent of plans held by pension-covered workers of all ages in the 1983 SCF, to 48 percent and 17 percent of all pension-covered workers with matched employer plans in the HRS in 1992 and private sector workers in 2004, respectively. Row 2 shows the corresponding increase in the proportion of respondents with DC plans from 8.5 percent in the 1983 SCF to 62 percent in the 2004 HRS, while row 3 shows the fraction holding both a DB and a DC plan, with an increase from 3.5 percent to 21 percent between the 1983 sample of all ages and the 2004 HRS sample of older workers only. Again, because these samples are selected to include only those respondents with matched employer data, because the SCF and HRS contain respondents of different ages, and because the 2004 HRS data include only private sector workers, these figures are meant to provide baseline indications of reports rather than the basis for calculating trends over these years.
- The fraction of respondents who do not know their plan type is lower in later years (table 2.4, line 4). Some of the difference probably reflects the younger age of the population in the 1983 SCF data than in the HRS data collected in later years.
- The fraction of respondents who correctly identify their plan type has no strong trend over time, running about 60 percent in 1983 and about 62 percent in 2004 (table 2.4, line 5). These numbers reflect the share of the sample that falls along

the main diagonal of tables 2.1A, 2.2A, and 2.3A, where respondent and firm reports for a given observation agree. Although the fraction saying they do not know their plan type is much lower in the HRS than in the SCF, the frequency of other errors appears to increase over time. The findings from 1983–2004 raise questions about one hypothesis for explaining systematic disagreement between respondent and firm reports of plan type. To the extent that data from secondary DC plans (that is, DC plans of lower value than the primary plan) are more difficult to collect from employers than are the data from DB plans, it might be argued that the frequency of DC plans is systematically understated in employer data. But the patterns of discrepancies are uneven. Moreover, in 2004 we find that coverage by DB plans is overreported by respondents, while coverage by DC plans is underreported by respondents, relative to the distributions in employer-produced plan descriptions.

- Rows 6, 7, and 8 of table 2.4 take the report from the employer pension plan description as correct and compare the probability of DB only, DC only, and both plan types being reported by the respondent with the corresponding probability from firm reports. There are no consistent patterns in these data indicating that the degree of either over- or understatement is consistent over time. Rather, when DB plans are the dominant plan, as in 1983, the frequency of DB only is understated by respondents, while in the period in which DC is the dominant plan type, the frequency of DC only is understated, as in 2004.

- Those whose firms reported they had a DB plan were less likely to claim erroneously that they had a DC plan in 1983 (column 1, rows 9 and 10) than in 2004. In 2004, with the DC as the dominant type of plan, those whose firms reported a DB plan only reported with greater frequency (in column 3, rows 9 and 10) that they had a DC plan only or both types of plans than in 1983.

- In 1983, when DB was the dominant type of plan, those who worked for firms reporting their plan was DC only were much more likely to report that they had a DB plan (column 1, row 11) than was the case for those who worked for a firm reporting DC only in 2004 (column 3, row 11), when DC was the dominant type of plan.

To summarize, errors in reporting are substantial. They are sufficiently complex and vary enough over time that they are not easy to characterize or remove. The complexity of the misclassifications by respondents does suggest important changes for the HRS. There will be an increased effort to collect employer-provided pension plan descriptions, and beginning with the 2008 respondent survey, there will be an increasing effort to condition as few questions as possible on respondent reports of pension plan type.

TABLE 2.4 **Summary of respondent and firm reports over time for respondents with matched firm data**

	1983	1992	2004[a]
1. DB only: employer data	88.1	48	17
2. DC only: employer data	8.5	21	62
3. Both: employer data	3.5	31	21
4. DK: respondent data	16.4	2	3
5. Share on diagonal: employee and respondent agree	59.7 percentage points on diagonal (despite high DK)	49 percentage points on diagonal	62 percentage points
6. Frequency of DB only in respondent compared with employer data	Badly understated (17.6 percentage points) in respondent report, after excluding DKs	Understated by 1 percentage point in respondent report, after excluding DKs	Overstated 8.8 percentage points in respondent report, after excluding DKs
7. Frequency of DC only in respondent compared with employer data	Overstated by 4 percentage points, after excluding DKs	Overstated 3.5 percentage points in respondent data after excluding DKs	Understated 8.8 percentage points in respondent data, after excluding DKs
8. Frequency of both in respondent compared with employer data	Overstated 17.2 percentage points, after excluding DKs	Understated 2.5 percentage points in respondent data after excluding DKs	Not overstated or understated in respondent data, after excluding DKs
9. Conditional on firm reporting DB only, respondent reporting DC only	4.5	15	13
10. Conditional on firm reporting DB only, respondent reporting both	17.1	27	20
11. Conditional on firm reporting DC only, respondent reporting DB	28.6	26	14
12. Conditional on firm reporting DC only, respondent reporting both	10.2	18	14
13. Conditional on firm reporting both, respondent reporting DB only	35	45	28
14. Conditional on firm reporting both, respondent reporting DC only	10	18	32

Note: DB = defined benefit; DC = defined contribution; DK = do not know.
[a] Private sector workers only.

5. Difference over Time in Respondent and Firm Reports among Those Reporting No Change in Their Pensions

One way to address reporting consistency is to consider reports over time only by those who indicate there has been no change in their plan. Accordingly, we turn to HRS respondents who reported in 1994, 1996, and 1998 that their pension plans did not change from the previous wave. Thus according to these respondents, their plans were identical in 1992 and 1998, two years for which employer plan reports are also available. Here we examine changes in both self-reports of plan type and in firm reports of plan type over the 1992–98 period.

For this exercise, it is important to determine whether those who report that their plans are unchanged over time between 1992 and 1998 have a similar distribution of plan type to all those with a pension in 1992. Comparisons indicate there is a close similarity in the fractions with DB only, DC only, and both types of plans in the two samples.[11]

If respondent reports were correct and plans matched correctly, there should be no change in plan type for anyone in this sample. Given the discrepancies we found in the previous section, it is not surprising to find that reported plan types vary over time for a significant minority of respondents who report no change in their plan. Moreover, when respondents report a different plan type from the one reported in 1992, they often misreport the nature of the change.

There are a number of possible reasons why the reported plan type changed even though a respondent said there was no change. The respondent may be wrong about the plan not having changed. Or, despite reporting correctly that the plan has not changed, the respondent may misidentify the plan type in one or another of the two years. A third possibility is that the respondent may have a DC plan but may participate in some years and not in others, failing to report plan type as DC in a year when not participating.

To avoid problems in cases in which the report of the most important plan changes over time because the respondent does not consistently value the plans, that is, in one year considers the DB plan to be the most important and in another year considers the DC plan to be the most important, we classify plans as DB only, DC only, and both. So if a person has both types of plans in different periods but considers the DB plan to be the most important in one period and the DC plan to be the most important in the other, we tabulate whether the respondent has reported on two plans and do not take account of which one was listed as most important in each period.

By contrasting the changes for the respondent sample and the firm sample, the evidence suggests that plans have changed in many more cases than respondents think. Table 2.5A shows the distribution of self-reported plan types between 1992 and 1998 for those who report no change in plan type. Along the diagonal, we see that 58 percent of respondents report the same plan type in 1998 as they did in 1992 (32 + 16 + 10). From row 1 of table 2.5B, among those who reported having a DB only in 1992, 72 percent continue to report a DB only in 1998, 16 percent report a DC plan only, and 11 percent report both. Thus there is a reported gain in DC plans only, replacing DB plans only, and an 11 percent increase in the frequency of both types of plans.

Since these changes are in the direction of trends in plan type, they cannot be dismissed out of hand. However, for the 25 percent of respondents reporting a plan type who reported a DC plan only in 1992, as seen from table 2.5B, row 2, 22 percent of respondents report that their plan type switched back to a DB plan only, and another 14 percent claim that they gained a DB plan as their firm adopted both types of plans. Yet we know there was almost no adoption of new DB pension plans after the mid-1980s (Ippolito and Thompson 2000). Similarly, from row 3 of table 2.5B, 50 percent of those who claimed to have both a DB and a DC plan in 1992 claim to have lost the DC plan in the intervening six years, while 15 percent of those with both types of plans claim to have lost their DB plan over the intervening period.

Now consider the changes in employer-reported plan type for this sample of employers who claim their plans were unchanged over the period. From table 2.5C, only 55 percent (14 + 16 + 25) of the observations lie along the diagonal, suggesting that plan type changed for the remaining 45 percent of the sample. The changes found in this table, and examined further in table 2.5D, are much more consistent with what is known about trends in pensions over the period. Thus while only 30 percent of those with a DB plan only in 1992 have employer reports suggesting they are covered by a DB plan only in 1998, the reason is that 64 percent of them now are covered by both types of plans. More importantly, among those with a DC plan only in 1992, their employer-provided data suggest they are covered by a DC plan only in 83 percent of the cases. In sharp contrast with the self-reported data in table 2.5B, where 36 percent of respondents with a DC plan only reported gaining a DB plan over the intervening

TABLE 2.5 **Self-report and provider report of pension plan type, over time**

A. Percentage distribution of self-reported plan type for respondents reporting the same pension plan from 1992 to 1998 and with matched 1992 and 1998 plan data (Health and Retirement Study 1992, 1998)

	Self-reported in 1998, %				
	DB	DC	Both	DK	Total
Self-reported in 1992	(1)	(2)	(3)	(4)	(5)
1. DB	32	7	5	0	45
2. DC	6	16	4	0	25
3. Both	14	4	10	0	28
4. Total	52	28	19	0	100
5. Number of observations	235	128	85	2	450

B. Distribution of self-reported plan type in 1998 by self-reported plan type in 1992, for respondents reporting the same pension plan from 1992 to 1998 and with matched 1992 and 1998 plan data (Health and Retirement Study 1992, 1998)

1. DB	72	16	11	1	100
2. DC	22	64	14	0	100
3. Both	50	15	35	0	100
4. Total	52	28	19	0	100

C. Percentage distribution of firm-reported plan type for respondents reporting the same pension plan from 1992 to 1998 and with matched 1992 and 1998 plan data (Health and Retirement Study 1992, 1998)

	Provider report in 1998, %			
	DB	DC	Both	Total
Provider report in 1992	(1)	(2)	(3)	(4)
1. DB	14	3	31	48
2. DC	1	16	2	19
3. Both	6	2	25	33
4. Total	21	21	58	100
5. Number of observations	95	94	261	450

D. Distribution of firm-reported plan type in 1998 by firm-reported plan type in 1992, for respondents reporting the same pension plan from 1992 to 1998 and with matched 1992 and 1998 plan data (Health and Retirement Study 1992, 1998)

1. DB	30	6	64	100
2. DC	5	83	13	100
3. Both	18	7	76	100
4. Total	21	22	58	100

Note: DB = defined benefit; DC = defined contribution; DK = do not know.

period, only 18 percent (5 + 13) of those whose employer reported they had a DC plan only in 1992 were seen to gain a DB plan over the six years. Although more in line with known trends, the gain in DB plans in the private sector among the employer data does suggest some difference in matching procedures over time or in the number of plan descriptions provided by employers over time. Of perhaps greater interest, according to this sample of respondents, there was no change in their plans between 1992 and 1998, yet the changes observed in employer-reported plan types mirror the strong changes observed among general holders of pensions.

We also find discrepancies when we consider results for a sample of 48 respondents who reported no change in their pension for the entire period between 1992 and 2004 and have matched plan data for both 1992 and 2004 surveys and for a comparable sample between 1998 and 2004.[12]

To summarize, we find misreporting by respondents on two fronts: they report their plan types have not changed when they have, and they misreport the types of plans that they hold. Of the respondents who reported no change in their pension for the period of 1992–98 and have matched plan documents, 58 percent of respondent reports indicate the same plan type(s) in those two periods. According to their plan documents, 55 percent of them had the same plan type in both years. Moreover, the changes observed in the employer sample correspond more closely to trends in pensions in the 1990s found in administrative data such as Form 5500 data from the Department of Labor, while those reported by respondents do not.

For the corresponding periods 1992–2004 and 1998–2004, the matches were better. For the respondent-reported plan types, among those who reported no change in their pensions, the plan types are the same over the period in 62 and 68 percent of the cases, respectively. For the plan documents, the same plan types are reported in 72 and 63 percent of the cases over the two time periods, respectively.[13]

6. Comparison with Payroll Data from a Sample Produced by Watson Wyatt

There are a number of potential problems that may result from the process of matching firm reports of plan type to the covered workers in the HRS sample. Although the SPDs describe the characteristics of covered workers and although HRS asks respondents about these characteristics (for example, hourly or weekly employee, union member, white collar or blue collar, history of employment, and coverage at the firm), there is always a chance for slippage in matching a plan to an individual. Moreover, despite requests that firms send HRS all their plans, they may not have supplied a full set of matched plans.[14]

Using payroll data matched with respondent reports of plan type can help to determine whether there are strong consequences from these limitations on the pension-matching process used by the HRS. HRS does not have payroll data for its covered respondents. But the Watson Wyatt Company has made available a matched sample with both payroll and respondent survey data. Because the payroll data reveal the worker's pension plans with certainty, comparisons of respondent reports of plan type with the plan types reported in the payroll data provides a reliable indication of the extent of misreporting of plan type by respondents. Since we find the same degree of misreporting by respondents whether the baseline from employer data is taken to be SPDs collected from respondent employers or the payroll data collected by Watson Wyatt, the suggestion is that most of the discrepancy between respondent- and firm-produced data is due to misreports by the respondent.

Steve Nyce (2007) of Watson Wyatt has followed this methodology by matching payroll data from the human resources departments of a number of firms with data from pension questionnaires administered to workers covered by those plans. Moreover, he has, at our request, reformatted his findings to allow a direct comparison with table 2.3, which relates employer and respondent data for the 2004 HRS.[15]

In table 2.3A, 62 percent of HRS observations are on the main diagonal, where respondent reports match firm reports. In table 2.6A, the comparable figure for the Watson Wyatt sample is 65 percent.[16] Because there are overall differences in the samples of covered workers, it is useful to focus on respondent reports of plan type conditional on the plan type reported in firm-provided data. When we do that, the two tables match remarkably well.

For convenience, the comparisons are summarized in table 2.6C. The bottom line from this table is that when respondents' reports of pension plan type disagree with the reports by their employers, the error is in the respondents' reports. Among those with a firm report of a DB only, in the HRS data, the percentages of respondents reporting DB, DC, and both are 65, 13, and 20. In the Watson Wyatt data, the percentages reporting DB, DC, and both are 62, 16, and 10, which when adjusted for the additional

TABLE 2.6 **Firm versus respondent reports of plan type using Watson Wyatt data purged of those with no pension coverage, age 20–64**

A. Percentage of total responses

Provider report (Watson Wyatt data)	Respondent report (Watson Wyatt data), %				
	DB	DC	Both	DK	Total
	(1)	(2)	(3)	(4)	(5)
1. DB	2	0	0	0	3
2. DC	0	18	6	2	26
3. Both	2	21	45	2	70
4. Total	5	40	52	4	100
5. Number of observations	344	2,958	3,876	253	7,471

B. Percentage of row total

1. DB	62	16	10	13	100
2. DC	2	68	24	7	100
3. Both	3	30	64	2	100
4. Total	5	40	52	4	100

C. Comparison of selected plan type outcomes between Health and Retirement Study and Watson Wyatt data, percent on the main diagonal

	2004 Health and Retirement Study	2003 Watson Wyatt
Firm reports DB only:		
Respondent says DB only	65	62
Respondent says DC only	13	16
Respondent says both only	20	10
Firm reports DC only:		
Respondent says DB only	14	2
Respondent says DC only	70	68
Respondent says both only	14	24

Note: DB = defined benefit; DC = defined contribution; DK = do not know.

10 percent DK in the Watson Wyatt sample, come relatively close to the HRS values. For those whose firms report DC only, the comparable fractions in the HRS are 14, 70, and 14, while the corresponding figures in the Wyatt sample are 2, 68, and 24. There is a larger tendency in the Watson Wyatt sample to mistakenly pick DC only, rather than to mistakenly pick DB only, as in the HRS. The largest discrepancy is in the fraction whose employers say they have both types of plans who report coverage by both. In the HRS, 37 percent of those whose employers report both also report both. In the Watson Wyatt data, when the employer reports both, 64 percent of respondents report both.

It is obvious that the findings from the HRS and Watson Wyatt survey are highly complementary. Much of the discrepancy remains between respondent and firm identification of plan type, even when the match is perfect between the respondent- and the employer-provided plan description. The comparisons between the Watson Wyatt and HRS findings indicate that most of the discrepancy between firm- and respondent-reported data results from errors or misunderstanding by respondents. This suggests that findings to date with HRS data are valid. Accordingly, findings with Watson Wyatt payroll data suggest that HRS data can be used to estimate and model the effects of imperfect knowledge in analyses of retirement and saving.

For the first time, results based on Watson Wyatt data also provide an indication of underreporting of pension coverage. HRS does not try to collect plan descriptions from those who report not having a pension. Findings with Watson Wyatt data suggest that underreporting of pension coverage amounts to about 5 percent. To allow comparisons, table 2.6 removes this 5 percent from the sample.

7. Plan Type in the Full Respondent Panel

In this section, we use the HRS panel to expand our analysis of changes in reported plan type by respondents who report that their plans have remained unchanged. The data allow us to consider both consistency across adjoining waves and cumulative consistency over a number of waves. Once again it will be apparent that many people who claim to have unchanging pension plans nevertheless change their reported plan types over time.[17]

Table 2.7 documents some of the inconsistencies that arise in the panel among respondent reports of number of plans and plan type for a sample of respondents who report that their pension plans have not changed since their previous interview. In this table, we see differences over two consecutive interviews. Comparing adjoining waves, typically one-fifth to one-third of those reporting no change in their pensions nevertheless report a different number of plans or plan type than they reported in the previous wave. For example, row 1, column 2, of table 2.7 indicates that there were 2,771 cases who reported how many pensions they held in wave 2 of the HRS. Out of this group, there were 752 cases (27 percent) who reported a different number of plans from the number they had reported in their

TABLE 2.7 **Number of respondents reporting the same pension across waves but reporting differ-ent plan numbers and plan types (Health and Retirement Study 1992–2006)**

Respondents with the same pension	Same pension (1)	Number of plans[a] (2)	At least one DB plan (3)	At least one DC plan (4)
1. Wave 2	2,786	2,771	1,790	1,110
Wave 1 different from wave 2		752 (27)	329 (18)	251 (23)
2. Wave 3	2,378	2,369	1,303	1,048
Wave 2 different from wave 3		566 (24)	267 (20)	356 (34)
3. Wave 4	2,125	2,098	1,019	983
Wave 3 different from wave 4		599 (29)	299 (29)	308 (31)
4. Wave 5	2,227	2,215	1,132	1,126
Wave 4 different from wave 5		559 (25)	317 (28)	268 (24)
5. Wave 6	1,817	1,809	875	862
Wave 5 different from wave 6		519 (29)	260 (30)	230 (27)
6. Wave 7	1,548	1,548	696	835
Wave 6 different from wave 7		443 (29)	217 (31)	229 (27)
7. Wave 8	2,144	2,135	959	1,165
Wave 7 different from wave 8		635 (30)	268 (28)	220 (19)

Note: Data in parentheses are percentages.
[a]Do not knows and refusals are excluded.

wave 1 interview. Similarly, row 1, column 3, shows that there were 1,790 cases who reported having at least one DB plan in wave 2. Of those, 329 (18 percent) reported not having any DB plans in wave 1. Row 1, column 4, shows the number of respondents (1,110 cases) reporting at least one DC plan in wave 2. There were 251 cases out of the 1,110 (or 23 percent) who did not report any DC plans in wave 1, even though they reported that their plan was unchanged since wave 1.

Cumulative changes since wave 1 are reported in table 2.8. For example, row 5, column 3, indicates that 383 respondents in wave 6 were working at the same employment since wave 1, reporting each period there had been no change in their pension since the last period. Out of this group, 206 cases reported having at least one DB plan in wave 6 (excluding DK/refusals), and 125 of them (61 percent) reported a plan type that did not include a DB plan in at least one previous wave. Row 5, column 4, shows the number of respondents (174) with at least one DC plan in wave 6 who reported no change in their pension since wave 1. Out of this group, there

TABLE 2.8 **Those with cumulative inconsistencies in respondent reports of number of plans and plan type for those reporting no change in their pensions since wave 1 (Health and Retirement Study 1992–2006)**

Respondents with the same pension[a]	Same pension (1)	Number of plans[b] (2)	At least one DB plan (3)	At least one DC plan (4)
1. Wave 2	2,786	2,771	1,790	1,110
Wave 2 different from wave 1		752 (27)	329 (18)	251 (23)
2. Wave 3	1,776	1,768	1,030	757
Wave 3 different from wave 2 or wave 1		635 (36)	303 (29)	353 (47)
3. Wave 4	1,120	1,113	609	511
Wave 4 different from wave 3, 2, or 1		473 (42)	241 (40)	282 (55)
4. Wave 5	663	660	362	323
Wave 5 different from wave 4, 3, 2, or 1		298 (45)	193 (53)	195 (60)
5. Wave 6	383	381	206	174
Wave 6 different from wave 5, 4, 3, 2, or 1		157 (41)	125 (61)	112 (64)
6. Wave 7	213	213	108	107
Wave 7 different from wave 6, 5, 4, 3, 2, or 1		92 (43)	69 (64)	78 (73)
7. Wave 8	119	119	55	53
Wave 8 different from wave 7, 6, 5, 4, 3, 2, or 1		51 (43)	36 (65)	40 (75)

Note: Data in parentheses are percentages.
[a]The sample in each wave includes respondents who were interviewed and reported the same pension since wave 1. For example, the wave 5 sample includes respondents who reported the same pension in wave 2, 3, 4, and 5. Respondents who have skipped an interview are not included in the samples.
[b]Do not know and refusals are excluded. Zero number of plans is not excluded.

are 112 cases (64 percent) who did not report any DC plans in one or more of the previous waves.

The cumulative results show the extent of misreporting in the panel. By wave 8, despite having reported no change from wave 1 to wave 8, two-thirds to three-quarters of respondents who consistently report no change in their plans over the entire period nevertheless are reporting a different plan type in at least one previous wave than they reported in wave 8, and 43 percent are reporting a different number of plans. One simply cannot take a report that the plan has not changed at face value, especially if one is trying to understand the evolution of a respondent's pension over the life cycle.

8. Evidence from the HRS Pension Modules

With an eye toward developing a procedure to improve identification of plan type, in 2004 the HRS administered a special supplement/module to the core survey inquiring about detailed pension plan characteristics including plan type or name.[18] In this module, in contrast to the core, plan types were not defined, but respondents were asked if they knew the technical name or the type of their plan.

If the response was affirmative, they were asked to name it. If the response was negative they were presented with a list of plan names to choose from. Those respondents who did not know the name of their plan and could not identify it from the list were read the definition of a DB plan and asked whether their plan was a DB.

Seventy-three percent of respondents reported they knew the plan name or type of their most important plan. About 49 percent of those reporting they knew their most important plan type reported a 401(k). Another 20 percent of them reported another type of DC plan. A respondent was much less likely to report having a DB plan if unprompted or being read the term "defined benefit" but without an explanation of that term.

Respondents did well in identifying 401(k) plans. They did much less well in identifying DB plans. Thus, when we paired respondent reports from the module with plan type from employer documents, about 84 percent of respondents who reported having a 401(k) only had a matched plan document from their employer indicating that the employer offered a DC plan only. Among respondents with a matched employer plan description for a DC plan only, about 80 percent of them reported a DC only. In contrast, among respondents who had a matched employer document for a DB plan only, about 42 percent of them reported a DB plan only. About 20 percent of respondents with a matched employer document for a DB plan only answered DK when asked their plan type. In contrast, 5 percent of respondents with a matched DC only answered DK when asked their plan type.

These findings again suggest that respondents have a good deal of information about their pensions but that a number do not know their plan type. The method used in the module may improve the accuracy of respondent answers. Nevertheless, it appears that respondent reports of plan type will continue to be characterized by errors.

Much of this study has focused on the reasons for discrepancies between respondent and firm reports of pension plan types, with much of the evidence pointing to reporting errors by respondents. Before concluding, we wish to consider the consequences of this finding for one approach to redesigning surveys such as the HRS. In particular, one might ask whether it is possible to skip the step of identifying plan type altogether. Why should surveys simply not ask all respondents all questions about pensions, whether the preponderance of evidence suggests they have a DC or a DB plan?

One answer is contained in table 2.9, which is based on an experiment HRS conducted in 2006. People were deliberately asked questions appropriate for plan types they did not have. It looks like respondents will move outside the current sequence to provide an answer, that is, will provide information about a plan other than the one he/she is currently reporting on, whether appropriate or not.

When respondents who report that their plan is DB are asked for the account balance, 62 percent of them provide an account balance, either directly or indirectly in the form of brackets. To further understand just what it means when someone who says they have a DB plan reports a plan balance, we did a preliminary analysis for three groups.

1. *Respondents who have both a DB and DC.* Among the respondents who reported their plan was DB, the balance some of them supplied was appropriate for their second plan, which was DC. More specifically, fourteen out of

TABLE 2.9 **Respondents with DB plans answering to DC questions and vice versa in 2006 (Health and Retirement Study 2006[a])**

Questions	Respondents (Rs)
Rs with DB: receiving quarterly report	Yes: 40% (466/1,153)
Rs with DB/both/DK: Receiving quarterly report	Yes: 43% (595/1,382)
Rs with DB: account balances	Reported:
	No account: 5% (61/1,138)
	Zero balance: 1% (12/1,138)
	An amount: 27% (300/1,138)
	Through brackets: 36% (410/1,138)
	Total: 62% (714/1,138)
Rs with DC: had automatic enrollment	30% (451/1,497)
Rs with DC: expecting lifetime benefits	49% (727/1,497)
Rs with DC: expected amount of benefits	Reported:
	An amount: 36% (534/1,497)
	Through brackets: 19% (281/1,497)
	Total: 55% (809/1,497)

Note: DB = defined benefit; DC = defined contribution; DK = do not know; Rs = respondents.
[a]The 2006 data are from the early-release version.

eighty-two in the selected sample report the amount in their secondary DC account when asked for their balance in their primary DB account.

2. *Respondents who report balances for DB plans.* Comparing the expected value of the benefit in 2006 with the value of the account balances when a person with a DB is asked how much is in the account, we would expect to see the account balance somewhere between ten and twenty times the expected yearly benefit. Again in a selected sample, the ratios of account balance to expected yearly benefit range from less than 1 to 50. Many ratios are in the low single digits.

3. *Respondents who report different plan types in 2004 and 2006.* Seventeen out of fifty-nine of them report a DB balance in 2006 that is very close to their DC balance in 2004.

Should surveys ask all pension-covered workers about their plan balance, users are going to find it very difficult to interpret what the respondent is reporting when he or she reports a DB plan and then a balance. In many cases, the report will simply reflect a misunderstanding or will be the result of the respondent assuming that a question that is not appropriate for a person having their plan type really does make sense.

As seen in table 2.9, other responses are also likely to be error ridden when respondents are asked questions appropriate for plan types they do not hold. Forty percent of respondents who report they have a DB plan also report they receive quarterly reports on their pension, when asked. But quarterly reports are common for those who hold a DC plan, and much less common for those with a DB plan. Forty-nine percent of those who report their plan is DC indicate they will receive lifetime benefits, when asked, even though annuities are rare for DC plans and most benefits take the form of an account balance that becomes available upon retirement. Fifty-five percent even reported an expected amount for the benefit (either directly or through brackets).

Thus a survey that is designed to very carefully separate the question sequences between different plans, trying hard to avoid any double counting, may hopelessly entangle certain answers pertaining to different plans if plans are not separated according to type. Moreover, some of the answers provided to irrelevant questions may simply be erroneous. Although many questions can be asked regardless of plan type, one cannot entirely skip the process of determining plan type before asking certain questions. Asking a respondent certain questions about a plan type he or she does not have is inviting error in the response.

9. Summary and Implications

Summary

Respondent reports contain a good deal of useful information about their pensions. Watson Wyatt data suggest that underreporting of plan coverage is not too severe. Moreover, on average, respondent reports do a good job of describing the overall distribution of pension plan type. Thus respondent reports of plan type often indicate the same frequency of occurrence for those with DB only, DC only, or both plans as do employer data.

However, our findings suggest there is also a great deal of error in respondents' reports of plan type. Although much of this error is offsetting in the aggregate, so that the overall frequencies of plan type are close to the values reported by employers, the errors have serious implications for respondent knowledge and understanding of their pensions.

Although section 3 includes eight reasons for discrepancies between respondent reports of plan type and firm reports gleaned from employer-produced SPDs matched by HRS staff, our findings suggest that most of the error is on the side of the respondent. Allowing the numbers in parentheses to refer to the reasons for mismatches noted in the list in section 3, (1) we find that discrepancies between the Watson Wyatt payroll data, which are not subject to significant error in matching the firm data, and employee responses look very similar to discrepancies found between employee responses and the plan type gleaned from matched SPDs produced by employers. This strongly supports a view that the error in reported plan type is on the respondent's side. Further evidence that the bulk of the error is due to the respondent includes our findings of inconsistencies in respondent reports over time among those who report no change in plan type and in comparison with known trends. (2) Our results also suggest that respondents have some difficulty in determining which is their most important plan. If questions are asked about the wrong plan type, our evidence suggests that respondents with more than one plan may become confused as to which plan the interviewer is referring to. We avoid the implied problem by categorizing the types of pensions covering a particular worker according to whether the plans are one type only, the other type only, or both types. However, there is a cost to this approach. By not focusing on each plan individually, the burden of trying to determine which plan is most important is lifted from the respondent, but at the cost of aggregating results that could be analyzed on a plan-by-plan basis. (3) We do find some undercounting of pension coverage in Watson Wyatt data, but the extent of undercounting is relatively small. (4) Panel data confirm that respondents do misreport whether their plan has changed over time. (5) Respondent errors in reporting their plan type are reduced if respondents are first asked the name or type of plan they have and are then read the definitions of various plan types. Respondents often remember the name of their plan, but they do not do a good job of deciding whether their plan is DB or DC. That distinction is best determined from employer data or from the respondents' recall of the name of their plan. (6) (7) (8) Evidence from the Watson Wyatt data suggests that problems in matching SPDs to respondents are not the main reasons for the mismatches between plan type reported by respondents and plan type found in SPDs from firms.

The bottom line from this evidence is that respondents frequently misreport pension plan type. Even if there is only one plan, if respondents answer questions that are not appropriate for their plan type (for example, even though they have a DB plan, they are asked to report the amount accumulated in their plan), they are likely to provide inappropriate answers that cannot be understood in the context of their plans. They misreport pension plan type because they do not understand their pensions well. As DB plans take on more of the features of DC plans, morphing through cash balance or related plans, and as DC plans take on more of the characteristics of DB plans, offering opportunities for annuitizing benefits and imposing defaults and participation requirements, it is even less likely that respondents will correctly categorize their plans.

Implications for Survey Design

Our findings suggest certain modifications in the design of surveys to reduce reporting error. One suggestion arises from our finding that respondents misreport whether their plans have changed over time. To save time, the HRS has conditioned the set of pension questions asked in particular waves on whether the respondent reports a pension change since the last wave of the survey. When the respondent reports no pension change, the set of questions asked is truncated and some responses from the previous wave are used. But if some of these plans have changed, it is inappropriate to use answers from a previous wave.

Another implication concerns the way the information about plan type is elicited. Plan type will be more accurately identified by those who have DC pensions if they are simply asked what type of pension they have. In contrast, respondents with a DB plan will be more accurate in reporting their plan type when the characteristics of a DB plan are read to them before they are asked about plan type. As a result of these findings, the 2008 version of the HRS will ask respondents first whether they know the name or type of plan they have and, if so, what it is. Then the definition of each plan type will be read to respondents, and they will be asked to identify plan type.

Although respondent reports of plan type are subject to errors, and these errors sometimes create systematic bias, we have also shown that respondent reports do contain a good deal of useful information. Given the information content of respondent answers, alternative approaches to identifying plan type within surveys become less attractive. For example, we have shown elsewhere (Gustman and Tabatabai 2006) that it would not help the situation much to try to identify plan type from respondent reports of characteristics that are disproportionately associated with either a DB or with a DC plan, for example, whether a respondent receives a report about the plan on a quarterly basis, whether the plan pays lifetime benefits, and others.

The evidence also shows that providing a person with the opportunity to report on the wrong plan type will invite the individual to present erroneous information. That means one cannot simply ask every person all questions: those pertaining to the plan type they have as well as those pertaining to the plan type they do not have. Each time a person is asked a question pertaining to a different plan type from their own, the effect is to introduce complex errors that are difficult to unscramble.

One might suggest that survey questions should use information on plan type from firm-reported data. However, firm-reported pension data are available with a lag. They can only be collected from firms or the Web once the main survey is completed. If they are to be collected indirectly from government sources such as Department of Labor files containing attachments to Form 5500 data, an additional lag is created by any delays in the release of the government data. Moreover, once plan descriptions are obtained, it takes time to process them. Consequently, firm-reported data are not available on a timely basis for use in a survey.

Notes

Support was provided by National Institute on Aging grant nos. UO 1 HL AG09740 (Robert J. Willis, principal investigator) to the University of Michigan through a subcontract to Dartmouth College, IPOIAG022481 (Arie Kapteyn, principal investigator) through the Rand Corporation, and 5R01AG024337 (Alan L. Gustman, principal investigator) through the National Bureau of Economic Research. We would like to thank Steven Nyce from Watson Wyatt Worldwide for providing data comparing respondent reports of plan type with plan type indicated from their payroll records and Karen Pence for her comments. Additional results are available in a working paper, Gustman, Steinmeier, and Tabatabai (2007).

1. Gustman and Steinmeier (1989) provide a detailed discussion of how the various features of pensions affect the present value of the plan.

2. For example, see Mitchell (1988), Gustman and Steinmeier (1989, 2004), and Chan and Huff Stevens (2006).

3. It appears that retirement behavior conforms to the incentives from pensions only for those who understand how their pensions work (Chan and Huff Stevens 2005).

4. In the next round of matches, HRS pension coders have been instructed to create an index indicating the degree of certainty or uncertainty they hold as to the quality of the match; that is, how well a particular plan description applies to a given HRS respondent.

5. In 2005, HRS was collecting employer-produced pension plan descriptions from a number of sources. Respondents were collecting the descriptions directly from their employers. Presumably, if these respondents sent in all their plans, matching would be exact and up to date. Comparisons of plans submitted by respondents with those obtained from other sources should indicate the extent to which collection of outdated SPDs accounts for discrepancies between firm- and respondent-provided plan descriptions.

6. Although the SCF covers a younger age group than the HRS, the trend in reported plan type is obvious in any data set and has been documented extensively in the literature. See Gustman and Steinmeier (1992) for early results.

7. Even though a large number of observations fall off the main diagonal, the survey asks most of those with a DB plan about the details of the plan and asks many of those with a DC plan about the details of a DC plan. So 91.6 percent (88.1 + 3.5) of employer documents reported coverage by a DB plan, while 72.9 percent (55.2 + 1.2 + 15.1 + 1.4) of respondents whose employer reported a DB plan also reported coverage by a DB plan, amounting to 87.2 (72.9/.836) percent of those who reported a plan type.

8. There appears to be little overall disagreement in the average plan type reported by respondents and their employers in 1992. In table 2.2A, 48 percent of provider reports indicate a DB plan only (row 1, column 5), roughly the same total (46 percent) as in respondent reports (row 4, column 1). The fraction with a DC plan only (row 2, column 5) is 21 percent in the firm data and 24 percent (column 2, row 4) in the respondent data. The fraction found with any DC plan in the employer data in 1992 (column 5, sum of rows 2 and 3) is the same as the fraction

found in respondent reports (row 4, sum of columns 2 and 3). Similarly, 79 percent
of employer reports indicate coverage by a DB plan, either via coverage by a DB
plan only (row 1, column 5) or by both a DB and a DC plan (row 3, column 5), while
74 percent of respondent reports suggest coverage by a DB plan either alone or in
addition to a DC plan (row 4, sum of columns 1 and 3).

   9. In the 2004 survey, there are 3,685 respondents who reported being included
in one or more pension plan(s) through their current employment. As of the present time, employer plan descriptions and respondent's statements or plan descriptions have been roughly matched for 797 (523 + 329 − 55) of those respondents.
Thus, this exercise begins with about 22 percent (797/3,685) of respondents reporting a pension in the current job. Plans for government employees are not included
in the data.

   10. Although half the plans held by members of retirement age cohorts who are
working full time are still DB, fully half of all DB plans are held by public employees. Once the pension plans for government workers are matched, we expect that
almost half of the respondents with a pension in 2004 will be covered by a DB plan,
corresponding to the share of plans that are DB as reported by respondents.

   11. In table 2.2A, where data for 1992 are reported, the percentages of respondents reporting a DB, DC, and both types of plans was 46, 24, and 28 percent,
respectively. In table 2.5A, where plan type is reported among respondents who
reported their plan type has not changed between 1992 and 1998, the proportions
of respondents with DB, DC, and both types of plans in 1992 are 45, 25, and 28 percent, respectively. Also note that the subsample of employer-reported plan types
for respondents who reported the same pension in 1992 and 1998 in table 2.5C
matches the distribution of employer-reported plan types in table 2.2A for the
larger sample of all respondents with matched pensions in 1992. Thus in table 2.2A,
the percentages reported in employer data of DB, DC, and both types of plans in
1992 are 48, 21, and 31 percent, respectively. In table 2.5C, the corresponding figures
are 48, 19, and 33 percent, respectively.

   12. See our working paper, Gustman, Steinmeier, and Tabatabai (2007).

   13. Percentages are not additive because of varying sample sizes over the periods.

   14. Even if the matches obtained were perfect, plan matches are obtained for
only two-thirds of HRS respondents who indicate they are covered by a pension.
This means that when generating descriptive data that apply to the overall population, pension plan type has to be imputed for one-third of respondents. Moreover,
a major reason for trying to improve identification of plan type is to ensure that the
respondent is being asked questions that are appropriate for whatever plan type
is covering the individual. Employer data cannot help with the matching process.
They are not obtained until a year after the respondent survey and thus cannot be
used to determine which plan type to quiz the respondent about.

   15. Some differences between the Watson Wyatt data and the HRS data should

be noted. Although some analysis with the Watson Wyatt data suggests that age is not a dominating factor, the Watson Wyatt data cover a full age range, while the HRS data cover those over the age of 50. With regard to the definitions of coverage, there is only a slight difference between the Watson Wyatt and HRS data. We classify the following two cases as DK, while the Watson Wyatt data classify them as DC or DB respectively.

	Have DB	Have DC
1.	DK	Yes
2.	Yes	DK

Our categories for HRS data are DB only, DC only, and both. So if a respondent says DK to either DB or DC, we cannot tell whether he or she has both or not and therefore classify the response as DK.

The two data sets also treat cash balance plans differently, and cash balance plans are more likely to be found in the Watson Wyatt sample of large firms. HRS treats hybrid plans as DC (they involve an account), while the Watson Wyatt data separate out 401(k) and 403(b) and call them DC and classify hybrid plans as DB. Thus in the Watson Wyatt sample, 73 percent of respondents have a DB plan, which includes hybrid plans, while 28 percent of the sample has a hybrid plan. So 38 percent of Watson Wyatt DB plans are hybrid. It is clear that there are more DB plans in the Watson Wyatt sample of firms than in the HRS sample and that the HRS is much less successful in identifying hybrid plans in its sample. Note the possibility that with respondents in the HRS sample all over the age of 50, many more in the HRS will have been grandfathered into their old DB plans than would be the case for the younger Watson Wyatt sample.

There also are other differences between the populations surveyed. The Watson Wyatt sample is not nationally representative. Moreover, voluntary respondent participation is lower in the Watson Wyatt sample than in the HRS sample. Those who participate may be better informed about their pensions than those who refuse to take part in the survey, creating another source of bias.

16. In the HRS data, 17 percent of the respondent-matched, firm-reported plan types are DB only, 62 percent are DC only, and 21 percent are both. In the Watson Wyatt sample, 3 percent of respondent-matched plan types from payroll data are DB only, 26 percent are DC only, and 70 percent are both. Thus 38 percent of the HRS firm reports indicate coverage by any DB plan, while for 73 percent of the respondents in the Watson Wyatt sample, the payroll data suggest coverage by any DB plan. Hybrid plans are not nearly numerous enough to account for this difference. Similarly, in the HRS sample, 83 percent of firm reports involve any DC, while in the Watson Wyatt sample, 96 percent of reports involve any DC.

17. Changes in plan type observed in panel data among those who report no change in their pensions tell us how those in relatively stable employment situations perceive their plan type over time. The remainder of pension-covered work-

ers, those with pensions that change between waves, may be in less stable employment, may be located in firms that have switched to cash balance or other hybrid
plans, may be covered by plans that are more suitable for job changers, or may
have plans that differ for other reasons from the plans of those who remain at the
same job with an unchanging pension. There also is a question about how having
experienced a recent plan change affects knowledge or learning about one's pension. Those whose plans are unchanged from period to period may have a longer
period to learn about their pension. On the other hand, those with a recent pension
change may have just recently been made more aware of their plan type by their
employer.

18. These questions were contained in the Pension Characteristics Module and
administered to all those in the survey who reported having a pension.

References

Chan, Sewin, and Ann Huff Stevens. 2005. What You Don't Know Can't Help You:
     Knowledge and Retirement Decision Making. Working paper. New York Uni-
     versity, New York.
———. 2006. New Measures of Pension Knowledge. Working paper. New York
     University, New York.
Gustman, Alan L., and Thomas L. Steinmeier. 1989. An Analysis of Pension Ben-
     efit Formulas, Pension Wealth and Incentives from Pensions. *Research in Labor
     Economics* 10: 53–106.
———. 1992. The Stampede toward Defined Contribution Pension Plans: Fact or
     Fiction? *Industrial Relations* 31: 361–69.
———. 2004. What People Don't Know about Their Pensions and Social Security:
     An Analysis Using Linked Data from the Health and Retirement Study. In
     Public Policies and Private Pensions, edited by William G. Gale, John B. Shoven,
     and Mark J. Warshawsky, 57–119. Washington, DC: Brookings Institution.
———. 2005. Imperfect Knowledge of Social Security and Pensions. *Industrial Re-
     lations* 44: 373–97.
Gustman, Alan L., Thomas L. Steinmeier, and Nahid Tabatabai. 2007. Imperfect
     Knowledge of Pension Plan Type. Working paper. Dartmouth College, Han-
     over, NH.
Gustman, Alan L., and Nahid Tabatabai. 2006. Determining Plan Type in the HRS
     Pension Sequence. Mimeo. Dartmouth College, Hanover, NH.
Ippolito, Richard A., and John W. Thompson. 2000. The Survival Rate of Defined-
     Benefit Pension Plans, 1987–1995. *Industrial Relations* 39: 228–45.
Lusardi, Annamaria. 1999. Information, Expectations, and Savings for Retirement.
     In *Behavioral Dimensions of Retirement Economics,* edited by Henry Aaron,
     81–115. Washington, DC: Brookings Institution.

Mitchell, Olivia. 1988. Worker Knowledge of Pension Provisions. *Journal of Labor Economics* 6: 28–39.

Nyce, Steven A. 2007. Behavioral Effects of Employer-Sponsored Retirement Plans. *Journal of Pension Economics and Finance* 6: 251–85.

Rohwedder, Susann. 2003. Measuring Pension Wealth in the HRS: Employer and Self-Reports. Unpublished manuscript. Rand Corporation, Santa Monica, CA.

CHAPTER THREE

The Trilateral Dilemma in Financial Regulation

Howell E. Jackson

Introduction

Consumers face numerous challenges in keeping their financial houses in order. How to invest one's retirement savings? What kind of insurance policies to purchase? How to finance a home or education? Where to open a checking account? These are all complicated decisions, requiring the balancing of many factors and the weighing of risk tolerances. Many consumers find these decisions so intimidating that they turn to others to make recommendations as to specific courses of action or at least to narrow the range of possibilities to a manageable number. Indeed, consumer education programs often recommend the use of financial advisers. Sometimes these advisers will be family friends or relatives, but more commonly consumers will turn to members of the financial services industry for advice and direction.

This reliance on the recommendations of the financial services industry creates a potential problem for consumers. By gaining control over some aspects of a consumer's financial decision-making process, a financial adviser may be tempted to steer the consumer's decision in a manner that serves the interest of the adviser and not the client. Often times, the temptation will involve the selection of a financial product or service that produces a collateral benefit for the adviser—either a direct cash payment or the provision of some ancillary service for the adviser. These collateral benefits will often be difficult for consumers to observe but can increase their costs and may also lead the adviser to steer consumers into less than optimal financial products.

This problem—which I call the trilateral dilemma of financial regulation—is surprisingly pervasive.[1] In multiple settings and in many sectors of the financial services industry, problems of inappropriate steering of financial choices have emerged over the years. If anything, the trilateral dilemmas are becoming more pronounced as more and more financial decisions are being placed in the hands of individual consumers, a prime example being the shift from traditional defined benefit pension plans to 401(k) plans (see chapter by Poterba, Venti, and Wise in this volume). The problem is also directly related to the low level of consumer understanding about financial services that is documented elsewhere in this volume (see chapters in this volume by Gustman, Steinmeier, and Tabatabai; Lusardi, Keller, and Keller; and Smith and Stewart). Because many consumers lack expertise in financial matters, representatives of the financial services industry have the opportunity to steer consumers toward financial decisions that advance the interests of financial firms and not the interests of their customers.

In this chapter, I review nearly a dozen examples of trilateral dilemmas and describe the many different ways in which legislatures, courts, and regulatory bodies have attempted to address the problem. I then discuss a number of common issues and recurring difficulties in evaluating the overall impact of trilateral dilemmas. I conclude with some thoughts about the implications of my analysis for devising regulatory responses to trilateral dilemma problems and for the role that consumer education might play in helping consumers work through these difficulties. Among other things, I suggest that more regulatory attention should be focused on the intermediaries who help consumers make financial decisions, that one promising approach is to require intermediaries to disclose aggregate information about their compensation arrangements with a wide range of customers, and that consumers should be better educated about how to determine which intermediaries are most likely to act in the consumers' best interests.

Mapping the Dilemma

In many different kinds of financial transactions, market professionals occupy positions that permit them to extract side payments as a result of their capacity to steer the financial decisions of members of the general

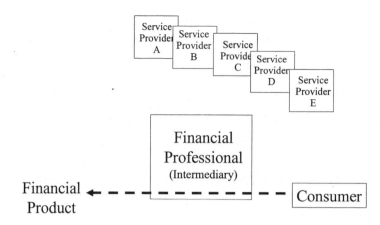

FIGURE 3.1 The trilateral dilemma.

public. Regulatory problems of this sort typically involve three separate parties: a consumer, a financial professional with authority to make or influence decisions made on the consumer's behalf (the intermediary), and a third party in competition to be selected to provide some service associated with the underlying transaction (the service provider). The dilemma arises when the service provider offers the intermediary a side payment of some sort in exchange for being selected to provide services to the intermediary's clients (see figure 3.1).

In this section, I review a range of regulatory contexts in which the trilateral dilemmas have arisen over the years and discuss briefly the wide range of legal tools that have been developed to solve the trilateral dilemma in each context. As the examples span the financial services industry, my descriptions will be cursory; more complete descriptions of the individual settings are available in sources cited in endnotes. The goal of this presentation is not to provide an exhaustive treatment of each example, but rather to demonstrate the pervasiveness of this category of problem, the complexities these arrangements pose for policy makers, and key features of the disparate regulatory approaches that have been employed to address problems of a similar functional form.

Real Estate Settlement Transactions

A good starting place to study the trilateral dilemma is residential real estate transactions, in which an individual or couple purchase a home and, in the process, obtain a number of separate services associated with the purchase (title insurance, inspections, various legal documents) and also often obtain a mortgage. The problem of consumer abuses in real estate settlement transactions first came to the attention of Congress in the early 1970s and led to the passage of the Real Estate Settlement Protection Act of 1974 (RESPA).[2] The legislative history of RESPA reveals that in the early 1970s real estate agents and closing attorneys often received side payments (kickbacks and unearned referral fees) as a reward for selecting particular third-party service providers to work on home closings. Figure 3.2 illustrates these relationships, noting (1) the real estate professional's selection of a service provider, (2) the consumer's payment of the provider's fees, and (3) the third party's side payment to the referring market professional. The dilemma for the consumer is that market professionals face strong incentives to select the settlement service provider that makes the largest side payment as opposed to the one that offers the best and most cost-effective services for the consumer.

To address the perceived vulnerabilities of consumers in the context of real estate settlement transactions, Congress considered a wide range of options, including a regulatory proposal that the federal government regulate the prices charged for real estate settlement services. In the end, Congress chose instead to adopt a three-pronged attack, including mandatory disclosure requirements for the costs of all real estate settlement services (both a final disclosure document distributed at closing and a preliminary "good faith estimate" provided to consumers earlier in the process), pro-

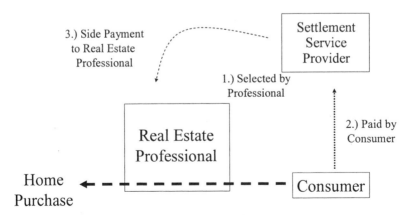

FIGURE 3.2 The real estate settlement transaction.

hibitions against certain unearned fees and kickbacks, and a liability regime that allowed both public officials and injured private parties to seek
injunctive relief and in some cases monetary damages.

Payment of Yield Spread Premiums to Mortgage Brokers

Another example of the trilateral dilemma in the real estate area arises
when a consumer who is in the process of purchasing or refinancing a home
or other property comes to a mortgage broker for assistance in obtaining
a mortgage. The mortgage broker provides an array of services to the consumer, including helping the consumer complete a variety of application
forms, hiring other providers of settlement services (such as appraisers and
title insurance companies), and working through various other issues that
may arise in the course of the transaction. One of the mortgage broker's
responsibilities is to recommend a lending institution to finance the consumer's mortgage (see figure 3.3). Typically, mortgage brokers have cor-
respondent relationships with a large number of lending institutions. As a
number of factors are relevant in determining which lending institution is
selected for any particular consumer, the mortgage broker has considerable latitude in selecting a lending institution for a particular consumer.

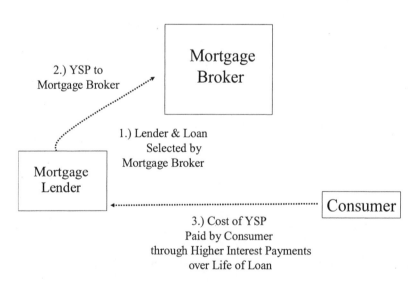

FIGURE 3.3 Mortgages with yield spread premiums (YSP).

Individual consumers, therefore, are heavily dependent upon mortgage brokers to select lending institutions in an appropriate manner.

As industry practices have evolved, mortgage brokers can now steer consumers into many different levels of interest rates for any particular kind of loan, such as a thirty-year fixed conventional loan or an adjustable-rate mortgage of some sort. The variation in rate does not reflect different levels of credit risk on the part of the borrower; rather it determines the price that the lending institution is prepared to pay for the loan. Par loans are loans that carry an interest rate for which the lending institution is prepared to pay (or fund) the face amount of the loan. For a loan with a higher interest rate, known as an above-par loan, the lending institution will pay a greater price, and the excess, which often amounts to thousands of dollars, is paid over to the mortgage broker when the loan is closed. The payment of yield spread premiums follows the pattern of the trilateral dilemma because the mortgage broker often has considerable control over the selection of the lending institution and interest rate on the loan selected; when the broker selects an above-par loan, the broker receives a side payment from the lending institution in the form of a yield spread premium, and the consumer bears the cost of the yield spread premium through higher interest payments over the life of the loan.

The payment of yield spread premiums has been controversial and the subject of numerous lawsuits over the past ten years. The lawsuits raised numerous questions about whether the payments, which are subject to RESPA's requirements, had been properly disclosed on appropriate Department of Housing and Urban Development (HUD) forms and also whether the payments constituted impermissible kickbacks in violation of RESPA's statutory prohibition. After a series of conflicting judicial rulings, the courts eventually accepted the interpretations of HUD that authorized the payment of yield spread premiums as long as the recipient mortgage broker performed some service to the underlying transactions and the total compensation paid to the mortgage broker was reasonable. This interpretation left open the possibility that some yield spread premiums might violate RESPA's requirements but that such determinations would be fact specific, so these cases have not generally been amendable to class action lawsuits.

Although litigation over yield spread premiums failed to result in any substantial damage awards for consumers, the lawsuits did produce a fair amount of data about mortgage broker compensation, which has led to several empirical studies of the relationship between yield spread premiums and mortgage broker compensation. In general, these studies suggest that mortgage brokers make significantly more money on loans in which yield spread premiums are charged as compared with loans in which the brokers are compensated through more visible direct payments from borrowers. The studies also suggest that there is greater variation in mortgage broker compensation when yield spread premiums are paid, as opposed to the variation that is found when the brokers are compensated through direct payment. Finally, this analysis reveals that mortgage broker compensation is lower on "no-cost" mortgages, that is, on loans for which the yield spread premium is structured to cover the full amount of mortgage broker compensation or the full amount of all real estate settlements and the borrower makes no additional direct payments for these services.

The controversy over yield spread premiums also led HUD to propose an amendment of RESPA regulations that would have required all yield spread premiums to be paid directly to consumers (as opposed to mortgage brokers). Under the proposal—which essentially would have assigned borrowers a property interest in yield spread premiums—consumers would be free to use the yield spread premium to compensate their mortgage broker or pay for other real estates settlement services. Placing these payments into the hands of consumers in the first instance would clarify the significance and magnitude of the payments. After an extensive period of public commentary, HUD eventually withdrew the proposal, partially out of concern that the proposed rules might confuse consumers and disadvantage them with respect to direct lenders, who do not receive yield spread premiums. The HUD proposal also would have included a reform to liberalize somewhat the regulatory requirements for firms that committed to fixed prices for all closing costs at the beginning of the settlement process (rather than adjusting prices at closing, as is now often the case). That aspect of the proposal was also withdrawn.

Investment Choices of Pension Plans

The selection of investment choices by the Employee Retirement Income Security Act of 1974 (ERISA) plan sponsors offers another fertile field for trilateral dilemmas as well as several recent examples of regulatory concern and response. An initial illustration in this setting is the practice by pension consultants to advise employer sponsors on the selection of investment options and then to receive compensatory payments from cer-

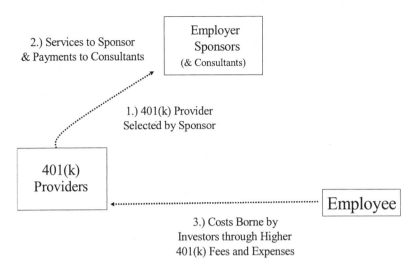

FIGURE 3.4 Investment choices for ERISA plans.

tain providers, such as financial services firms offering 401(k) programs (see figure 3.4). These arrangements, which have been the subject of Department of Labor scrutiny in recent years, pose risks to employee participants in 401(k) programs because the receipt of these payments may lead consultants to steer plan sponsors to less than optimal service providers and may also increase the cost of 401(k) programs, as additional payments to consultants are factored into higher fees and expenses for employee participants. The Department of Labor's solution to this problem has been to encourage pension plan sponsors to more carefully scrutinize the compensation arrangements of their consultants and to make a holistic evaluation of the appropriateness of the consultants' advice, taking into consideration a variety of factors (see U.S. GAO 2006). Under the Investment Advisors Act of 1940, many consultants also face legal obligations to disclose their compensation arrangements to their clients—that is, the employer sponsors.[3]

A more substantial, though less well-documented, example of the trilateral dilemma in the pension context concerns direct and indirect payments of 401(k) providers to employer sponsors. A few years ago, the Securities and Exchange Commission (SEC) instituted an investigation of pay-to-play practices in the 401(k) industry, exploring allegations that 401(k) providers might be paying for "shelf space" in employer-sponsored 401(k) programs, and, more recently, allegations have arisen that sponsors of 403(b) plans have also earned undisclosed fees from annuity providers.[4] While investigations into these practices have not yet been resolved, one can imagine how 401(k) providers might have an incentive to make such payments in anticipation of the costs of these payments being recouped through higher fees and expenses charged to plan participants. Moreover, 401(k) providers need not rely on direct cash payments to employer sponsors in order to win contracts. In supplying 401(k) services, providers often offer a number of administrative functions, many of which blur with payroll and human resource activities that would typically be the responsibility of the employer sponsors. By assuming a larger share of these administrative chores, a 401(k) provider indirectly subsidizes the employer sponsor, incurring costs that again would have to be borne through employee participants in the form of higher 401(k) fees and expenses (Economic Systems Inc. 1998; *Sun-Sentinel Ft. Lauderdale* 1997; see also Sayles 1999). Alternatively, plan sponsors can be relieved of the responsibility for payment of certain plan-related costs (for example, plan record keeping), and these expenses can be charged directly to plan participants.[5] To the best of my knowledge, no serious academic studies have documented the extent to which such cross subsidization does in fact occur.[6] Studies have, however, documented that employee participants may be naive in evaluating and choosing among the investment options provided in their 401(k) plans (see Choi et al. 2006; Brown and Weisbenner 2004), and one can easily imagine that competitive pressures would encourage 401(k) providers to compete for business by making side payments to employer sponsors with the expectation of recouping their costs through higher fees and expenses for the mutual fund options placed in the employers' 401(k) programs. Under ERISA, fiduciary obligations require employer sponsors to exercise their fiduciary duties (including the selection of 401[k] providers) for the exclusive benefit of plan participants, but these duties can often be satisfied through the balancing of multiple considerations, and plan sponsors are under no obligation to select providers with the lowest possible fees and expenses or even to justify with any rigor decisions to select providers with above-average fees and expenses.[7]

A final 401(k) context in which a trilateral dilemma might arise lies in the provision of investment advice directly to plan participants. For many years, plan sponsors have shied away from providing investment advice to plan beneficiaries out of fear of incurring legal liabilities if investment performance fails to meet participant expectations and allegations arise that the advice offered or the investment choices supplied violated the fiduciary duties of plan sponsors to safeguard the interests of plan participants.[8] Recently, however, the legal rules in this area have changed. Responding in part to mounting empirical evidence that 401(k) participants often make poor investment choices (see, for example, Choi, Laibson, and Madrian 2005), the Pension Protection Act of 2006[9] established a number of new statutory exemptions designed to encourage employers to hire independent investment advisers to assist their employees in making investment choices. These reforms include several safeguards intended to insulate these advisers from making recommendations that serve their own financial interests and not those of plan participants—that is to say, restrictions designed to ameliorate the trilateral dilemma in this context. Under one approach, the investment advice must be the product of a certified computer model that analyzes all investment options made available under the employee's plan and then makes recommendations in accordance with generally accepted investment theories. Under an alterative approach, the compensation of the investment adviser (but not the adviser's affiliates) must not vary based on the investment option that an employee chooses. As a result of these reforms, one might expect to see an increasing amount of professional investment advice becoming available to assist defined contribution plan participants in structuring their retirement savings. Whether the safeguards of the Pension Protection Act of 2006 will succeed in restraining the trilateral dilemma in this context remains to be seen.

Investment Management

The field of investment management is another area in which trilateral dilemmas proliferate. Typically, the structure of the problem here involves an asset management firm—either working directly for clients or indirectly through a mutual fund or other pooled investment vehicle. As a result of a manager's control over investment decisions, opportunities arise for the manager to obtain the kind of collateral benefits that characterize the trilateral dilemma and pass along the costs of those benefits to investors.

REBATES IN THE ERA OF FIXED BROKERAGE COMMISSIONS. An early example of this phenomenon emerged in the late 1960s and early 1970s when New York Stock Exchange (NYSE) member firms were still required to charge fixed commissions for brokerage transactions. At the time, mutual funds and other large institutional investors began to press brokers for

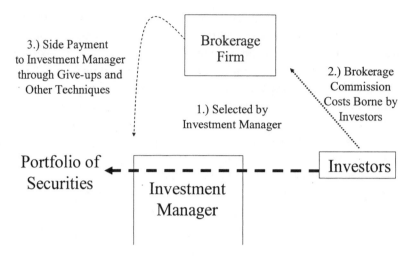

FIGURE 3.5 Investment managers and brokerage commissions.

rebates on commissions for their large trading volumes, which were considerably less expensive to execute than smaller transactions. As direct
cash rebates violated the fixed-commission rules, the securities industry
developed a variety of mechanisms to transfer value to institutional investors, with the most popular technique for mutual funds being the allocation of excess commission to securities firms that distributed the mutual
fund's shares. As the full cost of the fixed brokerage commissions was
borne by mutual fund shareholders and a portion of the commissions was
rebated for the benefit of the investment manager in facilitating distribution, these allocation practices follow the basic structure of a trilateral
dilemma. See figure 3.5.

The fixed-commission allocation practices prompted a series of legal
challenges, which produced a number of complicated and not fully consistent legal opinions.[10] At the root of much of the analysis was the question of whether the investment managers were violating fiduciary duties
to investors by utilizing excessive commissions for their own benefit. The
courts were much influenced by the law of trusts, which generally prohib-
its trustees from obtaining undisclosed compensation for their fiduciary
services without a client's consent (see Restatement of Trusts [Second]
1959, sections 170, 216). The judicial decisions were, however, divided on
whether investment managers were absolutely barred from benefiting
from the rebates (that is, whether the rebates belonged to investors) or

whether rebate practices simply needed to be disclosed to investors or (in the case of mutual funds regulated under the Investment Company Act of 1940) to the directors charged with safeguarding the investors' interests. As the rebate practices were often used to finance (or subsidize) distribution costs for new shareholders, some opinions also questioned whether the payments violated charter provisions or even statutory requirements that all investors be treated in the same manner.

CURRENT VARIANTS: SOFT DOLLAR PRACTICES AND 12B-1 FEES. The year 1975 marked the end of the era of fixed-rate commissions and ushered in the dramatic reduction of the financial incentives facing investment managers to recapture excessive commissions. But analogous practices have emerged. While the confused case that arose out of the fixed-commission era still establishes background legal requirements, most attention is focused on the statutory safe harbor that Congress established in 1975 for soft dollar practices under section 28(e) of the Securities Exchange Act of 1934, as amended (see 15 U.S.C.A. section 78bb [West 2007]), and also under the SEC rule 12b-1 under the Investment Company Act of 1940 (Commodity and Securities Exchanges 2007, title 17 C.F.R. 270.12b-1), which governs the use of mutual fund assets to finance the distribution of fund shares. Both legal regimes have been controversial and have generated a considerable amount of administrative gloss over the past two to three decades. They also offer interesting examples of regulatory efforts to constrain abuses from two prominent illustrations of trilateral dilemmas.

Section 28(e) of the 1934 Securities Exchange Act establishes a statutory safe harbor, which permits investment managers to utilize brokerage firms that charge commissions that are higher than required for pure execution services and for the investment managers to receive, in return, certain brokerage and research services. The SEC recently issued interpretive guidance on the permissible scope of section 28(e) arrangements and narrowed the range of permissible services that the safe harbor covers (see U.S. SEC 2006). But the basic structure of the safe harbor has always required generalized disclosure to customers of a manager's use of soft dollar practices and imposed an additional requirement that investment managers make a good faith determination that the amount of excess commission payments to brokerage firms for soft dollar benefits are reasonable in light of the additional services received. While section 28(e) is formally structured as a safe harbor—suggesting that other analogous arrangements might be consistent with the fiduciary duties of investment managers—other legal requirements make it difficult for many investment managers to undertake similar practices outside the safe harbor (see U.S. SEC 2006). In recent years, the SEC has explored developing more detailed disclosures designed to quantify the value of soft dollar payments for mutual funds—for example, by deconstructing the disclosure of commission expenses into execution services and excess commissions used to finance research and brokerage services and recognizing all excess commission as fund expenses—but no such comprehensive disclosure requirements have yet been imposed for the mutual fund industry.[11] Reform of the SEC's soft dollar rules has been complicated by the fact that the payments have become an important source of revenue for independent research firms, which claim that they would be disadvantaged with respect to full-service brokerage houses were soft dollar payments prohibited. In other words, the practice has come to be defended on the grounds that it promotes additional research and enhances competition in the financial services industry. In addition, some academic research has offered both theoretical and empirical evidence that soft dollar arrangements actually benefit investors by allowing investment managers to enter into more efficient contracts with brokerage firms (see Johnsen 1994; Horan and Johnsen 2004).

Rule 12b-1 represents a somewhat different solution to a similar problem: the use of mutual resources to finance distribution expenses. The central component of rule 12b-1 is its reliance on the independent directors of mutual funds to approve annually the imposition of 12b-1 fees and to monitor their use on a quarterly basis.[12] The SEC also specifies a variety of factors that these independent directors need to consider in reviewing 12b-1 plans and has imposed a series of supplemental corporate governance standards (for example, that at least 75 percent of fund directors be independent) that are designed to ensure the disinterestedness of the board. Disclosure and shareholder approval also figure into the oversight of 12b-1 fees, and the level of these fees must remain within the quantitative limits set by the old National Association of Securities Dealers, which, since July 2007, has become the Financial Industry Regulatory Authority. But the distinguishing feature of this regulatory structure is its reliance on independent directors to prevent abusive practices.

PAYMENT FOR ORDER FLOW.   A distinct regulatory problem in the area of investment management is the selection of execution services from trading markets. In the 1990s, various trading venues began to compete for order flow by offering side payments to brokers that directed order flow to these

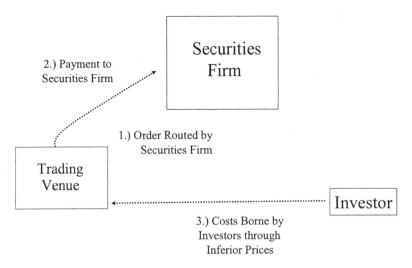

FIGURE 3.6 Payment for order flow.

alternative venues instead of to traditional markets such as the NYSE. Typically, in these arrangements, the order would be executed at the best posted price at the time the order was received, that is, the national best bid or offer (NBBO).[13] Critics of the practice complained that by routing orders in this way brokers were benefiting but were denying their customer the opportunity to get price improvement on the NBBO as was sometimes available in auction markets like the NYSE and possibly other venues.[14] As illustrated in figure 3.6, this arrangement followed the familiar pattern of other trilateral dilemmas and prompted a series of lawsuits in the 1990s.

As is often the case with controversies of this sort, there was initial confusion over whether the practice should be considered a wrongful taking of investor property or whether the payments should be evaluated as potential violations of a broker's duty to obtain best execution for a client. In addition, questions were raised as to whether the practice constituted a desirable example of competition among market centers or an undesirable instance of alternative venues free-riding off of price discovery and other valuable public functions of traditional exchange. Over time, the courts and the SEC accepted payment for order flow as a reasonable mechanism of competition but recognized that the practice did raise potential concerns of consumer confusion and emphasized the obligations of brokerage firms to provide best execution (measured with a multifactored test) and imposed disclosure obligations to ensure that investors were informed (as a general matter) that their brokers might sometimes receive payments in exchange for order flow.

One of the problems with the initial disclosure rules for payments of order flow was that the disclosures tended to be quite general in nature, and it was difficult for customers to determine whether payments had been made in particular cases or—more importantly—whether the customer's order might have been executed at a better price in another market. To address these (and other) concerns, the SEC in 2000 adopted new rules requiring market centers to produce monthly reports with aggregate data on trade execution, including information on the quality and speed of each market's execution of trades (see Commodity and Securities Exchanges 2007, section 240.11Ac1–5). The rules also require similar information from individual brokerage houses (see Commodity and Securities Exchanges 2007, section 240.11Ac1–6). While these monthly data do not allow individual investors to determine how well their particular orders were executed, they do allow customers to get an overall sense of the execution services of a brokerage house and the markets to which the customers orders have been routed. And there is both anecdotal and empirical evidence that market centers reporting better execution quality receive greater order flow (see Boehmer, Jennings, and Wei 2007).

Another interesting proposal regarding payment for order flow—from Professor Allen Ferrell of Harvard Law School—was to require that broker dealers give customers the option of having all their orders executed at the NBBO without any possibility of price improvement (see Ferrell 2001). While this solution is somewhat counterintuitive in that it prevents customers from getting better prices, Professor Ferrell's goal was to force brokerage firms to internalize the expected net value of price improvement generated through payment for order flow or other techniques into the brokerage commission charged to customers. The proposal thus represented a structured solution to this variant of the trilateral dilemma that would clarify for customers their total execution costs in a manner that could readily be compared across brokerage firms. The Ferrell proposal has not been adopted by the SEC, nor—to the best of my knowledge—has it been implemented voluntarily by any brokerage firm.

RECENT ENFORCEMENT ACTIONS OVER MUTUAL FUND SERVICE PROVIDERS. Another example of a trilateral dilemma involving investment management can be seen in recent SEC enforcement actions over side payments from transfer agents to mutual fund organizations in connection with transfer agent service contracts (see SEC 2000). The undisclosed side payments, which ran from the service providers to the mutual fund complexes, presumably increased the cost of transfer agency services, which mutual fund shareholders typically pay directly. Side payments of this sort are prohibited under federal securities laws but nevertheless sometimes still occur.[15] In addition, there is a fairly steady stream of cases in which the personnel working at investment management firms—as opposed to the firms themselves—have been found to extract gifts and other undisclosed remuneration from service providers, typically in violation of internal guidelines and also sometimes securities law strictures.[16]

Contingent Insurance Commissions

Yet another example of the trilateral dilemma can be found in the insurance industry, where investigations initiated by then New York attorney general Elliot Spitzer uncovered the payment of contingent commissions to insurance brokers from insurance underwriters.[17] When these transactions were announced, there was much public outcry over whether these often undisclosed payments were increasing the level of insurance premiums for the brokers' customers or inhibiting brokers from processing customer claims in order to maintain contingent commissions, which are often based on underwriter profits. Compensation practices in the insurance industry, however, made it a bit more difficult to assess the impact of contingent payments because brokers were typically compensated through fixed commissions paid by insurance companies out of revenues from premiums. As a result, the impact of contingent commissions was more to change the timing of broker compensation and not to change its sources (or provide an additional source). In addition, academic commentary on the payment of contingent commissions is divided on the question of whether the compensation arrangements actually harm consumers; at least one line of research suggests that contingent commissions help align the interests of brokers and underwriters, thereby reducing information asymmetries that arise from the fact that brokers tend to have better knowledge about the risks of their customers than do underwriters.[18] To date, a comprehensive response to contingent commissions has not emerged; the most commonly discussed approaches support some combination of disclosure and enhanced attention to broker duties to customers, and there have been a few calls for outright prohibitions of the practice, at least for insurance contracts involving consumers.

Student Loan Transactions

Recently, another trilateral dilemma has emerged in the student loan industry. In this context, the trusted intermediary is the financial aid office of universities, the side payments apparently have taken the form of benefits given to financial aid office personnel, the steering of consumer choice occurs in the form of the selection of preferred lenders for the student body, and the costs are passed along to the students through some combination of higher loan costs or poorer servicing to compensate lenders for the extra payments made to financial aid office personnel (see Cuomo testimony, House Committee on Education and Labor 2007; Zimmerman 2007). Again, no regulatory response to the practice has been imposed, and—to the best of my knowledge—no economic defense of the practice has been offered.

Confidential Consumer Information

A final example of a variant on the trilateral dilemma concerns misuse of private consumer information on the part of financial institutions. In the late 1990s, there were a growing number of reports of financial institutions selling private consumer financial information to third-party vendors—often telemarketing firms. This often included information about the consumer's finances and spending patterns, credit card information, and even (in the case of insurance companies) information about a consumer's health and medical conditions. The third parties then used this information to market products to the consumers and to recover the cost of purchasing the private information through the sale of products and services. The practice is analogous to a classic trilateral dilemma in the sense that the financial institution benefits (here through the receipt of cash payments) as a result of its control over confidential information it collects regarding its customers. The distinguishing feature of this trilateral dilemma is that a large portion of the cost imposed on consumers is the inconvenience associated with being approached by unwanted telemarketers, although consumers who purchase the telemarketers' products or services may also bear a cost in terms of higher prices to cover the cash payments to financial institutions. As with other instances of the trilateral dilemma discussed above, there are a host of reasons to suspect that these practices did not serve the best interests of consumers. To begin with, financial institutions seldom disclosed that they were selling information in this manner, nor did telemarketers typically disclose from where they had obtained a consumer's name or other contact information. In addition, even if a consumer somehow discovered that its financial institutions were disclosing information in this way, it might have been difficult or costly for the customer to change banks just because of this practice.

Because market forces did not seem likely to protect consumer interests in this area, in 1999 Congress passed a new law regulating how financial institutions deal with confidential consumer information.[19] Essentially, the legislative response has two components. First, financial institutions are now required to make periodic disclosures to consumers about their privacy policies and, in particular, whether they make private consumer information available to third parties. Second, Congress gave each consumer the unconditional right to "opt out" of any institution's plan to share private information about that consumer with third parties. If a consumer exercises this opt-out right—essentially a legal entitlement to deny a financial institution the authority to share confidential information—the financial institution is not allowed to profit from selling that consumer's private information to third parties. Again this substantive right is granted to consumers in addition to the right to obtain periodic disclosures about the privacy policies of banks and other financial institutions. The opt-out rules, however, do not apply to the transfer of confidential information among affiliated firms operating within the same financial holding company structure.

Summary of Regulatory Approaches

In short, trilateral dilemmas appear in multiple areas of the financial services industry and have generated a surprisingly diverse array of regulatory responses, which I have summarized in table 3.1. The responses can be organized into a few basic groups: prohibitions (P), price controls (PC), assignment of property interests or entitlements (PI), solutions that require transactions to be structured in a certain way (SS), fiduciary duties (FD), and disclosure rules. Within these basic divisions one can make further refinements. For example, disclosure rules can be subdivided into general disclosure requirements (GD), individualized disclosure requirements of the sort required in real estate settlement transactions (ID), and aggre-

gate disclosure requirements of the sort the SEC imposed on the execution services of marketplaces and brokerage firms (AD). Plus one can
distinguish mere disclosure from disclosure coupled with a requirement of
express consent or shareholder approval (C). On the fiduciary duty side,
one can distinguish between fiduciary duties imposed on firms directly
engaged in transactions and those policed in the first instance by more
disinterested parties, such as the independent directors of mutual funds
or 401(k) advisory firms whose compensation does not depend on recommendations (DFD). While generalizations are tricky given the range of
legal regimes covered in table 3.1, one might safely say that the modal
regulatory response to trilateral dilemmas is the imposition of some sort
of fiduciary duty on the financial professional who has power to steer consumer decisions (often requiring the balancing of a number of factors and
considerations) along with a generalized disclosure to the consumers who
are affected by the transaction.

Recurring Analytical Issues

The frequency with which segments of the financial services industry use
positions of trust and confidence to obtain side payments for the referral
of customer business presents a puzzle. On the one hand, from the high incidence of these arrangements and the considerable supervisory attention
that has been expended to police them over the past decade, one might
infer that the ethics of the financial services industry are systematically deficient. On the other hand, one could interpret the high incidence of these
arrangements as evidence that side payments of this sort have some sort
of economic function that explains their proliferation in so many sectors
of the financial services industry.

The array of regulatory responses to trilateral dilemmas poses another
puzzle. Is it plausible that a fairly similar set of agency problems—assuming,
of course, that these dilemmas do present problems—are best resolved in
such different ways in different contexts? Might there not be a dominant
regulatory response to the trilateral dilemma, such as the modal regime
of fiduciary duties and general disclosure, which should be adopted across
the board? Or might one of the less frequently applied solutions—perhaps
property interests or aggregate disclosures—be more widely applied?

In an attempt to get a handle on these larger questions, I now consider a range of recurring analytical issues that arise in policy debates over

TABLE 3.1 **Summary of regulatory approaches to the trilateral dilemma**

Area of regulation	Key regulatory strategies
Restatement of trusts	Ancillary benefits permissible only with disclosure (ID) and consent (C)
Real estate settlement service providers	Rate regulation (proposed but never imposed) (PC)
	Prohibitions on certain kickbacks and unearned fees (P)
	Disclosure requirements (HUD-1 and GSE) (ID)
Yield spread premiums for mortgage brokers	Judicial review of reasonableness of total compensation (FD)
	Mandatory assignment of payments to borrower (proposed) (SS/PI)
Selection of pension plan service providers	Fiduciary duties based on consideration of multiple factors (FD)
	Disclosure requirements (GD)
Investment advice for participants in 401(k) plans	Advice from certified computer model (SS)
	Compensation must not vary based on investment options (DFD)
Excess brokerage in era of fixed New York Stock Exchange commissions	Fiduciary duties (waivable if payments disclosed [GD] and justified [FD])
	Investor property interest in excessive commission (considered) (PI)
	Judicial oversight for equitable treatment of shareholders (considered)
Soft dollar payments	Safe harbor for certain brokerage and research services with good faith assessment of value and disclosure (GD)
	Receipt of other services effectively prohibited (P)
	Additional disclosure on value of benefits (proposed) (ID)
12b-1 fees for mutual funds	Primary reliance on oversight by independent directors to approve and oversee 12b-1 plans (DFD)
	Disclosure (ID) and approval of shareholders also required (C)
	National Association of Securities Dealers price caps (PC)
Payment for order flow	Duty of best execution (FD) and disclosure (GD)
	Monthly disclosure of execution quality for markets and brokers (AD)
	Requirement to execute at NBBO (proposed) (SS)
1940 Act service providers	Side payments to management firms prohibited (P)
Financial privacy	Disclosure (GD) and opt-out right granted to consumers (SS/PI)

Note: AD = aggregate disclosure requirements; C = requirement of express consent or shareholder approval; DFD = disinterested fiduciary duties; FD = fiduciary duties; GD = general disclosure requirements; ID = individualized disclosure requirements; P = prohibitions; PC = price controls; PI = assignment of property interests or entitlements; SS = solutions that require transactions to be structured in a certain way.

trilateral dilemmas in a variety of settings. In the course of this analysis, I also propose some potential distinctions in the types of transactions that give rise to trilateral dilemmas in the hopes of both identifying the subset of transactions in which public policy concerns are likely to be most pronounced and suggesting which of the many available regulatory responses might be the most efficacious in particular contexts.

Side Payments as Benign or Efficacious

An initial, but trenchant, question about trilateral dilemmas is whether they do in fact represent a problematic set of transactions. Putting aside for a moment the unfortunate optics of side payments, one must recognize that the business world abounds with discounts and rebates—from volume discounts for use of copying machines to frequent flyer awards that professional service providers routinely accumulate on travel expenses that are billed to clients. In these and many other similar contexts, our working assumption is that the savings are factored into the service provider's pricing strategy and that as a result of market pressures the savings are passed on to customers. A common defense of the payments received by intermediaries in trilateral dilemmas is that precisely the same offsets occur in the financial services industry and thus the side payments are in fact innocuous, notwithstanding their superficially unseemly nature.[20] In effect, this view is that these side payments are an acceptable means to help finance the cost of distributing financial services and products.

Defenders of industry practices in trilateral dilemmas also sometimes assert that the existence of side payments actually offers a superior form of contract for the intermediary, for example, because the payments solve a problem of adverse selection or allow the intermediary to make creditable commitments to service providers and thereby enhance cooperative efforts. In the case of mortgage broker compensation, yield spread premiums have been justified as a valuable tool that allows liquidity-constrained borrowers to finance closing costs. Side payments may also be used to correct artificial constraints on pricing, as was almost certainly the case in the era of NYSE fixed commissions, and thereby allow intermediaries to obtain on behalf of their clients more attractive prices for services than would have otherwise been available.[21] In other contexts, side payments are portrayed as being a necessary tool for specialized service providers to compete with integrated firms that engage in various forms of similarly motivated internal cross subsidies within operating divisions.[22] Finally, the practice of making side payments is also sometimes justified on the grounds that payment is used to promote a service (such as research) that has the quality of a public good.[23]

In short, defenders of side payments typically assert a general defense, resting on the notion that competitive forces will ensure that the payments are offset in the total prices individuals pay for their financial services and then on more context-specific claims that these payments address some more subtle contracting problems.

The Theoretical Case against Side Payments

Critiques of side payments typically respond to both of these defenses. As the more general defense of financial offset is the more ubiquitous and important, I will focus my discussion on that line of argument. I would note, however, that in many contexts the contracting advantages of side payments are contested and that in some contexts critics argue that the payments facilitate free-riding and the erosion of public goods.

CONSUMER CONFUSION AND UNJUSTIFIED RELIANCE. Perhaps the most common, if not fully theorized, explanation of why market forces do not adjust to side payments in trilateral dilemmas is that consumers do not understand the nature or significance of the payments, do not appreciate that they themselves ultimately bear the costs of the payments, and generally accept the recommendation of the market professional who chooses the service provider making the payment. Particularly where trilateral dilemmas involve retail consumers, one can well imagine why an individual without substantial financial expertise might readily defer to the recommendation of a professional adviser without scrutinizing too carefully the fine print of the transaction and the pricing of various ancillary services. Certainly, the evidence introduced elsewhere in this volume of the relatively low level of consumer understanding of financial matters would lend credence to this line of attack on trilateral dilemma payments.

MULTIDIMENSIONAL DECISIONS WITH CENTRAL FOCUS ELSEWHERE. A distinguishing feature of trilateral dilemmas that provides a somewhat more grounded explanation for consumer confusions in these transactions is the fact that payment is often associated with an ancillary service that may be overshadowed by another more salient transaction or decision confronting the customers. In the context of real estate settlements, the purchase of a new house, coupled perhaps with the sale of another property and the undertaking of moving and fix-up expenses, is almost certainly going to be of greater concern to most individuals than the price paid to an appraiser or title insurance company.[24] For an individual considering whether to accept a job offer, the nature of the employment opportunity and the salary offered is likely to overwhelm concern about fees charged on 401(k) plan offerings. Indeed, to the extent a potential employee inquires as to 401(k) issues, the focus is much more likely to be on the amount of the employer's contribution than the total annual fees and expenses to be charged on the plan. Similarly, when a consumer is picking a bank for a checking account and basic financial services, factors such as the location of the bank's offices and its hours of business are likely to be of more importance than the institution's policies on sharing confidential information. The behavioral economics literature offers ample evidence that, when confronted with multidimensional decisions, consumers tend to focus on one or two salient issues. This phenomenon may be even more acute when the transaction in question—such as the purchase of a home or the establishment of a new retirement savings program—is a new and unfamiliar experience. What the financial services industry may be exploiting in trilateral dilemma transactions is that the side payments at issue and their indirect impact on consumer costs will seldom have sufficient salience to attract consumer attention.[25]

TIME VALUE COMPLEXITIES.   Another recurring feature of problems involving trilateral dilemmas is that the underlying choices facing consumers often involve complex issues related to the time value of money, where consumers must value streams of payments—such as higher mortgage interest payments in the case of yield spread premiums or higher mutual fund fees and expenses in the case of 401(k) plans that subsidize sponsor costs. Again, the behavioral economics literature is instructive regarding the tendency of consumers to undervalue the costs of periodic payments made over an extended period of time, hence the proliferation of marketing schemes denominated in terms of pennies a day or dollars a week.

SEPARATE COSTS VERSUS BLENDED COSTS.   In classifying trilateral dilemmas, one can distinguish two subsets of cases. In the first, the consumer pays the ancillary service provider directly, and the costs of the side payment (from the service provider to the recommending intermediary) are factored into the price that the consumer pays. Traditional real estate settlement services (like title insurance and attorney fees) take this form as typically do transfer agent fees to mutual fund shareholders. While consumers may not pay too much attention to these payments given their relative unimportance compared with other aspects of the overall transaction, at least the costs are distinct and potentially susceptible to scrutiny. In the second category of trilateral dilemmas, the additional costs from side payments are blended into a pricing arrangement that covers many other services. Mortgage loans with yield spread premiums, for example, combine the cost of borrowing funds with the compensation of a mortgage broker for origination services. Similarly, total returns on an investor's portfolio are most heavily influenced by investment returns but also factor in the cost of commissions and execution services, which may also bear costs associated with side payments. Insurance premiums reflect both underwriting costs and the costs of broker commissions, whether fixed or contingent.

A priori, one cannot say with confidence whether trilateral dilemmas with blended costs are more or less problematic than those with separate costs. On the one hand, when all of the costs of a transaction are factored into a single price, it might be easier for a consumer to make comparisons across service providers. Indeed, in the context of mortgage broker compensation, there is some evidence that consumers do better with no-cost loans for which all mortgage broker compensation is blended into mortgage interest rates, as opposed to loans for which mortgage brokers receive both direct compensation and payments from yield spread premiums.[26] There are, however, also reasons to believe that consumers will have greater difficulty monitoring side payments when the costs of associated services are bundled with other items.

For example, in many of the cases in which trilateral problems have been identified, characteristics of the underlying product or service may make it difficult for consumers to make informed comparisons. In many transactions, the cost of a financial product or service will depend on the individual characteristics of consumers. This is most obviously the case with insurance contracts, for which pricing is so clearly dependent on the risk profile of the insured party, but the same holds true of loans, in which credit risk factors into pricing, and it may even be true for things like securities execution for which trading markets value uninformed traders over informed traders. In the area of active investment management too, it is often difficult to find appropriate market comparisons for portfolios that have distinctive investment strategies and risk profiles. Problems of this sort might explain why critics of the subprime lending industry claim that mortgage broker abuse with yield spread premiums is particularly pronounced for consumers with poor credit and little ability to ascertain the market costs of obtaining credit. Similar problems may also explain why expenses charged on mutual funds with active management strategies are so much greater than those paid on index mutual funds (for which market comparisons are readily available) and do not seem to reflect the actual incremental costs of active management compared with passive investment strategies.

A further complexity of blended costs is that, in some contexts, only a portion of an intermediary's compensation is incorporated into blended costs and another component is imposed as more traditional forms of direct payment. So, for example, mortgage brokers often receive direct payments in the form of origination points as well as yield spread premiums, whose costs are blended into mortgage interest rates. Similarly, brokerage firms often receive a direct commission as well as payment for order flow, whose costs are blended into inferior execution prices.

In short, while blended pricing may in some contexts facilitate price comparison and market constraints on abuses, other times the blending of costs may complicate such comparison and insulate firms from market pressures.

CAPACITY/PROCLIVITY TO PRICE DISCRIMINATE BASED ON CONSUMER KNOWLEDGE. An additional point to make about trilateral dilemma problems is the possibility that the practice facilitates price discrimination between sophisticated and unsophisticated consumers. Again, drawing on mortgage broker compensation as an example, the compensation paid to mortgage brokers has been found to be much more uniform (tightly distributed around a payment equal to one percent of loan value) when consumers pay only direct compensation. When mortgage broker compensation includes some amount of yield spread premium, not only does the average level of compensation increase, but the distribution of compensation widens dramatically with no obvious modal pricing point. It may well be that by complicating the mechanisms of compensation, side payments in trilateral dilemma transactions make it more difficult for consumers to monitor costs, which inhibits the operation of market forces and thereby increases the ability of financial services firms to exploit less sophisticated consumers. Again, the low level of consumer financial education may allow financial services firms to engage in more price discrimination than is possible in other areas.

COLLECTIVE ACTION PROBLEMS AND OTHER CONTRACTING DIFFICULTIES FAC-
ING SERVICE PROVIDERS AND INTERMEDIARIES. Another potential impediment to the natural operation of market forces in trilateral dilemmas is
the difficulties that service providers face in eliminating payments on a
unilateral basis. In various settings, one often hears complaints from those
making the side payments (that is, mortgage lenders making payments
to mortgage brokers or 401[k] providers making payments to employer
sponsors) that they would prefer not to engage in the practices at issue but
that competitive forces prevent them from ceasing unilaterally. Soft dollar
practices are also sometimes explained on the grounds that investment
managers insist that their brokerage firms offer this sort of pricing arrangement. Complaints of this sort presumably proceed from an assessment that
the intermediaries controlling the selection of service providers have some
sort of market power (typically control over distribution channels) that
individual service providers have difficulty resisting on their own.[27]

Intermediaries often face a distinct contracting problem in preventing their own employees from extracting side payments in exchange for
using their personal discretion to steer business to service providers that
offer gratuities or other benefits. Recent disclosures about the behavior
of personnel in university financial aid offices fall into this category, as do
enforcement actions against personnel in asset management firms who
have control over firm trading business. As with insider trading, the potential personal benefits are so large that it may be difficult for financial
intermediaries to effectively prevent their personnel from soliciting and
receiving side payments, which then increase the costs of ancillary services
for the intermediaries' clients.

Revisiting the Array of Regulatory Choices

The foregoing analysis of recurring analytical problems in debates over
trilateral dilemmas has several implications for regulatory responses. First,
a knee-jerk response that market forces will always or even generally protect consumers adequately in these contexts is contestable. There are a variety of theoretical and practical reasons why ordinary market forces may
not operate smoothly in these contexts, particularly where customers are
ordinary individuals. And the opportunities that side payments provide
to generate additional profits for some financial services firms may provide incentives to exploit transactions to increase revenues and discriminate against unsophisticated consumers. In contexts where the underlying

problems arise—that is, where market forces are not sufficient to protect consumers—one wonders whether the mere imposition of fiduciary obligations, which typically call upon the recipients of side payments to assess their reasonableness in light of numerous factors, is likely to be effective. It is conceivable that shifting the evaluation of reasonableness to disinterested third parties (such as independent directors in the case of 12b-1 fees or the courts in the case of mortgage broker compensation financed with yield spread premiums) offers somewhat stronger protections, but the efficacy of such ex post reviews may also be limited. One could raise similar concerns about generalized disclosure regarding the existence of payments to consumers. It is hard to understand how vaguely worded disclosure can assist most consumers.

To the extent that one of the sources of difficulty in trilateral dilemmas is the absence of clear information on the market price of services being financed through side payments, the imposition of structured solutions and the creation of mandatory property interests have intuitive appeal. For example, the HUD proposal that would have required yield spread premiums to be paid over to borrowers in the first instance would have helped borrowers to understand the total amount of compensation being paid to mortgage brokers and eliminated the need for them to estimate the costs of higher monthly interest payments over the life of a mortgage. The new ERISA provisions that encourage 401(k) investment advisers to utilize computerized models to recommend plan options based on established investment theories may also promote disinterested advice. To be sure, it may not always be possible to devise structured solutions that clearly reveal the costs of the ancillary financial services that are now subsidized through side payments, and one must always be mindful of potential problems that may arise from imposing regulatory requirements that disadvantage specialized firms compared with integrated organizations. But structured solutions and the assignment of property interests do seem to have a greater potential for getting to the heart of the trilateral dilemma than do malleable fiduciary duties and rules of general disclosure.[28]

Another potentially attractive line of regulatory intervention is the collection of aggregate data on the overall activities of service providers, similar to what the SEC requires of market centers and brokerage firms with respect to trading services. If, for example, mortgage brokers were required to maintain records on and disclose periodically their levels of compensation on all loan originations, then consumers would be in a much better position to compare firms and make informed evaluations of

compensation levels on their own loans. Similarly, one might imagine requiring 401(k) providers to publish information on the aggregate fees and
expenses of mutual funds and other investment options placed in pension
plans. Then it would be much easier for regulatory officials and employees
to evaluate the investment choices made by plan sponsors as well as the
recommendations made by investment advisers. The key here is to move
away from both generalized disclosure (that is, boilerplate) and individualized disclosure, which are difficult to evaluate, and to move in the direction of aggregate service provider information that would help facilitate
cross-market comparisons and stimulate competition.

The Role of Consumer Education

I conclude with a few remarks on the implications of this analysis for consumer education.

First, the foregoing discussion suggests that consumer education should
not be limited to financial products themselves, such as mortgages or investment vehicles. Consumers also need education on the intermediaries
that influence their selection of financial products and the temptations
those intermediaries face to profit from steering consumer choices inap-
propriately. Consumers need to be attentive to both financial products and
financial intermediaries.

Intermediaries are, however, difficult to evaluate. One of the critical
services that intermediaries provide is advice; indeed, consumer education
often recommends that consumers seek out financial advice. But advice
implies deference, and deference lies at the core of the trilateral dilemma.
So a challenge for consumer education is how to instruct consumers not
only to seek advice but also to scrutinize the advice for the conflicting
interests and exploitative pricing that side payments facilitate. This task
is made all the more difficult when one considers that a complete understanding of the functions of intermediaries requires a fairly detailed
analysis of the overall effect of side payments in a particular context. Has
an intermediary made an offsetting adjustment in its other charges to recognize the benefit received through side payments? Does the use of side
payments in the particular context offer some significant advantages in
contracting or solve some other economic problem? And, ultimately, does
the overall compensation received by the intermediary approximate its
fair market value?

Given the complexity of unpacking fair market pricing in the context of trilateral dilemmas, consumers might well be encouraged to consider aggregate information about the distribution of total compensation payments received by financial intermediaries as well as charges imposed by service providers. In many contexts, regulations may need to be adopted to require the collection and dissemination of this information, although in certain contexts one could imagine that market forces might cause some firms or groups of firms to publish this information voluntarily so as to distinguish themselves from other firms, especially in industries with reputational problems.[29] One might also imagine third-party rating services or consumer advocacy groups taking on the challenge of assessing these aggregate data and classifying the quality of intermediaries and service providers so as to assist consumers in making choices. To a considerable degree, private services like Lipper and Morningstar take on this function with respect to mutual funds, and one could imagine similar rating services emerging in other areas of consumer finance.

Finally, my analysis counsels strongly for more empirical studies into the overall effects of side payments in different contexts. As this discussion demonstrates, the economic impact of side payments in trilateral dilemma problems is ambiguous and depends on numerous, potentially crosscutting factors. In some contexts (like yield spread premiums), studies suggest that these side payments increase consumer costs, but in others (soft dollars), available studies suggest the payments may have economic value for consumers. Only through careful empirical investigations can these issues be resolved. The collection and dissemination of aggregate data on intermediaries and service providers is essential for work of this sort, and its development could greatly assist third-party rating services in making informed recommendations and facilitating better consumer choices.

Notes

This chapter benefited from suggestions and questions from participants at the May 2007 National Bureau of Economic Research conference, "Improving the Effectiveness of Financial Education and Savings Programs," as well as comments from Annamaria Lusardi, David Wray, Peter Tufano, Patricia McCoy, John Campbell, and Michael Barr. I would also like to express my thanks to the Leeds Research Fund for research support and to the John M. Olin Center for Law, Economics, and Business at Harvard Law School.

1. I first coined the term "trilateral dilemma" in early drafts of Jackson and Bur-

lingame (2007). See also Schwarcz (2007), applying the term to contingent payments in the insurance industry, which are discussed in this chapter.

2. See Jackson and Burlingame (2007), who review the legislative history of RESPA, the legal controversies over yield spread premiums, and an empirical study of the economic impact of these payments.

3. See U.S. SEC (2005). See also Lauricella (2007), reporting on Merrill's decision to rebate $2 million of side payments to pension fund clients in the face of both regulatory and market pressures.

4. See Morgenson (2004, 2007), discussing similar problems for annuities recommended for 403(b) plans.

5. See U.S. GAO (2006), noting a trend in the movement of record-keeping fees to plan participants.

6. For a recent press account documenting the potential high costs of 401(k) fees, see Laise (2007).

7. In addition to publishing a series of substantial studies of the subject, the department has produced a model disclosure form that employers can now use to explain 401(k) fees to employees (see Lerner 2001). The department clarified its position that the federal statute governing retirement savings—the Employee Retirement Income Securities Act of 1974—establishes substantive duties on corporate sponsors to act in the best interest of participating employees and to search for 401(k) plans that minimize costs for employees (see Economic Systems Inc. 1998). Corporate sponsors who breach these duties are subject to a variety of penalties, including government enforcement actions and private litigation.

8. Claims of this sort arose in the early 1990s when a number of defined contribution plan participants suffered losses on guaranteed investment contracts placed in individual accounts. Responding to employer sponsor concerns about the scope of potential liability, the Department of Labor adopted regulations that encouraged plan sponsors to place investment decisions squarely in the hands of individual participants. See Langbein, Stabile, and Wolk (2006), describing rules before the 2006 statutory amendments.

9. See Pension Protection Act of 2006, Public Law 109–280, 120 Statute 780 (2006). For an overview of the new investment advice rules and implementing the Department of Labor regulations, see St. Martin (2007).

10. For illustrative cases challenging these practices, see *Moses v. Burgin*, 445 F.2d 369 (1st Cir. 1971) and *Tannenbaum v. Zeller*, 552 F.2d 401 (2d Cir. 1977), discussed in Jackson and Symons (1999).

11. See U.S. SEC (2003), describing limited disclosures of certain kinds of soft dollar payments. Among other complexities, the SEC Concept Release noted the possibility of confusion in a disclosure rule that emphasized certain components of trading costs (like soft dollar payments) but not others, such as price impacts and spread costs.

12. See Commodity and Securities Exchanges (2007), section 270.12b-1. SEC officials have recently indicated that the commission may soon revisit the current structure of rule 12b-1 and may even repeal the rule, thereby preventing mutual funds from using fund assets (as opposed to adviser resources) to pay for distribution costs (see Anand 2007a, 2007b).

13. For a review of the controversy, see "The Perils of Payment for Order Flow" (1994). See also Ferrell (2001).

14. A separate line of criticism of the practices was based on the claim that alternative markets offering payments for order flow were free-riding off of price discovery and other activities of the major markets, such as the NYSE, and causing excessive market fragmentation and loss of liquidity.

15. Another form of side payments—from investment managers to mutual fund distributors to subsidize the cost of selling mutual fund shares—has been the subject of recent regulatory scrutiny. The SEC recently prohibited the use of directed brokerage to support the distribution of mutual fund shares (see SEC 2004). This practice was an example of a trilateral dilemma as the investors bore the cost of these payments through higher brokerage commissions on portfolio transactions. When the manager pays for distribution expenses, the implications for investors are less clear, although arguably the cost is also passed on to investors in the form of higher advisory fees.

16. Many of the mutual fund market timing cases had this characteristic, as do enforcement actions involving the receipt of inappropriate gratuities by investment firm personnel. Another recent example of this sort of employee misconduct can be seen in the secret side payments that lower level employees of brokerage firms made to firms that assisted them in finding illiquid securities for their firm's securities lending programs (see Davis 2007).

17. For a good introduction to the Spitzer investigations and subsequent debates, see Schwarcz (2007). See also Fitzpatrick (2006).

18. Compare Cummins and Doherty (2006), emphasizing the value of contingent commissions for solving adverse selection programs, with Schwarcz (2007), offering an alternative interpretation of contingent commissions and arguing for their prohibition.

19. See *Gramm-Leach-Bliley Financial Modernization Act of* 1999, Title V, Public Law 106–102, 113 Statute 1338 (1999). For an overview of the legislation, see Swire (2002).

20. An argument of this sort in the context of yield spread premiums is explored in Jackson and Burlingame (2007). See also Fitzpatrick (2006).

21. The emergence of so many strategies to circumvent NYSE fixed commission rules in the late 1960s and early 1970s in fact prompted the SEC and Congress to eliminate the practice in 1975. See Jackson and Symons (1999).

22. Soft dollar practices, for example, have been defended as necessary to support independent research firms, and regulatory tolerance of yield spread premi-

ums has been characterized as necessary to permit mortgage brokers to compete for loan originations with integrated mortgage lenders. See Jackson and Burlingame (2007).

23. For a review of these arguments in the context of NYSE fixed commissions, see *Gordon v. NYSE,* 422 U.S. 659 (1975), discussed in Jackson and Symons (1999).

24. For evidence that consumers focus on the larger issues associated with a home purchase and mortgage financing and not the smaller details, see Bucks and Pence (2006).

25. In some contexts, decisions on the purchase of ancillary services occur well after a consumer is locked into the overall transactions and switching costs may be high. See Jackson and Burlingame (2007) for discussion of this problem in the context of mortgage broker compensation. This timing mismatch—which may be engineered by the intermediaries in question—can further diminish for consumers the salience of ancillary services involving side payments.

26. See Jackson and Burlingame (2007), exploring this issue but also finding that consumers fared best when they made direct cash payments.

27. This point is analogous to John Campbell's claim that the presence of cross subsidies in the price of certain mortgages limits the ability of mortgage lenders to price mortgages more accurately for all consumers (see Campbell 2006).

28. In the area of 401(k) plans, one might imagine requiring providers to include a range of index funds for which total performance can more easily be measured against the underlying index and for which the net effect of expenses and fees is clear. Again, this would be a form of structured solution to the problem. Plan participants could then evaluate the expenses and fees for other actively managed funds against this somewhat more objective benchmark.

29. An interesting example of such voluntary disclosures are the "Upfront" Mortgage Brokers, a group that voluntarily pays over yield spread premiums to borrowers in the manner that the Department of Housing and Urban Development proposed a few years ago but never implemented. See http://www.upfrontmortgagebrokers.org/search_umb.asp.

References

Anand, Shefali. 2007a. SEC Will Review Mutual-Fund Sales Fee. *Wall Street Journal,* March 27.
———. 2007b. Independent Directors Tackling 12b-1 Fees. *Wall Street Journal,* May 8.
Boehmer, Ekkehart, Robert Jennings, and Li Wei. 2007. Public Disclosure and Private Decisions: Equity Market Execution Quality and Order Routing. *Review of Financial Studies* 20: 315–58.

Bucks, Brian, and Karen Pence. 2006. Do Homeowners Know Their House Values and Mortgage Terms? Federal Reserve Board of Governors Working Paper.

Brown, Jeffrey R., and Scott Weisbenner. 2004. Individual Account Investment Options and Portfolio Choice: Behavioral Lessons from 401(k) Plans. Working paper. University of Illinois at Urbana-Champaign.

Campbell, John Y. 2006. Household Finance. *Journal of Finance* 61: 1553–604.

Choi, James J., David Laibson, and Brigitte C. Madrian. 2005. $100 Bills on the Sidewalk: Suboptimal Savings in 401(k) Plans. Pension Research Council Working Paper No. 2006–4. Wharton School, University of Pennsylvania, Philadelphia, PA.

Choi, James J., David Laibson, Brigitte C. Madrian, and Andrew Metrick. 2006. Saving for Retirement on the Path of Least Resistance. In *Behavioral Public Finance: Toward a New Agenda,* edited by Ed McCaffrey and Joel Slemrod, 304–51. New York: Russell Sage Foundation.

Commodity and Securities Exchanges. 2007. *Code of Federal Regulations.* Title 17, section 270.12b-1.

———. 2007. *Code of Federal Regulations.* Title 17, section 240.11Ac1–5.

———. 2007. *Code of Federal Regulations.* Title 17, section 240.11Ac1–6.

Cummins, J. David, and Neil A. Doherty. 2006. The Economics of Insurance Intermediaries. *Journal of Risk and Insurance* 73: 359–96.

Don't Minimize Differences in 401(k) Expenses. 1997. *Sun-Sentinel Ft. Lauderdale.* November 17.

House Committee on Education and Labor. 2007. Testimony of Andrew Cuomo. 110th Congress, 1st session, April 25. Available at http://edworkforce.house.gov/testimony/042507AndrewCuomotestimony.pdf.

Economic Systems Inc. 1998. Study of 401(k) Plan Fees and Expenses. Report submitted to Department of Labor, Pension and Welfare Benefits Administration. April 13.

Davis, Paul. 2007. Former Wall Street Workers to Face Charges in Brooklyn. *Wall Street Journal,* September 21.

Ferrell, Allen. 2001. A Proposal for Solving the "Payment for Order Flow" Problem. *Southern California Law Review* 74: 1027–88.

Fitzpatrick, Sean M. 2006. The Small Laws: Eliot Spitzer and the Way to Insurance Market Reform. *Fordham Law Review* 74: 3041–71.

Gustman, Alan L., Thomas S. Steinmeier, and Nahid Tabatabai. 2008. Do Workers Know about Their Pension Plan Type? Comparing Workers' and Employers' Pension Information. This volume.

Horan, Stephen M., and D. Bruce Johnsen. 2004. Does Soft Dollar Brokerage Benefit Portfolio Investors: Agency Problem or Solution? George Mason Law and Economics Research Paper No. 04-50. George Mason University, Arlington, VA.

Jackson, Howell E., and Laurie Burlingame. 2007. Kickbacks or Compensation:

The Case of Yield Spread Premiums. *Stanford Journal of Law, Business and Finance* 12: 289–362.

Jackson, Howell E., and Edward L. Symons. 1999. *The Regulation of Financial Institutions*. West Group: 851–70.

Johnsen, D. Bruce. 1994. Property Rights to Investment Research: The Agency Costs of Soft Dollar Brokerage. *Yale Journal on Regulation* 11: 75–113.

Laise, Eleanor. 2007. What Is Your 401(k) Costing You? *Wall Street Journal*, March 14.

Langbein, John H., Susan Stabile, and Bruce A. Wolk. 2006. *Pension and Employee Benefit Law*, 4th ed. Foundation Press.

Lauricella, Tom. 2007. Merrill Adjusts Policy on Pension-Fund Fees. *Wall Street Journal*, March 12.

Lerner, Charles. 2001. Department of Labor Enforcement Developments. American Law Institute–American Bar Association, SF53 ALI-ABA 245, 251.

Lusardi, Annamaria, Punam Anand Keller, and Adam M. Keller. 2008. New Ways to Make People Save: A Social Marketing Approach. This volume.

Morgenson, Gretchen. 2004. S.E.C. Inquiry to Encompass 401(k) Plans. *New York Times*, July 7.

———. 2007. Lawsuit Says Teachers Are Overcharged on Annuities. *New York Times*, July 17.

The Perils of Payment for Order Flow. 1994. *Harvard Law Review* 107: 1675–92.

Poterba, James M., Steven F. Venti, and David A. Wise. 2008. The Changing Landscape of Pensions in the United States. This volume.

Restatement of Trusts (Second). 1959. Philadelphia, Penn.: The American Law Institute.

St. Martin, Andree M. 2007. Providing Investment Advice to Plan Participants Following the Pension Protection Act. ALI-ABA Course of Study on Pension, Profit-Sharing, Welfare and Other Compensation Plans, May 28–30.

Sayles, Yolanda. 1999. ERISA Section 404(C) Plan Fees and Expense: Is There an Affirmative Fiduciary Duty to Disclose? *William Mitchell Law Review* 25: 1461–500.

Schwarcz, Daniel. 2007. Beyond Disclosure: The Case for Banning Contingent Commissions. *Yale Law and Policy Review* 25: 289–336.

Smith, Barbara A., and Fiona Stewart. 2008. Learning from the Experience of Organisation for Economic Co-operation and Development Countries: Lessons for Policy, Programs, and Evaluations. This volume.

Swire, Peter P. 2002. The Surprising Virtues of the New Financial Privacy Law. *Minnesota Law Review* 86: 1263–325.

U.S. Government Accountability Office (GAO). 2006. Private Pensions: Changes Needed to Provide 401(k) Plan Participants and the Department of Labor Better Information on Fees. GAO Report 07-21. November.

U.S. Securities and Exchange Commission (SEC). 2000. Final Rule on Disclosure of Order Execution and Routing Practices. *Federal Register* 65: 75,414–542.

———. 2003. Concept Release on Measures to Improve Disclosure of Mutual Fund Transaction Costs. *Federal Register* 68: 74,819–28.

———. 2004. Final Rule Prohibiting the Use of Brokerage Commissions to Finance Distribution. *Federal Register* 69: 54,728–34.

———. 2005. Staff Report Concerning Examination of Select Pension Consultants. SEC Office of Compliance and Examinations, May 16.

———. 2006. Guidance Regarding Client Commission Practices under Section 28(e) of the Securities Exchange Act of 1934. *Federal Register* 71: 41,978–42,051.

Zimmerman, Rachel. 2007. Federal Student-Aid Official Steps Down. *Wall Street Journal,* May 9.

PART II

Portfolio Choice, Life-Cycle Funds, and Annuities

CHAPTER FOUR

Red, Yellow, and Green: Measuring the Quality of 401(k) Portfolio Choices

Gary R. Mottola and Stephen P. Utkus

Introduction

The shift over the past quarter century from professionally managed defined benefit (DB) plans to participant-directed defined contribution (DC) plans has meant that employees must take an active role in managing their retirement assets. However, some participants may not be willing or able to manage those assets. Surveys suggest that many plan participants are inexperienced in dealing with financial matters and have low levels of financial literacy. Some participants appear to make obvious portfolio errors, such as concentrating their portfolios in employer stock or holding too conservative portfolios. Many make subtle construction errors, failing to diversify their equity portfolios more broadly with small-capitalization or international stocks.[1] In response to these concerns, the 2006 Pension Protection Act (PPA) in the United States envisions a new type of 401(k) plan—the autopilot or automatic 401(k)—in which more participants are automatically enrolled into qualified default investments designed by investment professionals. The PPA also encourages greater provision of investment advice to participants. Yet even if automatic plan designs or advisory services grow quickly, it remains the case that the vast majority of nearly 60 million private sector DC plan participants have constructed their portfolios on their own, without professional help.

How well are participants faring in the task of portfolio construction? In this chapter, we assess investment literacy among 401(k) plan participants by measuring the quality of their portfolio decisions compared with professional investment advice. We use a simple stoplight color scheme—red, yellow, and green—to classify portfolio selection. In general, we find that many participants appear to adopt reasonable levels of equity exposure: specifically, nearly 45 percent of participants construct "green" portfolios with equity allocations consistent with expert advice, while just over 25 percent build "yellow" portfolios that have meaningful equity holdings but appear to be invested either too aggressively or too conservatively. At the same time, three in ten participants construct "red" portfolios with egregious portfolio errors, including zero participation in the equity markets or overexposure to single-stock risk. At a finer level of detail, many participants fail to take advantage of additional opportunities for diversification, such as diversifying holdings with international or small-capitalization stocks or high-quality bonds when they are offered. Few participants own more specialized asset classes (for example, high-yield bonds), which are not made available by plan sponsors in the first place.

Besides assessing the quality of portfolio choices, we are also able to estimate the cost of portfolio errors. Portfolio errors can be costly—on the basis of our estimate errors are anywhere from roughly 60 to 350 basis points in expected real return per year. Our demographic models also suggest that lower income, lower wealth, and less financially sophisticated participants incur the largest costs in terms of reduced expected returns because they are more likely to invest in an ultraconservative manner. This same population would be the largest beneficiary of strategies to improve 401(k) portfolio diversification. At the other extreme, older, affluent male participants, who typically invest quite aggressively, may see expected portfolio returns fall with a shift to "better" portfolios. But, overall, portfolio efficiency levels would still rise.

Plan sponsors and policy makers overseeing DC programs have several remedial strategies available for improving participant portfolio allocations. These include greater reliance on professionally managed default investment funds, the introduction of managed account advisory services, and the "mapping" of existing participant accounts to new default funds. Investment education may also be effective, but the impact of education on actual behavior is highly debated. Regardless of the remedial strategy adopted, our research suggests that through such approaches, a meaningful group of participants could improve expected returns or diversification levels (or both), thus enhancing their prospects for retirement security.

In this chapter, after reviewing the prior research on 401(k) investment decisions and describing our data set, we first assess the quality of portfolio decisions and then turn to estimating the costs of poor portfolio choices. We conclude by discussing implications for sponsors and policy makers overseeing DC retirement programs.

Prior Research on 401(k) Investment

Prior research on 401(k) investment decision making falls broadly under three themes: behavioral biases, portfolio allocations and trading activity, and financial literacy.

One of the most important themes of the behavioral finance research has been the impact of the employer-designed 401(k) menu on participant investment choices. With small menus, participants appear to follow a "naive $1/n$" heuristic, allocating their savings evenly among menu options; in larger menus, this effect appears in the form of a "conditional $1/n$" heuristic, in which participants tend to divide their savings equally among a subset of funds they select from the menu. In addition, menus with a higher proportion of equity funds tend to result in participant allocations with higher equity exposure. The same is true if the menu has more high-cost active equity funds. Meanwhile, 401(k) investment menus with many options appear to give rise to "choice overload," which either leads to lower plan participation or to reliance on familiar, conservative investment choices. One possible explanation for these effects is that, contrary to neoclassical models of revealed preferences and portfolio choice, participants may have unstable preferences—perhaps due in part to deficiencies in financial education—that are easily subject to framing effects.[2]

The role of procrastination or inertia as a decision heuristic is also evident in 401(k) portfolios. The inertia effects are best known in the context of automatic enrollment in 401(k) plans. But they also apply to the tendency of participants to fail to revisit their ongoing investment allocations. For example, 45 percent of plan participants in higher education never changed their asset allocation over a ten-year period. Research on 401(k) trading underscores this finding. These studies demonstrate that only 10 percent of participants trade in any given year, far below the rate that might be expected from periodic rebalancing of portfolios.[3]

Additional research places 401(k) portfolio choices in the context of overall questions of participant financial literacy or experience. According

to one national survey, 42 percent of 401(k) participants describe themselves as "novice" or "beginner" investors, and a similar percentage describe themselves as "little or somewhat experienced." Only 15 percent say
they are knowledgeable or experienced investors. Another survey demonstrates that some 401(k) participants believe money market funds include
stock investments; few understand the inverse relationship of bond prices
and yields; and many find their employer stock to be a safer investment
than a diversified portfolio. More broadly, one of the substantive "investment mistakes" made by some American households, particularly lower
income or lower wealth households, is the failure to participate in the equity markets—the failure to take any equity risk whatsoever. In addition,
while many older Americans understand basic percentages, they struggle
with basic financial calculations such as compound interest calculations.
Low levels of financial literacy tend to be associated with younger age,
lower income, lower levels of educational attainment, female sex, and
lower wealth.[4]

Approach and Data

In our analysis of 401(k) portfolios, we first develop a set of qualitative
measures of portfolio construction. The result is our red, green, and yellow
taxonomy reflecting the relative quality of portfolio decisions. This analysis
is based on a large data set drawn from Vanguard's 401(k) record-keeping
systems, which we refer to as our full sample. The full sample encompasses
over 2,000 DC plans and nearly 2.9 million 401(k) participants as of December 31, 2005.

The second part of our analysis develops first-order estimates of the
cost of portfolio choices—in terms of both forfeited return or reduced
diversification levels. This analysis is based on a much smaller data set,
called the managed account sample. It consists of nearly 12,000 participants drawn from the full sample who adopted a managed account service in the twelve months prior to September 2005.[5] A managed account
service is a third-party, professional advisory service authorized for 401(k)
plans by the U.S. Department of Labor in its 2001 *SunAmerica* advisory
opinion. Participants who sign up for the managed account cede all investment control to the adviser, who reallocates the participant's plan balance
to conform to the adviser's investment recommendations. The adviser also

TABLE 4.1 **Sample characteristics**

	Full sample	Managed account sample
n	2,857,089	11,729
Demographics:		
Median age, years	44.0	50.0
Percent male	64	48
Median job tenure, years	8.5	13.2
Median household income	$87,500	$95,951
Percent high wealth[a]	21	20
Percent Web registered	49	56
Investment:		
Median plan assets	$23,784	$38,572
Percent equity exposure	67	57
Percent company stock exposure	11	7

Note: Data from the IXI company were used to impute non–retirement plan household financial wealth at the ZIP+4 level.
[a]High-wealth participants are defined as participants with over $50,000 in nonretirement household wealth (the top 20 percent).

assumes control for ongoing management and rebalancing of the port-folio. For this sample, we were able to obtain portfolio risk and return measures from the third-party adviser, Financial Engines, both before and after the adoption of a professional advisory service. By definition, the managed account sample is not a random sample of the broader data set. But the results from our analysis of this smaller data set are, in our view, at least a good first-order approximation of the costs associated with various suboptimal portfolio strategies for a larger group of participants.

Table 4.1 summarizes characteristics of the two data sets. In the full sample, the median participant was 44 years old, was male, had worked for his employer for 8.5 years, had a household income of $87,500, and had accumulated nearly $24,000 in 401(k) savings at year end 2005. Half of participants in the sample were registered for online access to their 401(k) accounts. The managed account sample is broadly similar to the full sample, but with some marked differences. Participants in the man-aged account sample were somewhat older, were longer tenured, included more females, and were somewhat more likely to be registered for Inter-net access. They also tended to hold less in diversified equities overall and in company stock. They obviously differ from other participants in their willingness to adopt an advisory service when it was first offered.

Quality of Portfolio Decisions

The first part of our analysis examines the degree to which participants in the full sample conform to simple portfolio construction rules provided by portfolio experts. We begin by assessing the quality of "gross" portfolio construction—namely, participants' overall risk exposure to equities and their willingness to expose themselves to single-stock rather than diversified equity market risk. Specifically, we determine to what degree participant portfolios conform to the following three rules:

1. *The diversified equities rule.* We assume that portfolios with between 40 and 95 percent equity exposure are consistent with well-accepted standards of portfolio practice based on two independent investment methodologies. In our managed account sample, Financial Engines (Vanguard's managed account provider) generally recommends overall portfolio allocations to equities ranging from 40 to 95 percent of 401(k) account assets.[6] In addition, the equity allocations for Vanguard age-based life-cycle funds range from approximately 45 to 90 percent for individuals in their working years. Thus, we define as green diversified equity exposure ranging from 40 to 95 percent.

2. *The zero-equity error rule.* A common portfolio error cited in the financial economics literature is a household's decision to hold zero percent of financial wealth in equities. An approximation of this rule for 401(k) plans is for participants to hold zero percent of their 401(k) assets in equities.[7] As such, we define portfolios with zero equity exposure as making an egregious, or red, portfolio error.

3. *The company stock rule.* While neoclassical models of portfolio choice would suggest a zero allocation to single-stock risk, there are mixed findings on the motivational aspects of employer stock. As a result, we define as egregious, or red, any portfolio with more than 20 percent of assets in company stock. This rule is consistent with the limit also imposed by the Vanguard managed account service; it is also the rule included in mandatory disclosure to participants regarding company stock risk under the 2006 PPA.[8]

These portfolio construction rules, applied to our sample of 2.9 million accounts, result in five investor segments, which are shown in table 4.2. The simple stoplight color scheme reflects the extent to which participant portfolios conform to our three rules of portfolio construction. Forty-three percent of portfolios are in the green segment, with equity allocations ranging from 40 to 95 percent and company stock exposure less than 20

TABLE 4.2 **Investor segments**

A. Summary of segments

Investor Segment	Percent
A. Green	43.1
B. Yellow (conservative equity)	6.9
C. Yellow (aggressive equity)	19.3
D. Red (zero equity)	13.4
E. Red (company stock)	17.2

B. Segments in detail

Equity exposure		Company stock exposure, %					Total
	1. Zero	2. 1–19	3. 20–39	4. 40–99	5. 100	
1. Zero	D 13.4					13.4
2. 1–39	B 5.2	1.7	0.8			7.7
3. 40–94	A 37.5	5.7	E 3.7	3.9		50.7
4. 95–99	C 3.3	1.0	0.6	1.6		6.6
5. 100	C 13.7	1.3	1.1	1.4	4.2	21.7
Total	73.1	9.6	6.1	6.9	4.2	100.0

Note: Based on full sample.

percent.[9] Twenty-five percent of portfolios are in one of the two yellow segments because their equity exposure is outside our green 40–95 percent range but nonzero. Thirty percent are in one of two red segments, with either zero in equities or a concentrated stock position exceeding 20 percent.

This color scheme refers only to our three basic rules of portfolio construction. What about finer levels of portfolio construction, such as the decision to diversify equity holdings more broadly or to hold volatile bonds over principal-stable investments like guaranteed investment contracts (GICs) or money market funds? Table 4.3 demonstrates that most plans offer, and most participants in our full sample are offered, the opportunity to diversify their equity holdings using mid- and small-capitalization U.S. stocks and international developed market stocks and to diversify their fixed income holdings with high-quality bonds. Yet fewer than three in ten participants avail themselves of these three classes. Other specialized asset classes, such as emerging market stocks,[10] non-U.S. bonds, real estate investment trusts (REITs), and Treasury inflation protected securities (TIPS), are by and large not widely offered by sponsors in the first place. When offered, few participants take up these specialized options.

TABLE 4.3 **Type of investment options used**

Category	Percent of plans offering	Percent of participants offered	Percent of participants offered and using
Large-cap U.S. equities	99	98	65
Money market/guaranteed investment contract	98	98	44
Balanced/life-cycle/life-style	97	95	43
High-quality bond	97	95	26
International equities	95	96	25
Small/midcap U.S. equities	93	96	29
Real estate investment trusts	21	15	8
Speciality/sector	19	13	12
High-yield bonds	16	15	8
Treasury inflation protected securities	16	20	4
Emerging markets	13	15	6
Company stock	12	46	58
World bonds	0	2	1

Note: Based on full sample.

Overall, our results suggest that at a gross portfolio construction level, many participants have reasonably healthy portfolios. Forty-five percent construct portfolios consistent with third-party expert rules, and another 25 percent assume equity market risk, although they take levels of equity exposure that are either too aggressive or too conservative by the advisory rules we set forth. But an important minority fails at the extremes by constructing red portfolios that are too conservatively invested or too concentrated in employer stock. Of course, participants may be in a given portfolio for several reasons. For example, they may fail to understand rudimentary investment principles; they may have been defaulted into a given portfolio; or they may have applied some naive decision heuristic, like the $1/n$ rule. Alternatively, they may have well-established preferences for a particular allocation, whether extreme or not.

In terms of finer levels of portfolio construction, only three in ten appear to utilize more sophisticated diversification strategies.[11] Table 4.4 summarizes the main investment patterns for each of the five segments identified above. Not surprisingly, red (zero equity) investors invest almost exclusively in stable-principal investments such as money market funds and GIC funds and to a limited extent in bonds. Yellow (conservative equity) investors have a high weighting to stable-principal investments as well. Both of these segments no doubt reflect either high levels of risk aversion and a preference for capital stability or a lack of knowledge about the benefits, even for cautious investors, of investing in high-quality bond funds relative to shorter duration instruments. The participants who take on extended levels of diversification with international or mid- and small-capitalization U.S. stocks are largely in two segments, green and yellow (aggressive equity). One noteworthy finding is the high use of balanced, life-cycle, and lifestyle funds among the green segment—no doubt a reflection of the growing popularity of these funds and their increasing use as default investment options in 401(k) plans (see Viceira 2008, chapter 5 of this volume).

Which demographic characteristics are associated with membership in each of our five investor segments? Figure 4.1 graphically summarizes the relationship between demographic characteristics and investor type (see the appendix for technical details). After controlling for various demographic variables, the conservatively invested segments—that is, participant portfolios classified as red (no equity) and yellow (conservative)—are more likely to be held by older, less affluent, or unengaged participants.[12] This finding is consistent with studies that show financial literacy is particularly low for the less educated, those with low income, and minorities (see Smith and Stewart 2008, chapter 13 of this volume). The more aggressively invested yellow segment tends to have younger, more affluent, and engaged participants. Since financial literacy is associated with affluence, it would appear at first that affluence, financial literacy, and equity risk tak-

TABLE 4.4 **Participant asset allocations by investor segment (percentage of assets)**

Category	Red (zero equity)	Yellow (conservative equity)	Green	Yellow (aggressive equity)	Red (company stock)
Large cap	0	8	36	68	16
Balanced/life-cycle/life-style	0	16	34	1	6
Small and mid cap	0	1	7	16	4
Money market/guaranteed investment contract	92	55	7	0	8
Bond	7	14	7	0	3
International	0	1	5	9	2
Company stock	0	2	1	1	61
Other	1	2	2	4	0
Total	100	100	100	100	100
Percent equity exposure	0	21	73	99	87

Note: Based on full sample.

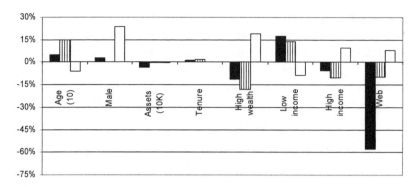

■ Red (Zero Equity) ⊞ Yellow (Conservative) □ Yellow (Aggressive)

FIGURE 4.1 Relationship between demographics and investor segment membership (relative marginal probabilities).

ing go hand in hand. Yet in our analysis, even these affluent and aggressive yellow investors may be taking too much risk according to our portfolio construction rules.

The Cost of Portfolio Choices

We next turn to developing first-order estimates of the costs associated with suboptimal portfolio decisions. This analysis relies on our managed account sample described earlier.

For the nearly 12,000 participants who signed up for the program, the managed account advisory service dramatically changed their portfolio allocations. Figure 4.2 depicts the before and after equity allocations for these participants. Prior to the adoption of the advisory service, 42 percent of participants were at three focal points: zero equities, 100 percent equities, and 50 percent equities (which represented the presence of a balanced default investment option in several of the large plans in this sample). The remaining participants were scattered across the equity allocation spectrum, with anywhere from 10 to 90 percent or more of account holdings invested in equities. After the advisory service took control of participant accounts, extreme equity holdings were entirely eliminated. Moreover, in a quite dramatic way, portfolio equity holdings became more normally distributed, with a mean equity exposure of 76 percent and a standard deviation of 12 percent.

To evaluate the impact of these dramatic changes, we first classified the participants in the managed account sample using our five red/green/yellow investor segments methodology. In turn, using data provided by the third-party adviser, Financial Engines, we estimated portfolio returns and Sharpe ratios both before and after adoption of the service.[13] The returns reported are real returns—expected returns after projected inflation. The returns are also net of fund expenses, but the cost of the managed account service has not been deducted from any of the returns. The Vanguard man-

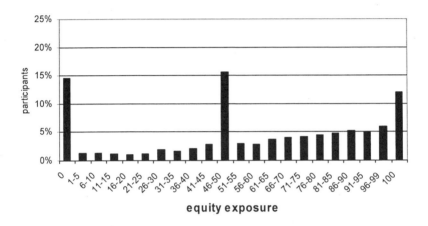

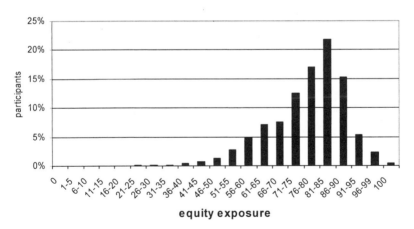

FIGURE 4.2 Impact of managed account on equity exposure (before managed account adoption [*above*] and after managed account adoption [*below*]).
Note: Based on managed account sample

TABLE 4.5 **Portfolio return and risk characteristics by investor segment**

A. Expected real returns after fund expenses[a]

Segment	Before managed account, %	After managed account, %	Methodology adjustment,[b] %	Change in expected return, %	Percent change
Red (zero equity)	1.76	5.41	−0.07	3.58	203
Yellow (conservative equity)	3.02	5.70	−0.10	2.58	85
Green	5.09	5.87	−0.15	0.63	12
Yellow (aggressive equity)	6.63	6.00	−0.19	−0.82	−12
Red (company stock)	7.68	6.14	−0.21	−1.75	−23
Total	4.86	5.83	−0.15	0.82	17

B. Sharpe ratios

Segment	Before managed account	After managed account	Methodology adjustment[b]	Change in Sharpe ratio	Percent change in Sharpe ratio
Red (zero equity)	0.111	0.316	−0.0064	0.198	179
Yellow (conservative equity)	0.250	0.318	−0.0025	0.066	26
Green	0.304	0.319	−0.0043	0.011	4
Yellow (aggressive equity)	0.289	0.318	−0.0049	0.024	8
Red (company stock)	0.233	0.313	−0.0081	0.072	31
Total	0.256	0.318	−0.0049	0.057	22

Note: Based on the managed account sample. Projected returns are based on Financial Engines' forecasting methodology, which projects the likelihood of various investment outcomes that are hypothetical in nature. The expected returns do not reflect actual results and are not guarantees of future results.
[a]Expected returns are after fund expenses but before the separate fee charged by the managed account service.
[b]These adjustments reflect changes over time in the subadviser's expected returns and/or covariance matrix. See note 13 in the text for more information.

aged account service has a base fee of 0.40 percent per year (with a sliding scale for high-asset accounts), but fees vary widely depending on the sponsor of the managed account program.

Table 4.5 presents before and after expected returns and Sharpe ratios for each of the five segments in the managed account sample. These results provide estimates of the costs or inefficiencies associated with a given type of portfolio strategy chosen by the participant compared with a portfolio selected by a professional adviser. For red (zero equity) participants, not surprisingly, the costs in terms of lower expected returns are dramatic: these participants forfeit 358 basis points in expected return. Even green portfolios experience gains in expected return of 63 basis points due to improvements in portfolio strategy. However, note that the adoption of professional advice does not lead to improvements in expected real returns across the board. The most aggressive investors—yellow (aggressive equity) and red (company stock)—actually see expected returns fall as their portfolios are diversified away from high levels of, respectively, diversified equities and company stock-specific risk. In both groups, however, expected returns per unit of risk improve. For all investor segments, Sharpe ratios (as a measure of portfolio efficiency) improve. The largest gains in Sharpe ratios occur for zero-equity holders and for those eliminating company stock risk.

In addition, we examined which demographic segments might benefit the most—in terms of improved portfolio risk and return characteristics—if they were to adopt "greener" portfolio strategies. Results from our model are shown in figure 4.3 (with details in table 4.6 in the appendix). All demographic groups experienced an improvement in performance after managed account adoption, but the relative size of the improvement varied. As shown in figure 4.3, a hypothetical managed account adopter—in this case defined as a non-high-wealth, medium household income, non-Web-registered female of average age, account balance, and tenure—experiences a 1.50 percent increase in her expected return. However, if we hold everything constant about this average participant but change her sex

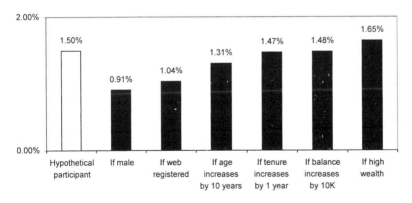

FIGURE 4.3 Relationship between demographics and portfolio improvement (change in expected return pre– and post–managed account implementation). *Note:* Based on managed account sample. Due to the interaction terms in our model, the hypothetical participant effect of 1.50% is a conditional effect for low wealth, medium household income, non-web registration, being a female of average age, account balance, and tenure. The unconditional effect is 0.97%.

to male, this hypothetical participant experiences a 0.91 percent increase in expected return after managed account adoption—an improvement in performance significantly greater than zero but also significantly less than that of a female participant. Similarly, if we hold everything constant but change the hypothetical participant to a high-wealth participant, he or she experiences a 1.65 percent increase in expected return instead of 1.50 percent.

Summary and Implications

Our analysis of participant portfolio choice indicates that nearly 45 percent of participants construct green portfolios based on their overall exposure to a diversified level of equity market risk, while another 25 percent or so construct yellow portfolios with possibly too aggressive or too conservative equity holdings. Another three in ten make egregious or red portfolio errors, either by not investing in equities at all or by overconcentrating their portfolio in employer stock. At a finer level of portfolio detail, most participants (with some exceptions) do not appear to engage in additional levels of portfolio diversification, such as holding mid- and small-capitalization U.S. and non-U.S. stocks or high-quality bonds, despite the widespread availability of these options and the potential for increased portfolio efficiency that they offer. Some portfolio diversification errors are clearly related to employer plan design (for example, the availability of company stock or the lack of specialized diversification options), although many participants in our sample have access to a wide range of broad asset classes.

Our estimates suggest that portfolio errors can be costly. The most costly errors are made by red (zero equity) participants, those who hold no equities in their 401(k) account; the potential gain from improving their portfolios is estimated at over 350 basis points in real return per year. Yet even green investors can improve portfolio performance by sixty basis points or more through better portfolio construction. Gains are also possible in terms of portfolio efficiency as measured by Sharpe ratios. For plan sponsors overseeing a given DC plan, the potential gains at the plan level will of course depend on the proportion of investor segments in the plan population. For example, a plan with a large proportion of red (zero equity) investors will experience more dramatic improvements in expected returns than, say, a plan with more green or yellow (aggressive equity) investors. Similarly, a plan with many aggressively oriented participants is likely to see expected returns fall, while efficiency measures improve.

The participants most likely to experience improvements in expected returns and Sharpe ratios from better portfolio strategies are those whose characteristics are typically associated with low levels of financial literacy—namely, lower income and less engaged participants. More aggressive investors, who are more often affluent men, may experience reductions in returns but still see improvements in overall portfolio efficiency.

There are a variety of strategies that sponsors and policy makers might pursue in order to improve participant portfolios and reduce the costs of portfolio errors. Continued financial education is one avenue, and indeed, investor education materials are already quite common within the 401(k) marketplace. However, their main drawback is that education programs appear to yield few actual changes in portfolio strategy because of the widespread prevalence of inertia among participants. Educational programs can alter people's attitudes and intentions regarding investment planning; the challenge arises with follow-through and executing on intentions (see Clark and d'Ambrosio 2008, chapter 8 of this volume). An alternative approach is to promote automatic enrollment of participants into well-designed default funds. This is the premise underlying the PPA, and in keeping with its provisions, the U.S. Department of Labor issued new regulations encouraging the greater use of "qualified default investment alternatives." Advice programs may also improve portfolios. They typically come with incremental costs for the advisory service, although those costs must be compared with the potential gains in portfolio expected returns and/or diversification levels that may occur, at least for some segments of participants.

Another possible strategy is the notion of mapping plan participants to better investment allocations. Under U.S. fiduciary law, plan sponsors generally remain the ultimate party responsible for the investment of plan assets. If they so choose, they are able to map (or shift) all plan participants' balances into other investment funds, such as professionally managed default investments.[14] Such a strategy could potentially improve portfolio allocations quickly, given the tendency of most participants to rely on default choices made by others. And by including a right to opt out of the mapping, such a strategy could address the needs of participants who have strong preferences for retaining their existing choices.

Addressing overconcentration of company stock is more difficult owing to the facts that some companies match in company stock and that such matching contributions appear to be the principal determinant of concentrated stock holdings. One option is for sponsors to match in cash (that is, into the funds the employee has selected) rather than in employer stock. A second strategy is to impose limits on concentrated holdings by employees. Advice programs like managed accounts are a third approach, as the advisory service takes responsibility for the liquidation of employer stock and the employer is not responsible for encouraging the sale of shares of employer stock. A final option is the "sell more tomorrow" program, in which participants are defaulted into a reverse dollar-cost averaging service that gradually liquidates their stock holdings down to a reduced level over time (see Benartzi et al. 2007).

One consideration in interpreting the results of our study is that we are assessing participant holdings based on a single 401(k) account, whereas participants could be constructing portfolios at the household level. For example, we might classify a participant portfolio as red (zero equity), but the participant or the participant's spouse or partner may have assets invested in equities in other accounts that we do not observe. In total, their household portfolio could be green. While we acknowledge that this is a possibility, our research suggests that for many participants their current 401(k) account is their only meaningful financial investment. Nearly 50 percent of our participants have less than $10,000 in nonretirement assets. Furthermore, a 2006 study from the Employee Benefit Research Institute found that for nearly a third of participants, their retirement savings in their employer plan represented "all or almost all" of their total retirement savings and that for another 15 percent, their employer plan represented three-quarters of their total retirement savings (see Helman, Copeland, and VanDerhei 2006). Given that most participants have no or few assets outside their plan, our belief is that this problem may be limited in scope and confined to the more affluent participants in our sample, who already construct yellow or green portfolios anyway.

An intriguing question raised by our research is whether or not informing participants of their color-coded segment (through their quarterly statements or on the Web) would influence their investment behavior. Given the widely demonstrated power of inertia in DC investing and the fairly limited effects of investor education, we believe that this knowledge would not impact participant investment behavior in a meaningful manner. However, informing a plan sponsor that 30 percent of their participants are in the red segment could motivate the sponsor to alter the design of the plan. In any event, future research might explore the impact of informing participants about their investor segment or plan sponsors about the distribution of segments within their plan.

Overall it seems that participant portfolios are quite heterogeneous, and efforts by sponsors to improve portfolio allocations will depend on the specific segments that predominate in a given plan. Any gains in expected real returns from improvements in portfolio strategy are likely to be largest among populations typically associated with low levels of financial literacy, especially low-wealth and unengaged participants. Meanwhile, participants who invest in an overly aggressive manner, such as affluent male investors, may benefit from greater portfolio efficiency and diversification.

Appendix

Investor Segments

Figure 4.1 summarizes marginal effects from a multinomial logit regression analyzing the impact of participant demographics on membership. The general form of the model is $\Pr(\text{Segment}_{i,j}) = \beta_0 + \beta_1 \mathbf{X}_{i,j} + \varepsilon_{i,j}$, where the dependent variable is the probability of being in one of the investor segments shown, with the green segment as the reference category. We excluded red (company stock) participants from the analysis since their holdings of company stock were not influenced by demographic factors but by the plan sponsor's decision to place company stock in the 401(k) menu.

Portfolio Changes and Demographics

Figure 4.3 summarizes changes from a difference-in-difference ordinary least squares model relating portfolio expected returns and Sharpe ratios to demographic characteristics. The sample is our managed account sample. The empirical model for $E(r_{i,j,t})$, the expected returns for the ith participant account in the jth plan at time t, is as follows: $E(r_{i,j,t}) = \beta_0 + \beta_1 \text{Treatment}_{i,j,t} + \beta_2 Y_{i,j,t} + \beta_3 Z_{i,j,t} + \varepsilon_{i,j,t}$. We observe each participant portfolio at two points in time: prior to the managed account adoption (September 2004) and after (December 2005). Our independent variables include a within-subject Treatment variable (that is, set to 1 if after adoption of the managed account and 0 before adoption) and a vector of demographic variables $Y_{i,j,t}$. Furthermore, we interact the Treatment variable with the between-group demographic variables such as gender, age, and Web registration in $Z_{i,j,t}$. Observations are clustered at the participant level to ensure robust errors. The complete regression results are shown in table 4.6.

TABLE 4.6 **Regression results supporting figure 4.3**

	Estimate when the dependent variable is the expected real return (means: before = .0486; after = .0583; difference = .0090)		Estimate when the dependent variable is the Sharpe ratio (means: before = .256; after = .318; difference = .062)	
Main effects:				
Intercept	0.0479	**	0.2639	**
Treatment	0.0299	**	0.0535	**
Age (10)	−0.0023	**	−0.0014	
Male	0.0073	**	0.0010	
Balance ($10K)	0.0002	**	0.0010	**
Tenure	0.0003	**	−0.0010	**
High wealth	−0.0020	**	0.0010	
Household income low	0.0003		−0.0016	
Household income high	0.0010	*	0.0024	
Web registered	0.0051	**	0.0121	**
Interaction terms:				
Treatment × Age (10)	−0.0019	**	0.0018	
Treatment × Male	−0.0059	**	−0.0017	
Treatment × Balance ($10K)	−0.0002	**	−0.0009	**
Treatment × Tenure	−0.0003	**	0.0009	**
Treatment × High wealth	0.0015	**	−0.0011	
Treatment × Household income low	−0.0004		0.0016	
Treatment × Household income high	−0.0007		−0.0022	
Treatment × Web registered	−0.0046	**	−0.0123	**
Clustering at participant level?	Yes		Yes	
R^2	20%		27%	

Note: Clustering at the plan level to ensure robust standard errors. Results do not account for the "methodology adjustment" referenced in the endnotes. There were 20,590 observations and 10,295 participants.
*Significant at the 10% level.
**Significant at the 5% level.

Notes

The authors thank Brigitte Madrian and Olivia Mitchell for helpful comments. Opinions expressed herein are those of the authors alone and not those of Vanguard or any other institution with which the authors may be affiliated.

1. See John Hancock (2002) and Vanguard (2002) for measures of financial literacy. For information on participant allocation patterns, see Vanguard (2006a) and Munnell and Sundén (2004).

2. For a discussion of behavioral biases in defined contribution plans, see Benartzi and Thaler (2001, 2002); Iyengar, Huberman, and Jiang (2004); Brown, Liang, and Weisbenner (2006); and Iyengar and Jiang (2006).

3. For a discussion of the role of procrastination and inertia in financial decision making, see Madrian and Shea (2001); Ameriks and Zeldes (2004); and Choi. et al. (2006). For 401(k) trading research, see Agnew, Balduzzi, and Sundén (2003); Mitchell et al. (2006); and Yamaguchi et al. (2006).

4. See Hancock (2002) and Vanguard (2002) for measures of financial literacy. For common household financial mistakes, see Campbell (2006). For a discussion of financial literacy among older Americans, see Lusardi and Mitchell (2007).

5. These participants were drawn from nineteen organizations with thirty-seven plans and 242,412 unique participant accounts.

6. In total, 95 percent of participant portfolios fell in this range after managed account implementation. See Vanguard (2006b) for full details about adoption of the managed account service.

7. This 401(k) approximation is a good measure of the overall market participation rule, since equity exposure in 401(k) plans can be obtained with no minimum balance constraints and with no transaction costs (such as sales loads) in our sample.

8. The Pension Protection Act requires that plans offering company stock notify participants of their "right to diversify." The Internal Revenue Service builds on this provision with Notice 2006-1-7, which states that "if you invest more than 20 percent of your retirement savings in any one company or industry, your savings may not be properly diversified."

9. Company stock classification superseded equity exposure classification, so, for example, a participant with between 40 and 95 percent equity exposure but over 20 percent company stock exposure would be classified as red (company stock).

10. In our sample, many international stock funds included an allocation to emerging market stocks.

11. Even among the participants diversifying their portfolios more broadly, we are not assessing whether their portfolios conform to detailed asset allocation rules, such as the proportion to be invested internationally, that our experts might recommend.

12. We use registration for 401(k) Internet access as a proxy for degree of financial engagement.

13. We estimated portfolio expected returns and variances at two points in time: September 2004, prior to the introduction of the managed account service in late 2004, and December 2005, the endpoint of our analysis. Expected real returns for the ith participant account at time t are simply the weighted average of expected real returns for the k assets in the plan: $E(r_i) = \sum_{k=1}^{N} \omega_{k,t} E(r_k)$. Portfolio variances based on the variance-covariance matrix $\hat{\Sigma}$ are: $\hat{\Sigma}_i = \omega'_{i,k,t} \hat{\Sigma} \omega_{i,k,t}$. Each ith account's Sharpe ratio is its excess return over the risk-free rate divided by its portfolio standard deviation, $r_i - r_f/\sigma_i$. Other details about the calculations, including the "methodology adjustment" needed to capture the "drift" in the Financial Engines return-covariance matrix, are summarized in Vanguard (2006b).

14. Sponsors may forfeit so-called 404(c) fiduciary protection in doing so. But they may choose to map the plan if, as plan fiduciaries, they judge such a move to be in the best interests of plan participants. There is anecdotal evidence that some sponsors have undertaken such mappings, usually providing participants with the right to opt out of such changes and retain their existing holdings.

References

Agnew, Julie, Pierluigi Balduzzi, and Annika Sundén. 2003. Portfolio Choice and Trading in a Large 401(k) Plan. *American Economic Review* 93: 193–215.

Ameriks, John, and Stephen P. Zeldes. 2004. How Do Household Portfolio Shares Vary with Age? Working paper. Graduate School of Business, Columbia University, New York.

Benartzi, Shlomo, and Richard H. Thaler. 2001. Naïve Diversification Strategies in Defined Contribution Savings Plans. *American Economic Review* 91: 79–98.

———. 2002. How Much Is Investor Autonomy Worth? *Journal of Finance* 57: 1593–616.

Benartzi, Shlomo, Richard H. Thaler, Stephen P. Utkus, and Cass R. Sunstein. 2007. The Law and Economics of Company Stock in 401(k) Plans. *Journal of Law and Economics* 50: 45–79.

Brown, Jeffrey R., Nellie Liang, and Scott Weisbenner. 2006. Individual Account Investment Options and Portfolio Choice: Behavioral Lessons from 401(k) Plans. Working paper. University of Illinois at Urbana-Champaign.

Campbell, John Y. 2006. Household Finance. *Journal of Finance* 61: 1553–604.

Choi, James J., David Laibson, Brigitte C. Madrian, and Andrew Metrick. 2006. Saving for Retirement on the Path of Least Resistance. In *Behavioral Public Finance,* edited by Ed McCaffrey and Joel Slemrods, 304–51. New York: Russell Sage Foundation.

Clark, Robert L., and Madeleine d'Ambrosio. 2008. Adjusting Retirement Goals and Saving Behavior: The Role of Financial Education. This volume.

Helman, Ruth, Craig Copeland, Jack VanDerhei. 2006. Will More of Us Be Working Forever? The 2006 Retirement Confidence Survey. EBRI Issue Brief 292. Employee Benefit Research Institute, Washington, DC.

Iyengar, Sheena, Gur Huberman, and Wei Jiang. 2004. How Much Choice Is Too Much? Contributions to 401(k) Retirement Plans. In *Pension Design and Structure: New Lessons from Behavioral Finance,* edited by Olivia S. Mitchell and Stephen P. Utkus, 83–96. Oxford: Oxford University Press.

Iyengar, Sheena, and Wei Jiang. 2006. The Psychological Costs of Ever Increasing Choice: A Fallback to the Sure Bet. Working paper under review at the *Journal of Personality and Social Psychology.*

John Hancock. 2002. *Eighth Defined Contribution Plan Survey.* Boston: John Hancock Financial Services.

Lusardi, Annamaria, and Olivia Mitchell. 2007. Retirement Security among Baby Boomers: The Role of Planning, Financial Literacy, and Housing Wealth. *Journal of Monetary Economics* 54: 205–24.

Madrian, Brigitte, and D. F. Shea. 2001. The Power of Suggestion: Inertia in 401(k) Participation and Savings Behavior. *Quarterly Journal of Economics* 116: 1149–87.

Mitchell, Olivia S., Gary R. Mottola, Stephen P. Utkus, and Takeshi Yamaguchi. 2006. The Inattentive Participant: Portfolio Trading Behavior in 401(k) Plans. Pension Research Council Working Paper No. 2006-05. The Wharton School, University of Pennsylvania, Philadelphia.

Munnell, Alicia H., and Annika Sunden. 2004. *Coming Up Short: The Challenge of 401(k) Plans.* Washington, DC: Brookings Institution Press.

Smith, Barbara A., and Fiona Stewart. 2008. Learning from the Experience of Organisation for Economic Co-operation and Development Countries: Lessons for Policy, Programs, and Evaluations. This volume.

Vanguard. 2002. Vanguard Participant Monitor: Expecting Lower Market Returns in the Near Term. Malvern, PA.: Vanguard Center for Retirement Research.

———. 2006a. How America Saves 2006: A Report on Vanguard 2006 Defined Contribution Plan Data. Malvern, PA: Vanguard Center for Retirement Research.

———. 2006b. Managed Accounts and Participant Portfolios. Malvern, PA: Vanguard Center for Retirement Research.

Viceira, Luis M. 2008. Life-Cycle Funds. This volume.

Yamaguchi, Takeshi, Olivia S. Mitchell, Gary R. Mottola, and Stephen P. Utkus. 2006. Winners and Losers: 401(k) Trading and Portfolio Performance. Pension Research Council Working Paper 2006-26. The Wharton School, University of Pennsylvania, Philadelphia.

CHAPTER FIVE

Life-Cycle Funds

Luis M. Viceira

Introduction

The U.S. retirement system has experienced a substantial transformation in recent years. It has evolved from a system in which employees rely mainly on Social Security and professionally managed defined benefit (DB) pension plans sponsored by their employers to provide for their retirement to a system in which employees must rely on their own saving and investment decisions to fund their own retirement.[1] Defined contribution (DC) plan participants and individual retirement account (IRA) holders decide how much to contribute (up to a legally established maximum limit) to their plan and how to invest their contributions and the contributions that their employer might make on their behalf. Thus the benefits they get at retirement depend on their own accumulation and investment decisions. DC plan sponsors are only responsible for the design of the plan and for its administration and record keeping. Current regulations grant sponsors considerable freedom in their selection of the number and type of investment options available to participants. In practice, most plan sponsors have chosen to offer a menu of plain vanilla mutual funds plus company stock. Thus mutual funds have become the main retirement investment vehicle in the United States, and mutual fund companies have become the main managers of retirement assets.

In recent years, plan sponsors have started including mutual funds geared toward offering "one-stop" solutions to retirement investment needs in their menu of investment options (see Viceira 2007). These funds have originated in response to what numerous sponsors, mutual fund industry executives, and pension and investment experts consider a disappointing experience with the way in which many participants in DC plans and IRAs manage their plan investments. There is concern that many employees might not be making saving and investment decisions conducive to maximizing the probability of getting adequate retirement income.[2]

In particular, there is evidence that a large number of DC plan participants, particularly among those with lower levels of education, wealth, and income, show a considerable degree of inertia in their contribution and investing decisions. They tend to adopt the default contribution and investment option chosen by the plan sponsor, which is typically either no contribution or a small contribution that is entirely invested in a money market fund. Those who actively move away from the plan default investment option tend to adopt naive diversification strategies, such as allocating equally among all the investment options in the plan, regardless of whether there are substantially more options in a particular asset class than in another. They also tend to invest heavily in company stock. Moreover, they fail to rebalance regularly (see Mottola and Utkus 2008).

In response to this concern, plan sponsors have begun adopting mutual funds that aim at providing investors with one-stop solutions to their long-term asset allocation and portfolio rebalancing needs. These funds fall into two main categories: balanced, or "life-style" funds, which follow a risk-based asset allocation strategy, and "life-cycle" funds, which follow an age-based asset allocation strategy. This chapter reviews modern theories of long-term investing and explores their implications for the design of investment products that help investors save for retirement.

Risk-based investing and age-based investing are at odds with the asset allocation recommendations that emerge from traditional mean-variance analysis. However, recent developments in the theory of asset allocation show that these strategies are optimal under realistic assumptions about investment opportunities and about the composition of investors' wealth. Based on these considerations, and the inertia that many investors exhibit in their portfolios, this chapter argues that properly designed life-cycle funds are better default investment choices than money market funds in DC pension plans.

However, the predictions of modern portfolio theory also suggest changes in the way that these funds are currently structured. Among other changes, this chapter argues that life-style and life-cycle funds should consider increasing substantially their allocation to inflation-indexed bonds at the expense of their current allocations to long-term nominal bonds, which are exposed to considerable inflation risk. Inflation-indexed bonds are also safer investment choices than money market funds for plan participants because money market funds, while safe at short horizons, can be highly risky at long horizons when investors face real interest rate (or reinvestment) risk.

This chapter also argues for the creation of industry-specific or company-specific life-cycle funds. These funds can help solve some of the design shortcomings of the current generation of life-cycle funds in a cost-effective way. The creation of "conservative," "moderate," and "aggressive" life-cycle funds can also help investors choose the equity profile that best fits their appetite for risk. This chapter also suggests that investors who expect to receive Social Security benefits and pension income after retirement should choose a target retirement date for their funds based on their life expectancy, not on their expected retirement date.

Finally, this chapter argues that, while life-cycle funds are better default investment choices than money market funds in DC plans, they should not be the only choice available to plan participants. For example, life-cycle funds can be a tax-inefficient way of implementing an age-based investment strategy for plan participants who have the ability to save outside the plan. These employees might want to build their own tax-efficient life-cycle investing strategy. Similarly, employees who feel financially educated enough might want to build an asset allocation strategy specifically designed for their own risk profile and retirement spending goals.

Life-Style Funds and Life-Cycle Funds

Balanced or life-style funds have a long tradition in the mutual fund industry, while life-cycle funds are relatively new to the industry. Life-style funds are mutual funds built on the idea of risk-based investing, or the notion that the fraction of savings allocated to stocks should be a function of investors' risk tolerance and independent of their investment horizon. Life-cycle funds are a variant of life-style funds built on the idea of age-based investing, or the notion that investors should allocate a larger share of their long-term savings to stocks when they are young and have long retirement horizons and decrease this allocation as they approach retirement.

Life-style funds automatically rebalance their holdings, typically a portfolio of underlying funds representing different asset classes and investment styles, so as to keep a constant asset target mix over time. These funds provide investors with diversified portfolios whose risk exposure does not change over time. For example, the Vanguard Balanced Index Fund tracks the investment performance of a portfolio that is 60 percent invested in the U.S. stock market and 40 percent in the U.S. bond market.[3] Mutual fund companies typically offer several of these funds and use words such as "aggressive," "moderate," or "conservative" in the fund name to indicate the fund's tilt toward equities.

Similar to balanced funds, life-cycle funds automatically rebalance the investments in the underlying funds to keep the overall portfolio composition of the fund in line with a prespecified asset target mix. Unlike balanced funds, however, life-cycle funds do not keep their target mix constant over time; instead, they change their target mix according to a predefined "roll-down" schedule until they reach a date called the target date or target maturity date of the fund. This roll-down schedule becomes more conservative over time in the sense that it tilts the target mix away from equities and toward bonds and cash. After the target date, these life-cycle funds are typically folded into a life-style fund that keeps its target asset allocation constant. Table 5.1, figure 5.1, table 5.2, and figure 5.2 show the life-cycle fund offerings, including asset allocation glide paths and returns, of the two largest life-cycle fund families ranked by assets managed in 2006, Fidelity's Freedom Funds and Vanguard's Target Retirement Funds, respectively.

Life-cycle mutual funds are one of the fastest growing segments in the mutual fund industry. Assets under management in these funds were about $120 billion at year end 2006, from about $1 billion in 1996, when Fidelity, the industry leader in this segment, launched its own version of these funds. This growth has accelerated in recent years with inflows of $15 billion in 2004, from less than $5 billion in 2001 and 2002.

This growth has taken place mostly through both IRAs and DC plans, as sponsors of DC plans have added these funds to their plan offerings. In the future, industry experts expect numerous plans to adopt these funds as the plan default investment option as a result of the enactment of the Pension Protection Act of 2006, which gives sponsors more flexibility in guiding participants in their fund selection.

TABLE 5.1 **Fidelity Freedom Funds asset allocation (May 30, 2006)**

Underlying Fidelity fund	Income	Freedom Fund										
		2000	2005	2010	2015	2020	2025	2030	2035	2040	2045	2050
Domestic equity funds												
Blue Chip Growth	3.0	3.6	5.8	5.8	7.2	8.1	8.9	9.7	10.0	10.0	10.4	10.5
Disciplined Equity	3.1	4.0	5.9	6.0	7.1	8.2	8.9	9.8	10.2	10.0	10.4	10.5
Equity-Income	3.1	4.0	5.9	6.0	7.1	8.3	8.9	9.8	10.1	10.0	10.4	10.5
Fidelity Fund	1.6	1.7	1.9	3.5	2.1	4.9	2.5	5.2	2.5	3.5	0.0	0.0
Growth and Income Portfolio	3.2	3.9	6.5	6.5	7.9	9.0	9.9	10.8	11.3	11.1	11.8	11.9
Fidelity Growth	2.0	2.6	3.7	3.9	4.6	5.2	5.6	6.2	6.3	6.4	6.7	6.8
Company Fund	0.0	0.0	0.0	0.0	0.0	0.0	0.0	0.0	0.0	0.0	0.0	0.0
Mid-Cap Stock	2.1	2.7	3.8	4.1	4.6	5.5	5.7	6.3	6.6	6.4	6.7	6.8
OTC Portfolio	1.6	1.9	2.9	3.0	3.6	4.1	4.5	4.9	5.0	5.1	5.3	5.4
Small Cap Growth	0.1	0.1	0.2	0.2	0.2	0.3	0.3	0.3	0.4	0.3	0.4	0.4
Small Cap Independence	0.3	0.2	0.8	0.7	1.0	1.1	1.2	1.3	1.4	1.4	1.4	1.4
Small Cap	0.1	0.1	0.2	0.2	0.3	0.3	0.3	0.4	0.4	0.4	0.4	0.4
Value Fund	0.9	0.7	2.3	1.9	2.8	2.9	3.4	3.5	3.9	3.8	5.3	5.4
Total	21.1	25.5	39.9	41.8	48.5	57.9	60.1	68.2	68.1	68.4	69.2	70.0
International equity funds												
Diversified International	0.0	0.2	1.9	1.9	2.6	3.0	3.3	3.7	3.9	4.1	4.9	5.0
Europe	0.0	0.2	2.7	2.6	3.6	4.2	4.4	5.1	5.2	5.5	6.8	7.0
Japan	0.0	0.1	0.8	0.8	1.1	1.2	1.4	1.5	1.6	1.7	1.9	2.0
Overseas	0.0	0.1	1.9	1.9	2.6	3.0	3.0	3.7	3.8	4.1	4.9	5.0
Southeast Asia	0.0	0.0	0.4	0.4	0.5	0.6	0.7	0.8	0.8	0.8	1.0	1.0
Total	0.0	0.6	7.7	7.6	10.4	12.0	13.1	14.8	15.3	16.2	19.5	20.0

Investment grade fixed-income funds

Government Income	13.5	13.0	12.1	12.8	10.2	7.9	6.4	3.4	2.9	1.8	5.0	5.0
Intermediate Bond	8.8	8.6	8.3	8.6	7.1	5.4	4.5	2.3	2.0	1.2	5.0	5.0
Investment Grade Bond	13.9	13.4	13.1	13.4	11.2	8.5	7.1	3.7	3.1	1.9	0.4	0.0
Strategic Real Return	1.0	0.9	2.0	1.2	2.0	1.0	1.3	0.4	0.6	0.3	0.3	0.0
Total	37.2	35.9	35.5	36.0	30.5	22.8	19.3	9.8	8.6	5.2	10.7	10.0

High-yield fixed-income funds

Capital and Income	0.9	0.8	2.5	2.6	3.3	3.6	3.8	3.6	4	5.1	0.5	0
High Income	0.8	0.8	2.5	2.5	3.2	3.6	3.7	3.6	4	5.1	0.1	0
Total	1.7	1.6	5	5.1	6.5	7.2	7.5	7.2	8	10.2	0.6	0

Short-term funds

Retirement Money Market Portfolio	26.3	25.6	7.5	5.8	2.6	0.1	0	0	0	0	0	0
Short-Term Bond	13.7	10.8	4.4	3.7	1.5	0	0	0	0	0	0	0
Total	40	36.4	11.9	9.5	4.1	0.1	0	0	0	0	0	0

Note: Data are percentages.
Source: Fidelity Freedom Funds Prospectus, May 30, 2006.

TABLE 5.2 **Vanguard Target Retirement Funds asset allocation (June 7, 2006)**

Underlying Vanguard Fund	Income	2005	2010	2015	2020	2025	2030	2035	2040	2045	2050
							Target Retirement Fund				
Total Stock Market Index	24.0	40.0	48.0	53.3	60.0	66.0	72.0	72.0	72.0	72.0	72.0
European Stock Index	3.5	5.9	7.1	7.9	8.8	9.7	10.6	10.6	10.6	10.6	10.6
Pacific Stock Index	1.7	2.8	3.3	3.7	4.2	4.6	5.0	5.0	5.0	5.0	5.0
Emerging Markets Stock Index	0.8	1.3	1.6	1.8	2.0	2.2	2.4	2.4	2.4	2.4	2.4
Total Bond Market Index	45.0	40.0	40.0	33.3	25.0	17.5	10.0	10.0	10.0	10.0	10.0
Inflation-Protected Securities	20.0	10.0	0	0	0	0	0	0	0	0	0
Prime Money Market	5.0	0	0	0	0	0	0	0	0	0	0

Note: Data are percentages.
Source: The Vanguard Group.

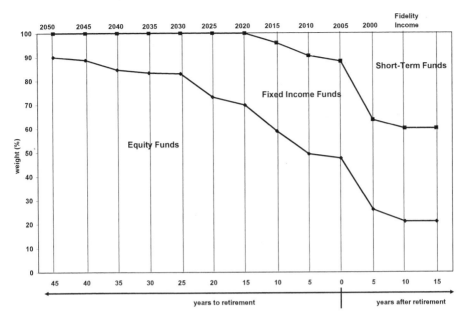

FIGURE 5.1 Fidelity Freedom Funds asset allocation change over time, May 30, 2006. (Source: Fidelity Freedom Funds Prospectus.)

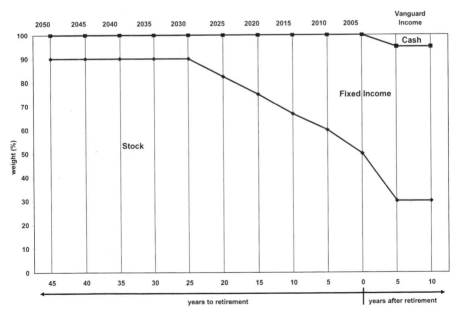

FIGURE 5.2 Vanguard Target Retirement Funds asset allocation change over time, June 7, 2006. (Source: The Vanguard Group.)

The main characteristic of life-style funds is that they change the stock exposure of the fund as a function of the investor's risk tolerance. Life-cycle funds reduce the stock exposure of the fund as their target maturity date approaches. Both approaches to asset allocation are in line with the advice that financial planners traditionally give to their clients and with conventional investing wisdom.

A different question, however, is whether these allocation strategies have any fundamental scientific basis. This is an important question given the relevance of asset allocation decisions to investors' welfare. Poor investment and saving decisions can seriously undermine the long-term welfare and wealth accumulation of investors. Thus, providing investors with sound portfolio advice is of first-order importance. What does academic finance have to say about the investment decisions of long-term investors? What are the prescriptions of the theory of long-term investing for the design of life-style and life-cycle funds? I explore these questions in the remaining sections of this chapter.

Asset Allocation in a Mean-Variance Framework

The analysis of portfolio decisions has a great academic tradition in finance. In fact, modern finance is often thought to have originated with the mean-variance analysis that Harry Markowitz (1952) developed more than fifty years ago. Markowitz showed how investors should pick assets if they care only about the mean and variance—or equivalently, the mean and standard deviation—of portfolio returns over a single period.

Mean-variance analysis has transcended its academic origins to become the basic paradigm guiding portfolio advice. Mean-variance usefully emphasizes portfolio diversification, the principle that investors should eliminate exposure to risk that is not rewarded. Mean-variance analysis, however, also makes asset allocation recommendations that are often at odds with conventional wisdom.

One of the most famous results in mean-variance analysis is the mutual fund theorem of portfolio choice first formulated by the late James Tobin (1958). According to this theorem, all investors should combine cash with a single portfolio or "mutual fund" of risky assets. Consider the basic problem of allocating a portfolio among three broad asset classes: stocks, long-term bonds ("bonds"), and short-term bonds or money market funds ("cash"). The mutual fund theorem directs all investors, conservative or aggressive, to hold the same portfolio of stocks and bonds, mixing the portfolio with more or less cash depending on the investor's tolerance to risk. This portfolio advice is at odds with conventional investing wisdom as well as with the way that life-style funds allocate assets between aggressive and conservative funds. In practice, both conservative investors and conservative life-style funds favor bonds relative to equities, so the ratio of bonds to stocks increases as portfolios become more conservative. In the previous example, the more conservative investor might be advised to hold a portfolio consisting of 40 percent equities, 40 percent bonds, and 20 percent cash, with a 1:1 ratio of stocks to bonds.

Another implication of mean-variance analysis is that it directs investors to maintain the same asset allocation regardless of their age or investment horizon. This advice is at odds with the advice that financial planners traditionally give their clients and with the asset allocation patterns embedded in life-cycle funds, all of which suggest that the allocation to equities should be directly related to investment horizon.

Thus, traditional mean-variance analysis does not seem to provide scientific support for the risk-based investing approach and the horizon-based investing approach to asset allocation that characterize life-style funds and life-cycle funds, respectively. However, the asset allocation advice that emerges from mean-variance analysis is based on two critical assumptions. First, mean-variance analysis assumes that investors live in a parsimonious world of constant risk and return. In such a world, it is optimal for long-term investors to act as short-term investors, ignoring the long term (see Merton 1969, 1971; Samuelson 1969, 1991). Second, mean-variance analysis treats financial wealth independent of income.

For decades, the assumption of constant investment opportunities constituted a good approximation of reality to academics and practitioners alike. But in recent years, both academic research and industry research has shown through careful empirical analysis that changes in investment opportunities are quantitatively important. Long-term investors typically receive a stream of income and use it, along with financial wealth, to support their standard of living. In recent years, academic finance has explored the impact of these considerations on long-horizon investing, building on the early theoretical insights on dynamic portfolio choice of Robert Merton (1969) and Paul Samuelson (1969) in the late 1960s (see Markowitz 1952). In particular, it has shown that they provide a qualified support for risk-based investing and age-based investing. This issue is explored next in greater detail.

The Case for Risk-Based Investing: Interest Rate Risk and the Optimal Bond Allocation of Long-Term Investors

A traditional idea in investment theory and practice is that cash (for example, short-term default-free bonds or bills) is the safe asset for all investors. Traditional mean-variance analysis treats cash as the riskless asset and considers bonds as another risky asset like stocks. Bonds are valued only for their potential contribution to the expected short-run excess return, relative to risk, of a diversified risky portfolio.

This idea is rooted in the perception that real interest rates are constant. In reality, real interest rates change over time, and future real interest rates are far from certain. In such circumstances, cash is safe for short-term investors, provided that short-term inflation risk is small, but it is not safe for long-term investors. If future real interest rates eventually decline, these investors need to worry about the impact on their long-term welfare of constantly reinvesting wealth in short-term instruments.

A strategy of constantly reinvesting wealth in short-term bonds will preserve investors' initial wealth but not necessarily their ability to spend out of this wealth. If real interest rates decline, investors will have to either reduce their spending to accommodate this reduction in the yield on their wealth or deplete part of the principal to maintain their spending, with the subsequent impact that this reduction in wealth might have on their future well-being.

An article in the *Wall Street Journal* on July 7, 2003, provides a vivid example of the importance of reinvestment risk for long-term investors. The article recounts the stories of several people in Florida who retired during the last twenty years and followed the conventional strategy of continuously investing their retirement assets in certificates of deposit and other short-term fixed-income instruments and living off the interest income produced by these investments. As nominal interest rates fell faster than the prices of services and goods they consume—that is, as real interest rates declined—during the 1980s, 1990s, and early 2000s, these retirees were forced to substantially reduce their standards of living. The title of the article says it all, "As Fed Cuts Rates, Retirees Are Forced to Pinch Pennies—With Interest Income Down, Seniors in Florida Complex Are Facing Tough Choices—A $1.63 Splurge at Burger King."

In contrast to a strategy of constantly reinvesting wealth in short-term bonds, a strategy of investing in long-term bonds will protect spending, since these bonds will increase in value as real interest rates decline, thus providing the extra cushion investors need to maintain their spending plans without depleting the initial principal.

This analysis, while enlightening and helpful, is still incomplete. In practice, the coupons and principal payments of long-term bonds such as Treasury bonds are typically fixed in nominal terms. This means that the value of these bonds is also affected by an additional factor: inflation. If inflation is volatile, the ability of long-term bonds to protect spending plans on an inflation-adjusted basis can be seriously undermined. Larger than expected inflation rates will erode the purchasing power of these bonds, even if real interest rates do not move at all. By contrast, inflation-indexed bonds, which the U.S. Treasury started issuing in 1997 under the denomination of TIPS (Treasury inflation protected securities), are immune to the potentially devastating effects of unexpected inflation. Thus investors need to be aware that regular Treasury bonds are safe investments only when inflation risk is low.

Establishing the extent to which real interest rate risk and inflation risk are important is of key importance to investors because it determines which financial instruments are safest at long horizons. In a study of portfolio selection with inflation risk and real interest risk, Campbell and Viceira (2001) find that real interest rates vary enough over time to make cash a risky investment at long horizons, and that, except for the Volcker-Greenspan period of the last twenty years, inflation risk is large enough to make long-term Treasury bonds poor substitutes for inflation-linked TIPS (see Campbell and Viceira 2001, 2002, chapter 3). They show that, in an environment of changing real and nominal interest rates, long-term investors should optimally allocate a larger fraction of their wealth to long-term inflation-indexed bonds as they become more conservative. The ratio of bonds to stocks increases with risk aversion, and in the limit when investors' risk tolerance approaches zero, long-term investors allocate all their financial wealth to long-term inflation-indexed bonds, not to cash.

Extremely conservative long-term investors prefer long-term inflation-indexed bonds to cash because, while T-bills help investors preserve capital, they do not necessarily preserve long-term standards of living. Long-term inflation-indexed bonds, not cash instruments, are the riskless asset for conservative investors who care about financing their long-term spending plans or liabilities.

The analysis of Campbell and Viceira has significant implications for the design of investment vehicles for long-term investors. First, this analysis provides support for the idea of risk-based investing, that is, the idea that the portfolio share of bonds should be larger in conservative portfolios than in aggressive portfolios. However, this support is qualified. These bonds should be inflation-indexed bonds (or TIPS). Nominal bonds play an important role in conservative portfolios only when inflation risk is low, and they are close substitutes of inflation-indexed bonds.

Table 5.3, which reproduces selected columns from table 3.3 in Campbell and Viceira (2002), illustrates this result. The table shows the optimal percentage allocation to stocks, bonds, and cash of investors with different degrees of risk aversion. The left columns in the table consider a problem in which investors can choose among cash, stocks, and inflation-indexed long-term bonds. The right columns consider a problem in which inflation-indexed bonds are not available, and instead investors can choose among cash, stocks, and nominal long-term bonds. Panel A shows optimal allocations to each asset class implied by the dynamics of real interest rates and inflation in the post–World War II period, which was characterized by significant inflation risk. Panel B shows the allocations implied by the dynamics of real interest rates during the last two decades of the twentieth century, which was characterized by much lower inflation risk than the rest of the postwar period.[4]

The first row in each panel shows the optimal allocations of investors with the coefficient of relative risk aversion equal to 1. These are aggressive investors who value bonds only for their short-run properties (that is,

TABLE 5.3 **Optimal percent allocation to stocks, bonds, and cash for investors with different degrees of relative risk aversion**

Relative risk aversion	Equity	Indexed	Cash	Equity	Nominal	Cash
A. 1952–99						
1	100	0	0	100	0	0
2	100	0	0	100	0	0
5	65	35	0	73	6	21
10	32	68	0	35	8	57
5,000	0	94	6	0	10	90
B. 1983–99						
1	100	0	0	100	0	0
2	86	14	0	87	13	0
5	38	62	0	36	64	0
10	22	78	0	19	81	0
5,000	0	93	7	1	98	1

Source: Campbell and Viceira (2002), table 3.3.

the contribution they make to their portfolio expected excess return and short-run volatility) and not for their long-term properties. As we move down the columns, the rows show the optimal allocations for increasingly conservative long-term investors.

Table 5.3 shows that the portfolio share of inflation-indexed bonds relative to the portfolio share of stocks increases with risk aversion and is basically 100 percent for investors with extremely high risk aversion coefficients. By contrast, the allocation to nominal bonds in panel A is very small for all investors, including those who are extremely conservative. These investors prefer to move away from equities and into cash because nominal bonds in this period are subject to considerable inflation risk and in practice are poorer substitutes for inflation-indexed bonds than cash itself. This picture changes completely in panel B, in which low inflation risk makes nominal bonds close substitutes of inflation-indexed bonds.

Second, the mutual fund industry has designed life-cycle funds so that they are folded into a balanced retirement fund at or shortly after their target maturity date. These balanced funds tend to have very small allocations to equities and inflation-indexed bonds and large allocations to nominal bonds and cash (see tables 5.1 and 5.2). The allocations shown in table 5.1 suggest that these retirement funds and in general all balanced funds except the most conservative ones should contain a considerable allocation to equities. They also suggest that balanced funds, particularly conservative balanced funds, should contain significant allocations to inflation-indexed bonds. Substitution of nominal bonds for inflation-indexed bonds makes an implicit bet that inflation risk will stay low in the future, which might or might not happen.

Third, this analysis suggests that the long-standing practice of sponsors of DC pension plans choosing a money market fund as the default option for plan participants might not be appropriate if the goal is to choose a safe investment. With that goal, the choice should instead be a portfolio of long-term bonds, preferably inflation indexed. Of course, plan sponsors might be simply responding to a legal and regulatory environment that is mistakenly focused on preservation of initial principal as the safe choice. If so, this analysis suggests that there should be a discussion of what the regulatory concept of a safe long-term investment should be.

Fourth, this analysis also suggests that the issuance of inflation-indexed bonds by the Treasury has a significant impact on welfare, as it provides long-term investors with a truly riskless long-term investment vehicle.

The Case for Age-Based Investing

Mean Reversion in Stock Returns

The standard theory of asset allocation treats equities as a risky asset class whose high historical average returns represent compensation for commensurately high risk. In recent years, however, it has become commonplace to argue that equities are actually relatively safe assets for investors who are able to hold them for the long term. This view is based on evidence that stock returns are less volatile when they are measured over long holding periods (see Campbell and Shiller 1998).[5] As illustrated in figure 5.3, the annualized volatility of real (or inflation-adjusted) U.S. stock returns appears to decline with holding horizon, from about 16 percent per annum at a one-year horizon, to about 8 percent per annum at horizons of twenty-five years or longer.[6] Similarly, the range of U.S. stock returns experienced by investors since 1926 changes depending on the holding horizon, with short horizons exhibiting a much wider spread than long horizons, as shown in figure 5.4. Similar patterns are visible in some international markets (see Dimson, Marsh, and Staunton 2002).

This evidence has been used to promote a strategy of buying and holding equities for the long-term and to support the horizon-based allocations

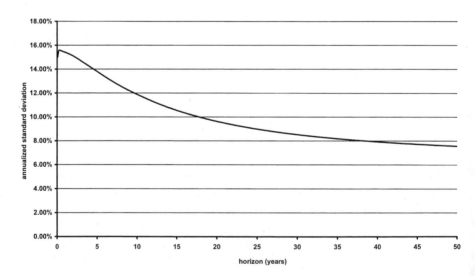

FIGURE 5.3 Annualized percent standard deviation of monthly real returns on U.S. stocks, January 1959 to December 2004.

of life-cycle funds (see Siegel 1998; Greer 2004; and Cheng and Shelon 2004). Indeed, several studies show that these findings imply that buy-and-hold long-term investors should hold more equities in their portfolios than buy-and-hold short-term investors (see Campbell and Viceira 2005; Jurek and Viceira 2006).

A different question, however, is whether a strategy of aggressively buying and holding stocks for the long-term or the deterministic rebalancing strategy implemented in life-cycle funds are desirable long-run investment strategies if stock returns behave the way the data suggest. The key to answering this question resides in understanding what makes stock market risk decrease significantly at long horizons.

In a world of time-invariant risk and return, risk per period (measured as the annualized variance of holding period returns) is constant across all investment horizons. Thus, if expected returns were constant, the line shown in figure 5.3 would be horizontal, not decreasing.[7] Therefore, the evidence for reduced risk of stocks at long horizons is inconsistent with constant expected returns. In fact, it is indirect evidence for predictable variation in stock returns.

Empirically, times of unusually high stock prices relative to dividends or earnings appear to be followed by periods of low average stock returns, and, conversely, times of low stock prices relative to dividends or earnings tend to be followed by periods of high average stock returns. Figure 5.5 illustrates this evidence. It plots ten-year real returns on the Standard and Poor's 500 when stocks are purchased at different initial price-to-earnings multiples and dividend-to-price ratios.[8] This figure is constructed from Robert Shiller's annual data set for the period 1871–2004.

Figure 5.5 shows that when stock market valuations relative to earnings or dividends were in their lowest quintile in this period, real returns over the following ten years were about 10–11 percent per annum on average. This average return was more than twice as large as the average return in ten-year periods following times in which stocks relative to earnings or dividends were in their highest quintile. Thus stock returns appear to revert toward a long-run average or mean, and stocks are said to be mean reverting.

But if returns are predictable, then why would long-term investors want to pursue a buy-and-hold investment strategy or a strategy of mechanically rebalancing away from equities as their investment horizon shortens? Should they not instead change their allocation to stocks as a function of prevailing market conditions? For example, they might want to

Stock Returns

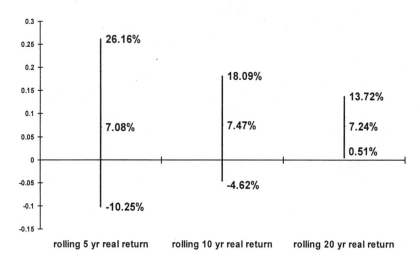

Bond Returns

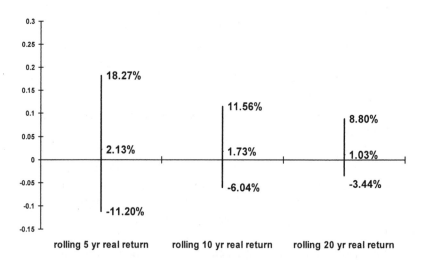

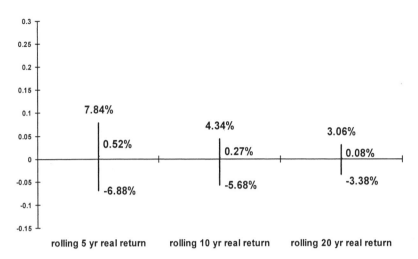

FIGURE 5.4 Spread of annualized returns at different horizons, 1926–2005. This figure plots annualized mean returns on U.S. stocks, bonds, and T-bills at horizons of five, ten, and twenty years.

decrease their allocation to stocks when expected future stock returns are low (for example, at times when stock prices are high relative to earnings of dividends) and conversely increase it when expected future stock returns are high (for example, when stock prices are low relative to earnings or dividends).

Several academic studies have addressed this question in depth using formal models of long-term portfolio choice under time-varying expected stock returns (see Campbell and Viceira 1999, 2002; Campbell, Chan, and Viceira 2003; Campbell et al. 2001). These studies show that long-horizon investors should indeed vary their allocation to stocks in response to changes in expected stock returns. However, these changes are only gradual, not the type of volatile high-frequency trading that is often recommended by "tactical asset allocation" programs. The reason for this gradual approach is that empirically expected stock returns seem to change slowly. The variables that proxy for expected returns, such as dividend yields, smoothed price-to-earnings ratios, and interest rates, are highly persistent, slow-moving variables.

This research also finds that, at the same time, it is optimal for long-term investors to introduce a strategic tilt toward equities in their portfolios,

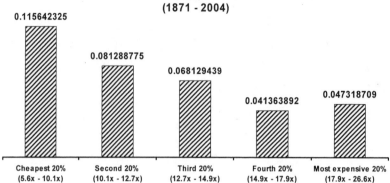

The Future 10-Year Real Rates of Return When Stocks are Purchased at Alternative Initial Price-to-Earnings (P/E) Multiples (1871 - 2004)

0.115642325

0.081288775

0.068129439

0.041363892

0.047318709

| Cheapest 20% (5.6x - 10.1x) | Second 20% (10.1x - 12.7x) | Third 20% (12.7x - 14.9x) | Fourth 20% (14.9x - 17.9x) | Most expensive 20% (17.9x - 26.6x) |

Initial P/E Multiples Range

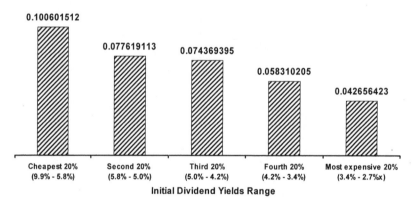

The Future 10-Year Real Rates of Return When Stocks are Purchased at Alternative Initial Dividend Yields (D/P) (1871 - 2004)

0.100601512

0.077619113

0.074369395

0.058310205

0.042656423

| Cheapest 20% (9.9% - 5.8%) | Second 20% (5.8% - 5.0%) | Third 20% (5.0% - 4.2%) | Fourth 20% (4.2% - 3.4%) | Most expensive 20% (3.4% - 2.7%x) |

Initial Dividend Yields Range

FIGURE 5.5 The empirical relation between smoothed price-to-earnings (P/E) multiples and dividend yields (D/P) and future ten-year real returns on the S&P 500, 1871–2004. P/E multiples are based on ten-year moving averages of earnings. (Source: Stock market annual data from Robert Shiller.)

even as they vary their actual allocation at shorter horizons. This strategic tilt reflects a positive intertemporal hedging demand for stocks, and it is relatively insensitive to changes in expected returns. If stocks mean revert, realized stock returns are high at times of low expected future stock returns. It is in this sense that stocks provide a good hedge against a deterioration in their own expected future return and are relatively safer assets for long-term investors.

Stock return predictability also affects the composition of equity portfolio. Jurek and Viceira (2006) show that at times when expected aggregate stock returns are low, growth stocks—stocks with high prices relative to earnings or dividends—tend to deliver higher realized returns than value stocks—stocks with low prices relative to earnings or dividends—do (see Jurek and Viceira 2006). This makes growth stocks less risky than value stocks from the perspective of long-horizon investors, since they provide a better hedge against market downturns. Thus the strategic tilt toward equities in long-horizon portfolios should be itself biased toward growth stocks.

In sum, this research suggests that long-term equity investors should invest more on average in equities than their short-horizon counterparts, but they should also consider periodic revisions of this allocation as market conditions change. It is logically inconsistent to count on reduced long-term risk while ignoring the variation in returns that produces it. This market-sensitive allocation policy is very different from the asset allocation policy of life-cycle funds, whose target mix moves mechanically away from stocks as an inverse function of investment horizon, regardless of market conditions. Thus mean-reversion arguments provide, if anything, only a partial justification for the roll-down schedule characteristic of life-cycle funds.

The idea of age-based investing focused on mean reversion is further challenged by the ongoing debate in empirical finance about the robustness of the statistical evidence on stock return predictability. Some research disputes this evidence (see Goyal and Welch 2008), while other research claims that the observed time series variability in dividend yields and the lack of empirical evidence that aggregate dividend growth is predictable are consistent with stock return predictability (see Campbell and Thompson 2008; Cochrane 2008; Lewellen 2004).

A body of research has explored the implications of uncertainty about the existence of mean reversion in stock returns on asset allocation (see Barberis 2000; Brennan 1998; Xia 2001; Wachter and Warusawitharana

2007). This research finds that this uncertainty should make investors more cautious when changing their equity allocation in response to changes in market conditions compared with investors who take the estimated stock return processes at face value. However, investors are still willing to engage in market-dependent asset allocation strategies. This uncertainty also dampens, but does not eliminate, the long-term strategic tilt toward equities induced by mean reversion. Of course, the magnitude of these effects depends on investors' initial uncertainty. In a model with fixed underlying parameters, the learning effect is transitional and will eventually disappear as investors become more and more confident about the true data-generating process.

Human Capital and Asset Allocation

I have noted that mean-variance analysis ignores that investors have additional sources of wealth besides their financial wealth. One of these sources, arguably the most important for most individual investors, is human capital, or the present discounted value of their expected future labor earnings.

Unlike other types of capital, human capital is not tradable. Investors cannot sell claims against their future labor earnings, but they can extract value from their human capital through the earnings it produces over time, which they can then use either to finance their current spending or to save and thus increase their financial wealth.

Just because human capital is not tradable does not mean that investors should ignore it when deciding how to invest their financial wealth (or savings). In fact, Bodie, Merton, and Samuelson (1991) have shown that human capital considerations should lead investors to change the target asset allocation for their financial portfolios as they age. This is because as investors age, their human capital gets depleted as it is transformed into consumption and savings.

The relation between human capital and asset allocation is easiest to see if we consider an investor who knows his income in advance with perfect certainty. For this investor, human capital is equivalent to an implicit investment in bonds. When the investor is young and has many years of earning labor income ahead of him, but little wealth saved, human capital represents a large share of his total wealth. The investor should then tilt his financial portfolio toward risky assets to offset the large bond position he already holds through his human capital.

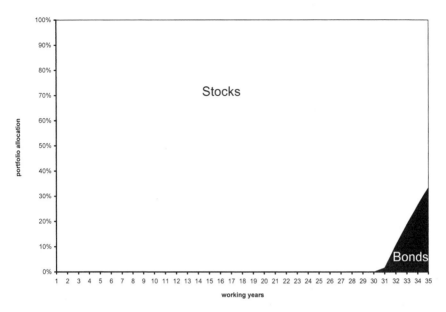

FIGURE 5.6 Life-cycle allocation to stocks and bonds when human wealth is riskless.

As the investor ages, the value of his human wealth declines (he has fewer years left to earn labor income), while his financial wealth grows. Thus the bond investment represented by his human wealth becomes less important relative to his total wealth, and the investor will want to attenuate the tilt toward risky assets in his financial portfolio.

Figure 5.6 illustrates this principle using a stylized example. This figure plots the asset allocation of a life-cycle investor along the expected path of labor earnings and expected returns during the investor's working years. The figure is built under the following assumptions: First, it assumes that the investor wishes to hold a 60/40 percent stock/bond portfolio. Second, it assumes that the investor works for thirty-five years. He starts with an initial salary of $60,000 per annum, which grows at a real (or inflation-adjusted) rate of 4 percent per annum. Third, it assumes that the investor starts with initial financial wealth of $75,000. This wealth grows through the returns he obtains on his investments and through the savings he adds every year. The figure assumes that he saves 15 percent of his salary every year and that equities return 6 percent per annum on average and bonds 2.3 percent per annum in real terms. The real riskless rate is also 2.3 percent.[9]

Under these assumptions, when the investor still has thirty-five years left until retirement, his human capital is worth \$2.864 million. This is the present value of all his future earnings discounted at the riskless rate of 2.3 percent. Since he also has \$75,000 in savings, his total wealth equals \$2.939 million. Given his target mix, this investor would like to hold \$1.764 million in stocks, and \$1.175 million in bonds. But he has already an implicit investment in bonds through his human capital worth \$2.864 million, which is well above his target allocation. Thus this investor will opt to invest the entirety of his financial wealth (\$75,000) in stocks in an effort to get as close as possible to his 60 percent target allocation to stocks.

Interestingly, this investor will appear to an outside observer as a very aggressive investor because he allocates 100 percent of his financial wealth to stocks. In practice, however, his overall wealth portfolio is actually heavily tilted toward bonds: 97.4 percent of his total wealth is invested in bond-like wealth.

As he grows older and approaches retirement, the value of his human capital declines, and his financial wealth grows. However, the ratio of financial wealth to human capital does not grow fast enough for the investor's desired bond holdings to be larger than the value of his human capital until year thirty-one. At that point, his financial wealth has grown to \$1.6 million, and his human capital is still worth \$1.022 million. Thus his total wealth is \$2.6022 million, of which he would like to hold \$1.050 million in bonds. Since his bond-like human wealth is worth less than his desired allocation to bonds, at this point he starts investing part of his financial wealth in bonds and moves away from stocks. The investor starts investing 2 percent of his financial wealth in bonds, which grows to 34 percent in the last year of his working life.

Figure 5.6 shows a path for asset allocation in which the share of financial wealth allocated to equities declines as the investor approaches retirement. Thus human capital considerations provide support for age-based investing. However, there are some important caveats to this conclusion.

First, figure 5.6 shows an asset allocation path that is much more aggressive than the asset allocation path typical of life-cycle funds (see tables 5.1 and 5.2). Despite the fact that the investor aims at a relatively conservative target allocation for his total wealth (60 percent stocks/40 percent bonds), the resulting asset allocation path for financial wealth is fully invested in stocks for thirty years of his thirty-five years of his retirement horizon. In the remaining five years, the allocation to equities is always above 65 percent. This suggests that the asset allocation path of life-cycle funds is perhaps too conservative.

Of course, one could argue that this example is unrealistic. In practice, future labor income is uncertain for most investors, which makes human wealth a risky nontradable asset. This might make investors wish to invest their financial wealth more conservatively than in the case with perfectly safe human capital. However, this conclusion does not hold for plausible representations of labor income risk.

In a study of optimal asset allocation with labor income uncertainty, Viceira (2001) finds that investors with risky labor income should still tilt their portfolios toward stocks when they are young, provided that labor earnings are not too volatile and that they are uncorrelated with the stock market (see Viceira 2001; see also chapter 6 of Campbell and Viceira 2002). For these investors, the risk in their human capital is largely idiosyncratic and as such is more similar to an investment in bonds than to an investment in stocks. The resulting asset allocations for investors with typical earnings volatility (around 10 percent per annum) and low correlation with stock returns are still more aggressive than the asset allocations typical of life-cycle funds. Labor earnings must be highly volatile to significantly reduce the investors' willingness to hold equities in their portfolios.

Second, while idiosyncratic, risky labor income might ameliorate the pronounced tilt toward stocks that riskless labor income suggests, there are other considerations that actually work in the opposite direction. Most investors receive Social Security benefits, and many receive other pension benefits when they retire. Pension income is also bond-like, and should make investors even more willing to tilt their portfolios toward equities.[10]

Another consideration is the ability of many working investors to influence the value of their human wealth by varying how hard they work. The ability to vary work effort allows individuals to hold riskier portfolios because they can work harder if they need extra labor income to compensate for losses in their financial portfolios. In their study, Bodie, Merton, and Samuelson (1991) emphasize that the tilt toward risky financial investments with riskless labor income is strengthened if investors have the ability to adjust their labor supply. Chan and Viceira (2000) have shown that this result carries over when labor income is idiosyncratically risky.

Third, recent research on portfolio choice with risky labor income shows that realistic calibration of labor earnings profiles leads to asset allocation paths in which stock portfolio shares are not necessarily monotonically

164	VICEIRA

decreasing with retirement horizon. Cocco, Gomes, and Maenhout (2005) show empirical evidence that, unlike the stylized example I have just presented that assumes that earnings grow at a steady rate over the working life of the investor, the earnings profile of a typical working investor exhibits a hump shape. Labor earnings grow at increasingly higher rates until employees are about 45 years old, at which point they stop growing or even decrease until they retire.

They next note that this also implies a hump shape for the value of human wealth, which in turn implies a hump shape for the optimal asset allocation path for equities as investors age. That is, investors should hold portfolios that are more conservative early in their working lives, become more aggressive as they approach middle age, and then become increasingly more conservative. However, they find that the share of human capital on total wealth at young ages for a typical working investor is so large relative to financial wealth that these investors still want to hold almost if not all of their financial wealth in equities. Thus their findings suggest that life-cycle funds should perhaps exhibit a slightly hump-shaped equity allocation path instead of a monotonically declining path.

Fourth, asset allocation is highly sensitive to the correlation of labor earnings with stock returns. In his study of optimal asset allocation with labor income uncertainty, Viceira (2001) shows that small correlations significantly reduce the portfolio tilt toward equities in financial portfolios and that large correlations might even reverse this tilt and make younger investors less willing to hold equities in their financial portfolios than older investors. In fact, Benzoni, Collin-Dufresne, and Goldstein (2007) argue that aggregate labor income and dividends exhibit a large, positive long-run correlation, even though they exhibit a low short-term correlation. This positive long-run correlation implies a hump-shaped allocation to stocks over the working life of the investor.

This is so because in this case human capital is more stock-like than bond-like, and young investors should compensate by tilting their financial portfolios toward bonds and away from stocks. In the extreme case in which labor income is perfectly positively correlated with the return on stocks, human wealth is in fact an implicit investment in stocks. Thus life-cycle funds will not be appropriate for investors whose labor earnings are highly correlated with the stock market.

Correlation considerations are important in other aspects of the design of DC plans. Current regulations allow corporate sponsors to include company stock as part of the menu of investment options available to plan participants. Arguably, employees' labor income is likely to be highly correlated with the fortunes of the company they work for. They should not only avoid holding an undiversified position in their employer's stock, but they should actually underweight the company stock relative to its weight in an index fund. If employees fail to understand this point, or mistakenly think they have superior information about company stock, they might allocate too large a fraction of their retirement savings to company stock. The recent bankruptcy of Enron and the subsequent negative effect on employee retirement benefits has made some investors painfully aware of the risks of investing in company stock.

Finally, it is important to note that while all these models support the notion that retirement horizon matters for asset allocation, they do not prescribe a unique asset allocation path for all investors with identical human capital characteristics. This asset allocation path is a function of both human capital and the investor's risk tolerance. Thus these models imply that life-cycle funds should be both age based and risk based. These studies also ignore important factors that affect the ability of individuals to work in the future such as health risk and mortality risk. A recent study by Edwards (2005) suggests that health risk considerations effectively increase the risk aversion of investors.

The Design of Life-Cycle Funds

General Considerations

The previous two sections of this discussion have explored what modern financial economics has to say about long-run asset allocation strategies and its implications for the design of life-cycle funds and the life-style or balanced funds into which these funds fold once they reach their target maturity date. In general, the findings of modern financial economics provide support for a notion of age-based investing, for which age (or retirement horizon) is a proxy for human capital, but they provide weaker support for a notion of age-based investing that builds on the idea of mean reversion in stock returns.

Research on long-run investing suggests that life-cycle funds should adopt an asset allocation path heavily tilted toward equities until they are fairly close to their target date. This asset allocation path is based on the typical labor earnings profile, which exhibits low volatility and low correlation with stock returns and is more aggressive than the asset allocation path of most life-cycle funds currently available to investors. However, employees whose earnings are highly volatile or exhibit significant correlation with stock returns should adopt life-cycle investment strategies with a much less pronounced tilt toward equities.

This research also suggests that the retirement horizon of the investor (a proxy for his human capital) should not be the only variable that determines the asset allocation path of life-cycle funds. Market conditions should induce low-frequency adjustments to the path, as expected returns change over time.

Risk tolerance should also influence this allocation path. To the extent that investors systematically differ in their risk tolerance, it makes sense to consider creating aggressive, moderate, and conservative life-cycle funds instead of offering a single life-cycle fund per target date. For example, Poterba et al. (2005) have conducted simulations suggesting that the asset allocation of a typical life-cycle fund can produce lower expected utility (or welfare) than a 100 percent stock allocation for aggressive investors.

It is also important to give consideration in life-cycle fund design to the term structure of target maturity dates. Long maturity dates that match current life expectancy projections instead of expected retirement dates should probably be considered. Investors who expect to receive pension income from other sources, such as Social Security or traditional DB pension plans, should probably choose life-cycle funds with target dates well beyond their expected retirement date to account for the fact that their pension income represents a bond-like investment just as their labor earnings do. Of course, investors with no significant pension income should choose target dates that match their expected retirement date.

The findings of modern financial economics also have clear suggestions about the assets that should be included in these funds. First, modern financial economics shows that long-term inflation-indexed bonds, not cash, are the safest assets for long-term investors. Long-term nominal bonds are subject to inflation risk and are safe only when this risk is low; otherwise they are risky assets and poor substitutes for inflation-indexed bonds. This strongly suggests that long-term inflation bonds should play an important role in these funds, particularly conservative funds, while cash should probably not play a role. In fact, the simulations conducted in the study of Poterba et al. (2005) show that all investors would consistently experience a gain in welfare if they adopted life-cycle funds, which replace nominal bonds with TIPS. This is in sharp contrast to the allocations of most, if not all, of the life-cycle funds available to investors, where inflation-indexed bonds play only a marginal role.

Second, the equity allocations of life-cycle funds and life-style funds are typically heavily biased toward U.S. stocks. They typically define the "stock market" as the U.S. stock market and include only small allocations to international stocks, which are typically defined as being riskier than U.S. stocks. However, it is hard to see why the stock of GM or Ford is inherently safer than the stock of Toyota or Honda. The empirical evidence available suggests that a well-diversified portfolio of equities should include a healthy allocation to international equities (see French and Poterba 1991). In a recent study, Campbell, Serfaty-de Medeiros, and Viceira (2007) show evidence that such a portfolio should have its currency exposure fully hedged, except for the European and Swiss component of the portfolio, which should be left unhedged.

Third, the equity allocations of life-cycle funds should probably be tilted toward growth stocks and away from value stocks at long horizons. This tilt should decrease as the funds approach their target maturity date. Growth stocks appear to be safer than value stocks at long horizons (see Jurek and Viceira 2006). This tilt should be more pronounced for moderate and conservative life-cycle funds.

These design considerations for life-cycle funds are all based on three premises: first, that investors are homogeneous in their human capital characteristics and in their risk tolerance; second, that they use these funds as their only long-term saving vehicle; and third, that tax considerations are irrelevant. Under those premises, one single life-cycle fund per retirement horizon is enough. I explore next the implications of relaxing these premises.

Heterogeneity in Human Capital Characteristics and Risk Tolerance

Life-cycle funds are designed to provide investors with a one-stop solution to their investment needs. However, arguably there is considerable heterogeneity among investors with respect to their risk tolerance and the characteristics of their human capital. Factors such as health risk, expected longevity, family composition, job changes, and others are individual specific and might change over the lifetime of an individual. These considerations would suggest that the "one size fits all" approach of life-cycle funds is inadequate and that individually managed accounts would be

more appropriate than a single asset allocation fund since they can take
into account these individual-specific characteristics when making asset
allocation recommendations.

It is important to note that this individualized approach is different
from the "interior decorator" approach to investing popular among some
financial advisors, who build concentrated, investor-tailored stock portfolios for their clients instead of well-diversified stock portfolios, thus expos-
ing them to considerable idiosyncratic risk. Here the goal is to use asset
allocation to help investors hedge systematic risk through asset allocation
risk. Investors should still hold a well-diversified portfolio of equities (see
Bernstein 1992).

Ultimately, separate managed accounts might be the right approach
in an ideal world. In practice, however, managing separate accounts is an
expensive process whose cost is driven by the need for intensive human
intervention. Currently, separate managed accounts are cost-effective only
at sizable account balances. Thus in considering adopting an individual approach, investors need to weigh the cost of these accounts against the cost
of adopting a fund whose asset allocation path might not fit exactly their
human capital characteristics and risk tolerance. Of course, in addition
to the cost of deviating from what is optimal for them in an ideal world,
investors also need to consider the fees on life-cycle funds. However, most
mutual fund companies do not charge an extra layer of fees on their life-
cycle funds.

It is also an open question how much personalization is needed to
provide investors with reasonable asset allocation advice. It is possible
that heterogeneity in human capital risk and in risk tolerance is such that
a relatively small number of model asset allocation portfolios suffice to
serve most investors' needs.

There are also ways to help capture more investor diversity at a relatively lower cost than full personalization. One is the suggestion already
mentioned of creating aggressive, moderate, and conservative life-cycle
funds to capture disparity in risk tolerance. This raises the question of
whether employees can identify their own risk tolerance. However, employees might be able to better identify which risk-return trade-off they
are comfortable with if that trade-off is framed as questions about potential replacement ratios of their current income at retirement and uncertainty about those ratios.

Another way is for sponsors of DC pension plans to consider adopting life-cycle funds specifically designed for their firms. These funds might

be able to better capture the human capital risk characteristics of their typical employee, particularly the correlation of wages with stock returns. For example, these company-tailored funds might consider investing in stock portfolios that underweigh the exposure to stocks in the industry in which the company competes and avoid exposure to company stock altogether. They might also adopt asset allocation paths whose equity tilts take into account the correlation of wages in the industry with aggregate stock returns.

Wealth Heterogeneity and Tax Efficiency

Investors are heterogeneous not only regarding their human capital and risk tolerance. They also differ along other important dimensions such as wealth and tax status. Many investors, particularly small investors, do not typically save outside their retirement account, except to own a home and perhaps to hold some precautionary savings. Thus it might make sense for these investors to simply allocate their DC plan contributions to a life-cycle fund that appropriately reflects their risk tolerance and retirement horizon—or their life expectancy if they expect to receive traditional pension benefits in retirement. Sponsors can allow this practice by including life-cycle funds in their plan investment options, and, more importantly, they can encourage it by making these funds the default allocation of the plan.

It is interesting to consider how homeownership should affect asset allocation decisions. A home is both an asset and a durable consumption good since it provides its owner with a stream of housing services. Since a home provides its owner with insurance against fluctuations in the cost of housing services, one can view a home as a real (or inflation-indexed) consol bond that pays coupons in the form of housing services. As such, homeownership might make long-horizon investors more willing to hold equities in their financial portfolios.

At short horizons, however, home prices fluctuate, and these fluctuations might be positively correlated with investors' labor earnings. This makes residential housing a risky asset and can make homeowners less willing to take equity risk in their financial portfolios. However, empirically home price volatility and its correlation with labor earnings does not seem large enough to significantly impact asset allocation in practice (see Cocco 2005; Yao and Zhang 2005).

Tax considerations, however, can have a significant impact on how investors "locate" their assets. Many employees, particularly those in the upper levels of the wage distribution, have the ability to save outside their retirement accounts. Tax efficiency considerations make life-cycle funds an inappropriate investment vehicle for these investors, even if age-based investing is still an appropriate asset allocation strategy for them to follow.

Instead, these investors should use regular funds to build their own tax-efficient life-cycle allocation strategy. Tax regulations typically tax fixed-income assets more heavily than equities. From this perspective, investors should place as much of their fixed-income asset allocation as possible in their tax-exempt retirement accounts and equities in their taxable account (see Dammon, Spatt, and Zhang 2004).

For this reason, life-cycle funds should probably not be the only investment option available to investors within a DC plan, even if they are appropriately designed to match the human capital characteristics and risk tolerance of plan participants. In particular, tax efficiency considerations suggest that plan participants who have the ability to save outside the plan should have plain vanilla funds available to them, particularly fixed-income investment options, so they can make their own asset allocation plan and, given this plan, locate these assets in their tax-exempt and taxable accounts in a tax-efficient manner.

Conclusions

This chapter has reviewed recent advances in academic models of asset allocation for long-term investors and explored their implications for the design of investment products that help investors save for retirement, particularly life-cycle funds and life-style funds. The modern theory of long-term asset allocation shows that the type of risk-based and age-based asset allocation strategies that characterize life-style funds and life-cycle funds, respectively, are conceptually sound under specific circumstances relating to investment opportunities and investors' wealth. Simultaneously, it also offers a number of suggestions about both the design of these funds and the types of investors for whom these funds are appropriate.

Real interest rate risk (or reinvestment risk) can give rise to risk-based asset allocation strategies. This risk makes short-term bonds (or cash) risky assets and long-term inflation-indexed bonds (or TIPS in the United States) the riskless asset at long horizons. Thus it is optimal for long-term investors to increase their allocation to these bonds as they become increasingly risk averse. Thus these considerations provide support for the risk-based approach of life-style funds, which provide investors with a menu of funds that differ in their relative allocation to bonds and thus allow them to select the fund that best fits their risk tolerance.

However, there is an important caveat. Long-term nominal bonds are subject to inflation risk, and they are safe assets at long horizons only to the extent that this risk is low, in which case they become close substitutes for inflation-indexed bonds. Life-style and life-cycle funds should therefore consider increasing substantially their allocation to inflation-indexed bonds at the expense of their current allocations to nominal bonds. Their current fixed-income allocations implicitly assume that inflation risk will be insignificant in the foreseeable future.

The interaction of human wealth (the capitalized value of expected future labor earnings) with financial wealth can give rise to "age-based" asset allocation strategies of the sort used by life-cycle funds. However, these strategies are appropriate only for working investors whose labor earnings exhibit low volatility and low correlation with equity returns. For these investors, it is optimal to allocate a large fraction of their savings to equities when they have long retirement horizons and their bond-like human wealth accounts for most of their wealth and to decrease this allocation as their retirement horizon shortens and their human wealth is depleted.

Employees with volatile labor earnings or labor earnings that are highly correlated with equity returns should avoid investing in the current generation of life-cycle funds, which exhibit significant equity tilts. For these investors, their human wealth is less bond-like and more equity-like. Therefore they already have exposure to equities through their human wealth and should avoid excessive exposure, or any exposure at all, to equities in their portfolios. Since the correlation of labor earnings with stock returns is likely to be similar for employees within the same industry or company, these considerations suggest that there is a benefit to the creation of industry-specific or company-specific life-cycle funds.

Mutual fund companies might want to consider offering life-cycle funds that exhibit different equity tilts. That is, they might want to offer conservative, moderate, and aggressive life-cycle funds. These funds will help capture investor heterogeneity in risk tolerance and in the correlation between human wealth and equity returns.

Stock return predictability, or mean reversion, makes it optimal for investors to strategically tilt their portfolios toward equities at long horizons. However, it also suggests that investors should tactically change the equity tilt of their portfolios based on market conditions. It is logically inconsistent to invest more in equities because of mean reversion but then ignore the short-term implications of holding such a view of the world.

These considerations do not mean that mutual fund companies should discard their current life-cycle fund offerings or that DC plan sponsors should ignore them. Instead, they offer suggestions on how to modify the current design. In evaluating the merit of an investment vehicle, one needs to consider which alternatives are realistically available to investors.

One alternative is the status quo. The U.S. retirement system is moving toward a system fundamentally based on DC pension plans. In that system, employees are responsible for financing their own retirement. The existing empirical evidence indicates that many DC plan participants, particularly those on the low end of the education and income distribution, appear to make suboptimal saving and investing decisions. In particular, they exhibit a significant degree of inertia in their decisions, and they disproportionately tend to adopt the default investment option offered in their plans, which very often is cash in the form of a money market account.

Thus the status quo for many investors is investing in a money market account. One can argue that life-cycle funds, even if imperfectly designed, are a better investment choice for long-term investors than a money market account. As such, employers could use the inertia that overwhelms so many investors positively and adopt life-cycle funds, possibly tailored to their own needs, as default investment options.

Another alternative would be to implement individually managed accounts for everyone. While this might be the best approach to capture individual characteristics regarding risk tolerance, human wealth, tax status, and other types of wealth, these accounts are costly to manage. This cost is high enough at this point that they are not a plausible alternative for the vast majority of working investors. Life-cycle funds, on the other hand, are inexpensive to manage, and most mutual fund companies do not charge fees on top of the fees they already charge to the underlying funds. A more diverse menu of life-cycle funds might be a more cost-effective way of avoiding the "one size fits all" approach of the current generation of life-cycle funds. This menu can also help as employee circumstances (for example, job changes) and, thus, demand for equities change over their life cycle.

A third alternative would be to educate investors so they can make their own choices, adapted to their personal characteristics. However, the existing empirical evidence suggests that it is investors on the low end of the income and education distribution that tend to make more mistakes.

There is also evidence that the average person has difficulty understanding relatively simple financial concepts and ideas. Thus one has to wonder to what extent it is cost-effective to try to educate people to become sophisticated investors. However, it might be cost-effective to educate people to be discriminating consumers of financial products and services.

Life-style funds and life-cycle funds are part of a first generation of products that try to help individuals meet their financial goals, without requiring them to become investment professionals. Financial engineering is in many ways conceptually and practically as difficult as other types of engineering. Just as we do not require people to build their own personal computers or electronic devices, we should probably not require them to build their own investment strategies. And just as people can become highly discriminating buyers of electronic products, despite the fact that they are not engineers, they might also become discriminating consumers of financial products and services.

Until the next generation of investment products is available, individually managed accounts are a reality for everyone, and until investment education becomes widespread, we need to evaluate whether life-cycle funds can improve on the status quo. Arguably they do, and as such, adopting them as default investment options in DC pension plans might help a significant number of individuals. Doing nothing just because these funds are not perfect might be a worse solution than adopting them. The best is often the enemy of the good.

Notes

I am grateful to the Division of Research of the Harvard Business School for generous financial support. I am also grateful to John Campbell, Jim Poterba, Annamaria Lusardi, and participants of the conference "Improving the Effectiveness of Financial Education and Saving Programs" for helpful comments and suggestions.

1. For a more complete description of the changes in the U.S. pension landscape, see the chapter by Poterba, Venti, and Wise in this volume.

2. For a more complete description of employee savings and investment choices in defined contribution plans, see the chapter by Mottola and Utkus in this volume.

3. Specifically, with 60 percent of its assets, the fund seeks to track the investment performance of the Morgan Stanley Capital International (MSCI) U.S. Broad Market Index, which represents 99.5 percent or more of the total market capitalization of all the U.S. common stocks regularly traded on the New York and American Stock exchanges and the Nasdaq over-the-counter market. With 40 percent of its assets,

the fund seeks to track the investment performance of the Lehman Brothers Aggregate Bond Index, which measures a wide spectrum of public, investment-grade, taxable, fixed-income securities in the United States—including government, corporate, and international dollar-denominated bonds as well as mortgage-backed and asset-backed securities, all with maturities of more than one year.

4. These are allocations where the weight of each asset class is constrained to be between 0 and 100 percent.

5. Earlier work on mean reversion includes Fama and French (1988a, 1988b), Campbell and Shiller (1988), and Poterba and Summers (1988).

6. The line shows the volatility (or standard deviation) of stock returns at different holding horizons properly scaled by dividing by the square root of the number of years in the holding horizon.

7. In a world of constant expected return and risk, the volatility of K-holding period returns is precisely equal to the volatility of one-period returns times the square root of K, the number of holding periods. Since the line shown in figure 5.3 is the volatility of K-holding returns divided by the square root of the number of holding periods, this line should be flat in that world.

8. Earnings and dividends in these ratios are averages over the previous ten years, to smooth out seasonal and business-cycle variation in these variables.

9. This is approximately the current yield on long-term inflation-indexed bonds. Note that the implied equity premium (around 3.7 percent) is low relative to the historical average equity premium, which is around 6.5 percent.

10. However, uncertainty about future pension benefits can make investors less willing to take equity risk. See Kotlikoff, Gomes, and Viceira (2006).

References

Barberis, N. C. 2000. Investing for the Long Run When Returns Are Predictable. *Journal of Finance* 55: 225–64.
Benzoni, L., P. Collin-Dufresne, and R. S. Goldstein. 2007. Portfolio Choice over the Life-Cycle When the Stock and Labor Markets Are Cointegrated. *Journal of Finance* 62: 2123–67.
Bernstein, P. L. 1992. *Capital Ideas: The Improbable Origins of Modern Wall Street.* New York: Free Press.
Brennan, M. J. 1998. The Role of Learning in Dynamic Portfolio Decisions. *European Finance Review* 1: 295–306.
Bodie, Z., R. Merton, and W. Samuelson. 1991. Labor Supply Flexibility and Portfolio Choice in a Life Cycle Model. *Journal of Economic Dynamics and Control* 16: 427–49.
Campbell, J. Y., Y. L. Chan, and L. M. Viceira. 2003. A Multivariate Model of Strategic Asset Allocation. *Journal of Financial Economics* 67: 41–80.

Campbell, J. Y., J. Cocco, F. Gomes, P. J. Maenhout, and L. M. Viceira. 2001. Stock Market Mean-Reversion and the Optimal Equity Allocation of a Long-Lived Investor. *European Finance Review* 5: 269–92.

Campbell, J. Y., K. Serfaty-de Medeiros, and L. M. Viceira. 2007. Global Currency Hedging. NBER Working Paper No. 13088. National Bureau of Economic Research, Cambridge, MA.

Campbell, J. Y., and R. Shiller. 1988. Stock Prices, Earnings, and Expected Dividends. *Journal of Finance* 43: 661–76.

———. 1998. Valuation Ratios and the Long-Run Stock Market Outlook. *Journal of Portfolio Management* 28(2): 11–26.

Campbell, J. Y., and S. Thompson. 2008. Predicting Excess Stock Returns Out of Sample: Can Anything Beat the Historical Average? *Review of Financial Studies* 21: 1509–31.

Campbell, J. Y., and L. M. Viceira. 1999. Consumption and Portfolio Decisions When Expected Returns Are Time Varying. *Quarterly Journal of Economics* 114: 433–95.

———. 2001. Who Should Buy Long-Term Bonds? *American Economic Review* 91: 99–127.

———. 2002. *Strategic Asset Allocation: Portfolio Choice for Long-Term Investors.* New York: Oxford University Press.

———. 2005. The Term Structure of the Risk-Return Tradeoff. *Financial Analysts Journal* 61(1): 34–44.

Chan, Y. L., and L. M. Viceira. 2000. Asset Allocation with Endogenous Labor Income: The Case of Incomplete Markets. Mimeo. Harvard University, Cambridge, MA.

Cheng, R., and J. Shelon. 2004. Putting Lifecycle Investing Theory into Practice. Investment report, Fidelity Investments.

Cocco, J. F. 2005. Portfolio Choice in the Presence of Housing. *Review of Financial Studies* 18: 535–67.

Cocco, J. F., F. J. Gomes, and P. J. Maenhout. 2005. Consumption and Portfolio Choice over the Life Cycle. *Review of Financial Studies* 18: 491–533.

Cochrane, J. H. 2008. The Dog That Did Not Bark: A Defense of Return Predictability. *Review of Financial Studies* 21: 1533–75.

Dammon, R. M., C. H. Spatt, and H. H. Zhang. 2004. Optimal Asset Location and Allocation with Taxable and Tax-Deferred Investing. *Journal of Finance* 59: 999–1038.

Dimson, E., P. Marsh, and M. Staunton. 2002. *Triumph of the Optimists: 101 Years of Global Investment Returns.* Princeton, NJ: Princeton University Press.

Edwards, R. D. 2005. Health Risk and Portfolio Choice. Mimeo. University of California, Berkeley, and Rand Corporation, Santa Monica, CA.

Fama, E., and K. French. 1988a. Permanent and Temporary Components of Stock Prices. *Journal of Political Economy* 96: 246–73.

———. 1988b. Dividend Yields and Expected Stock Returns. *Journal of Financial Economics* 22: 3–27.

French, K. R., and J. M. Poterba. 1991. Investor Diversification and International Equity Markets. *American Economic Review* 81: 222–26.

Goyal, A., and I. Welch. 2008. A Comprehensive Look at the Empirical Performance of Equity Premium Prediction. *Review of Financial Studies* 21: 1455–1508.

Greer, Boyce. 2004. The Case for Age-Based LifeCycle Investing. Viewpoint Investment Concepts White Paper, Fidelity Investments.

Jurek, J., and L. M. Viceira. 2006. Optimal Value and Growth Tilts in Long-Horizon Portfolios. NBER Working Paper No. 12017. National Bureau of Economic Research, Cambridge, MA.

Kotlikoff, L., F. J. Gomes, and L. M. Viceira. 2006. The Excess Burden of Government Indecision. Mimeo. Harvard University, Cambridge, MA.

Lewellen, J. 2004. Predicting Returns with Financial Ratios. *Journal of Financial Economics* 74: 209–35.

Markowitz, H. 1952. Portfolio Selection. *Journal of Finance* 7: 77–91.

Merton, R. C. 1969. Lifetime Portfolio Selection under Uncertainty: The Continuous-time Case. *Review of Economics and Statistics* 51: 247–57.

———. 1971. Optimum Consumption and Portfolio Rules in a Continuous-time Model. *Journal of Economic Theory* 3: 373–413.

Mottola, G., and S. Utkus. 2008. Red, Yellow, and Green: Measuring the Quality of 401(k) Portfolio Choices. This volume.

Poterba, J., J. Rauh, S. Venti, and D. Wise. 2005. Lifecycle Asset Allocation Strategies and the Distribution of 401(k) Retirement Wealth. Working paper. Massachusetts Institute of Technology, Cambridge, MA.

Poterba, J., and L. Summers. 1988. Mean Reversion in Stock Returns: Evidence and Implications. *Journal of Financial Economics* 22: 27–60.

Poterba, J., S. Venti, and D. Wise. 2008. The Changing Landscape of Pensions in the United States. This volume.

Samuelson, P. A. 1969. Lifetime Portfolio Selection by Dynamic Stochastic Programming. *Review of Economics and Statistics* 51: 239–46.

———. 1991. Long-run Risk Tolerance When Equity Returns Are Mean Regressing: Pseudoparadoxes and Vindication of "Businessman's Risk." In *Money, Macroeconomics, and Economic Policy: Essays in Honor of James Tobin,* edited by William C. Brainard, William D. Nordhaus, and Harold W. Watts, 181–204. Cambridge, MA: MIT Press.

Shiller, Robert. Online data. Available at http://www.econ.yale.edu/~shiller/data.htm.

Siegel, J. 1998. *Stocks for the Long Run.* 2d ed. New York: McGraw-Hill.

Tobin, J. 1958. Liquidity Preference as Behavior towards Risk. *Review of Economic Studies* 25: 68–85.

Viceira, L. M. 2001. Optimal Portfolio Choice for Long-Horizon Investors with Nontradable Labor Income. *Journal of Finance* 56: 433–70.

———. 2007. The Vanguard Group, Inc., in 2006 and Target Retirement Funds. HBS Case 9-207-129, Harvard Business School Publishing.

Wachter, J. A., and M. Warusawitharana. 2007. Predictable Returns and Asset Allocation: Should a Skeptical Investor Time the Market? Working paper. The Wharton School, University of Pennsylvania, Philadelphia.

Wall Street Journal. 2003. As Fed Cuts Rates, Retirees Are Forced to Pinch Pennies—With Interest Income Down, Seniors in Florida Complex Are Facing Tough Choices—A $1.63 Splurge at Burger King. July 7.

Xia, Y. 2001. Learning about Predictability: The Effects of Parameter Uncertainty on Dynamic Asset Allocation. *Journal of Finance* 56: 205–46.

Yao, R., and H. H. Zhang. 2005. Optimal Consumption and Portfolio Choices with Risky Housing and Borrowing Constraints. *Review of Financial Studies* 18: 197–239.

CHAPTER SIX

Understanding the Role of Annuities in Retirement Planning

Jeffrey R. Brown

It is a well known fact that annuity contracts, other than in the form of group insurance through pension systems, are extremely rare. Why this should be so is a subject of considerable current interest. It is still ill-understood.
—Franco Modigliani, Nobel Prize acceptance speech (December 9, 1985)

Introduction

Individuals engaged in financial planning for retirement have no shortage of resources available to provide guidance on how much to save and how to invest those savings. If one does a Google search on the term "retirement planning," the lion's share of the over 1.2 million hits appear to guide one to Web sites that discuss various features of saving and investment decisions. Given the dominant focus on saving and investment, the typical worker could be forgiven for believing that "retirement planning" is synonymous with "wealth accumulation."

While wealth accumulation is an important ingredient in any financial plan, it is not sufficient to ensure financial well-being in retirement. A particularly glaring shortcoming of the focus on wealth accumulation is that it fails to consider how a worker's assets will be converted into a stream of consumption in retirement. A comprehensive retirement planning strategy requires that one think about more than how to save: it also requires thinking about how to spend.

Converting wealth into consumption is made difficult by the various risks that people face, such as uncertainty about how long one will live. Life annuities are financial contracts designed to insure against the financial risk created by length-of-life uncertainty by allowing an individual to exchange a lump sum of wealth for an income stream that is guaranteed to last for the rest of the annuitant's life. While life annuities play an important role in the economics literature, the insurance features of life annuities appear to be poorly understood and/or "undervalued" by the general public, as evidenced by the very small size of the market. Many financial-planning calculators simply ignore uncertainty about length of life or handle it in a naive way, such as by creating a financial plan with a horizon equal to one's average remaining life expectancy plus five or ten years. Because these approaches ignore uncertainty, the retirement planning process becomes framed in a manner that does not provide a clear role for insurance against low consumption at advanced ages. Anecdotal evidence suggests that the lack of clarity on the benefits of annuities in reducing longevity risk also applies to financial planners and others who are engaged in the business of advising clients on how to prepare for retirement.

This chapter examines the role of annuities in the financial-planning process, including both the normative judgment about what role annuities "should" play (as guided by economic theory), as well as empirical evidence about the role that annuities actually do play. A key point is that there is a large gap between these two perspectives: much of the economics literature suggests that most individuals would find annuities welfare enhancing, and yet the empirical evidence suggests that individuals do not value them very highly. The economics literature that seeks to solve this annuity puzzle within a strictly rational framework has uncovered some important insights. However, to better understand why consumers behave as if they do not value annuities, it appears that the literature may need to move beyond the fully rational paradigm. This chapter discusses several working hypotheses about behavioral biases that may influence annuity demand, while recognizing that these hypotheses have not yet been adequately tested in the literature. The chapter concludes with a discussion of new developments in the annuity market that may overcome some of these demand limitations in the future.

Uncertain Lifetimes and the Role of Annuities

In a world of certainty, financial planning for retirement would be easy: an individual could simply spread his wealth over a fixed time horizon. For example, an individual who prefers equal consumption in every period could simply amortize his wealth to provide constant real income each month until running out of wealth on precisely the last day of life.

In reality, of course, an individual faces several significant sources of uncertainty, including uncertainty about how long he will live, future expenditure needs (such as for uninsured medical expenses), and future real rates of return, among others. The financial implication of length-of-life uncertainty is that an individual must balance the risk of consuming too aggressively, potentially resulting in a large consumption drop at advanced ages, against the risk of consuming too conservatively, subjecting him to a lower level of consumption than he could otherwise afford.

Life annuities are designed to eliminate longevity risk by allowing an individual to exchange a lump sum of wealth for a stream of payments that continue so long as the individual (and possibly a spouse) is alive. Economic theory suggests that life annuities can substantially increase individual welfare by eliminating the financial risks associated with uncertain lifetimes and provide consumers with a higher level of lifetime consumption. One early and influential study showed that in the absence of bequest motives, risk-averse individuals would find it optimal to annuitize 100 percent of their wealth.[1]

To understand this result, consider an individual without a bequest motive who cares only about her consumption in the current period and one period hence. If this individual invests $1,000 in a nonannuitized asset with an 8 percent rate of return, in the next period she will be able to consume $1,080. On the other hand, if she invests $1,000 in an annuity, and assuming a probability of 0.02 that the individual will not survive to receive the payment next period, then the insurer is able to pay $1,080/(1−0.02) = $1,102 to the annuitant, conditional on survival. The extra return provided to surviving annuitants is sometimes called the "mortality premium" or "mortality credit" because it is provided in return for giving up one's right to the wealth upon death.[2] For an individual who does not value bequests, the fact that the rate of return on the annuity is greater than the rate of return on the nonannuitized asset for individuals who survive should lead to annuitization.

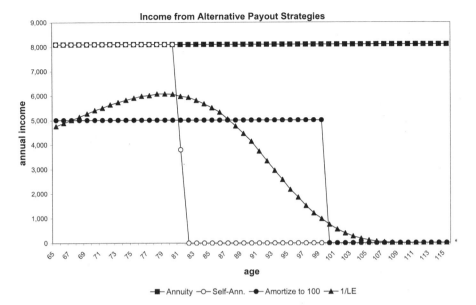

FIGURE 6.1   Income from alternative payout strategies.

This potential for higher returns can be seen in figure 6.1, which shows
the amount of income that would be available to an individual under several alternative strategies for converting one's nest egg into retirement income. The "annuity" line shows the $8,100 of annual income that would be
available for life to a 65-year-old man who purchased a standard life annuity contract with an initial premium of $100,000.[3] This strategy is then com-
pared with three alternatives. The "self-annuitization" alternative shows
a 65-year-old man who invests his $100,000 in a nonannuitized account
earning the market rate of interest but who consumes the same $8,100 per
year in income that the life annuity would have provided. Because this
individual is not benefiting from the mortality premium, this strategy is
unsustainable: he would run out of money before age 82.

   The "amortization" line shows another case in which the 65-year-old
man invests his wealth at the going market interest rate and amortizes it
(that is, spreads it evenly) over 35 years, from age 65 to 100. This strategy
provides income that is 38 percent lower than that provided by the annuity. Furthermore, the amortization strategy still imposes some risk; in the
event that the individual lives beyond age 100, he will have no money left

to consume under this approach, whereas he would still have income if he had purchased a life annuity.

The $1/LE$, or "1 divided by life expectancy," line shows what happens if the 65-year-old man follows a more sophisticated draw-down strategy that is similar to one of the methods permitted by the Internal Revenue Service (IRS) for meeting minimum distribution requirements from qualified pension plans. In particular, the strategy is based on consuming a fraction of remaining wealth that is proportional to the individual's remaining life expectancy (according to IRS life tables). The important feature of this approach is that, once again, the income stream is always lower than that provided by a life annuity. Indeed, the income from this approach never exceeds 76 percent of the annuity income level and falls to less than 50 percent by the time the person is in his early 90s.

These stylized results extend to more complex models, at least as long as the market for annuities is sufficiently well developed that individuals can match the annuity payouts to their desired consumption levels across time and across various resolutions of uncertainty (Davidoff, Brown, and Diamond 2005). We know, of course, that the annuity market is not well developed: for example, most annuities offered in the private sector lack inflation protection.[4] Nor is there a rich market for products that combine annuities with other forms of insurance, such as the combined annuity and long-term care product that has recently been suggested (see, for example, Murtaugh, Spillman, and Warshawsky 2001). Still, simulations show that even when there is an extreme mismatch between the annuities provided by the market and the desired consumption path, a risk-averse consumer would still find it optimal to annuitize the majority of her wealth (Davidoff, Brown, and Diamond 2005). These simulations also show that while a bequest motive reduces the demand for annuities, it does not eliminate it in general. In short, the economic literature provides a strong theoretical foundation for the normative conclusion that annuities ought to be of substantial value to retirees. It also has the positive empirical implication that annuities should comprise a large component of individual and household portfolios.

Do Consumers Behave as If They Value Annuities?

The empirical evidence on annuitization suggests that individuals do not behave as if they value annuities as highly as theory would predict. This is evidenced by the fact that the private market for immediate annuities, or payout annuities, was only $11.8 billion in 2005 (National Association of Variable Annuities 2006). Even this may overstate the size of the payout annuity market because included in the immediate annuity figures are some period-certain products that pay out for a specified number of years with no life contingency.[5] The conclusion that the market is small is supported by standard household data sets that are used to track asset ownership, such as the Survey of Consumer Finances or the Health and Retirement Study (HRS). The frequency with which annuity owners appear in these data sets is so low that empirical work on private market annuity purchases in the United States has been severely limited.

While annuitization is limited in the individual market, there has traditionally been a high level of annuitization provided through the group market via employer-sponsored pension plans. Over the last few decades, however, defined benefit plans have been steadily declining in importance relative to hybrid plans (for example, cash balance plans) and defined contribution plans (for example, 401[k] plans; see Poterba, Venti, and Wise 2008). One study reports that as of 2002, "nearly all of the over 500" cash balance, or hybrid, plans offer lump sum distributions as a payout option (Salisbury 2002). It is also well-known that in many defined contribution plans, such as the 401(k), participants often do not have the option of annuitizing. For example, survey evidence of 401(k) plan sponsors conducted by Hewitt Associates found that the fraction of 401(k) plans offering annuities as a payout option fell from 31 percent in 1999 to only 17 percent in 2003.[6] Even in those defined benefit plans that still exist, it is now very common for participants to have the option to take their benefits as a lump sum; over half of all defined benefit plans now offer a lump sum distribution at retirement (Salisbury 2002). As a result of these three factors, the Congressional Research Service reports that 85 percent of the 61.1 million workers age 21 or older who were included in a retirement plan at work participated in a plan that offered a lump sum distribution as a payment option (Congressional Research Service 2005).

With a tiny individual annuity market and a small and declining group annuity market, the only meaningful source of annuitization left in the United States today is the Social Security system. Evaluated solely as an annuity product, the Social Security benefit is quite good, in that it is inflation indexed (that is, every January 1, benefits are increased by the amount of the Consumer Price Index [CPI]) and provides spousal benefits. While individuals are permitted to claim Social Security benefits as early as age 62, they are not required to do so. Individuals who delay claiming are essentially purchasing (at better than market prices) a larger inflation-indexed annuity for the future. Research on benefit claiming behavior, however, suggests that very few individuals avail themselves of this opportunity, with only one out of ten men retiring before their sixty-second birthday delaying benefits claiming for at least a year (Coile et al. 2002).

While public support for the Social Security program has historically been high, new survey evidence suggests that many individuals would prefer to receive their benefit as a lump sum. In an experimental module from the Health and Retirement Survey, a subset of participants was asked the following question:

> Imagine you are 65 years old, and you are receiving $1000 per month in Social Security benefits. Suppose you were given the choice to lower that benefit by half, to $500 per month. This one-half benefit reduction will continue as long as you live. In return, you would be given a one-time, lump sum payment of $87,000. Would you take the $1000 monthly benefit for life or the lower monthly benefit with the lump sum payment?

The $87,000 lump sum is approximately actuarially fair for a 65-year-old single individual (the assumed age in the question), given average unisex population mortality rates and a 3 percent real interest rate.[7] Respondents were then asked a follow-up question that either increased or decreased the lump sum amount by approximately 25 percent. A large fraction of respondents stated a preference for the lump sum payment when priced at an approximately actuarially fair level, and many respondents preferred the lump sum even when it was substantially below its actuarial value. Clearly, if a large share of respondents are willing to give up the best annuity they own for a lump sum that is less than or equal to the actuarially fair level, then these individuals are not behaving as if they place a high insurance value on the annuity.

Importantly, the limited degree of annuitization is not unique to the United States. A series of World Bank studies in 1999 examined annuity markets in Canada, the United Kingdom, Switzerland, Australia, Israel, Chile, and Singapore. The summary report states "annuities markets are still poorly developed in virtually all these countries" (James and Song 2001).

In addition to the primary puzzle discussed here—that individuals do not annuitize as often as theory would predict—a secondary puzzle pertains to those who do annuitize: the prevalence of "guarantees." The vast majority of private annuity products sold in the United States include guarantees, such as a "ten-year period-certain" feature that promises that the annuitant and/or the policy beneficiary will receive at least ten years of payments, even if the annuitant dies during that period. This feature is somewhat puzzling in the standard life-cycle framework because it is easy to show that a life annuity with a ten-year period-certain guarantee is simply a combination of two distinct products: (1) a non-life-contingent bond that pays back its principal plus interest over ten years and (2) a life annuity with a deferred payout date of ten years.[8] Given that the loads charged for annuities with a ten-year guarantee are not substantially different from the loads charged for products that are entirely life contingent, it is not clear why individuals want to purchase the first of these products at existing loads, when plenty of alternative investments exist that would provide a better payout at comparable risk for the period of the guarantee. Another way to view this part of the annuity puzzle is that even when individuals are annuitizing, they are explicitly unraveling part of the annuity by including the guarantee.

Can Rational Models Explain the Limited Demand for Annuities?

An extensive literature has developed in recent years that attempts to explain the lack of annuitization within the framework of a fully rational, optimizing agent. In this section, I argue that while it is possible to generate more limited annuitization by extending the rational model in several directions, such an approach does not seem to provide the complete answer to the puzzle. In some cases, the hypothesized explanations run counter to established empirical findings. In other cases, the explanations reduce the theoretical demand for annuities, but not by enough to explain such low observed levels. In still other cases, the explanations solve one puzzle at the expense of creating new ones.

Adverse Selection and High Prices

It has been well documented that annuity prices (payouts) tend to be higher (lower) than actuarially fair levels. One commonly used metric for evaluating annuity prices is the "money's worth" (MW) concept, which is simply defined as

$$\text{Money's Worth} = \frac{\text{Expected Net Present Value of Payouts}}{\text{Premium}}$$

The numerator is the sum of all future annuity payments, weighted by the probability that an individual will be alive to receive them and discounted back to present at a risk-free interest rate. The denominator is the premium paid for the annuity. Thus, when the MW ratio is less than 1.0, it indicates that individual annuitants will, on average, receive less in annuity payments than they paid in premiums. Analysis of market prices in 1999 found that the MW ratio for a single premium immediate annuity for a 65-year-old male in the United States was approximately 0.85 when it was evaluated using general population mortality and a Treasury yield curve (Brown, Mitchell, and Poterba 2002). By computing the MW separately using general population and annuitant mortality tables, studies show that most of the load (where load = 1 – MW) arises from the fact that the mortality rate of annuitants is substantially below that of the general population. These mortality differences reflect both adverse selection arising from private health information about expected longevity (that is, "active" selection) and differences arising from the fact that annuitants tend to have higher income and wealth than nonannuitants, factors that are also correlated with mortality (that is, "passive" selection; Finkelstein and Poterba 2002). Several papers reinforce the idea that active selection may matter by showing that individuals with poor self-reported health are less likely to express an interest in annuitizing (see, for example, Brown 2001; or Brown, Casey, and Mitchell 2007). More recently, several papers have argued that part of the annuity load may also arise from the fact that insurance companies are unable to adequately hedge aggregate mortality risk in the population and therefore must charge a higher price to compensate for bearing this risk (see, for example, Blake and Burrows 2001; Blake, Cairns, and Dowd 2006; Blake, Burrows, and Orszag 2002; Friedberg and Webb 2006; Brown and Orszag 2006).

Regardless of the source of the price markup, however, the implicit assumption behind the belief that prices drive down annuity demand is that consumers are price sensitive, that is, that they have a price elasticity of demand that is rather large (in absolute value). Perhaps surprisingly, we have relatively little in the way of empirical estimates about the price elasticity of demand for annuities.[9] However, there are several pieces of data that suggest that existing loads are not the most important explanation of limited demand. First, simulation work suggests that the loads are not large enough to offset the utility gains from annuitization (see, for example, Mitchell et al. 1999). Second, evidence suggests that few individuals are willing to postpone the claiming of Social Security benefits, despite the fact that Social Security actuarial adjustments for early retirement are roughly actuarially fair on average (see Coile et al. 2002). Finally, a recent study finds that many individuals state a preference for a lump sum to the Social Security annuity even when the annuity is favorably priced (Brown, Casey, and Mitchell 2007). Of course, this study did find some evidence of price sensitivity: when the lump sum was reduced, the proportion preferring the lump sum declined. Specifically, a 33 percent increase in the monthly annuity payout per dollar spent on the annuity induced only one out of five individuals to switch their stated preference from the lump sum to the annuity. Given that most estimates of the MW of annuities in the private U.S. market suggest loads in the neighborhood of 10–15 percent, a simplistic linear extrapolation suggests that less than 10 percent of the population would switch to an annuity if annuities suddenly became offered at actuarially fair prices.

Another way to view the pricing problem is that it may create an incentive to delay annuitization. Higher than actuarially fair prices, the irreversibility of the annuity contract, and the potential arrival of asymmetric information may provide an advantage to delaying the purchase of annuities (Milevsky and Young 2007). For example, it may be optimal to delay annuitization if returns on investment in the future might exceed current returns or if annuities purchased later in life are priced more favorably than those purchased earlier. Relatedly, an "all or nothing" annuitization decision at a single point in time is suboptimal, and consumers would be better off initially annuitizing a lump sum (if they do not already have this minimum level from preexisting defined benefit pensions like Social Security) and then gradually purchasing additional life annuities over time (Milevsky and Young 2007). Of course, while these models provide excellent guidance about how people "ought to" behave when faced with realistic institutional restrictions on the timing and type of annuitization, they share the shortcoming of being unable to explain how people actually behave: empirically, we do not observe many households following a strategy of gradual annuitization at older ages.

Preexisting Annuitization

Given standard models of lifetime expected utility, the marginal value of additional annuitization typically declines with the amount of wealth already annuitized. Numerous authors have made the point that high levels of preexisting annuitization from Social Security or private defined benefit plans may lead to low demand for additional annuitization.[10]

For individuals at the low end of the wealth distribution, this explanation certainly rings true. For example, the Social Security Administration states that 21 percent of married couples and 43 percent of unmarried persons rely on Social Security for more than 90 percent of their income (Social Security Administration 2007). It should not be surprising that these households would not wish to annuitize what little savings they have remaining. Higher up the wealth distribution, however, where Social Security represents a much smaller portion of wealth, it is more difficult to argue that all private annuity purchases are crowded out. As recently noted, "for the vast majority of retirees, however, for their optimal annuitization strategy to equal the amounts provided by Social Security and DB [defined benefit] pensions would be a miraculous coincidence" (Hu and Scott 2007, 71).

Risk Sharing in Couples

It has long been noted that families who share a common budget constraint can effectively substitute for a formal annuity market.[11] By pooling their resources, a married couple is able to capture a large share of the gains from a formal annuity market. As a result of this risk-sharing potential, a couple's willingness to pay for joint-and-survivor annuities is substantially lower than a single individual's willingness to pay for an annuity (Brown and Poterba 2000).

One recent paper combines several of the preceding insights—high prices, high levels of preexisting annuities, and risk sharing within couples—into a set of simulated annuity demands by individuals in the HRS and finds that it is possible to explain observed low levels of annuitization (Dushi and Webb 2004). This suggests that while many of these explanations are inadequate, on their own, to explain limited annuity demand, the combination of multiple factors may have more success. However, this paper also confirms that annuity demand should be higher for single individuals than for couples. One implication of this is that we should observe individuals choosing to annuitize upon the death of a spouse, and yet we do not.

Bequests

Naturally, if a person wishes to leave an inheritance to her children, and if an annuity product has no value at death, then the individual will not find it optimal to annuitize all of her wealth. This is why the classic "full annuitization" result requires that there be no bequest motive (Yaari 1965). There are two problems, however, with viewing bequest motives as the answer to the annuity puzzle. First, while bequests clearly lead one away from the full annuitization result, this does not mean that individuals will not value partial annuitization. Indeed, under certain assumptions, an individual will simply wish to divide her wealth between "own consumption" and "heirs' consumption" and then fully annuitize the "own consumption" piece. The value of annuitizing the own consumption part of one's wealth would be particularly important if the individual (or, depending on the bequest function, the individual's children) were risk averse over the size of the bequest. The reason is that, in the absence of annuitization, the size of the bequest becomes a draw from a very disperse distribution—for example, the bequest might be quite large if the individual dies young but quite small if the individual dies at age 95.

Second, the empirical evidence in favor of bequest motives mattering for marginal annuity decisions is essentially nonexistent, at least in the widely used HRS. For example, one study found that self-reported measures of the strength of the bequest motive could not explain intentions about the likelihood of annuitizing defined contribution account balances at retirement (Brown 2001). Another found that older adults with children are equally likely to annuitize as older adults with no children (Johnson, Burman, and Kobes 2004).

Bequest motives are sometimes also posited as an explanation for the frequency with which individuals purchase annuities with period-certain guarantees. This explanation also seems unsatisfactory, however, due to the odd distribution of bequests that results from such a contract. Suppose, for example, that an individual purchased an annuity with a monthly payout of $1,000, and a ten-year period-certain guarantee. If the annuitant dies immediately after purchasing the annuity, the beneficiary receives 120 payments of $1,000. If the annuitant dies after one year, the beneficiary receives only 108 payments of $1,000. At the end of ten years, the beneficiary receives nothing. Standard parameterizations of a bequest motive (whether a "warm glow" model or an altruistic model) have difficulty explaining why this particular distribution of bequests would be optimal. If there is any risk aversion over the size of the bequest, it is easy to show that a guarantee is dominated by purchasing a $1,000 per month annuity with no guarantee and using the savings from the reduced annuity premium to make an immediate gift to the beneficiary. Indeed, if there were any load paid on the guarantee, even a risk-neutral recipient would prefer the immediate gift.

Incomplete Annuity Markets

Recent theoretical work shows that as long as markets are complete, full annuitization is optimal (Davidoff, Brown, and Diamond 2005). In reality, existing annuity markets in the United States and elsewhere are far from complete: most of the life annuity products that are sold today offer a fixed nominal payout, which leaves individuals exposed to other risks, such as from inflation or unexpected medical expenditures.

Inflation risk arises because most privately available annuity products are fixed in nominal terms. Simulation work shows that under a specific process for inflation, a moderately risk-averse consumer would find nominal annuities less attractive than inflation-indexed annuities.[12] However, it is difficult to conclude that the lack of inflation protection is the major culprit for the lack of annuity demand. Empirically, we know that when inflation-indexed annuities are provided—such as through the Teachers Insurance and Annuity Association, College Retirement Equities Fund's (TIAA-CREF's) inflation-linked bond account or through the CPI-indexed product offered by Vanguard/AIG—demand does not suddenly increase. Further, in the United Kingdom, where inflation-linked annuities have been widely available for many years, they represent a very small share of the market (Finkelstein and Poterba 2002). Also, when individuals in the HRS were given the opportunity to choose between an inflation-indexed Social Security annuity and a lump sum, a large fraction of individuals prefer the lump sum payment (Brown, Casey, and Mitchell 2007).

A second problem with incomplete markets is that most annuity contracts are structured in a manner that imposes constraints on the degree of liquidity provided. It is generally not possible to borrow against the future value of an annuity or to alter the timing of annuity payouts once a contract has commenced. Reversing an annuity, such as by selling it to a third-party buyer, is quite costly and often is not possible. Concerns about liquidity often arise in the context of health-care expenditures. Health expenditures are highly uncertain, not fully insured, and can be quite large especially at older ages. If expenditures are concentrated very late in life, then because annuities are able to provide a higher level of income in the years prior to the shock, annuities might be an effective way to save for such expenditures (see Davidoff, Brown, and Diamond 2005). Alternatively, if the expenditures come early in life, they may well reduce the value of annuities. Several papers analyze the role of medical expenditure shocks and find that they tend to reduce annuity demand.[13] Of course, forgoing annuitization is an inferior strategy to buying both annuities *and* insurance against the shocks, such as long-term care insurance in the case of nursing homes. Similarly, one could offer a single product that combines annuities and long-term care, which in addition to providing both types of insurance also has the potential benefit of improving pricing due to offsetting forms of adverse selection.[14] Whether this approach would work depends in part on whether individuals will find the long-term care benefits valuable in their own right. For example, Medicaid imposes a large implicit tax on the purchase of private long-term care contracts, and to the extent this limits the market, this implicit tax would afflict combination products as well.[15]

A more general problem with blaming the limited annuity market size on the incompleteness of the product space is that it begs the question of why insurance companies are not providing a richer mix of products in the first place. In some cases, it is easy to trace the blame to institutional barriers, such as the difficulty of obtaining level tax treatment of the combination annuity plus long-term care product (Brazell, Brown, and Warshawsky 2007). Similarly, it is understandable that many insurance companies have historically been reluctant to offer inflation-indexed annuities owing to the lack of securities with which to hedge their inflation exposure. With the introduction of Treasury Inflation Protected Securities (TIPS) in the late 1990s, followed more recently by the "stripping" of the principal and interest from TIPS into separate securities, a few insurance companies have begun creating inflation-indexed products. In many other cases, however, the market has been very slow to evolve, despite the lack of any obvious external impediment to innovation. For example, aside from TIAA-CREF, insurers have been somewhat slow in providing lifetime annuity payouts linked to risky asset portfolios, such as stock indices. Another example is the limited availability of true deferred payout annuity contracts, in which an individual contributes gradually over time in exchange for a life-contingent payout that starts at some future date in exchange for forfeiting the money if one dies prior to the payout date.

Possible Behavioral Hypotheses

In recent years, insights from the field of psychology have increasingly been used to explain consumer behavior that deviates from what standard economic models would suggest in a very wide range of contexts. Just within the area of retirement planning, numerous papers have demonstrated the power of "behavioral economics" to explain saving rates, 401(k) plan participation rates and contribution levels, portfolio decisions, and much more.

The literature on applying behavioral economics to the annuitization decision is just beginning to emerge. Nonetheless, there are several reasons to believe that our understanding of annuity decisions will likely be informed by research in this area. First, the mixed success of explaining annuitization behavior in a fully rational context suggests that other factors are at play. Second, the insights from behavioral economics have been very influential in other aspects of the retirement and household finance literature, and there is little reason to believe that consumers who are exhibiting psychological biases during their work lives will instantly switch to becoming fully rational optimizers at retirement. Finally, anecdotal evidence (for example, conversations with financial services providers, financial planners, and consumers), as well as some industry research, provides reason to believe that behavioral considerations loom large.

In this section, I outline an incomplete list of possible behavioral hypotheses that appear to be worth exploring in future research. While there are several research programs that are starting to apply behavioral economics to the annuity decision, few results are yet available, and thus it is too early to know which insights, if any, will prove most powerful and robust. As such, the discussion that follows is necessarily speculative.

The Framing of Annuity Choice

For more than two decades, psychologists and economists have understood that the framing of a choice can influence decisions. Recent work provides evidence that when individuals are asked to choose between an annuity and a savings account, this choice is heavily influenced by the frame (Brown et al. 2008).[16] In particular, when the annuity is presented in an investment frame that highlights rates of return, liquidity, and so forth, most individuals prefer the savings account. In sharp contrast, when the annuity is presented in a consumption frame that highlights the sustainability of consumption after retirement, most individuals prefer the annuity. If these results, which are based on stated preferences in a survey, prove robust when tested in actual market conditions, the implications for financial education and planning are significant.

Complexity and Financial Literacy

Determining how to provide for a sustainable retirement income stream in the face of uncertainty is a complex task, especially when the annuity product space is extremely confusing (such as the fact that the majority of products that are called "annuities" do not provide any life-contingent payouts). In general, complexity and information problems may be rational barriers to annuitization if the transaction costs associated with obtaining the necessary information are sufficiently high. In this context, however, where the potential welfare gains from optimizing one's retirement income plan are quite large, it is unlikely that consumers are making fully rational decisions to forgo educating themselves about annuities because of the perceived costs of doing so.

More likely, the average individual may simply lack the financial sophistication to make a fully informed decision about payouts.[17] Evidence abounds regarding the lack of financial sophistication in the population (Lusardi and Mitchell 2007).

Complexity is one of several hypotheses as to why default options have been found to have such power in influencing a wide range of behaviors associated with retirement planning. There is some evidence that defaults influence behavior in the wealth decumulation phase: in 1984, the federal government began requiring a spouse's notarized signature if a married retiree wished to opt out of the joint-and-survivor annuity and take a single-life annuity instead, a change that increased joint-and-survivor annuitization by 5–10 percentage points (Aura 2001). Of course, complexity is only one possible explanation for the importance of defaults, but all of them rely on behavioral, rather than fully rational, insights.[18]

Mental Accounting and Loss Aversion: "Annuities Are a Gamble"

In focus groups conducted by the American Council of Life Insurers, some participants viewed the purchase of an immediate annuity as "gambling on their lives."[19] This view is hard to reconcile with the standard life-cycle consumer whose lifetime utility derives from his or her consumption each period and for whom the elimination of mortality risk is a form of insurance.

Mental accounting and prospect theory's loss-aversion concept may help to explain this finding. Rather than evaluating the annuity as part of an overall optimization exercise, individuals may use a narrow framing along the lines of "will I live long enough to make back my initial investment?"[20] If the question is framed in this manner, it is easy to see why the product is viewed as a risky gamble. Without the annuity, the individual has $100,000 for certain. With the annuity, there is some probability that the individual will receive only a few thousand dollars in income (if he or she were to die within a few months), some probability that the individual will receive far more than $100,000 (if he or she lives well past life expectancy), and numerous possibilities in between. This line of reasoning suggests that if one applies the cumulative prospect theory approach to a narrow framing of the annuity, annuities do not look attractive because the "losses" from the annuity (if one dies young) loom larger in the individual's value function than do the potential "gains" from living a long time.[21]

In addition to providing a possible explanation of limited demand, proponents of this view argue that it can explain the prevalence of guarantees, which are essentially a way to hold less of the "risky" annuity. Of course, the use of prospect theory to explain why people purchase guarantees along with their annuity suffers from the difficulty that individuals who approach annuities from this perspective would prefer not to annuitize at all. There are a number of questions that need more research attention in this context, such as determining which reference point consumers use to evaluate gains and losses when evaluating an annuity. Nonetheless, this model provides a useful starting point for thinking about these issues.

Misleading Heuristics: "Insurance Is for Bad Events"[22]

An economist's view of insurance is that it is a mechanism for transferring resources from states of low marginal utility of income (that is, times when additional money is less valuable) to states of high marginal utility of income (that is, times when additional money is more valuable). An annuity does this by transferring resources from states of the world in which an individual has died young (and thus has a low marginal utility of income) to states in which they have lived past their expected lifespan and therefore presumably have a high marginal utility of income.

Casual empiricism suggests, however, that many noneconomists use a different framing for buying insurance, such as, "I buy insurance against bad events." In other words, many individuals appear to buy insurance to pay off when the level of utility is low rather than when the marginal utility of income is high. In many cases, low utility and high marginal utility correspond, which is why this heuristic works well in cases such as life insurance, health insurance, casualty insurance, disability insurance, and so forth. To the extent that living a long time is viewed as a good or high-utility outcome, this insurance heuristic may lead individuals to forego annuities, even though the marginal utility of income in this state may also be high. Of course, a good marketing strategy should be able to overcome this objection by reframing the outcome as a negative event, along the lines of insuring against "being a widow living in extreme poverty because you outlived your money." Unfortunately, there is no empirical evidence to date that sheds any light on this hypothesis.

Regret Aversion: "I Should Not Have Bought That Annuity"

A common explanation proffered by financial planners as to why their clients do not like annuities, and for the popularity of period-certain guarantees for those who do buy them, is the desire to avoid regret. One possible response to this notion is that the time in which the individual should most regret the annuity purchase is after he is dead, at which time the capacity for regret seems speculative at best. This response, however, ignores the possibility that if an individual converts the majority of his retirement savings into an annuity and then subsequently learns he has only one year to live, the potential for regret during that final year of life may be significant. Even if the probability of this outcome is very small, individuals may inflate the probability in making the annuity decision. For example, research in psychology has shown that events that are more easily imagined (such as dying right after an annuity purchase) are overweighted in the decision process (Tversky and Kahneman 1974).

However, a formal application of the regret-aversion model to annuities does not necessarily imply that individuals will not value annuities. In

a study that examines insurance decisions within a formal model of regret aversion, researchers find that regret aversion leads individuals away
from extreme outcomes, meaning that regret-averse individuals are less
likely to fully insure but are also less likely to forego insurance completely
(Braun and Muermann 2004). In this context, just as individuals might regret the decision to purchase an annuity, a regret-averse individual might
also fear the possibility of living to age 110 after having failed to purchase
one. More research needs to be done to determine whether or not regret
aversion matters for the annuity purchase decision.

The Illusion of Control

One recent industry study finds that "loss of control" of one's assets is the
most commonly cited disadvantage of annuitization (Drinkwater 2006). To
the extent that individuals are really expressing a concern about liquidity,
there is a rational element to this objection. As noted earlier, the "costly
reversibility" feature of life annuities and the difficulty borrowing against
future annuity streams means that individuals who may face uninsured expenditure shocks may not want to fully annuitize. It may also be rational to
be concerned about control if one is concerned about entering into a long-
term contract with an insurance company that may go bankrupt sometime
during the life of the annuity contract (Babbel and Merrill 2006). However, the strength of the objections often registered about control suggests
that there is something deeper than a rational concern about liquidity.

It is possible that these objections may be related to the extensive psychology literature on the "illusion of control," or the tendency of individuals to believe they can control outcomes even when they have no such
control (Langer 1975). Individuals may well believe that they have more
control over their financial future by holding wealth rather than by receiving income. It is worth noting that during one's working life, much of the financial advice that one receives emphasizes individual choice and control.
Thus, it would not be surprising to think that individuals would have a difficult time handing over their wealth to an insurance company in exchange
for a monthly income stream over which they have little control.

Other Behavioral Factors

There are numerous other potential behavioral explanations as well, including models of ambiguity aversion (for example, people do not even know

the relevant probabilities of survival), models that suggest that individuals do not like to think about unpleasant events (for example, dying young or being old but poor), and models focusing on how individuals discount the future (for example, a hyperbolic discounting model).[23] As with the other hypotheses outlined above, however, much more research is needed to determine which of these factors, if any, are empirically relevant.

The Future of Annuitization

New Products[24]

With nearly 80 million baby boomers approaching retirement, the issue of how to convert wealth into a secure stream of retirement income is increasingly on the minds of individuals, insurance companies, and policy makers. In the last few years, insurance companies have started introducing several new products that focus on the payout phase, a small subset of which will be described below. The diversity of approaches being followed in the industry suggests that there is not unanimity about the underlying cause of limited annuitization. As the market evolves in the coming years, it will provide us with additional information to assess the underlying determinants of, and barriers to, annuitization.

DEFERRED PAYOUTS.   Several companies have begun to offer products that are designed to provide life annuity payments that start at some future date.[25] At least one company (Hartford) has structured a product to be similar to having a defined benefit option within a 401(k) plan: as a person contributes, she is buying a guaranteed amount of future annuity income. One possible advantage of this approach is that because the individual is gradually buying units of income, rather than accumulating wealth per se, she may not face the same psychological barrier of converting a large accumulated stock of wealth into income at the time of retirement.

A related product was introduced by MetLife in 2004. The idea behind this product is that a consumer at age 65 can use a small portion of his wealth to buy an annuity that does not begin paying out until age 85. In this sense, the product feels more like insurance in that it pays off only in the event that the person lives a long time. Because payouts commencing twenty years in the future are being discounted by both interest rates and nontrivial mortality rates, it appears relatively "cheap" to buy income at older ages. By providing insurance against outliving one's resources, this product captures a disproportionate share of the welfare gains from annuitization.[26] One way to view it is as a form of partial annuitization where the annuitization is concentrated in those periods where the mortality credits are the largest. While these products seem to be generating a fair amount of interest in the financial-planning community, only time will tell if they have a major impact on the market.

GUARANTEED MINIMUM WITHDRAWALS FOR LIFE. As noted earlier, variable annuity products have traditionally been used as asset accumulation devices, with little attention paid to the payout features. Recently, however, a "new generation of variable annuity products (is) proliferating in the market" (Prudential Financial 2006). An increasingly popular feature of these contracts is a guaranteed minimum withdrawal benefit (GMWB) that guarantees a minimum level of withdrawals over one's lifetime. Because these contracts typically guarantee that the individual will receive a fixed percentage (for example, 5 percent) of the account balance at a point in time (for example, a particular birthday, a high-water mark, and so on), they are essentially providing the owner with an annuity floor below which the income cannot fall. These contracts typically provide individuals with a reasonably high level of liquidity (for example, they may modify their withdrawal amount or even cash in the product) as well as some control over the portfolio allocation. GMWBs were available on nearly 80 percent of the variable annuities sold in the first quarter of 2006, up from 44 percent in 2003 (Prudential Financial 2006). Industry sources suggest that these products are becoming increasingly popular, although it is too early to know whether these products will ultimately provide a substantial share of overall retirement income.

ANNUITIES WITH LIQUIDITY. At least one insurance company offers a fixed life annuity with an option to withdraw, on a one-time-only basis, up to 30 percent of the expected value of the remaining annuity payments based on mortality rates at the time of purchase. This option is limited to being exercised only on the fifth, tenth, or fifteenth anniversary of the first payment or upon a "significant, non-medical loss."[27] It is not yet clear whether the potential for adverse selection in this context has affected the pricing in a significant way.

Another idea that has been floated is that of combining an annuity with long-term care insurance as a way of addressing concerns about liquidity in the context of long-term care expenditure risk.[28] The product would provide life annuity benefits with a significant "pop-up" benefit (for example, additional cash payments) when the annuitant meets the benefit triggers typically associated with long-term care insurance policies. While the Pension Protection Act of 2006 provided this combination product with some tax benefits beginning in 2010, it is too early to know whether this market will evolve in a substantial way.

Public Policy toward Annuitization

Whether policy makers should be actively encouraging annuitization is unclear because it depends on why individuals are choosing not to annuitize on their own. If the observed lack of annuitization represents optimal behavior by fully rational individuals, then the scope for welfare-increasing government intervention is more limited. Even if individuals are failing to fully optimize as a result of behavioral biases, it is not clear that government intervention is necessary or desirable in overcoming it, as private sector annuity providers may have sufficient incentive to determine how to promote annuitization on their own.

On the other hand, given that pensions and insurance are heavily regulated at the federal and state levels, respectively, there is no question that the government is already influencing the annuity landscape, and not always for the better. For example, an important reason for the lack of annuities in 401(k) plans is that legal advisors "strongly advise their clients against them. In their view, annuities expose plan sponsors to significant and long-term risk of liability. And plan sponsors, more often than not, heed their advice" (Perun 2004). While plan sponsors are at no fiduciary risk for choosing not to provide an annuity option, the decision to offer an annuity creates such risk because of a provision requiring plan sponsors to choose the "safest annuity available." At a minimum, it would seem desirable for the government not to discourage annuitization. Fortunately, the Pension Protection Act of 2006 took an important step by directing the Department of Labor to clarify that the selection of an annuity contract would no longer be subject to this standard. A new interim final rule limiting the "safest annuity available standard" to defined benefit plans and providing a new fiduciary safe harbor for plan sponsors when selecting an annuity provider for defined contribution plans took effect in November 2007. It remains unclear whether the rules will have a substantial positive impact on annuity offerings within defined contribution plans, but the new rule is clearly a step in the right direction.

The Pension Protection Act also took significant steps to encourage the use of default options in the accumulation phase of 401(k) plans. Given the demonstrated power of default options, it is perhaps worth considering whether firms ought to be required to offer an annuity as a default payout option. Structuring an optimal annuity default would arguably be more challenging than designing a default for contributions due to the issues of irreversibility, but such issues could likely be addressed by allowing for a richer set of annuity options (for example, gradual annuitization, liquidity options, and so on).

Conclusions and Implications for Financial Education

It has been more than two decades since Nobel Laureate Franco Modigliani stated that the reasons individuals do not annuitize more are still "ill-understood." Since that time, numerous scholars have contributed to a significant increase in our understanding of how annuity markets operate, the decisions that individuals make, and the implications of these decisions for individual welfare. Nonetheless, while we have a much greater understanding of how we think consumers ought to optimally behave and of how they actually do behave with respect to annuity decisions, we still do not have a fully developed sense of *why* they behave the way that they do.

The answers to these questions are critical for understanding the appropriateness and/or potential efficacy of financial education in this area. If future research were to show that consumer aversion to annuities is well informed and rational, then there is minimal scope for financial education or other forms of government intervention to alter outcomes (nor in this case would altering outcomes be desirable). If research confirms that consumer aversion is driven primarily by complexity, confusion, or various psychological biases, then the next question is whether scarce societal resources are better spent on financial education or on creating products and policies that mandate or encourage annuitization by appealing to or overcoming such biases. Until we have a better understanding of why consumers act as if they place so little value on annuitization, it will remain unclear whether individual and social welfare will be enhanced by policies that promote annuitization or even which policies would be successful at doing so. As such, the economics and psychology of the annuitization decision remain a very fruitful area for additional research.

Notes

The author thanks John Ameriks, Andrew Caplin, Annamaria Lusardi, and participants in the "Improving the Effectiveness of Financial Education and Savings Programs" conference for helpful conversations.

1. Yaari (1965) is the classic reference in this area. Later papers, including Bernheim (1987) and Davidoff, Brown, and Diamond (2005), have shown that the central result holds even after relaxing many of the original assumptions.

2. For a discussion of mortality credits, see Milevsky (1998).

3. Figure 6.1, and the accompanying text, is an updated version of that found in Brown (2004) and is based on the following assumptions: on March 31, 2008, a 65-year-old male resident of Illinois could receive monthly income of $675 from a $100,000 initial premium according to http://www.annuityshopper.com. The yield on a ten-year government bond for the week of March 28, 2008, which is used as the market rate of interest for nonannuitization strategies, was 3.52 percent according to http://www.federalreserve.gov/releases/H15/data/Weekly_Friday_/H15_TCMNOM_Y10 .txt. The IRS life table used in calculating the 1/LE rule is taken from the appendix to IRS publication 590.

4. An exception is the inflation-indexed life annuity offered by AIG/Vanguard, although even this product caps the inflation protection at 10 percent per year. A second exception is TIAA-CREF's Inflation Linked Bond Account, although this option is not available to retail investors.

5. One must be careful to distinguish life annuities from other "annuity" products that do not provide lifetime payouts. According to the National Association of Variable Annuities (2006), over 94 percent of the $212.3 billion of total annuity purchases was made up of deferred annuities, which are sold primarily as tax-deferred saving vehicles (Brown and Poterba 2006) and which do not require conversion to lifetime payouts. Less than 0.8 percent of these contracts were converted into fixed life annuities in 2003 (Beatrice and Drinkwater 2004).

6. One reason for this—the legal environment—is discussed later in the text.

7. The results are analyzed in detail by Brown, Casey, and Mitchell (2007). Different lump sum amounts were used for married individuals.

8. This point has also been made by Scott, Watson, and Hu (2006).

9. See Gentry and Rothschild (2006) for further discussion of the issues involved.

10. This factor plays a particularly large role in Dushi and Webb's (2004) model of limited annuity demand.

11. Kotlikoff and Spivak (1981) were the first to rigorously evaluate this argument.

12. Brown, Mitchell, and Poterba (2001) report these calculations for a moderately risk-averse individual, assuming that inflation roughly captures the distribu-

tion of inflation outcomes over the period 1926–97 and that inflation is correlated across periods.

13. For example, see Sinclair and Smetters (2004) and Turra and Mitchell (2005).

14. This idea has been suggested by Murtaugh, Spillman, and Warshawsky (2001).

15. See Brown and Finkelstein (2008) for a rigorous treatment of Medicaid's implicit tax.

16. For additional discussion of how men and women react differently to alternative annuity frames, see Agnew et al. (2008).

17. Smith and Stewart (2008) document that financial illiteracy is widespread.

18. These issues are more fully explored by Beshears, Choi, Laibson, and Madrian (2008).

19. These findings are discussed by Brown and Warshawsky (2004).

20. Hu and Scott (2007) discuss this hypothesis in detail.

21. Hu and Scott (2007) discuss in detail how the application of Tversky and Kahneman's (1992) cumulative prospect theory to annuities might explain some of the observed behavior.

22. I thank David Laibson and Richard Zeckhauser for suggesting this hypothesis.

23. Laibson (1997) provides a formal modeling of hyperbolic discounting.

24. Warshawsky (2007) provides a more detailed discussion of many of these new products.

25. Milevksy (2005) refers to these products as "advanced-life delayed annuities."

26. This has been shown by Scott, Watson, and Hu (2006).

27. Warshawsky (2007) discusses this product in more detail.

28. Murtaugh, Spillman, and Warshawsky (2001) have promoted this idea.

References

Agnew, Julie R., Lisa R. Anderson, Jeffrey R. Gerlach, and Lisa R. Szykman. 2008. Who Chooses Annuities? An Experimental Investigation of the Role of Gender, Framing and Defaults. *American Economic Review* 98: 418–422.

Aura, Saku. 2001. Does the Balance of Power within a Family Matter? The Case of the Retirement Equity Act. IGIER Working Paper No. 202. Innocenzo Gasparini Institute for Economic Research, Milan, Italy.

Babbel, David F., and Craig B. Merrill. 2006. Rational Decumulation. Working Paper No. 06-14. Wharton Financial Institutions Center, Philadelphia, PA.

Beatrice, Dan Q., and Matthew Drinkwater. 2004. The 2003 Individual Annuity Market: Sales and Assets. Windsor, CT: LIMRA International.

Bernheim, B. Douglas. 1987. The Economic Effects of Social Security: Toward a

Reconciliation of Theory and Measurement. *Journal of Public Economics* 33(3): 273–304.

Beshears, John, James J. Choi, David Laibson, and Brigitte C. Madrian. 2008. The Importance of Default Options for Retirement Saving Outcomes: Evidence from the United States. In *Lessons from Pension Reform in the Americas*, edited by Stephen J. Key and Tapen Sinha, 59–87. Oxford: Oxford University Press.

Blake, David, and William Burrows. 2001. Survivor Bonds: Helping to Hedge Mortality Risk. *Journal of Risk and Insurance* 68: 339–48.

Blake, David, William Burrows, and J. Michael Orszag. 2002. Survivor Bonds and Compulsory Annuitization: Reducing the Costs of Pension Provision. In *Innovations in Retirement Financing*, edited by Olivia Mitchell, 222–33. Philadelphia: Pension Research Council.

Blake, David, Andrew J. G. Cairns, and Kevin Dowd. 2006. Living with Mortality: Mortality Bonds and Other Mortality-Linked Securities. *British Actuarial Journal* 12(1): 153–97.

Braun, Michael, and Alexander Muermann. 2004. The Impact of Regret on the Demand for Insurance. *Journal of Risk and Insurance* 71: 737–67.

Brazell, David, Jason Brown, and Mark J. Warshawsky. 2007. Tax Issues and Life Care Annuities. Pension Research Council Working Paper No. 22. The Wharton School, University of Pennsylvania, Philadelphia, PA.

Brown, Jeffrey R. 2001. Private Pensions, Mortality Risk, and the Decision to Annuitize. *Journal of Public Economics* 82(1): 29–62.

———. 2004. The New Retirement Challenge. White paper for *Americans for Secure Retirement*. Available at http://www.paycheckforlife.org.

Brown, Jeffrey R., Marcus Casey, and Olivia S. Mitchell. 2007. Who Values the Social Security Annuity? Evidence from the Health and Retirement Study. Working paper. University of Illinois.

Brown, Jeffrey R., and Amy Finkelstein. 2008. The Interaction of Public and Private Insurance: Medicaid and the Long-term Care Insurance Market. *American Economic Review* 38: 1083–1102.

Brown, Jeffrey R., Jeffrey R. Kling, Sendhil Mullainathan, and Marian Wrobel. 2008. Why Don't People Insure Late Life Consumption? A Framing Explanation of the Under-Annuitization Puzzle. *American Economic Review* 98: 304–9.

Brown, Jeffrey R., Olivia S. Mitchell, and James M. Poterba. 2001. The Role of Real Annuities and Indexed Bonds in an Individual Accounts Retirement Program. In *Risk Aspects of Investment-Based Social Security Reform*, edited by J. Campbell and M. Feldstein, 321–60. Chicago: University of Chicago Press.

———. 2002. Mortality Risk, Inflation Risk, and Annuity Products. In *Innovations in Retirement Financing*, edited by O. Mitchell, Z. Bodie, B. Hammond, and S. Zeldes, 175–97. Philadelphia: University of Pennsylvania Press.

Brown, Jeffrey R., and Peter Orszag. 2006. The Political Economy of Government-Issued Survivor Bonds. *Journal of Risk and Insurance* 73: 611–31.

Brown, Jeffrey R., and James M. Poterba. 2000. Joint Life Annuities and the De-
    mand for Annuities by Married Couples. *Journal of Risk and Insurance* 67:
    527–53.
———. 2006. Household Demand for Variable Annuities. *Tax Policy and the Econ-
    omy* 20: 163–91.
Brown, Jeffrey R., and Mark J. Warshawsky. 2004. Longevity-Insured Retirement
    Distributions from Pension Plans: Regulatory and Market Issues. In *Public
    Policies and Private Pensions*, edited by W. Gale, J. Shoven, and M. Warshawsky,
    332–82. Washington, DC: Brookings Institution.
Coile, Courtney, Peter Diamond, Jonathan Gruber, and Alain Jousten. 2002. Delays
    in Claiming Social Security Benefits. *Journal of Public Economics* 84: 357–85.
Congressional Research Service. 2005. Pension Issues: Lump-Sum Distributions
    and Retirement Income Security. Congressional Research Service Report for
    Congress.
Davidoff, Thomas, Jeffrey R. Brown, and Peter A. Diamond. 2005. Annuities and
    Individual Welfare. *American Economic Review* 95: 1573–90.
Drinkwater, Matthew. 2006. Retirement Income Preferences. Windsor, CT: LIMRA
    International.
Dushi, Irena, and Anthony Webb. 2004. Household Annuitization Decisions: Simu-
    lations and Empirical Analysis. *Journal of Pension Economics and Finance* 3:
    109–43.
Finkelstein, Amy, and James Poterba. 2002. Selection Effects in the United King-
    dom Individual Annuities Market. *Economic Journal* 112: 28–50.
Friedberg, Leora, and Anthony Webb. 2006. Life Is Cheap: Using Mortality Bonds
    to Hedge Aggregate Mortality Risk. CRR Working Paper No. 2005-12. Boston
    College Center for Retirement Research, Boston, MA.
Gentry, William, and Casey Rothschild. 2006. Lifetime Annuities for US: Evaluat-
    ing the Efficacy of Policy Interventions in Life Annuity Markets. Paper pre-
    pared for the American Council for Capital Formation. Available at http://www
    .accf.org.
Hu, Wei-Yin, and Jason S. Scott. 2007. Behavioral Obstacles to the Annuity Market.
    Financial Analysts Journal 63(6): 71–82.
James, Estelle, and Xue Song. 2001. Annuities Markets around the World: Money's
    Worth and Risk Intermediation. Working Paper No. 16. Center for Research on
    Pensions and Welfare Policies, Turin, Italy.
Johnson, Richard W., Leonard E. Burman, and Deborah Kobes. 2004. Annuitized
    Wealth at Older Ages: Evidence from the Health and Retirement Study. Wash-
    ington, DC: Urban Institute.
Kotlikoff, Laurence J., and Avia Spivak. 1981. The Family as an Incomplete Annui-
    ties Market. *Journal of Political Economy* 89: 372–91.
Laibson, David. 1997. Golden Eggs and Hyperbolic Discounting. *Quarterly Journal
    of Economics* 62: 443–77.

Langer, Ellen J. 1975. The Illusion of Control. *Journal of Personality and Social Psychology* 32: 311–28.

Lusardi, Annamaria, and Olivia S. Mitchell. 2007. Baby Boomer Retirement Security: The Roles of Planning, Financial Literacy, and Housing Wealth. *Journal of Monetary Economics* 54: 205–24.

Milevsky, Moshe Arye. 1998. Optimal Asset Allocation towards the End of the Life Cycle: To Annuitize or Not to Annuitize? *Journal of Risk and Insurance* 65: 401–26.

———. 2005. Real Longevity Insurance with a Deductible: Introduction to Advanced-Life Delayed Annuities. *North American Actuarial Journal* 9: 109–22.

Milevsky, Moshe Arye, and Virginia R. Young. 2007. Annuitization and Asset Allocation. *Journal of Economic Dynamics and Control* 31: 3138–77.

Mitchell, Olivia S., James M. Poterba, Mark J. Warshawsky, and Jeffrey R. Brown. 1999. New Evidence on the Money's Worth of Individual Annuities. *American Economic Review* 89: 1299–318.

Modigliani, Franco. 1986. Life Cycle, Individual Thrift and the Wealth of Nations. Nobel Prize acceptance speech. Reprinted in the *American Economic Review* 76: 297–313.

Murtaugh, Christopher, Brenda Spillman, and Mark J. Warshawsky. 2001. In Sickness and in Health: An Annuity Approach to Financing Long-Term Care and Retirement Income. *Journal of Risk and Insurance* 68: 225–54.

National Association of Variable Annuities. 2006. *Annuity Fact Book.* 5th ed. Reston, VA: National Association of Variable Annuities.

Perun, Pamela. 2004. Putting Annuities Back into Savings Plans. Working paper presented at the Society of Actuaries Symposium on Managing Retirement Assets, Las Vegas, April 1.

Poterba, James M., Steven Venti, and David A. Wise. 2008. The Changing Landscape of Pensions in the United States. This volume.

Prudential Financial. 2006. Learning the Two-Step: A New Approach to Asset Allocation for the Retiree. Prudential Financial white paper.

Salisbury, Dallas. 2002. June 20 statement before the committee on Ways and Means, subcommittee on Oversight, United States House of Representatives. Hearing on retirement security and defined benefit pension plans.

Scott, Jason S., John G. Watson, and Wei-Yin Hu. 2006. Efficient Annuitization with Delayed Payout Annuities. Working paper. Financial Engines Inc., Palo Alto, CA.

Sinclair, Sven H., and Kent A. Smetters. 2004. Health Shocks and the Demand for Annuities. Congressional Budget Office Technical Paper Series 2004-09.

Smith, Barbara, and Fiona Stewart. 2008. Learning from the Experience of Organisation for Economic Co-operation and Development Countries: Lessons for Policy, Programs, and Evaluations. This volume.

Social Security Administration. 2007. Fact sheet. Available at http://www.ssa.gov/pressoffice/factsheets/basic-factalt.pdf.

Turra, Cassio M., and Olivia S. Mitchell. 2005. The Impact of Health Status and Out-of-Pocket Medical Expenditures on Annuity Valuation. Research Brief (RB) 2005-079. University of Michigan, Retirement Research Center.

Tversky, Amos, and Daniel Kahneman. 1974. Judgment under Uncertainty: Heuristics and Biases. *Science* 185: 1124–31.

———. 1992. Advances in Prospect Theory: Cumulative Representation of Uncertainty. *Journal of Risk and Uncertainty* 5: 297–323.

Warshawsky, Mark J. 2007. Recent Developments in Life Annuity Markets and Products. Watson Wyatt working paper.

Yaari, Menahem E. 1965. Uncertain Lifetime, Life Insurance, and the Theory of the Consumer. *Review of Economic Studies* 32: 137–50.

PART III

Improving Financial Education and Saving Programs

CHAPTER SEVEN

New Ways to Make People Save: A Social Marketing Approach

Annamaria Lusardi, Punam Anand Keller, and Adam M. Keller

Introduction

There exists a voluminous literature on saving. However, while several studies have examined barriers to saving, few studies have focused on helping people who want to save but do not know how. In this study, we use a social marketing approach to develop a planning aid to help new employees at a not-for-profit institution open and contribute to supplementary retirement pensions. To inform development of the planning aid, we employed different methods—from survey methods to focus groups and in-depth interviews—to "listen" to employees' needs and understand their barriers to saving. Moreover, we targeted specific groups that were less likely to save and contribute to supplementary pensions. Most important, we devised a cost-effective program to facilitate saving and contributions to supplementary pensions. We observed a sharp increase in supplementary retirement accounts after the implementation of our program: the election rate more than tripled in a thirty-day period and doubled in a sixty-day period. While this program was implemented at a single institution, it is suitable for application to a variety of employers and demographic groups.

Literature Review

The literature indicates that several individual characteristics are responsible for saving deficits. Households reporting low saving are disproportionately those with low income and low education (see, among others,
Hubbard, Skinner, and Zeldes 1995). The Retirement Confidence Survey
(2007), which covers a representative sample of U.S. workers, indicates
that, excluding the value of any defined benefit plans and a primary home,
49 percent of all workers (and 68 percent of workers under age 35) had
savings under $25,000, while only 14 percent of all workers had savings
above $250,000. The reason many households have little private wealth
is not because they have large employer pensions. In fact, many households, and particularly those with low income, have low amounts of private
wealth and also have no pensions at all (see Gustman and Steinmeier
1999). There are very wide differences in pension wealth and, again, many
households get close to retirement with very low levels of pension wealth.
Women are a particularly vulnerable group. According to the estimates
of Weir and Willis (2000), the death of a husband often precipitates his
widow's entry into poverty.

When examining the reasons why so many households do not save,
Lusardi (2005) found that a high proportion of older respondents had
not even thought about retirement. This finding is confirmed in another
study by Lusardi and Mitchell (2006) that shows that only one-third of
older respondents have ever tried to calculate how much they need to
save for their retirement. Widespread lack of planning is also evident in
studies about workers' knowledge of Social Security and pensions, two of
the most important components of retirement wealth. As many as half of
older workers do not know or are wrong about the type of pensions they
have (whether defined benefit, defined contribution, or a combination or
the two), and even fewer know how much money they have in their pensions (see Gustman and Steinmeier 2004 and the chapter by Gustman,
Steinmeier, and Tabatabai in this volume). Only a small fraction of workers know about the rules governing their Social Security benefits. As noted
in the Employee Benefit Research Institute report on the 2007 annual
Retirement Confidence Survey, even though it has been twenty-four years
since legislation was passed that increased in increments the normal retirement age for Social Security, and despite eight years of annual mailings
of individual benefit statements from the Social Security Administration,

only 18 percent of workers know the age at which they will be entitled to full Social Security benefits.

Lack of information and knowledge is also present in other important aspects of household financial decision making. For example, according to Campbell (2006) and Bucks and Pence (2006), many mortgage borrowers are confused about the terms of their mortgages. Borrowers with adjustable rate mortgages, in particular, did not know or were incorrect about the amount by which their interest rate could change. Low-income and low-education households were disproportionately more likely to be incorrect about their mortgages and much less likely to refinance their mortgages during a period of falling interest rates (Campbell 2006).

Lusardi and Mitchell (2006, 2007a) have traced lack of planning and low wealth holdings to lack of financial literacy. Many of the respondents to the module on planning and financial literacy they designed for the Health and Retirement Study did not have a grasp of the effects of inflation and the workings of risk diversification. Not only older but also middle-age respondents (51–56 years old) lacked an understanding of basic financial concepts, such as interest compounding, and often failed to succeed in very simple numeric calculations. The chapter by Mandell in this volume also shows that financial literacy is deficient among high school students, and Agarwal, Driscoll, Gabaix, and Laibson (2007) show that financial mistakes seem to be concentrated among the young and old, which are the groups that display the lowest amount of financial literacy.[1]

Given these challenges, employers have resorted to new programs to foster saving and participation in pension plans. Increasingly, employers have relied on automatic enrollment of employees in pension plans. With automatic enrollment, employees have to decide whether or not to *opt out* of pensions rather than decide whether or not to *opt in* to a plan. Moreover, the employer sets a default contribution rate and an asset allocation for every employee. This simple but ingenious scheme has been very successful in achieving very high participation rates (see Madrian and Shea 2001; Choi et al. 2004, 2006). However, automatic enrollment of employees into pensions is not without shortcomings. First, the contribution rate is the same for every type of employee, irrespective of the many differences in needs and economic circumstances we observe among individuals. Second, the contribution rate is often set very low, such as at 2 or 3 percent, and asset allocation refers to conservative assets, such as money market mutual funds or stable value funds.[2] It is not clear that these contributions and asset allocation rules help employees save adequately for their retirement. Moreover, because employees may passively accept this decision, they may not learn how to plan and save for other reasons, such as for their children's education or to support their aging parents.

Most of the surveys covering whole or large sections of the U.S. population result in limited information about the many difficulties households may face in their financial decision-making and their impediments to saving and contributing to pensions. Few surveys go beyond information about demographic and economic characteristics. Moreover, differences in saving behavior are so large that it may be preferable to focus on specific groups of the population and study them in detail.

A Social Marketing Approach

In this study, we deviate from previous work on saving and undertake a new approach that combines methods from both economics and social marketing. A social marketing approach requires several steps: (1) identify the target population, (2) "listen" to that population via multiple data-collection methods to discern barriers to saving, (3) design an offering (planning aid) that overcomes identified barriers, (4) pretest the planning aid within a subset of the target population, (5) modify the planning aid to maximize effectiveness for the target population, and (6) design a customized offering for other segments of the population (figure 7.1). We describe these steps in the next sections.

Target Population

Our first step toward identifying an employee segment at risk because of inadequate saving was to meet with the top administrators and the head of the human resources (HR) department at the institution where we conducted the study. The institution had been discussing changes to the benefit packages offered to employees that would require heightened individual responsibility, particularly concerning health benefits after retirement, and was eager to investigate new programs for their employees. Note that all employees at this institution are covered by a pension. The large majority of employees have a defined contribution pension, but all can contribute to a supplementary pension.

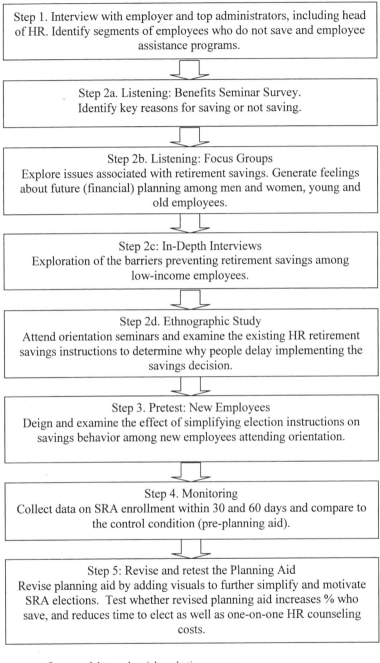

Step 1. Interview with employer and top administrators, including head of HR. Identify segments of employees who do not save and employee assistance programs.

Step 2a. Listening: Benefits Seminar Survey. Identify key reasons for saving or not saving.

Step 2b. Listening: Focus Groups
Explore issues associated with retirement savings. Generate feelings about future (financial) planning among men and women, young and old employees.

Step 2c: In-Depth Interviews
Exploration of the barriers preventing retirement savings among low-income employees.

Step 2d. Ethnographic Study
Attend orientation seminars and examine the existing HR retirement savings instructions to determine why people delay implementing the savings decision.

Step 3. Pretest: New Employees
Deign and examine the effect of simplifying election instructions on savings behavior among new employees attending orientation.

Step 4. Monitoring
Collect data on SRA enrollment within 30 and 60 days and compare to the control condition (pre-planning aid).

Step 5: Revise and retest the Planning Aid
Revise planning aid by adding visuals to further simplify and motivate SRA elections. Test whether revised planning aid increases % who save, and reduces time to elect as well as one-on-one HR counseling costs.

FIGURE 7.1 Sources of data and social marketing process.

All administrators voiced difficulties about how to best serve the needs of the employees. For example, while the institution hosts financial education and information sessions supplied by three pension providers, including one-on-one counseling, only a handful of employees attend these sessions and take advantage of individual counseling. The administrators identified three groups in the employee population that are disproportionately less likely to contribute to the supplementary pensions: employees with low income (less than $35,000), young employees, and employees with short tenures. As in data sets covering other institutions or more representative samples of the U.S. population, these characteristics (income, age, and tenure) are clearly correlated with saving and contributions to pensions (Madrian and Shea 2001).

Together with other researchers, Prochaska identifies five main stages individuals go through for successful self-change (see Prochaska and DiClemente 1983; Prochaska, Norcross, DiClemente 1994). The stages are precontemplation, contemplation, preparation, action, and maintenance. The sixth stage is possible relapse. Compared with precontemplators who resist change and often do not see or deny the problem, contemplators acknowledge they have a problem but are not quite ready to do anything about it (see Block and Keller 1998). Many have indefinite plans to take action in the next six months. Individuals in the preparation stage plan to take action within a definite time frame. A good example would be the familiar, "I'll start saving next month." We selected new employees as our target market. New employees were targeted because they are in the contemplation or preparation stage of decision making.

New employees who attend the orientation meeting that describes their medical and pension benefits were viewed as being in the contemplation or preparation stage because they have to review their employer benefit plan options. Both medical and retirement benefits require action on the part of new employees; they have to select the level of medical benefits desired as well as decide on a financial carrier and how they want to allocate their retirement assets. Thus, new employees were viewed as more motivated to contribute to a pension via a supplementary retirement account than existing employees.

Listening

We used several methods to understand the barriers that prevent employees from opening supplementary retirement accounts (SRAs). As mentioned before, few existing surveys offer detailed information about the many barriers to saving, particularly among specific segments of the population. We overcame this limitation by devising our own survey and collecting information on employee characteristics and barriers to saving. Because short tenures are identified as an important determinant of participation in supplementary pensions, we chose to administer our survey during the orientation program that the institution organizes for new employees. This test site also increased our access to the female employee population since they are more likely to attend the orientation seminar than male employees.

During orientation, employees are asked to attend sessions at the HR office, where they hear explanations of the benefits (health, pension, supplemental pensions, and other) that the institution offers. Asking questions during orientation provided us with an opportunity to listen to employees' needs. Moreover, and in general, orientations are a time when the attention and interest of employees is high; they can provide "teachable moments," making them an ideal time to administer intervention.

In addition to administering the survey, we conducted focus groups, in-depth interviews, and ethnographic studies to gain additional insights into barriers to saving and to better target the groups of employees at this institution least likely to contribute to supplementary pensions.

As expected, the surveyed employees had a disproportionate representation of low-income individuals. The size of the lower income groups (annual salary of less than $35,000) was 48.5 percent and was significantly larger than other income groups. Furthermore, new employees were more likely to be young: 53.9 percent were 35 years old or younger and, again, these age differences are statistically significant. Finally, our sample consisted of a high proportion of women, 57.8 percent. Thus, we present the results for the overall sample, as well as for these different income, age, and gender segments.

The survey questions we focus on here were part of a large set of questions designed to understand the beliefs, attitudes, and saving behavior of participating employees. One hundred sixty-seven surveyed employees were asked to identify the most difficult barriers to their saving decisions. They were presented with seven options: (1) I do not have enough information. (2) There is too much information to process. (3) I do not have enough knowledge about finance/investing. (4) I do not know where to start. (5) I do not have enough income. (6) It is hard to think far away into the future. (7) Other reasons. Respondents were allowed to select multiple barriers (see the sample survey in the appendix).

The percentages that listed each barrier are shown in table 7.1. A sizable portion of respondents indicate a lack of adequate information as a barrier to saving. The fraction of respondents pointing to lack of information increases when looking at subgroups of employees, such as those with low income and the young. Close to a quarter of low-income and young employees cite lack of information, and differences between groups are statistically significant.

Lack of adequate information can have many meanings. In fact, a third of those who chose this response also indicated that, when considering their saving decision, they do not know where to start. Close to 18 percent of the total sample indicated they do not know where to start, and this proportion increases to more than 22 percent when we consider young respondents and those with low income (table 7.1). Differences between groups are statistically significant at the 5 percent level of significance.

Not enough income is the reason cited most often by the employees (43.5 percent) as a barrier to saving. Note that this fraction is high not only among the total sample of new employees but also in all subgroups. However, differences are not statistically significant: both men and women, young and old, state that lack of income is what makes saving difficult. Even among higher income groups, the proportion of employees that cite lack of income as a difficulty remains high and differences are only statistically significant for those in the two highest income groups (corresponding to a salary greater than $75,000).

Lack of knowledge about finance and investing is another response chosen most often by employees (38 percent). As for income, the fraction of those who feel they do not have knowledge of saving and investing re-

TABLE 7.1 **Percentage of employees reporting difficult parts of saving decisions in total sample and across groups**

	Total sample	Female	Male	Young	Old	Low income	High income
Not enough information	15.9	18.3	12.8	22.7	8.0	22.8	9.5
Too much information	12.3	11.8	12.8	11.3	13.3	10.1	14.2
Not enough knowledge	38.0	39.8	35.7	37.5	38.7	40.5	35.7
Do not know where to start	17.8	19.3	15.7	22.7	12.0	22.8	13.1
Not enough income	43.5	46.2	40.0	43.2	44.0	45.6	41.7
Hard to think far into the future	3.7	5.4	1.4	6.8	0.0	5.1	2.4
Others	9.2	11.8	5.7	9.1	9.3	6.3	11.9
No. of observations	163	93	70	88	75	79	84

Source: Author's calculations using data from the survey distributed to new hires.

mains high when we consider subgroups of the population, but differences are not statistically significant.

The "barriers to saving" questions were followed by brief descriptions of hypothetical plans to assess which of two plan characteristics would prompt employees to take immediate saving action or to delay the decision to save. In particular, we tested whether employees were willing to take immediate action to open a new savings account or whether they would prefer to wait for one year. In addition, we varied whether they were required to rely on self-control to save or relinquish control by committing to a plan, such as to walk to central administration at a specific day of every month to make a personal deposit (see Ashraf, Karlan, and Yin 2006; Fujita et al. 2006). These data were used to determine the effect of planning on timing of saving and to determine the optimal amount of plan flexibility.

The key barriers gleaned from the survey were further investigated in separate focus groups of men and women in different age cohorts. The appendix contains sample focus group prompts. As we had difficulty getting low-income employees to participate in the focus groups, we relied on several in-depth interviews to understand their barriers to saving and opening an SRA. The appendix contains sample in-depth interview questions.

Designing the Planning Aid

The barriers identified in the listening stage were used to develop a planning aid for new employees. Research by Gollwitzer and others (Gollwitzer 1999; Gollwitzer and Brandstatter 1997) identifies lack of planning as the main reason individuals do not implement their goals. We identified three key saving barriers from our survey data that we could work with in devising a planning aid: (1) not having enough information and not knowing where to start, (2) not having enough income, and (3) not having enough self-control.[3] The results from the survey are followed by sample anecdotes from the focus groups and in-depth interviews. Implications of the data for the planning aid are discussed after the results for each barrier are identified and illustrated.

THE ROLE OF INFORMATION AND KNOWING WHERE TO START.   The first key saving barrier identified was lack of sufficient information on how to save. Surveyed employees reported that they could not save because there was not enough information. Moreover, several employees indicated they did

TABLE 7.2 **Percentage of female and male employees in two age cohorts reporting not having enough information to save**

	Younger employees, age ≤ 35	Older employees, age > 35
Female	28.3	5.0
Male	14.3	11.4

Source: Authors' calculations.

not know where to start. There were significant differences among employees according to age and income level. While we did not find major differences between men and women, we found a significant interaction between gender and age: women younger than 35 years were significantly more likely than men in the same age range to state they did not have enough information (28.3 percent of women versus 14.3 percent of men). By contrast, older men (older than 35) were more likely than older women to state they did not have enough information (11.4 percent of men versus 5 percent of women), and again differences are statistically significant (see table 7.2). We believe this pattern occurred because older women may give some thought to their retirement before men of a similar age. By contrast, as men age, they realize they do not have the information or ability to start saving. Our focus group results support this premise.[4]

> I retired a little earlier than 63 because my husband was retiring and it was a happy decision because after six years, he had a stroke which stopped us from doing any travel after that, but we had those six years to do some traveling. We spent some time in Greece. We also traveled in this country to see Alaska, Hawaii, and then I got very involved in volunteer work at the Hitchcock as a patient resource volunteer . . . also at the Hopkins Center, St. Thomas Church . . . I have always felt the need to give back to the community where I have lived and at times haven't been able to do community work. I am active; I still play tennis three times a week. I do gardening . . . I am very active in taking care of the house and the yard . . . we downsized the house after retiring. So basically they have been good years. (Focus group: retired female employee)

> I guess so. I have always been aware that I have to prepare for something. . . . My sources of income now that I am retired come from several different sources— one thing goes in jeopardy it isn't all in one basket . . . so it's a combination of little bit here and little bit there—from this employer, then Social Security, and then

I had arranged to have a new lease . . . everything together, then I had investments and then I had put some of it into the new lease . . . so a combination of things worked out for me. I have always disliked being in debt. . . . I never buy anything that I don't have money in the bank for—I avoid running up any credit card debts. One time my husband and I did get into a little difficulty that way but we paid it off as quickly as we could. I don't know if that's a generation thing because it seems now everyone is in debt! (Focus group: retired female employee)

I did feel I had information. Here again, I was always a little bit interested in finance. I was a little interested in the stock market—how it worked and we always bought a few stocks to see how it would come out. We didn't depend on them exactly . . . so my interest was always there. I selected the stocks myself. It was a secure thing for me to get a steady income. By reading and I think the (employer) seminars were good as far as I am concerned. I also thought the information they sent out from time to time was also very good. I have someone who I speak to occasionally but it's not like a professional as such. I was a Rotarian and still am—in that group there is a CPA—I have talked with him a couple of times but not specifically . . . just about some general information. (Focus group: elderly female)

These people think I am crazy . . . if you don't want to retire and want to keep working, it's a choice some people make—I don't know why if it occurred by accident, there's no point telling someone what they should have done—it's all done now. Some choices pan out better than others, if the whole investment system crashed, we would be without any money. (Focus group: elderly male)

Being not quite 50 yet, it still seems a long way away and so I still have in my mind a sort of model . . . age 65 and for some people a little earlier . . . somewhere in your 60s you stop working and you have confidence that you have income to make choices. If you choose to continue working, it's either because it interests you or just to keep yourself in the mainstream but then it's not primarily to earn money—that's the model. You are active but you are not feeling under the gun—you have more or less got your base income settled for the duration. And the duration seems to get longer as people live longer so imagine for 20 years you are going to have a somewhat active, somewhat secure life in this last quarter of your living. (Focus group: elderly male)

Focus groups and in-depth interviews also support the fact that lack of information is an important barrier to saving, particularly among those with low income and the young.

Having more available opportunities to speak to somebody would help. (In-depth interview: low-income male)

I don't have a structured plan at this time. I don't take time out to use the tools I have at my hand. Eric. . . . has done different presentations on planning. I can't say I go to those. I don't have time to use the tools. (In-depth interview: low-income female)

This phone call is useful because it reminds me that I should be thinking about the future and saving for retirement. Really, anything that brings it to people's attention. (In-depth interview: young, low-income male)

I don't really know how to budget all that well so I would love to have information that would tell me how to do so. (In-depth interview: low-income female)

In order to overcome lack of information and not knowing where to start as barriers to saving, we relied on established tactics to reduce task complexity and procrastination (Malcov, Zauberman, and Bettman 2007; Trope and Liberman 2003). Overall, our goal was to simplify the SRA election process by making the planning steps easier and more concrete. Note that the retirement saving information received by employees is provided in the same packet as the health information. Moreover, employees are asked to elect supplementary retirement saving before receiving their first paycheck. It is not clear that many employees know their net salary (net of taxes and all other contributions) prior to receiving their first check. The process for enrolling in the supplemental pension presents several additional complexities: employees have to access a provider Web site(s) to make their investment allocation, *and* they have to be able to complete the enrollment process in twenty minutes. For security reasons, the enrollment process automatically restarts if more than twenty minutes elapse. To be able to complete the enrollment in the allocated time, employees need to have prepared in advance. In developing our planning aid, we focused on providing information on how to enroll and ways to simplify enrollment by dividing the task into small, manageable steps.

THE ROLE OF INCOME.   Income was reported as a key reason for not saving (see table 7.1). While women are more likely to be low-income employees (in our sample 57 percent of female versus 37.1 percent of male employees earn less than $35,000), both women and men state that lack of income is a major barrier to saving. Note again that even higher income respondents have indicated lack of income as a major barrier. Our focus groups and in-depth interviews also show that employees feel they cannot save because they do not have enough income.[5]

> If I made enough money, I would set some aside. But there were times in my life when I didn't have enough money and sometimes no money ... so I think the biggest one is the perception that I don't make enough money, which might not be true because I think you can always set something aside every week. But I think that's an obstacle because it's a perception. (Focus group: female employee)

> We still made money, we were not poor but we were never going to be filthy rich like our college classmates. We planned our lives to live fairly modestly yet we discovered that you could make a heck of a lot more money in stocks than being a professor. Not maybe a fortune but it was better—I guess it might boil down to what you are targeting but if a person can't really afford to save any money, there is no program that will convince them to do that. This is a general problem but if you can save some money ... it just happens sometimes. (Focus group: female employee)

> I think my parents were a very happy couple ... as a family my brother and I, they were very interested in us, they were very happy and we did a lot of fun things together especially in the summer time. My father built a trailer ... a smaller one so we traveled all around the country on summer vacations as a family and we always had such a good time as a family. And money was not ... he wasn't trying to buy things to make us happy ... it was doing a lot of things together and being together that made us happy. (Focus group: male employee)

> Regardless of whether you have a lot of proceeds or assets or earnings, the time factor to me is the most important. If you are relatively less wealthy than your neighbor, but if you have time, you are much better off. So, even buying that Roth IRA when you are 20 is a brilliant thing to do. There are so many more vehicles to implement simple strategies and to get time on your side and so putting aside $2000 when you are 25 and doing that once a year or something like a Roth IRA—it's huge. So, that to me is the key feature I would like to communicate to someone in their 20s or 30s—it's not just a good habit to get into, but it's a huge lever, a mechanical advantage of that is immense. (Focus group: male employee)

We do not have any real savings other than what we have invested or in retirement funds. We are luckily able to make enough to cover the expenses, if the dishwasher breaks and replace it. (In-depth interview: low-income female)

We do not save as much as we should. Expenses are so that by the time we pay for all the things we need, there isn't much left to save. I guess you could say that our monthly expenses hinder our saving yes. (In-depth interview: low-income female)

No we do not save. We are a typical family and spend within our means but don't really keep money aside since we use all our income for daily/weekly expenses. (In-depth interview: low-income male)

In order to overcome the income barrier, we investigated ways to provide information on the minimum and maximum amounts one can put into an SRA. Note that the minimum is very low: $16 per month, which is roughly the cost of one dinner out in the restaurants surrounding the institution. We also specified the maximum because, as the research we reviewed at the beginning of the paper and our discussion with the HR office confirmed, many employees are rather uninformed of the rules governing pensions. The income issue also determined when we could test the effectiveness of the planning aid. Specifically, we had to wait until the second paycheck (after the medical expenses and other costs were deducted) in order for employees to have adequate information about their income to make saving decisions. For this reason we examine the number who elected to enroll in a supplemental pension thirty days after attending the orientation, which is also the time when employees have to elect health benefits, and the number who enroll after sixty days, to allow for the fact that employees had to know their net income to determine how much they could afford to contribute.

THE ROLE OF SELF-CONTROL.   Another key barrier to saving is low self-control. Several studies have pointed to lack of self-control as a critical determinant of saving (see, in particular, Laibson 1997). Moreover, several recent programs on how to stimulate saving have relied on methods that overcome the self-control problem (see Thaler and Benartzi 2004; Ashraf, Karlan, and Yin 2006). Rather than asking employees about their self-control, we devised a series of hypothetical scenarios with different saving plans. A sample plan was as follows:

We would like you to imagine that you are interested in increasing your personal wealth. Your employer tells you about a *hypothetical* program that recommends you contribute $20/month. You will need to put your money in an envelope with your name and deposit it in the central administration office once a month on any day of the month.

You have the choice of contributing immediately or after one year. Which would you prefer?

_____ Now   _____ One year later

Several different variations of this scenario, including reducing flexibility and temptations, were tested to examine how lack of self-control may be responsible for decisions to delay saving. The evidence shows that employees are less likely to procrastinate if they are given a plan rather than left to their own devices.

We used the spirit of this approach to design a planning tool that would not be too reliant on self-control. Our planning aid is a simple step-by-step guideline for how to open an SRA (see figure 7.2). Several features of this aid are worth noting. First, we provide general information on what needs to be done to open an account. Second, we make a fuzzy, abstract goal, such as "I do not want to depend on my kids when I am older," which was voiced by many employees, more specific and concrete (see Locke and Latham 1990). Third, our aid offers details about time commitment, homework, locations, and other information needed in order to open the retirement account. Our findings show that these features increase the likelihood of employees following through on intentions to open an account. Furthermore, our planning aid can be effective because proximal goals are better than distant goals (see Bandura and Schunk 1981). Finally, we focus on the effect of saving rather than of recommending not spending.

Pretest the Planning Aid

We examined the effectiveness of the eight-step plan by comparing the group that received this plan to a control group of new employees who attended employee orientation and received the standard packet but not the eight-step plan. The control period was selected from January 1, 2006, to July 30, 2006.[6] One hundred eighty-three new employees were eligible for the control condition. We compare the SRA election within thirty and sixty days between the control and the treatment group (see table 7.3). The

My Retirement Savings Account

Most people plan on filling out their supplemental retirement form, but feel they don't have the time or information right now. We have outlined **8** simple steps to help you complete the application. It will take between 15 – 30 minutes, from start to finish. It will take less time for you to start to insure your future than it takes you to unload your dishwasher!

1. Select a 30 minute time slot right now to complete the online contribution to your Supplemental Retirement Account (SRA) during the next week. Write down the reserved time slot in your date book or monthly planner.

2. 3 minutes. Check to see if you have the following materials: a) worksheet in your benefits packet √, and b) the name and social security number of a beneficiary √.

3. Select the amount you want to invest for 2006 (minimum: $16/month, maximum: $1,666.67/month), even if you don't know your take-home pay in your first month. The minimum investment is low (price of one dinner out per month) and within the reach of most employees. If you want, you can change this amount at a later date. This voluntary contribution is tax-deferred, you will not pay taxes on it until you withdraw the funds.

4. 5 minutes. Select a carrier. You have 3 options: a) TIAA-CREF, Fidelity, and Calvert. All three offer a variety of funds (stocks, bonds, short-term investments); if you are interested you can get more information on their websites. FYI, if you do not select a carrier, the employer will invest the non-voluntary portion of your funds in a Fidelity Freedom Fund, a fund that automatically changes asset allocation as people age.

5. 5 minutes. Now you are ready to complete your worksheet. Select an uncluttered place with few distractions like the dining table at home or your desk at work. Complete the worksheet even though you may be unsure of some options. You can change the options in the future.

6. Take your completed worksheet to a computer that is available for 20 minutes. If you like, you can use the one in the Human Resources office (address: XXX).

7. 15-20 minutes. Log on to Flex Online and complete your online SRA registration within the 20 assigned minutes. Be sure to click on the investment company (TIAA-CREF, Fidelity, or Calvert) to complete the application. You need to set up your account – otherwise your savings will not reach the carrier.

8. Don't give up! Contact the Benefits Office (tel: XXX) if for any reason you could not complete the online application.

FIGURE 7.2 Eight-step planning tool.

two groups have comparable demographic characteristics. For example, the average age in the control group is 37.4 (standard deviation, 10.5), the proportion of low-income employees is 0.428 (standard deviation, 0.49), and the proportion of women is 0.427 (standard deviation, 0.49). The corresponding figures in the treatment groups are 36.42 (standard deviation, 11.0), 0.48 (standard deviation, 0.50), and 0.57 (standard deviation, 0.49).

TABLE 7.3 **Percentage of new employees electing supplementary retirement before and after the initial planning aid**

	Thirty days after hiring date	Sixty days after hiring dates	Number of observations
Control groups: 2006			
January	9.52	26.19	42
February	8.33	30.56	36
March	4.35	26.09	23
April	7.41	33.33	27
May	7.69	26.92	26
June	3.45	31.03	29
July	10.7	28.6	27
Intervention period 1: 2006			
August:			
August 7 and 14	21.8	43.7	32
August 21 and 28	15.8	52.6	19
September:			
September 5 and 11	20	46.6	30
September 18 and 25	28.6	39.3	28
October:			
October 2 and 9	28.1	50	32
October 16 and 23	16	36	25

Source: Authors' calculations.

TABLE 7.4 **Percentage of new employees electing supplementary retirement before and after the modified planning aid**

Intervention period 2: 2006–7	Thirty days after hiring date	Sixty days after hiring date	Number of observations
December and January:			
December 8 and January 22	32.2	48.4	31
February:			
February 5 and 19	15.6	25	32
March and April:			
March 5 and April 2	35	50	20

Source: Authors' calculations.

Table 7.4 contains the effect of the modified planning aid on enrollment at thirty days and sixty days. With respect to the control group, in which 7.3 percent of employees enrolled in an SRA after thirty days, the percentage of employees who opened an SRA in thirty days tripled (21.7 percent) after being exposed to our intervention. A much higher fraction, 44.7 percent, opened an SRA in sixty days, versus an enrollment of 28.9

percent in the control group after sixty days. Thus, this simple planning aid
was rather effective in inducing employees to enroll in SRAs.

Modify the Planning Aid

Our next step was to redesign the planning aid based on employee feed-
back. Specifically, we simplified the aid by adding pictures depicting each
step. We also changed the format, switching from a flat, single sheet to a
folded brochure that was more convenient to carry (especially for women,
who could put it in their purses). To prevent the online registration from
"blowing up" because the registration was not completed within the allot-
ted twenty-minute time frame, we provided more specific time guidelines
for each step. Moreover, we simplified further the descriptions of the steps,
and we reduced the steps from eight to seven. Finally, we added a picture
of an elderly man and a younger woman exchanging gifts with their family. The picture choice was motivated by the saving challenges faced by
these two subsegments of the target population. Figure 7.3 contains the
revised plan.

Table 7.5 provides a summary of the employees electing SRAs under
the control condition, with the eight-step planning aid, and with the redesigned planning aid (in brochure format) for enrollment at thirty and
sixty days. There was an increase in participation following the addition
of the picture to the brochure (27.6 percent versus 21.7 percent), but, as
expected, the picture was helpful in grabbing attention in the immediate
run (thirty days) but not for the sixty-day period. Thus, providing employees with a plan for how to enroll in pensions was a powerful way to induce
employees to make decisions about their pensions.

TABLE 7.5 **Percentage of employees electing supplementary retirement before and after the original and modified planning aids**

	Thirty days after hire date	Sixty days after hire date	Number of observations
Control group	7.3	28.9	210
Eight-step intervention (1)	21.7	44.7	166
Seven-step/brochure intervention (2)	27.6	41.13	83

Source: Authors' calculations.

Don't give up! Contact the Benefits Office (6-3588) if for any reason you could not complete the online application.

It takes no time to prepare for your lifetime!

Most people plan on electing a supplemental retirement account, but feel they don't have the time or information right now. We have outlined 7 simple steps to help you complete the election process. It will take between 15 – 30 minutes, from start to finish. It will take less time for you to start to insure your future than it takes you to unload your dishwasher!

FIGURE 7.3A Brochure.

Discussion

A cost-effective planning tool significantly motivated employees to take immediate action to save in an SRA. We observed a sharp increase in SRA election for the first intervention compared with a control condition: the

We have outlined 7 simple steps to help you complete the application.

1. Select a 30 minute time slot right now to complete the online contribution to your Supplemental Retirement Account (SRA) during the next week.

2. 3 minutes. Check to see if you have the following materials: a) worksheet in your benefits packet _√ _, and b) the name and social security number of a beneficiary _√ _.

3. Select the amount you want to invest for 2006 (minimum: $16/month, maximum: $1,708.33/ month), even if you don't know your take-home pay in your first month. If you want, you can change this amount at a later date. This voluntary contribution is tax-deferred, you will not pay taxes on it until you withdraw the funds.

4. 5 minutes. Select a carrier. If you do not select a carrier, Dartmouth will invest the non-voluntary portion of your college funds in a Fidelity Freedom Fund, a fund that automatically changes asset allocation as people age.

5. 5 minutes. Now you are ready to complete your worksheet. Complete the worksheet even though you may be unsure of some options. You can change the options in the future.

6. Take your completed worksheet to a computer that is available for 20 minutes. If you like, you can use the one in the Human Resources office at 7 Lebanon Street, Suite 203.

7. 15-20 minutes. Log on to Flex Online and complete your online SRA registration within the 20 assigned minutes. Be sure to click on the investment company (TIAA-CREF, Fidelity, or Calvert) to complete the application. You need to set up your account – otherwise your savings will not reach the carrier.

FIGURE 7.3B Brochure.

election rate more than tripled in the thirty-day period and doubled in the sixty-day period. The second intervention further improved SRA election (from 21.7 percent to 27.6 percent) in the thirty-day period and sustained the lift obtained with the first intervention in the sixty-day period.

Our research provides valuable insights into designing saving programs.

The social marketing approach we employ is atypical for designing saving programs, but it is well suited to deal with the many differences in saving behavior that we observe among individuals. The program relies on motivating employees to overcome barriers to saving. Similar processes can be undertaken to identify barriers and customize programs for different target audiences.

Even though the sample is small and not representative of the population of employees, our eight-step program was effective in changing behavior relating to saving and pensions. Our pretests indicate that addressing the three key barriers related to (1) insufficient information on how to save, (2) the amount of income needed to open a savings account, and (3) control of employees in planning for retirement were effective in significantly increasing savings.

We used a variety of data collection methods to identify saving barriers and to guide development of our planning aid. The survey highlighted the three key barriers and also alerted us as to how these barriers posed greater saving difficulties for young female and older male employees. We also realized the role of insufficient income. Our planning aid highlighted the point that very low amounts are needed to get started and open an account. This can be useful information because many employees, particularly the young, state they do not know where to start. The survey also provided insights into the importance of self-control. Accordingly, our plan sought to confer control to the employee by giving them the planning aid. We use this cost-effective planning aid to remove these key barriers to saving.

Our approach to the problem of self-control is a significant departure from other initiatives that have been undertaken to promote saving and contributions to pension plans. Most of these initiatives rely on automatic enrollment in pension plans (see the review in Benartzi and Thaler 2007). However, contribution rates and asset allocations set by employers hardly match employees' needs. Rather than taking away control, in our approach we conferred control to employees with the help of an implementation plan. We relied on the psychology literature for guidelines on substitutes for low self-control. Gollwitzer (1996, 1999) suggests that specifying ways to implement plans makes individuals more likely to follow through with their intentions. More generally, actions that are integrated into an established routine tend to be performed efficiently.

The planning aid is not a substitute for automatic enrollment. In fact, with small modification, our aid can complement automatic enrollment programs very well. For example, it can keep employees motivated to stay

in pension plans as well as modify their contribution rate and asset allocation to best fit the employees' specific needs. We plan to continue working in this direction and to motivate employees to make plans for their
retirement.

Appendix

Sample Survey

This survey aims to collect information about saving and investment decisions of
employees.

1. Have you ever been to benefits orientations at this or other institutions?
   ☐ Yes   ☐ No

2. Were you previously contributing to an SRA/403(b) plan?
   ☐ Yes   ☐ No   ☐ I do not know

3. What represents the MOST difficult part of your saving decision? Please pick
   ONE below. If the list does not mention it, please explain in the last line.
   a. I feel I do not have enough information.
   b. I feel there is too much information to process.
   c. I do not have enough knowledge about finance/investing.
   d. I do not know where to start.
   e. I do not have enough income.
   f. It is hard to think far away into the future.
   g. Other, please explain _____

4. Which source of information do you use the MOST when making saving or
   investment decisions? Pick the most relevant ONE below or explain in the last
   line.
   a. Family and relatives
   b. Colleagues and friends
   c. Magazines and newspapers
   d. Internet
   e. Financial advisor/banker/CPA/other professional help
   f. Planning books
   g. I do not need to collect information to make saving and investment
      decisions
   h. Other, please explain _____

5. How would you classify yourself, that is, which type of investor are you?
   a. Sophisticated investor, I know a lot about bonds and stocks.

b. Average investor, I know about bonds and stocks.

c. Simple investor, I know a little about bonds and stocks.

d. I know very little or nothing about bonds and stocks.

e. Other, please explain _____

6. What kind of saver do you perceive yourself to be?
   ☐ Low saver   ☐ Average saver   ☐ High saver

7. How important are the following features of your retirement saving plan:

	Not at all				Extremely
1. Flexibility (e.g., can withdraw money)	1	2	3	4	5
2. Structure (e.g., same amount/same time)	1	2	3	4	5
3. Guidance (e.g. how to invest)	1	2	3	4	5
4. Commitment (e.g., a contract to invest)	1	2	3	4	5
5. Control (e.g., choice on whether to save or not)	1	2	3	4	5
6. Certainty (e.g., value of future savings)	1	2	3	4	5
7. Ease of implementation (e.g., scheduled payments)	1	2	3	4	5

Some information about you:

1. How old are you?
   ☐ 20–29   ☐ 30–39   ☐ 40–49   ☐ 50–59   ☐ 60–69
   ☐ Older than 69

2. What sex are you?
   ☐ Male   ☐ Female

3. Marital Status?
   ☐ Single   ☐ Married/no children   ☐ Married/children < 21
   ☐ Married/children > 21   ☐ Divorced/no children
   ☐ Divorced/children < 21   ☐ Divorced/children > 21

4. Are you: ☐ Level I   ☐ Level II   ☐ Other (please explain)

5. How many years have you had full-time employment?
   ☐ < 1 year   ☐ 1–3 years   ☐ 3–6 years   ☐ 6–10 years   ☐ > 10 years

6. Are you a returning employee?
   ☐ Yes   ☐ No

7. Are you a part-time or full-time employee?
   ☐ Full-time   ☐ Part-time

We would like you to imagine that you are interested in increasing your personal wealth. Your employer tells you about a *hypothetical* program that recommends you contribute $20/month. You will need to put your money in an envelope with your name and deposit it in the central administration office once a month on any day of the month.

You have the choice of contributing immediately or after one year. Which would you prefer?

☐ Now   ☐ One year later

How do you feel about your choice:

	Disagree					Agree	
1. I feel confident.	1	2	3	4	5	6	7
2. I feel committed.	1	2	3	4	5	6	7
3. I will need to plan.	1	2	3	4	5	6	7
4. I will lose the opportunity to increase my wealth.	1	2	3	4	5	6	7
5. I don't want to waste time.	1	2	3	4	5	6	7
6. I like this program.	1	2	3	4	5	6	7
7. This program is important.	1	2	3	4	5	6	7
8. The program design is simple.	1	2	3	4	5	6	7
9. I want to get this decision over with.	1	2	3	4	5	6	7
10. I will need self-control to implement this.	1	2	3	4	5	6	7

Thank you.

Focus Group Questions

1. What would you like to do after you retire?
2. Do you think you should plan for the future (in general) or accept things as they happen?
3. What kinds of things should you plan for? Why?
4. What kinds of things are difficult to plan for? Why?
5. Do you think you should plan for retirement saving or accept things as they happen?
6. What obstacles prevent you from planning for retirement?
7. What do you do if you do not know how to plan for retirement?
8. Having a plan does not mean one sticks to it. What types of things make you stick to the plan or not?
9. Where do you get information to help you with retirement saving planning?
10. Does knowledge about investing play a role in your retirement planning decision?
11. How much control over retirement saving do you feel you have?
12. When you think about your retirement savings, how do you feel?
13. Do you think your savings will determine when you retire?
14. Does anyone have a story about someone who did a good job in planning for his or her retirement? Bad job?

15. If you were interested in designing communications to help people to save for retirement, whom else would you speak to?
16. Are there any questions we should have asked but did not?

Thank you.

In-depth Interviews

1. What would you like to do after you retire?
2. Do you like to think about retirement?
3. Tell me about your parents. Are your father and mother retired? (If both dead, then ask if they retired before dying.)
4. Let us discuss retirement planning.
   Which of the following apply to you? Please listen to all four:
   a. I am not doing any planning for retirement.
   b. I have thought about it, but I have not done anything yet.
   c. I have taken some initial steps.
   d. I have been doing retirement planning for the last couple of years or longer.
5. Do you know anyone who has done a really good job or a really bad job in planning for retirement? Can you describe his/her/their story to me?
6. Have you thought at all about medical expenses after retirement?
7. Which sources of information do you use in making your financial decisions?
8. Let us turn now to saving. Does your household save/put money aside?
9. Have you ever tried to change your saving behavior, that is, how much you save?
10. Let us talk about your family situation
    a. What is your current marital status?
    b. Do you have children? (If yes, how many and of which age?)
    c. Do you have aging parents/parents-in-law you have to take care of?
    d. How much control do you feel you have in your family spending patterns?
    e. Would you like to have information, say, on things like how to budget, how to speak to kids about expenses, how to be a role model?
11. If you could pick two things that can help you in your financial decision making, what would they be?

Notes

We would like to thank Nava Ashraf, Robert Cialdini, Petia Petrova, and participants of the conference "Improving the Effectiveness of Financial Education and Saving Programs," Cambridge, Massachusetts, and the Transformative Consumer Research Conference, Tuck School of Business, Hanover, New Hampshire, for suggestions and comments. We would also like to thank the staff of the HR office of the not-for-profit institution we worked with for their help and support. Financial support from Dartmouth College and the National Endowment for Financial Education is gratefully acknowledged. Anna Dev provided able research assistance.

1. For a review of the evidence on financial illiteracy, see Lusardi and Mitchell (2007b) and Hogarth (2006).

2. For example, a survey by the Profit Sharing/401(k) Council of America in 2001 reports that 76 percent of automatic enrollment companies have either a 2 or 3 percent default contribution rate and that 66 percent of automatic enrollment companies have a stable value or money market default fund. See Choi et al. (2004) for a discussion of these findings.

3. Many employees have indicated they lack knowledge in saving and investment. We face many limitations in considering this barrier in our intervention because of regulatory constraints. While the Pension Protection Act of 2006 has relaxed some of these constraints, an intervention in this field requires some coordination with the pension providers. We plan to pursue this venue in future work.

4. In order to hear from many different age groups and to obtain insights from those who are facing retirement, we also invited a group of retired employees from the institution to attend one focus group.

5. More anecdotal evidence of the importance of income was provided by one of the administrative support staff members who volunteered to explain that her family does not save because the combined income of her household is only enough to cover all monthly expenses. Such views about saving were also voiced in the in-depth interviews.

6. Because online registration started for the first time in the fall 2005, we chose the period January until June to allow for some adjustment to a new system.

References

Agarwal, S., J. Driscoll, X. Gabaix, and D. Laibson. 2007. The Age of Reason: Financial Decisions over the Lifecycle. Mimeo. Harvard University, Cambridge, MA.

Ashraf, N., D. Karlan, and W. Yin. 2006. Tying Odysseus to the Mast: Evidence from a Commitment Savings Product in the Philippines. *Quarterly Journal of Economics* 121: 635–72.

Bandura, A., and D. H. Schunk. 1981. Cultivating Competence, Self-efficacy, and Intrinsic Interest through Proximal Self-motivation. *Journal of Personality and Social Psychology* 41: 586–98.

Benartzi, S., and R. Thaler. 2007. Heuristics and Biases in Retirement Savings Behavior. *Journal of Economic Perspective* 21: 81–104.

Block, L. G., and P. Keller. 1998. Beyond Protection Motivation: An Integrative Theory of Health Appeals. *Journal of Applied Social Psychology* 28: 1584–606.

Bucks, B., and K. Pence. 2006. Do Homeowners Know Their House Values and Mortgage Terms? Working paper. Federal Reserve Board of Governors.

Campbell, J. Y. 2006. Household Finance. *Journal of Finance* 61: 1553–604.

Choi, J., D. Laibson, B. Madrian, and A. Metrick. 2004. For Better or for Worse: Default Effects and 401(k) Savings Behavior. In *Perspective in the Economics of Aging,* edited by D. Wise, 81–121. Chicago: University of Chicago Press.

———. 2006. Saving for Retirement on the Path of Least Resistance. In *Behavioral Public Finance: Toward a New Agenda,* edited by E. McCaffrey and J. Slemrod, 304–51. New York: Russell Sage Foundation.

Employee Benefits Research Institute (EBRI). 2007. Retirement Confidence Survey. Washington, DC: EBRI.

Fujita K., Y. Trope, N. Liberman, and M. Levin-Sagi. 2006. Construal Levels and Self-Control. *Journal of Personality and Social Psychology* 90: 351–67.

Gollwitzer, P. 1996. The Volitional Benefits of Planning. In *The Psychology of Action: Linking Cognition and Motivation to Behavior,* edited by J. Bargh and P. Gollwitzer, 287–312. New York: Guilford Press.

———. 1999. Implementation Intentions: Strong Effects of Simple Plans. *American Psychologist* 54: 493–503.

Gollwitzer, P., and Veronika Brandstatter. 1997. Implementation Intentions and Effective Goal Pursuit. *Journal of Personality and Social Psychology* 73: 186–99.

Gustman, A., and T. Steinmeier. 1999. Effects of Pensions on Savings: Analysis with Data from the Health and Retirement Study. *Carnegie-Rochester Conference Series on Public Policy* 50: 271–324.

———.2004. What People Don't Know about Their Pensions and Social Security. In *Private Pensions and Public Policies,* edited by W. Gale, J. Shoven and M. Warshawsky, 57–125. Washington, DC: Brookings Institution.

Gustman, A., T. S. Steinmeier, and N. Tabatabai. 2008. Do Workers Know about Their Pension Plan Type? Comparing Workers' and Employers' Pension Information. This volume.

Hogarth, J. 2006. Financial Education and Economic Development. Paper presented at the international conference, "Improving Financial Literacy," which was hosted by the Russian G8 presidency in cooperation with the Organisation for Economic Co-operation and Development, November 29–30.

Hubbard, G., J. Skinner, and S. Zeldes. 1995. Precautionary Saving and Social Insurance. *Journal of Political Economy* 103: 360–99.

Keller, P., and A. Lusardi. 2006. Message Design to Change Behavior. Working paper. Dartmouth College, Hanover, NH.

Laibson, D. 1997. Golden Eggs and Hyperbolic Discounting. *Quarterly Journal of Economics* 112: 443–78.

Locke, E. A., and G. P. Latham. 1990. Work Motivation and Satisfaction: Light at the End of the Tunnel. *Psychological Science* 1: 240–46.

Lusardi, A. 2005. Planning and Saving for Retirement. Working paper. Dartmouth College, Hanover, NH.

Lusardi, A., and O. S. Mitchell. 2006. Financial Literacy and Planning: Implications for Retirement Wellbeing. Working paper. Pension Research Council, Wharton School, University of Pennsylvania, Philadelphia.

———. 2007a. Baby Boomer Retirement Security: The Role of Planning, Financial Literacy, and Housing Wealth. *Journal of Monetary Economics* 54: 205–24.

———. 2007b. Financial Literacy and Retirement Preparedness: Evidence and Implications for Financial Education. *Business Economics* 42: 35–44.

Madrian, B., and D. Shea. 2001. The Power of Suggestion: Inertia in 401(k) Participation and Savings Behavior. *Quarterly Journal of Economics* 116: 1149–525.

Malcov, S., G. Zauberman, and J. R. Bettman. 2007. Its in the Mindset! The Effect of Processing Specificity on Consumer Impatience. Mimeo. University of Pennsylvania, Philadelphia.

Mandell, L. 2008. Financial Education in High School. This volume.

Prochaska, J. O., and C. C. DiClemente. 1983. Stages and Processes of Self-Change of Smoking: Toward an Integrative Model of Change. *Journal of Consulting and Clinical Psychology* 51: 390–95.

Prochaska, J. O., J. C. Norcross, and C. C. DiClemente. 1994. *Changing for Good.* New York: William Morrow.

Thaler, R., and S. Benartzi. 2004. Save More Tomorrow: Using Behavioral Economics to Increase Employee Saving. *Journal of Political Economy* 112: 164–87.

Trope Y., and N. Liberman. 2003. Temporal Construal. *Psychological Review* 110: 403–21.

Weir, D., and R. Willis. 2000. Prospect for Widow Poverty. In *Forecasting Retirement Needs and Retirement Wealth,* edited by O. Mitchell, P. Hammond, and A. Rappaport, 208–34. Philadelphia: University of Pennsylvania Press.

CHAPTER EIGHT

Adjusting Retirement Goals and Saving Behavior: The Role of Financial Education

Robert L. Clark and Madeleine d'Ambrosio

Introduction

The adult life of most Americans is divided into years primarily devoted to work followed by a period mostly devoid of paid employment. Although the United States is a wealthy country, the majority of Americans generate most of their lifetime income through paid employment. Thus, individuals usually must develop, either implicitly or explicitly, a lifetime plan based on two retirement goals: the age at which they will stop working[1] and the desired level of income during retirement. In order to achieve their goals, individuals must refrain from consuming all of their income while working and save a portion of their earnings for retirement. Workers must decide how to invest these retirement funds based on their risk preferences. Annual saving and the compounded return on investments create a fund that—in addition to the federal government's Social Security program and employer-provided pensions—can be used to finance consumption in retirement.

To develop an adequate lifetime plan for working, retiring, consuming, and saving, an individual needs a basic understanding of financial mathematics, the risk-return characteristics of financial markets, and the economic environment in which they work. There is considerable evidence that many Americans do not possess the essential knowledge needed to develop realistic retirement goals and that they are not familiar with the saving and investment strategies necessary to attain retirement goals.[2] Some financial relationships are easily understood:

- The lower the desired retirement age, the more one must save each year to attain any specific retirement income goal.
- The higher the desired income replacement rate in retirement, the more one must save each year to be able to retire at any specific age.

However, other aspects of financial mathematics are more complex and more difficult to implement. For example,

- How much does one need to save each year to be able to retire at the desired retirement age with the desired income replacement rate?
- How should funds be invested in order to achieve one's retirement goals, given the uncertainty of returns on various types of investments?

A fundamental economic principle is that greater income in retirement is not free; in most cases higher consumption in retirement is financed through lower consumption (increased saving) during the working years. Thus, in developing retirement saving strategies, individuals must weigh the lower satisfaction of reduced consumption today against the gain in lifetime well-being associated with greater consumption during retirement. In developing personal saving plans, individuals should also consider sources of retirement income, such as Social Security and pension plans, that are earned through their employment or the government. Virtually all American workers are covered by Social Security, which promises a lifetime retirement benefit adjusted for inflation. However, for most households, Social Security benefits will be far less than the desired level of retirement income.

Given the low level of saving by many American households, the need for enhanced financial education to improve financial literacy is an important policy issue. Employer-sponsored education programs can play a major role in disseminating specific information to increase knowledge related to retirement planning, and government regulations and programs may be needed to stimulate broad-based financial education programs. It seems obvious that increased financial awareness would be beneficial to workers planning for retirement; however, it is important that financial literacy programs be monitored, evaluated, and continually improved.

This chapter reviews one such effort to evaluate the impact of financial education seminars on retirement income goals and retirement saving behavior. Our findings indicate that participants in financial education seminars respond to the knowledge and information gained by altering their retirement goals and changing their saving behavior. The results suggest that if more employers offered such programs to their workers, Americans would be better able to achieve their retirement goals.

Planning for Retirement

Two of the most important life-cycle choices facing workers are the age at which they plan to retire and the level of desired retirement income, which lead to a calculation of the amount of saving needed to achieve those goals. Economists have attempted to examine these choices by developing life-cycle models of time and resource allocation. These models assume that individuals decide on the optimal path of earnings and saving to achieve their desired level of consumption in each period of their expected life. Consumption and saving decisions determine income in retirement. For the most part, economic models assume that individuals have adequate information to make these important decisions. But contrary to the assumptions imbedded in these models, most workers do not have the level of financial literacy required to make good decisions. Using their existing knowledge, they may develop retirement goals and establish saving plans that are inconsistent, that is, a low expected retirement age accompanied by a high desired income replacement rate while saving relatively little each month. With incomplete or inadequate financial knowledge, workers may be confident that they will achieve the impossible dream of high consumption in retirement with little saving. Of course, the result will be unanticipated, and unpleasant, surprises at retirement (see Bernheim, Skinner, and Weinberg 2001).

Inadequate financial knowledge may cause workers to start saving too late in life or to save too little to realize their stated retirement goals. As a result, they are unlikely to achieve an optimal balance between consumption while working and consumption in retirement. In addition, a lack of information concerning the risk-return distribution of various investments might lead them to misallocate retirement portfolios.[3] If this situation is true for most workers, then financial education programs should enhance lifetime well-being and improve the retirement saving process. Of course, financial education may also confirm that some individuals are on track to achieve their retirement goals and therefore need no changes in plans or saving behavior or that others are wealthier than they think and have saved more than necessary to achieve their retirement goals, enabling them to save less or retire earlier.

Recognizing a lack of financial knowledge, some employers now offer financial education programs for their employees[4] that consist of written or online explanations of company retirement saving options and general information about financial markets and economic conditions. Other firms provide funds for their employees to hire outside financial advisors to help develop financial plans for retirement. There is some evidence that these employer-provided retirement-planning programs are effective in enhancing the financial knowledge of workers and improving their retirement planning.

In a series of studies, Bernheim and his colleagues found that workers employed by firms that offered financial education programs had higher participation rates in and contribution rates to 401(k) plans compared with workers at firms that did not provide these types of programs. Their analysis indicated that seminars were the most effective type of communication.[5] Clark and Schieber (1998) examined employment records from nineteen firms covering over 40,000 employees and concluded that company-provided written communications played a significant role in increasing the probability of participating in a 401(k) plan and in increasing the contribution rate to that plan.[6] Madrian and Shea (2001) examined the administrative records of a large employer and reported that employees who attended a financial education seminar tended to have increased rates of participation in the 401(k) plan and greater diversification in their retirement plan portfolios.[7]

Arguments that question the positive responses to financial education on retirement saving behavior have been made. A few authors assert that changes in retirement saving behavior after attending education events are the product of social effects, differential incentives to participate in these events, and any other motivational influences.[8] While there is some disagreement about whether financial education programs are cost-effective methods of enhancing retirement saving, most studies find that financial education does encourage workers to reassess their retirement goals and consider altering their saving behavior.[9]

Learning the Basics of Financial Planning

Individuals can increase their understanding of financial mathematics and markets using a variety of methods and types of programs. Financial education events that can be used to augment financial literacy include seminars, face-to-face sessions with financial planners, printed materials and lessons, and online programs. Currently, many employers offer one or more of these programs to their employees (see Arnone 2002), however, there seems to be very little evaluation of the usefulness of these programs. It is important that we learn more about the successes and failures of different aspects of financial education programs so that they can be improved upon and to insure that employers and employees receive maximum benefit for the dollars allocated to these programs. Over a three-year period, we participated in a research program with the objective of assessing the impact of financial education seminars on the retirement goals and saving behavior of workers employed at colleges and universities throughout the United States. The results of this project are summarized below, and the implications of the findings are considered.

Teachers Insurance and Annuity Association, College Retirement Equities Fund (TIAA-CREF) Financial Education Seminars

TIAA-CREF conducts financial education seminars at institutions where they offer basic or supplemental pension plans. The seminars are open to all employees of these institutions, participation is voluntary, and no incentives are provided to encourage employees to attend the meetings other than invitations sent by local TIAA-CREF consultants or human resources personnel of the institution. Attendees may be covered by a defined contribution plan offered by TIAA-CREF or another pension provider or be participants in a defined benefit plan. The objective of the seminars is to provide financial information that can assist individuals in the retirement-planning process.

The seminars are self-contained, meaning that a person attending only one meeting would learn about a broad range of issues that might affect their retirement saving behavior. Of course, individuals are free to attend multiple seminars throughout their careers. Seminar leaders discuss retirement goals, such as the amount of money needed in retirement to maintain a desired standard of living and the relationship between the age of retirement and the annual amount of saving needed to achieve the retirement income goal. Seminar leaders also examine the risk-return characteristics of alternative investments.

The evaluation of the effectiveness of these seminars was limited to examining responses of individuals to participation in a single financial education seminar.[10] The analysis is based on information obtained in three surveys.[11] Participants completed the first survey prior to the start of the seminar. The second survey was completed at the end of the seminar, before participants left the room, and the third survey was sent to participants several months later. Clearly, attendees should not be considered a random sample of the population of employees at these institutions. To generate baseline information on retirement goals and saving behavior, survey 1 requested that participants provide the age at which they hope to retire and the annual retirement income (as a percentage of their final working year's earnings) that they hope to have in retirement. They were also asked to indicate the likelihood that they would achieve these goals, how strongly committed they were to achieving these goals, and whether other priorities might make it difficult for the goals to be achieved. In addition, the first survey gathered baseline demographic and economic information on the respondents.

After participants completed the first survey, the seminar began, and discussion continued for approximately one hour. At the conclusion of the seminar, participants were asked to complete the second survey. Respondents were asked whether they had changed their retirement-age goals or revised the desired level of retirement income. The second survey asked whether individuals intended to change their allocation of invested funds in their basic defined contribution plans. Respondents with a supplemental retirement plan were asked if they expected to increase their contributions or change their investment allocations. Individuals who did not currently contribute to a supplemental plan were asked if they planned to establish one.

The research project was based on seminars conducted from March 2001 to May 2002. A total of thirty-six seminars at twenty-four institutions, along with twenty-four community-based seminars in eight different locations, are included in the analysis. A total of 633 usable responses in which participants completed both survey 1 and survey 2 were obtained.[12] The responses to the first two surveys are described below. We received 110 completed questionnaires for the third survey, or only 17 percent of the 633 respondents who completed the first two surveys.[13]

The average age of participants was 54, and women accounted for slightly more than half of the attendees. Of the attendees, 11 percent held only a high school degree, 25 percent a college degree, 31 percent a master's degree, 27 percent a doctoral degree, and 6 percent a professional degree. Mean annual household income was $102,677, with $63,823 coming from the respondents' earnings. Respondents indicated on the first survey that they were, on average, 72 percent sure that they would achieve their retirement-age goal and 63 percent certain that they would achieve their retirement income goal.

Altering Retirement Plans

After the seminars, respondents who completed survey 2 reported on the chances that they would alter their retirement goals and saving behavior.[14] The responses of individuals obviously depended on how they rated the quality of the information they had received. In general, participants thought they had been part of a high-quality financial education program, with 36 percent rating the seminar "excellent" and 54 percent "good." In response to the statement that the seminar had improved their understanding of the need for retirement saving, 32 percent strongly agreed with the statement and 58 percent agreed with the statement.[15]

During the seminar, participants may have acquired new information concerning how much money is needed to maintain consumption in retirement, the basic mathematics of retirement saving, and the risk-return characteristics of investment alternatives. On the basis of this new information, participants could be expected to reconsider their retirement plans and possibly alter their saving behavior. A comparison of retirement goals after the seminar to those stated prior to the seminar indicates how participants adjusted their retirement goals on the basis of the new information. Many respondents also indicated that they expected to change their saving behavior in the future. Participants might also have learned more about the mathematics of retirement saving, thus gaining a more realistic assessment of the amount of retirement income that they will have based on their current saving rates. This new information could result in respondents deciding to increase or decrease their contributions to retirement plans. Finally, participants may have obtained a better understanding of the risk associated with various types of financial instruments, inflation, and longevity. These new data might lead them to alter the investment allocations in their retirement accounts.

A small percentage of respondents changed their desired retirement age, while more than a quarter of participants altered their retirement income goal. The patterns of changes in desired retirement age are shown in tables 8.1 and 8.2. After the seminar, 7.4 percent of the sample reported having increased their retirement-age goal by an average of 3.5 years, and 4.3 percent of respondents reported reducing their expected retirement age by an average of 4.1 years. As one might expect, a larger proportion of people with relatively low initial desired retirement ages intended to increase them. For example, 15.1 percent of participants who initially set a retirement-age goal younger than age 60 indicated plans for a later retirement-age goal after the seminar. The average increase was 4.3 years. In contrast, less than 2 percent of those with an initial expected retirement age greater than age 65 indicated an older retirement age after the seminar. The tendency to lower retirement ages was greatest for participants whose preseminar retirement-age goal was 65. On average they lowered their age goals by 4.8 years.

In a series of papers concerning the survey results, we examined the impact of seminar participation on retirement goals and expectations of change in saving behavior. Empirical analysis indicates that compared with older seminar participants, respondents under age 45 were less likely to increase their desired retirement ages. Individuals without advanced degrees were more likely to increase their target ages of retirement while secretarial, clerical, and maintenance workers were more likely to lower their retirement ages (see Clark et al. 2006).

There was a much greater tendency to adjust retirement income goals than age goals (see table 8.2). A little more than 20 percent of the re-

TABLE 8.1 **Changes in retirement age goals**

Change	All respondents	< 60	60–64	65	65+
Sample percentage		10.9	39.5	27.7	21.8
No change, %	88.3	81.1	88.4	85.7	95.3
Age goal	63.7	56.1	61.4	65.0	69.6
Raise age goal, %:	7.4	15.1	8.7	6.8	1.9
New age goal	64.9	59.6	64.6	68.7	69.5
Amount of increase	3.5	4.3	3.2	3.7	2.0
Lower age goal, %:	4.3	3.8	2.9	7.5	2.8
New age goal	60.0	57.0	56.8	60.2	68.0
Amount of decrease	−4.1	−1.0	−5.0	−4.8	−2.0

Note: All data are means.
Source: Clark and d'Ambrosio (2003).

TABLE 8.2 **Changes in retirement income goals**

Change	All respondents	Less than 65	65–85	Over 85
Sample percentage		18.8	47.1	34.1
No change, %	71.4	59.8	66.4	84.5
Income goal	83	53.4	76.6	101.1
Raise income goal, %:	20.4	36.8	25.3	4.8
New income goal	85.1	70.9	89.1	111.3
Amount of increase	14.8	18.9	12.3	17.5
Lower income goal, %:	8.3	3.4	8.3	10.7
New income goal	69.9	40.0	63.5	81.9
Amount of decrease	−15.2	−19.0	−13.3	−16.7

Note: All data are means.
Source: Clark and d'Ambrosio (2003).

spondents increased their income goals, while another 8 percent decreased their income objectives. Of the participants who set low income goals (that is, less than 65 percent of their final year's earnings) before the seminar, almost 37 percent revised their retirement income goals upward by an average of 19 percentage points. This suggests that based on the information provided in the seminar these individuals determined that their goals were too low and that they should attempt to achieve a higher standard of retirement consumption. About one-fourth of those participants with preseminar goals of between 65 and 85 percent of their final working year's earnings revised their retirement income goals upward, while less than 5 percent of those with initial targets greater than 85 percent revised their income goals upward. People with higher initial retirement income goals were more likely to revise their income targets downward.

Results from the empirical analysis estimating changes in income goals as a function of individual and household characteristics showed significant differences across participants. Women were 6 percentage points more likely to increase their income goals compared with men. Participants with higher earnings were also more likely to raise their desired income replacement rates. Compared with respondents with annual earnings of $50,000, those earning $60,000 were 1 percentage point more likely to raise their income goals after the seminar. Individuals with defined benefit plans were 12 percent more likely to raise their income goals (see Clark et al. 2006).

In response to the seminars, the proportion of participants who changed either of their retirement goals was relatively small. This low probability of amending the retirement targets could be due to any of the following reasons:

- After learning that their goals were inconsistent with their saving behavior, participants had a strong desire to maintain these goals accompanied by a willingness to alter saving behavior in order to achieve them.
- Because the seminar had provided participants with reassurance that they were on track to attain their retirement goals, there was no need to change their goals.
- The participants achieved limited learning during the seminar and thus did not conclude that their goals and saving behavior were inconsistent.

However, the respondents who changed their target retirement ages and retirement income goals made rather large changes, suggesting that these participants did in fact increase their financial literacy and proceeded to act on their new knowledge.

Altering Saving and Investment Behavior

On the basis of the information provided in the seminar, respondents indicated that they expected to be more active in planning for their retirement. Forty percent of those who did not have a supplemental pension plan said that they planned to establish one with their employer. Among respondents who currently had supplemental plans, 37 percent stated that they would increase their contributions to them.[16] Empirical analysis showed that respondents in basic defined benefit pension plans had a 30-percentage-point higher chance of wanting to start a new supplemental plan compared with respondents in basic defined contribution plans. Compared with younger individuals, respondents aged 60 and older were less likely by 21 percentage points to want to start a new plan. Women were more likely than men by 22 percentage points to say that they planned to start a new supplemental plan, and married respondents had a 28-percentage-point higher likelihood than others of wanting to start a new plan. As one might expect, individuals with longer term saving horizons were more likely to report that they now wanted to establish a pension plan.

Compared with respondents between the ages of 45 and 59, individuals aged 44 or younger were more likely by 17 percentage points to report that they were going to increase their contributions to their supplemental plan after participating in the seminar. Those 60 and older were less likely by 29 percentage points to indicate a desire to increase their contributions. Once again, women had a greater likelihood of wanting to increase contributions than men did; the difference was 14 percentage points. Secretarial, clerical, and maintenance workers had a much higher desire to increase contributions after the seminar than did faculty, other professionals, and administrators.

In addition to changing their saving rate, some individuals expressed a desire to alter their choices of assets in their pension accounts. Ten percent of all respondents with basic defined contribution plans indicated that they intended to increase the proportion of their investment in equities, while 20 percent reported that they intended to increase their investment in bonds. In addition, one-third of those with supplemental retirement plans intended to change their investment allocations in those plans. The change in investment allocations is estimated separately for balances in the basic retirement plan and in supplemental plans. Women were more likely to plan to alter their investment allocations, especially in their supplemental plans, than men were. Married individuals had a higher probability of changing their investment patterns in both plan types. Those with basic defined benefit plans were less likely to indicate a desire to reallocate their investment allocations in their supplemental plans. Respondents attending a financial seminar for the first time were more likely, after the seminar, to plan to reallocate their investments.

Several other interesting relationships were found based on risk preferences and the past use of financial advisors by those attending the conference. Individuals who reported favoring conservative or moderate levels of investment risk were more likely to· enter the seminar with a lower retirement-age goal. After the seminar, these individuals who did not already have a supplemental retirement plan were less likely to say that they were going to establish one compared with individuals who were more willing to take investment risks. However, among individuals who already had a supplemental plan, those favoring conservative to moderate risk in their investments were more likely to report that they were going to increase their annual contributions to these plans.

Participants who had previously worked with a financial advisor entered the seminar with lower retirement-age goals. In addition, they were more likely to reduce their desired age of retirement after the seminar. Such a reaction could signal that these individuals had accumulated sufficient wealth to meet or exceed their stated goals. Those individuals who had consulted a financial advisor but did not have a supplemental retirement plan were less likely to state that they would establish such a plan after the seminar compared with individuals who had not worked with an advisor (perhaps indicting that they already had a well-established wealth accumulation plan and did not think they needed to open a supplemental retirement plan).

In survey 2, immediately following the seminar, respondents provided information on their desire to change their saving behavior. Of course, desire and intent do not always produce action. Survey 3, sent approximately three months after the seminar, assessed whether seminar participants actually changed their behavior in the months following the seminar.

At the time of the seminar, half of the respondents reported that they did not have a supplemental retirement plan. Of these, 41 percent had indicated that in response to the seminar they planned to establish a supplemental plan. Of the individuals who returned the third survey and who had indicated that they planned to open a new account, 25 percent had actually established a new plan and 63 percent stated that they still intended to open a new supplemental plan. Of those who did not initially have a supplemental plan and who did not express a desire to establish such a plan, 72 percent reported that they had not yet and still did not plan to open a plan, while 22 percent now indicated that they intended to establish a supplemental plan.

Among those who had preexisting supplemental plans, 37 percent had expressed a desire to increase future contributions. Of the respondents who completed the final survey, 42 percent had increased contributions. In contrast, 30 percent of those who stated that they were not going to increase contributions had actually increased their contributions to the supplemental plan. These findings indicate that there was limited follow-through on the plans developed during the seminar. The lack of change in saving behavior could be due to changed circumstances in the months following the seminar, insufficient time to complete the desired adjustments, or inertia, which characterizes many of us.

Gender Differences

The preseminar survey revealed that female participants had different retirement goals and different levels of retirement saving, as was also shown in the chapter by Lusardi, Keller, and Keller in this volume. Furthermore, statistical analysis showed that women were more likely to alter goals and behavior after the seminar.[17] Prior to the seminar, women had a slightly lower expected retirement age and a lower desired income replacement rate compared with male respondents. Before participating in the seminar, women also had less confidence in their abilities to attain their retirement goals. On a scale of one to ten, women indicated that they had a 6.7 confidence level in being able to retire at the desired age but only a 5.7 confidence level in their ability to achieve the retirement income goal. In comparison, the men had a confidence level of 7.7 on their retirement-age goal and a confidence level of 7.0 on achieving the retirement income goal.

After the financial education seminar, 16 percent of female respondents modified their expected age of retirement, while only 6 percent of male respondents reported a change in their desired retirement ages. Women were twice as likely to increase their expected retirement age than to lower it, while men were split almost equally between those that raised and those that lowered their retirement-age goal. Among women, many of those who had initially hoped to retire before age 65 raised their expected retirement age after learning more about financial markets and the saving process. Almost one-quarter of women who had initially indicated a desired retirement age of less than 60 raised this target after the seminar, and the increase was by an average of more than four years. Regardless of their initial retirement goal, relatively few men altered their expected retirement age.

In response to the new knowledge obtained in the seminar, women were also much more likely to alter their retirement income goal. Approximately 35 percent of female respondents changed their income target compared with only 20 percent of male respondents. Almost three-quarters of women who modified their goal raised their desired income replacement rate. Almost half of women who had initially reported a desired replacement rate of less than 65 percent of final earnings raised their retirement income goal. Similarly, men with relatively low retirement income goals were more likely to increase their desired replacement rate after the seminar.

Female respondents had much lower account balances in their retirement plans than did men. Building on the new information provided in the seminar, women were much more likely to have stated an intent to increase their retirement saving and alter their investment choices. Among respondents without a supplemental retirement plan, 48 percent of the women but only 33 percent of the men indicated that they would establish such a plan in the future. Of those who already had a supplemental plan, 53 percent of women compared with only 33 percent of men were planning on increasing their annual contributions. Women were also more likely to report that they were going to alter their investment choices in both basic and supplemental pension plans.[18]

Australian Survey Findings

Throughout our research project, we attempted to interest several large employers in partnering with us to develop an evaluation of their existing or planned financial education programs. To date, we have developed an international partnership to study the responses to financial education programs. After reviewing the findings reported above, the leaders of Uni-Super Management Pty. Ltd. decided to replicate our research methodology in Australia.[19] UniSuper is a pension provider in Australia with $15 billion (Australian) in assets. The mission of UniSuper is to provide the staff and families of all Australian universities and related organizations with a high standard of financial and superannuation services to enable them to achieve security in retirement. UniSuper also has a history of offering financial education seminars to its members. After several conversations with UniSuper chief executive officer Ann Byrne and executive manager of marketing and business development Paul Murphy concerning their research interests, we gave them permission to use the three surveys discussed above in a project to evaluate the effectiveness of Uni-Super's seminars.

After revising the surveys to better fit the Australian context, Byrne and Murphy integrated the surveys into a total of nineteen seminars held at Australian universities between April and June 2005. They obtained a sample of 961 respondents. In comparison with the sample in the TIAA-CREF data, the Australian sample had the same proportion of women and an equal proportion of persons attending the first seminar; however, the Australian respondents were younger by about eight years. The average retirement-age goal of these respondents was 60, and the retirement income goal was 68 percent of preretirement income. In comparison, the TIAA-CREF respondents had a higher retirement-age goal (64 years) and a higher income replacement goal (80 percent). The Australians indicated that they were more conservative investors than their U.S. counterparts; however, similar to the U.S. sample, Australian women tended to be more conservative investors than men.

Following the seminar, respondents reported changes in their retirement goals. The average desired retirement age increased by one year. This rather small change was the result of substantial changes in this goal by 25 percent of the sample, with 19 percent increasing the desired retirement age by an average of 5 years and 6 percent reducing their retirement age by 4 years. Half of the respondents reported that they had changed their retirement income goal, with 31 percent lowering their goal and 19 percent increasing their retirement objective. Byrne and Murphy also found that about one-third of the respondents indicated an intention to change their retirement saving rate, and following the seminar, 38 percent of those who had never made voluntary contributions to a retirement plan reported that they would begin to make such contributions.

Approximately 38 percent of the respondents to the first two surveys also completed a third survey approximately three months after the seminar. Comparing the actions reported in the final survey to intentions stated at the end of the seminar, Byrne and Murphy found that the lack of follow-through observed in the TIAA-CREF respondents was also exhibited by the Australians. Only about one-quarter of those who had stated that they would begin making or increasing contributions to retirement plans had actually done so by the time of the third survey. Thus, both the American and the Australian respondents seem to be exhibiting the very human trait of inertia.

Implications for Financial Education and Plan Sponsors

This project shows that financial education can cause workers to reconsider their retirement goals and alter their saving behavior. Discovering that they have based their desired retirement-age and income goals on inadequate saving behavior can lead to the development of more realistic retirement goals and to changing their saving for retirement. Importantly, individuals with low desired retirement ages often increased their expected retirement ages based on the information provided, while those with low retirement income goals also tended to raise their income target to a level more consistent with having a retirement income similar to their net income while working.

Many participants stated that they intended to alter their saving behavior by opening new retirement savings plans and increasing contributions to existing plans. Presumably, they are considering making these changes to increase the likelihood that they achieve their retirement goals. Frequently, plans to alter retirement savings were not immediately executed. This lack of follow-through suggests that it would be useful if arrangements were made so that participants in financial education programs could open new supplemental plans or alter contribution rates at the conclusion of educational programs. The ability to make on-site changes in their savings plans at the end of a seminar would tend to reduce the forces of inertia and procrastination. The addition of postseminar communications and encouragement could also increase the likelihood that participants will adopt their new retirement plans.

The results of this study are interesting and have direct policy implications for plan sponsors and workers. The analysis indicates that financial education matters. Quality educational programs encourage workers to reassess their retirement goals, to make more realistic plans, and to change their behavior in order to achieve their objectives. Follow-through on plans made during a seminar remains problematic, and introducing methods for immediate action would be a useful addition to educational programs. Finally, the research shows the importance of evaluating financial education programs and the need to modify these programs to maximize their benefits.

Knowing that on-the-job financial education programs can be effective in improving retirement planning is only part of the solution. Several important questions still remain. First, we need to know more about why some companies offer these types of plans and others do not. A survey by Ernst & Young (2004) indicates that many employers are concerned about the potential liability associated with providing this type of benefit to their employees. While the Pension Protection Act addresses some of these issues, firms may still be awaiting a clear statement of safe harbors for financial education programs. Second, financial education programs come in many shapes, and a better understanding of the costs and benefits of alternative programs might lead firms to conclude that some programs are more cost-effective than others, and, thus, they might be more interested in offering them. Third, the government could consider whether financial education should be required of those companies that offer pension plans.

The lack of financial literacy has also led to movements to automate the retirement saving process. Automatic enrollment in 401(k) plans, increasing contribution rates, default into life-cycle funds, and reliance on managed accounts are just some of the methods being considered and adopted by firms to increase the retirement saving of their employees, as discussed in previous chapters.[20] However, most of these innovations are voluntary, and contribution rates are often set at minimum levels. Thus, the need for more extensive financial education is not eliminated by the implementation of these policies.

Can companies offering financial education programs increase interest in and attendance at company-provided financial education programs? Because it may be easier for some workers to take time off during the workday to attend a program, companies could consider methods of providing equal access to programs. Tailoring information and programs to individuals[21] or types of workers may be more effective than offering general programs. Companies should consider programs specially aimed at low-income workers, women, minorities, or specific work units. Small monetary incentives or prizes for attending financial education programs might also increase participation and lead to more significant changes in retirement planning.

Notes

The research described in this paper was conducted as part of a grant from the TIAA-CREF Institute and in collaboration with Ann McDermed and Kshama Sawant. We would like to thank and acknowledge the TIAA-CREF consultants who administered the surveys as part of regularly scheduled retirement seminars. We would also like to thank Gary Engelhardt for providing many useful suggestions and comments.

1. Increasingly, retirement is not an all-or-none decision. Instead, many Americans are now transitioning into retirement through phased retirement programs in their career jobs or by moving from a career job to a bridge job before retiring completely. This period of partial retirement adds a new dimension to the lifetime planning process in which the individual continues to have some earnings but those earnings must be augmented by retirement savings to prevent a sharp decline in consumption.

2. For evidence on financial illiteracy and the incidence of financial education programs, see Smith and Stewart (this volume); Hilgert and Hogarth (2002); Hilgert, Hogarth, and Beverly (2003); National Council on Economic Education (2005).

3. For example, Bernheim (1998) presents evidence that questions whether the typical household has enough financial literacy to make appropriate saving decisions in its pension plans.

4. Arnone (2002) estimates that 40 percent of employers with more than 1,000 employees offer some type of educational program; however, he believes that only half of these companies provide a high-quality educational program. He defines such a program as "an employer-paid program available throughout the year during working hours and including both education that is custom tailored to the employer's specific benefit plans and counseling that is individualized to each employee" (Arnone 2002, 36). It is his assessment that most of the 42 million participants in 401(k) plans are, in effect, "on their own" as they plan for retirement.

5. These results are found in Bayer, Bernheim, and Scholz (1996) and Bernheim and Garrett (2003).

6. See Clark and Schieber (1998) for a discussion of these findings.

7. See Madrian and Shea (2001) for a more extensive discussion of these results.

8. Duflo and Saez (2003, 2004) provide a more negative assessment of the positive impact of learning from an education event.

9. For a comprehensive review of the literature assessing the influence of financial education on retirement saving behavior, see the review article by Lusardi (2004).

10. Some of the participants previously had engaged in other forms of financial education or had attended previous seminars. Participation in multiple seminars or other forms of educational events has been found to have positive effects on participation rates in 401(k) plans (Bayer, Bernheim, and Scholz 1996). Prior financial education activities were used as control variables in this analysis to account for this effect.

11. Clark and d'Ambrosio (2002) provide a more detailed description of the seminars and the surveys.

12. In total, 2,157 people attended part or all of these seminars, and 725 individuals completed some parts of the surveys, a response rate of 34 percent. The sample included in the analysis has 633 usable surveys in which participants completed both survey 1 and survey 2. It is important to recognize that some individuals arrived after the seminar had begun and were not included in the surveys. Some participants who had completed the first survey left the seminar early and did not complete the second survey. The basic economic and demographic characteristics of those responding to the final survey were similar to all of those who completed survey 1 and survey 2.

13. The decline in the number of respondents can be attributed to several factors, including the following: (1) not all respondents provided a contact address, so they could not be sent survey 3, (2) some incorrect addresses were given or individuals had moved, and (3) some simply did not want to provide the additional information requested.

14. This discussion of the research findings from this project draws heavily on Clark and d'Ambrosio (2003) and Clark et al. (2004, 2006).

15. Respondents also indicated that they now had a greater chance of achieving their retirement-age goal and their retirement income goal.

16. After completion of the seminar, 29 percent of the respondents stated that they planned to open new individual retirement accounts (IRAs) or increase their contributions to an existing IRA.

17. This section draws heavily on Clark and d'Ambrosio (2003) and Clark et al. (2004).

18. Statistical tests, reported by Clark et al. (2004), confirm that there are sig-

nificant differences in how men and women responded to the financial education seminars.

19. This section reviews the findings reported by Byrne and Murphy (2006).

20. For discussions of some of these issues and policies, see Mottola and Utkus (this volume) and Viceira (this volume).

21. A report by Ernst & Young (2004) concludes that "When programs include personalized assistance . . . the impact on employee behavior is significantly greater than in traditional or general programs."

References

Arnone, William. 2002. Financial Planning for Employees Post-Enron. *Benefits Quarterly* Fourth Quarter: 35–41.

Bayer, Patrick, Douglas Bernheim, and Karl Scholz. 1996. The Effects of Financial Education in the Workplace: Evidence from a Survey of Employers. Unpublished paper. Stanford University, Stanford, CA.

Bernheim, Douglas. 1998. Financial Illiteracy, Education, and Retirement Savings. In *Living with Defined Contribution Plans,* edited by Olivia Mitchell and Sylvester Schieber, 38–68. Philadelphia: University of Pennsylvania Press.

Bernheim, Douglas, and Daniel Garrett. 2003. The Effects of Financial Education in the Workplace: Evidence from a Survey of Households. *Journal of Public Economics* 87: 1487–519.

Bernheim, Douglas, Jonathan Skinner, and Steven Weinberg. 2001. What Accounts for the Variation in Retirement Wealth among U.S. Households? *American Economic Review* 91: 832–57.

Byrne, Ann, and Paul Murphy. 2006. Does Financial Education Influence Retirement Savings. Paper presented to Conference of Major Superannuation Funds CMSF 06—Striking the Balance, Queensland, Australia.

Clark, Robert, and Madeleine d'Ambrosio. 2002. Saving for Retirement: The Role of Financial Education. Working Paper No. 4-070102-A. TIAA-CREF Institute, July. Published online in *Retirement Implications of Demographic Family Change Symposium,* Society of Actuaries. http://www.soa.org/library/ monographs/retirement_systems/m-rs02-2_tableof contents.html.

———. 2003. Ignorance Is Not Bliss: The Importance of Finance Education. *Research Dialogue* no. 78, TIAA-CREF Institute.

Clark, Robert, Madeleine d'Ambrosio, Ann McDermed, and Kshama Sawant. 2004. Sex Differences, Financial Education, and Retirement Goals. In *Pension Design and Structure,* edited by Olivia Mitchell and Stephen Utkus, 185–206. Oxford: Oxford University Press.

———. 2006. Retirement Plans and Saving Decisions: The Role of Information and Education. *Journal of Pension Economics and Finance* 5: 45–67.

Clark, Robert, and Sylvester Schieber. 1998. Factors Affecting Participation Rates and Contribution Levels in 401(k) Plans. In *Living with Defined Contribution Plans,* edited by Olivia Mitchell and Sylvester Schieber, 69–97. Philadelphia: University of Pennsylvania Press.

Duflo, Esther, and Emmanuel Saez. 2003. The Role of Information and Social Interactions in Retirement Plan Decisions: Evidence from a Randomized Experiment. *Quarterly Journal of Economics* 118: 815–42.

———. 2004. Implications of Pension Plan Features, Information, and Social Interactions for Retirement Saving Decisions. In *Pension Design and Structure: New Lessons from Behavioral Finance,* edited by Olivia S. Mitchell and Stephen Utkus, 137–53. Oxford: Oxford University Press.

Ernst & Young. 2004. *The Role that Financial Education Programs Play in Influencing Participant Behavior in 401(k) Plans.* Ernst & Young LLP Human Capital Practice.

Hilgert, Marianne, and Jeanne Hogarth. 2002. Financial Knowledge, Experience and Learning Preferences: Preliminary Results from a New Survey on Financial Literacy. *Consumer Interest Annual* 48: 1–7.

Hilgert, Marianne, Jeanne Hogarth, and Sondra Beverly. 2003. Household Financial Management: The Connection between Knowledge and Behavior. *Federal Reserve Bulletin* 89: 309–22.

Lusardi, Annamaria. 2004. Savings and the Effectiveness of Financial Education. In *Pension Design and Structure: New Lessons from Behavioral Finance,* edited by Olivia S. Mitchell and Stephen Utkus, 157–84. Oxford: Oxford University Press.

Madrian, Brigitte, and Dennis Shea. 2001. Preaching to the Converted and Converting Those Taught: Financial Education in the Workplace. Unpublished paper. University of Chicago, Chicago, IL.

Mottola, Gary R., and Stephen P. Utkus. 2008. Red, Yellow, and Green: Measuring the Quality of 401(k) Portfolio Choices. This volume.

National Council on Economic Education. 2005. What American Teens and Adults Know about Economics. Washington, DC.

Smith, Barbara, and Fiona Stewart. 2008. Learning from the Experience of Organisation for Economic Co-operation and Development Countries: Lessons for Policy, Programs, and Evaluations. This volume.

Viceira, Luis M. 2008. Life-Cycle Funds. This volume.

CHAPTER NINE

Financial Education in High School

Lewis Mandell

Introduction

Financial literacy generally refers to the ability of consumers to make financial decisions in their own best short- and long-term interests. There is general agreement that many, if not most, American consumers could benefit by being more financially literate. This need has been driven home most recently by low (even negative) rates of personal savings as well as by the high rates of default on adjustable-rate, subprime mortgages.

A number of factors have contributed to the increased need for financial literacy. These include the proliferation and increased complexity of financial products as well as the increased unwillingness of employers to assume liability for the future welfare of their workers, who have therefore had to assume greater responsibility for their own financial well-being.

While few of these trends or issues are in dispute, effective remedies appear to be in short supply. A logical starting point would appear to be the teaching of personal finance in high school. Students completing high school are on the verge of adulthood and many have made or are making important financial decisions, such as the choice of credit cards, auto insurance, and student loans. The recent turmoil in the student loan market appears to suggest that many young people had little or no understanding of the contracts they undertook and may have been misled by those whom they trusted.

Equally important is the fact that high school is the last opportunity society has to mandate education for students. Few college-age students opt to take courses in personal finance, even when those courses are available, and many students do not attend college at all.

Since the 1997–98 academic year, the Jump$tart Coalition for Personal Financial Literacy has run large-scale, national, pencil-and-paper surveys of high school seniors every other year to measure financial literacy. A total of 16,128 have participated in the five surveys to date.[1] Scores on the standard, thirty-one-question, age-appropriate, multiple-choice (four possible answers) exam have never exceeded 60 percent and, since 2000, have tended to hover just above 50 percent. Making matters worse is the finding that full-semester high school classes devoted to teaching personal finance or money management are *not* helpful in raising financial literacy scores.

Since financial literacy has been shown to be positively related to self-beneficial financial behavior, the ineffectiveness of high school classes in boosting financial literacy questions the current relevance of the well-known finding by Bernheim, Garrett, and Maki (2001) that such classes are related to increased saving in middle age and simultaneously questions the efficacy of the current push to mandate the teaching of financial literacy to all students.

Attempts to mandate financial education are numerous. For example, the recent report of the National Association of State Boards of Education (NASBE) Commission on Financial and Investor Literacy recommends that states "consider financial literacy and investor education as a basic feature of K–12 education" (see NASBE 2006). In 2004, according to the National Council on Economic Education (NCEE), thirty-eight states had personal finance standards or guidelines, twenty-one required these standards to be implemented, eight states required a course with personal finance content, seven states required students to take a personal finance course, and nine states tested personal finance knowledge (see NCEE 2005).

This paper reviews the existing literature on the effectiveness of high school education in personal finance or money management in raising levels of financial literacy and/or self-beneficial financial behavior. It also examines, for the first time, the relatively small number of high school seniors who *are* financially literate in order to learn how they differ from their non–financially literate counterparts and to see the extent to which educational intervention at the high school level is likely to be effective in enhancing the proportion of students who are financially literate. It finds that financially literate high school seniors are disproportionately white, male, and the children of well-educated parents, indicating the existence of hard-to-change cultural variables that may predispose select youngsters toward a mastery of their own finances.

The Importance of Financial Literacy

The deregulation of the U.S. financial services industry, which began in earnest in the 1970s, eliminated interest rate ceilings on both debt and as-set products and lowered barriers to entry for new types of vendors. The concomitant increase in consumer discretionary income and advances in financial engineering have created a proliferation of financial products that are seemingly capable of meeting the complex needs of every con-sumer. There is a question, however, as to the ability of consumers to un-derstand and choose, from among these complex product offerings, those that are in their own short- and long-run best interests. The recent collapse of the subprime mortgage market is being seen as a combination of lack of understanding by many borrowers of the dangers of taking on loans with temporarily low "teaser rates," the inability or unwillingness of mortgage lenders and brokers to "educate" these customers, and the eagerness of the bond markets to absorb these loans as collateral for debt instruments with enhanced returns.

The inability of consumers to make self-beneficial decisions has many policy implications:

- Human and nonhuman capital may be suboptimally deployed.
- Consumer debt levels could exacerbate economic cycles.
- If the ability of consumers to make self-beneficial decisions is correlated with income or wealth, the inequality in the distribution of overall "consumer wel-fare" (a product of resources and the ability to utilize those resources) will be further exacerbated.
- Saving for retirement could be inadequate, creating huge fiscal and social prob-lems in the future.
- Financial product–enhanced consumption could weaken the value of the dollar, resulting in future inflation.

For many of these reasons, the Federal Reserve has begun to focus on the importance of financial education and understanding ("literacy") in the functioning of the financial markets (for example, see Morton 2005; Greenspan 2003, 2005; and Hilgert, Hogarth, and Beverly 2003).

For more than a decade, surveys have demonstrated that American youth and adults do not possess the basic knowledge needed to make good financial choices (see Chen and Volpe 1998; Volpe, Chen, and Liu 2006 for reviews). A 2001 Harris poll found that only 8 percent of college seniors believed that they were "very knowledgeable" about investing and financial planning, while about half that believed they were "not very" or "not at all" knowledgeable. This lack of basic financial literacy has been shown to result in poor financial decision making. Citing a Nellie May report, Murray (2000) states that 25 percent of undergraduate college students have four or more credit cards and about 10 percent carry outstanding balances of between $3,000 and $7,000.

Garman, Leech, and Grable (1996) and Joo and Grable (2000) have found that poor financial decisions can hurt productivity in the workplace. Volpe, Chen, and Liu (2006) surveyed corporate benefit administrators who identified basic personal finance as a critical area in which employee knowledge is deficient and recommended educational programs that focus on improving knowledge of basic personal finance.

Lusardi and Mitchell (2006) used the 2004 U.S. Health and Retirement Study (HRS) to test the basic financial knowledge of adults over the age of 50. They developed questions related to an understanding of interest compounding, the effects of inflation, and risk diversification and found that financial illiteracy is widespread and particularly severe among females, the elderly, and those without much education. These results were particularly surprising since most respondents over age 50 have had experience with bank accounts and credit cards and have taken out at least one mortgage.

A study by the Organisation for Economic Co-operation and Development (2005) and the work by Lusardi and Mitchell (2007) review the evidence on financial literacy across countries and show that financial illiteracy is common in many other developed countries, including European countries, Australia, Japan, and Korea. These findings are not unlike those of Christelis, Jappelli, and Padula (2006), who use microdata from European countries that are similar to the HRS data from the United States and find that most respondents in Europe score low on financial literacy scales.

Financial Literacy and Financial Behavior

Financial literacy does appear to be positively related to self-beneficial financial behavior. For example, Hilgert, Hogarth, and Beverly (2003) formed a "financial practices index" based upon self-benefiting behavior in cash-flow management, credit management, saving, and investment practices. When they compared the results of this index with scores on a financial literacy quiz, they found a positive relation between financial literacy scores and financial practices index scores. Their results suggest that financial knowledge is related to self-beneficial financial practices.

Van Rooij, Lusardi, and Alessie (2007) found in a study of Dutch adults that those with low financial literacy are more likely than others to rely on friends and family for financial advice and are less likely to invest in stocks. Using the 2006 Jump$tart survey, Mandell (2006a) found that high school seniors who never bounced checks or who balanced their checkbooks had substantially higher financial literacy scores than others with checking accounts.

Financial Education and Behavior

While financial behavior seems to be positively affected by financial literacy, the effects of financial education on financial behavior are less certain. Bernheim, Garrett, and Maki (2001) found that those who took a financial management course in high school tended in middle age to save a higher proportion of their incomes than others. On the other hand, Mandell (2006b) found little positive impact of a well-regarded high school personal finance course on objective, post–high school financial behavior from one to five years after taking such a course and also found that self-beneficial behavior did *not* improve with increased age and presumably greater experience.[2]

Danes (2004) measured changes in subjectively reported financial behavior[3] immediately after and three months after high school student exposure to the part-semester personal finance curriculum supplied to teachers by the National Endowment for Financial Education (NEFE). She reported positive change. By contrast, a multivariate analysis based on data from the 2006 Jump$tart survey regarding high school seniors who had bounced a check finds that while financial literacy scores, race, and aspiration are significant determinants of such non-self-beneficial behavior, financial management education has no effect.

It is useful to note that high school programs designed to change or modify behavior in other important areas have been no more successful than those related to financial literacy. For example, a meta-analysis by DiCenso et al. (2002) found that educational interventions designed to reduce unwanted pregnancies among adolescents did not delay initiation of sexual intercourse among young women or young men or reduce pregnancy rates among young women.

Studies of adult behavior modification education also produce results with mixed outcomes. The efficacy of retirement education through retirement seminars has been studied by a number of scholars with mixed results. Bayer, Bernheim, and Scholz (1996) found that employer retirement seminars increased both participation in and contributions to voluntary savings plans. Lusardi and Mitchell (2007) found that retirement seminars have a positive wealth effect, but mainly for those with less wealth or education. Duflo and Saez (2003) found retirement seminars to have a positive effect on participation in retirement plans but also found the increase in contributions to be negligible. Choi et al. (2006) and Madrian and Shea (2001) found participants in retirement seminars to have much better intentions than follow-through.

Outside of retirement planning, Elliehausen, Lundquist, and Staten (2007) found that credit counseling tended to improve borrowing behavior and improve creditworthiness. Hirad and Zorn (2001) found that prepurchase counseling programs for those about to buy a home decrease delinquency rates.

Determinants of Young Adult Financial Literacy

Demographics

Table 9.1 summarizes the results of the five Jump$tart surveys by various demographic and aspiration variables. Only recently have students from families with higher incomes (income greater than $80,000) tended to do better than others on the exam, making the relationship between mean financial literacy scores increase with income. In the first two surveys (1997 and 2000), students from families in the $40,000–$79,999 income range did *better* than students in the top family income range. We attributed it to the

notion that students from more affluent homes did not have to be as financially literate as their less-affluent counterparts since they were almost
universally college bound and would probably be insulated from most financial responsibilities for at least four more years. While we have no hard
data to explain why students from the highest income families suddenly
appear more financially literate than others, it may be the result of a higher
level of awareness of the importance of financial literacy by these wealthier and better-educated families. In any event, whenever financial literacy
scores are regressed on family income and a number of other explanatory
variables, income shows no significant relationship to financial literacy.

There is also a strong and monotonic relationship between financial
literacy scores and parents' education. The average score in 2006, if neither
parent completed high school, was 44.5 percent. This increased to 55.6
percent for those who had at least one parent who completed college. In
addition, while less than half of 1 percent of those whose parents had less
than a high school education scored a C or better on the exam (at least
75 percent of correct answers), 10.1 percent of those with parents in the
highest education category did this well.

The surveys have found little difference in financial literacy by gender.
In 2006, males did marginally better than females (52.6 percent versus 52.3
percent) as they did in 2000 and 2004. However, in two of the five surveys
(1997 and 2002), females did slightly better than males. As we will see later
in this chapter, gender equality in financial literacy breaks down when we
focus on those who are truly financially literate.

Differences in financial literacy appear to be more closely related to
race than to any other demographic variable. White students have consistently outperformed all others, while African Americans and Native
Americans have tended to do least well. The difference of approximately
ten points in financial literacy scores between whites and African Americans represents close to a 20 percent differential and underscores one
important but little noticed cause of racial inequality. Since racial groups
with fewer financial resources are shown by the Jump$tart surveys to have
lower financial literacy, overall economic well-being, which may be viewed
as a product of financial resources and financial literacy, is more poorly
distributed than either component.

Students from the Midwest region of the United States did best on the
exam, with a mean score of 54.2 percent. Those from the South did the
least well, with a mean score of 49.9 percent.

TABLE 9.1 **Test results by various factors**

	1997 Mean score	2000 Mean score	2002 Mean score	2004 Mean score	2006 Mean score	2006 Proportion of students	2006 Grade C or better	2006 Percent failing
	57.3	51.9	50.2	52.3	52.4	100	6.9	62.0
A. Demographics								
Parents' income:								
<$20,000	55.2	46.3	45.7	49.5	48.5	8.0	2.9	74.2
$20,000–$39,999	58.2	52.0	50.7	51.3	50.8	17.0	5.6	67.3
$40,000–$79,999	59.6	57.2	52.3	54.1	53.7	29.1	8.1	57.5
$80,000+	59.0	55.0	52.7	55.9	55.6	27.0	10.5	52.0
Highest level of parents' education:								
Neither finished high school	51.4	47.0	43.7	44.6	44.5	6.4	0.4	82.7
Completed high school	57.1	49.7	47.5	51.5	50.6	24.6	4.5	66.7
Some college	55.8	53.8	51.7	52.6	51.8	21.0	6.4	63.2
College grad or more	59.3	55.1	53.5	55.4	55.6	43.7	10.1	53.4
Sex:								
Female	57.9	51.6	50.7	52.2	52.3	53.1	4.9	62.6
Male	56.9	52.2	49.8	52.4	52.6	46.6	9.3	60.8
Race:								
White	60.9	54.5	53.7	55.5	55.0	71.3	8.9	54.6
African-American	50.4	47.0	42.1	44.0	44.7	10.1	1.6	79.8
Hispanic American	55.1	45.3	44.8	48.3	46.8	8.6	2.0	79.6
Asian-American	55.8	53.5	50.6	48.3	49.4	4.4	2.2	71.9
Native American	48.8	38.6	45.5	46.7	44.1	1.5	5.1	86.6

B. Aspirations

	C1	C2	C3	C4	C5	C6	C7	C8
Educational plans:								
No further education	43.8	39.7	32.2	41.9	37.9	2.0	2.7	91.5
Two-year or junior college	53.8	43.3	46.4	48.0	47.5	14.7	1.7	76.6
Four-year college	60.0	54.5	53.5	55.0	54.9	70.9	8.8	55.3
Planned occupation:								
Manual work	45.5	38.7	39.4	40.0	41.0	2.7	1.4	87.9
Skilled trade	55.7	43.6	45.7	47.1	47.8	6.2	4.0	71.4
Service worker	54.4	41.3	43.3	49.0	49.5	10.6	5.6	67.4
Professional worker	59.6	55.0	53.1	55.2	54.9	50.3	8.9	54.9
Expected full-time income:								
< $15,000	47.4	40.6	39.0	45.1	42.5	2.8	1.4	82.2
$15,000–$19,999	53.3	41.7	46.6	48.8	46.4	6.1	2.4	78.8
$20,000–$29,999	58.5	53.4	50.3	51.3	51.6	13.5	5.7	63.7
$30,000+	59.5	54.4	52.6	53.8	53.9	20.4	6.9	58.8
$40,000+[a]	NA	NA	NA	54.1	54.1	41.4	9.3	57.5

C. Education classes in high school

	C1	C2	C3	C4	C5	C6	C7	C8
Entire course, money management/ personal finance	51.4		48.2	53.5	51.6	16.7	6.8	62.4
Portion of course, money management/ personal finance	52.9		49.8	52.7	53.4	29.3	7.3	59.7
Entire course, economics	51.0		49.8	53.0	53.2	38.1	7.8	59.9
Portion course, economics	52.1		51.1	53.2	53.0	27.4	7.9	60.0
Stock market game in class	55.1		52.4	55.8	55.0	27.7	10.0	55.0

Note: Data are percentages. NA = not available.
[a] The $40,000+ bracket was added in 2004.

Aspirations

Students were asked about their educational plans and occupational aspirations as well as about the full-time income they anticipated making from their first job. The results are shown in table 9.1B. Jump$tart surveys have found consistently that students who expect to attend four-year colleges and those who intend to become professionals tend to do much better than others in financial literacy. Those who expect to become professional workers also display much higher scores, as do those who expect to earn high incomes in the future: the relationship between scores and expected full-time income is monotonically increasing.

Money Management Education

Table 9.1C summarizes results from the four surveys (2000–2006) that have included a question about courses related to financial literacy that the student may have taken. In three of the surveys, students who took a full-semester course in money management or personal finance actually had slightly *lower* mean financial literacy scores than all students. In 2006, for example, the 16.7 percent of high school seniors who reported having had an entire course in money management or personal finance scored an average of 51.6 percent on the exam, in contrast to the average score of all students of 52.4 percent. While the differences are not large enough to support a statistical conclusion that students who have had such a course are *less* financially literate than those who have not, there is no evidence to show that courses in money management or personal finance, as they are now taught, improve the financial literacy of their students.

Evaluations of part-semester high school programs in financial literacy that used pre- and post-tests have reported positive impact in both financial knowledge and financial behavior. Danes, Huddleston-Casas, and Boyce (1999) evaluated the NEFE's High School Financial Planning program, which could be taught in as little as two weeks or in as long as a semester, and found increases in knowledge and savings rates. Thus far, however, the names of specific part-semester programs have not been included in the Jump$tart surveys, so the relative effectiveness of these programs has not yet been determined.

Teachers and Schools

The finding that high school classes in financial management or personal finance are ineffective in raising levels of financial literacy elicited a number of hypotheses to explain this phenomenon. The first was that students who opted to take such classes were less likely to be academically talented and college bound. This was disproved by 2002 Jump$tart data showing no differences in the proportions of college-bound and non-college-bound students taking such a class.

A second hypothesis was that teachers of financial management or personal finance were not very well trained to teach in this area. However, a survey of participating schools conducted as part of the 2004 Jump$tart survey found that teachers who taught full-time courses in money management or personal finance tended to be well educated in the area and experienced. More than 90 percent of schools used the same teachers to teach these full-semester courses year after year, two-thirds of whom had a graduate degree in business, consumer economics, or related fields. Nearly all of these teachers were shown to have had at least an undergraduate degree in the appropriate field.

A third hypothesis was that many students took the course as an elective rather than as a required course and did so because it was structured to be easier than required courses and, consequently, did not study the material with equivalent rigor. In fact, students who took a *required* course in money management or personal finance did better than all other students (54.2 percent compared with 52.3 percent) on the financial literacy test, perhaps because required courses are taken more seriously. However, just 6 percent of all U.S. high school students were required to take such a course in 2002.

It was surprising to learn that students who took a course in personal finance or money management were primarily freshmen, sophomores, and juniors rather than seniors, who could presumably gain the most from it. In fact, the course was taken primarily by seniors in just 21.6 percent of the schools. This may lower Jump$tart scores for two reasons: low levels of recollection by the time students take the test in their senior year and the lack of relevance of courses taught to younger students who make few personal finance decisions of much consequence.

Stock Market Games

The stock market game is the only school-based educational program that is consistently related to higher financial literacy scores. Starting with the 2000 Jump$tart survey, when it was first measured, students who play a stock market game in class do 3–4 percentage points better than all students. On a mean score base just above 50 percent, this translates to a 6–8 percent increase in financial literacy. Although reasons for the success of this activity are not clearly known, playing such an interactive game appears to stimulate general interest in personal finance. The 2006 survey shows that students who played a stock market game in class outscored the average in every subject category, not just in areas related to saving and investments.

Motivation to Be Financially Literate

The possibility exists that courses in money management do not improve financial literacy because students do not realize how important this material is to their futures. To test this hypothesis, the 2006 Jump$tart survey added three new questions to see how young adults felt about three issues: the importance of one's own actions in avoiding financial distress; the degree of discomfort caused by the financial inability to pay one's bills; and the perceived difficulty of retiring without a pension (other than Social Security) or savings.

Regarding the first motivational issue, slightly more than two-thirds of the students attributed personal financial difficulty to the consumer's personal actions, largely to too much credit (28.9 percent) and no financial plan (also 28.9 percent). An additional 9.4 percent felt that the greatest cause of financial difficulty was not enough savings. Only 8.6 percent of students felt that "bad luck" was the greatest cause of financial difficulty, and those students had average financial literacy scores of 49.1 percent. The best financial literacy scores were recorded by students who felt that the greatest cause of financial distress was buying too much on credit (56 percent) and by those who felt that it was due to the lack of a financial plan (53.8 percent).

The second motivational issue relates to the fact that some young people may not regard financial distress and insolvency as being particularly bad or unusual in today's society. Perhaps most of their acquaintances are from overconsuming, credit-dependent families who have adjusted to unpaid bills and calls from credit collectors. However, only 8.5 percent of students feel that it is not so bad if you cannot pay your bills, and these tend to have very low financial literacy scores, averaging just 43.2 percent.

The third motivational issue was addressed by asking students how hard it is to survive in retirement entirely on Social Security. Just 7.5 percent responded that one could "live well" on Social Security, and their financial literacy scores were very low, just 39.9 percent. About half the students felt that it was tough to retire on Social Security alone, and they had the highest scores (56 percent). The remaining 42.3 percent of students took the middle view that people could get by on Social Security if they were willing to cut back on expenses; their average financial literacy score was 50.4 percent.

Mandell and Klein (2007) found in a regression analysis that, after controlling for many other important variables, such as aspiration, the three motivational variables had significant and positive relationships to financial literacy. The addition of these variables added about a third to the explanatory power of the regression. This suggests that the effective teaching of money management and personal finance involves continual emphasis on the importance of financial literacy to students' own futures.

Parental Involvement

Periodically, the Jump$tart survey has included questions to test commonly held ideas about imparting financial literacy through parental involvement. For example, the 2000 survey found that young adults who spend a lot of time discussing finances with parents are no more financially literate than those who spend a little amount of time, and students who receive a regular allowance from their parents tend to be *less* financially literate than those who are paid for doing chores or who receive no regular allowance (see Mandell 2001). The 2004 survey found that students who own stocks in their own name know no more about investments than do students who own stocks in their parents' name or who do not own stocks, and students who do not have credit cards know more about credit than students who do have credit cards (see Mandell 2004). In short, there is no evidence that common methods of parental involvement result in a significant improvement to the financial literacy of high school seniors.

The Financially Literate

While a great deal has been written about the inability of young people to cope with the complex financial decisions they will be forced to make, little attention has been paid to those who have become financially literate, that is, to examine the factors that have made them successful and to see what can be done to replicate their success among the general population of their cohorts.

In this study, the cutoff score for being financially literate was set at 75 percent for two reasons. First, a grade of C is generally regarded as a minimally acceptable grade in high schools and colleges, and a C average is often required for graduation. Second, a score of 75 percent on the Jump$tart survey test reflects nearly twice the average increment due to knowledge.[4]

To better focus on the financially literate, table 9.1 has been condensed and rearranged and an additional column has been added to show which groups contain a preponderance of financially literate students (table 9.2). It is most useful to contrast mean financial literacy scores to the proportion of C+ students, by category, in order to see how the financially literate stand out. In the 2006 survey, the percentage of literate students is 6.9%.

Demographics

Table 9.2A reveals some startling insights into the demographics of the financially literate high school seniors. They are overwhelmingly white (92.1 percent), male (63 percent), and the children of college graduates (64.3 percent). The gender differences are most surprising since there is virtually no difference in *mean* scores between young men and young women. This implies that there is greater variance in the scores of males than of females, but it also suggests the existence of cultural factors that tend to attract twice as many young men as young women to a more intense interest in their finances.

Aspiration

Student aspiration also tends to strongly differentiate the financially literate, C+ students from the others (table 9.2B). Nearly 90 percent of financially literate students intend to attend a four-year college, and 64.6 percent expect to be professional workers.

Personal Financial Education

Table 9.2C shows classes related to personal finance that have been taken by students. Since students may have taken more than one such class, totals do not add to 100 percent. The best way to understand the findings in this part of the table is to contrast the proportion of students taking a particular class with the proportion earning a score of C+ on the test. This shows that taking a full-semester class in personal finance neither increases mean financial literacy scores nor increases the proportion of financially literate students. This removes a hypothetical justification for such courses in that they may not raise the *average* level of financial literacy but instead may motivate a few students to become financially literate.

The stock market game again is found to be important: 40.2 percent of all financially literate students played a stock market game in class.

Motivation Variables

Table 9.2D shows that while just over half of all students felt that it was "tough" for a retired person to live on Social Security alone, this group accounted for 73.6 percent of the financially literate students. Also, while 28.9 percent of all students felt that too much credit was the greatest cause of financial difficulty, 41.1 percent of the financially literate felt this way.

Performance by Subject Category

Table 9.3 examines the performance of the financially literate students by subject category to see the areas in which they have relatively greater strengths or weaknesses. In all subject categories combined, the C+ students have mean scores that are 152 percent those of all students. The financially literate students stand out especially in money management (budgeting, insurance, and so on), with scores that were 163 percent of the average of all students, and in savings and investments, with scores that were 162 percent of the average of all students. They did relatively the "worst" in spending, with scores that were 143 percent of the average of all students.

TABLE 9.2 **Financially literate students by various factors**

	Mean score	Proportion of students	Proportion scoring C+	Proportion of C+
A. Demographics				
Parents' income:				
< $20,000	48.5	8.0	2.9	3.2
$20,000–$39,999	50.8	17.0	5.6	13.5
$40,000–$79,999	53.7	29.1	8.1	34.1
$80,000+	55.6	27.0	10.5	41.3
Parents' education:				
Neither finished high school	44.5	6.4	0.4	0.0
Completed high school	50.6	24.6	4.5	15.9
Some college	51.8	21.0	6.4	19.8
College grad or more	55.6	43.7	10.1	64.3
Sex:				
Female	52.3	53.1	4.9	37.0
Male	52.6	46.6	9.3	63.0
Race:				
White	55.0	71.3	8.9	92.1
African-American	44.7	10.1	1.6	2.4
Hispanic American	46.8	8.6	2.0	2.4
Asian-American	49.4	4.4	2.2	1.6
Native American	44.1	1.5	5.1	0.8
Region:				
Northeast	53.8	20.0	6.7	19.5
Midwest	54.2	29.2	7.5	32.0
South	49.9	37.8	5.1	28.1
West	52.8	13.0	10.9	20.3
B. Aspirations				
Educational plans:				
No further education	37.9	2.0	2.7	0.8
Two-year or junior college	47.5	14.7	1.7	3.9
Four-year college	54.9	70.9	8.8	89.8
Planned occupation:				
Manual work	41.0	2.7	1.4	0.8
Skilled trade	47.8	6.2	4.0	3.1
Service worker	49.5	10.6	5.6	8.7
Professional worker	54.9	50.3	8.9	64.6
Expected full-time income:				
< $15,000	42.5	2.8	1.4	0.8
$15,000–$19,999	46.4	6.1	2.4	2.3
$20,000–$29,999	51.6	13.5	5.7	10.9
$30,000+	53.9	20.4	6.9	20.3
$40,000+	54.1	41.4	9.3	55.5

TABLE 9.2 (*continued*)

	Mean score	Proportion of students	Proportion scoring C+	Proportion of C+
C. Classes in high school				
Entire personal finance course	51.6	16.7	6.8	16.5
Portion of personal finance course	53.4	29.3	7.3	31.3
Entire economics course	53.2	38.1	7.8	43.3
Portion of economics course	53.0	27.4	7.9	31.5
Stock market game in class	55.0	27.7	10.0	40.2
D. Motivation				
Major cause of financial difficulty:				
Bad luck	49.1	8.6	3.8	4.8
Not enough savings	48.1	9.4	4.2	5.6
Too much on credit	56.0	28.9	9.9	41.1
No financial plan	53.8	28.9	7.7	32.3
Income too low	50.6	24.0	4.7	16.1
How bad if cannot pay bills?:				
No so bad	43.2	8.5	2.6	3.2
Pretty bad	53.5	49.0	8.2	58.4
Very bad	52.9	42.5	6.2	38.4
How hard to live on Social Security:				
Live well	39.9	7.5	2.2	2.4
Get by	50.4	42.3	3.9	24.0
Tough	56.0	50.1	10.1	73.6

TABLE 9.3 **Performance by subject category**

	Income	Money management	Savings	Spending	Debt	All subjects
Below C	56.9	44.3	40.6	55.1	49.9	50.3
C+	89.7	75.8	68.7	81.2	77.6	79.4
All	59.2	46.4	42.6	56.9	51.8	52.3
% of All	152	163	162	143	150	152

Multivariate Analysis

In order to see which student characteristics were most closely associated with the attainment of financial literacy, a multivariate analysis (binary probit regression reported in the appendix) was run, making it possible to consider many determinants of financial literacy simultaneously. The dependent variable was whether or not students were "financially literate" (scores of 75 percent or more). Among the demographic variables, sex, race, and education of parents were all statistically significant. Family income was not significant. Those who lived in the West were 3 percentage points more likely to achieve financial literacy than those from all other regions, in spite of the fact that students from the West had mean scores that were close to the national average. Race and gender were particularly significant, reiterating the strong tendency of white males to outperform other groups.[5]

Aspiration variables, which do so well predicting financial literacy scores, are not as powerful in predicting who is financially literate. The aspiration variable that is most important is the intention to attend a four-year college; those who plan to attend a four-year college are 3 percentage points more likely to be financially literate. Among the three motivation variables that were found to predict overall scores, the feeling that it would be "tough" to retire solely on Social Security proves to be most important in predicting who is financially literate.

Finally, playing the stock market game is again found to be related to being financially literate; those who have played a stock market game in class are 2 percentage points more likely to be financially literate.

Summary and Conclusions

Young adults finish high school with low mean levels of financial literacy, and there is little evidence that high school courses in personal finance or money management are currently helpful in raising those levels.[6] There are some changes that could be made to the way in which such courses are taught that could raise financial literacy levels, somewhat. These changes include playing a stock market game (or other activities that are interactive, fun, and relevant), having the course required and taught by teachers trained in the discipline, and stressing the importance of the subject matter to the students' own lives. It also appears logical to assume that teaching such a course in the student's senior year may be more effective than the current practice of teaching it primarily to younger high school students for whom the subject has even less relevance, although we do not yet have empirical data supporting this assertion.[7]

When we attempt to establish the factors that are useful in making 6.9 percent of high school seniors financially literate, we find that current, full-semester high school classes in money management or personal finance are of no significant value, the stock market game is of some value, and only the fear of retiring poor has any motivational value.

Regardless of whether we examine financial literacy scores or the achievement of financial literacy competence, the impact of variables that cannot be controlled in school, such as race, parental education, region, gender, and aspiration, appears to overwhelm those variables that we can influence through education.[8] This raises serious policy questions about whether we can entrust the financial literacy of our population solely to secondary schools or whether other types of education, in earlier[9] grades or at the point of sale, are necessary to supplement what we can teach to high school students.

It may be useful to hypothesize why these results appear to differ so dramatically from those of Bernheim, Garrett, and Maki (2001), who found that mandated high school instruction on topics related to household financial decision making resulted in increased asset accumulation once the exposed students reached adulthood. The first hypothesis is that some of what students learn (and promptly forget) in high school may lie dormant for many years, materializing only when, as adults, they have sufficient resources to utilize what they learned. This may explain the authors' findings that the effects are gradual and are probably due to implementation lags. These findings are similar to those of Currie and Thomas (1995) who found that positive effects of the Head Start preschool program for economically disadvantaged children may not be apparent for nearly twenty years (see Currie and Thomas 1995).

A second hypothesis is that the respondents included in the survey analyzed by Bernheim, Garrett, and Maki (2001) graduated from high school between 1964 and 1983, when many fewer families had much discretionary income, when the parents of these students may have lived through the difficult years of the Depression and World War II, and when the proliferation of easy-to-use debt vehicles, such as credit cards, had not yet begun. If the importance of saving was stressed at home, it is possible that it was much easier to reiterate effectively at school. Today, when aggregate consumer saving rates are zero or negative, a consumer-oriented culture may be much more difficult for teachers to overcome.

Given the conflicting results and the important policy implications of these studies with respect to the effectiveness of high school financial education, additional studies on adults who graduated from high school in the past two decades would be very useful.

Appendix

Binary probit analysis on the financially literate (marginal effects)

	Estimate	Standard error
Male	.031	.007***
White	.048	.006***
Parents' income > $80,000	.004	.007
West	.033	.009***
Parent is college graduate	.022	.007***
Plans to be a professional	.016	.006**
Expected income > $40,000	.012	.007*
Plans four-year college	.034	.006***
Financial problems due to too much credit	.015	.007**
Many people have troubles paying bills	−.023	.009**
Tough to live on Social Security	.037	.006***
Played stock market game	.022	.007***

Note: Pseudo R^2 = 0.144
*Significant at the 10% level.
**Significant at the 5% level.
***Significant at the 1% level.

Notes

I would like to thank Shawn Cole for providing suggestions and comments on an earlier draft of this paper.

1. The survey and the sampling methodology are described in detail by Mandell (2006a).

2. Questions asked included whether the respondent always paid credit card bills in full, never made a late credit card payment, never bounced a check, balances checkbook at least weekly, and does own income tax.

3. Questions included "I compare prices when I shop," "I repay the money I owe on time," "I set aside money for future needs/wants," "I make goals for managing my money," "I track my expenses," "I achieve my money management goals," "I discuss money management with my family," and "I use a budget."

4. Since, in a four-question multiple-choice exam, a score of 25 percent may be expected by chance, the average score of just over 50 percent shows that just over 25 percent is due to knowledge. A score of 75 percent demonstrates that the increment due to knowledge is nearly twice that of the average student.

5. See the table in the appendix for detailed results of this analysis.

6. Results of the national economics exam administered for the first time by the U.S. Department of Education in 2006 showed similar results. High school seniors who had taken courses in economics scored only marginally better than students who had not. See www.nces.ed.gov/nationsreportcard/nde/ for data on results of the exam.

7. The 2008 Jump$tart survey will ask students who have taken such a course the year in which it was taken.

8. It is possible that financial literacy relates most closely to academic ability. To find this out, the 2008 Jump$tart survey will ask students about their combined scores on the SAT or ACT college examinations.

9. There is limited but promising evidence that teaching the value of saving has more effectiveness with students in sixth grade than with those in grades seven or eight; see Mandell (2007).

References

Bayer, Patrick J., B. Douglas Bernheim, and John Karl Scholz. 1996. The Effects of Financial Education in the Workplace: Evidence from a Survey of Employers. NBER Working Paper No. 5655. National Bureau of Economic Research, Cambridge, MA.

Bernheim, B. Douglas, Daniel M. Garrett, and Dean M. Maki. 2001. Education and Saving: The Long-Term Effects of High School Financial Curriculum Mandates. *Journal of Public Economics* 80: 435–65.

Chen, Haiyang, and Ronald P. Volpe. 1998. An Analysis of Personal Financial Literacy among College Students. *Financial Services Review* 7: 107–28.

Choi, James, David Laibson, Brigitte Madrian, and Andrew Metrick. 2006. Saving for Retirement on the Path of Least Resistance. In *Behavioral Public Finance: Toward a New Agenda,* edited by Edward J. McCaffrey and Joel Slemrod, 304–51. New York: Russell Sage Foundation.

Christelis, Dimitris, Tullio Jappelli, and Mario Padula. 2006. Cognitive Abilities and Portfolio Choice. CSEF Working Paper No. 157. University of Salerno, Italy.

Currie, Janet, and Duncan Thomas. 1995. Does Head Start Make a Difference? *American Economic Review* 85: 341–64.

Danes, Sharon M. 2004. Evaluation of the NEFE High School Financial Planning Program® 2003–2004. University of Minnesota, Minneapolis, MN.

Danes, Sharon M., Catherine Huddleston-Casas, and Laurie Boyce. 1999. Financial Planning Curriculum for Teens: Impact Evaluation. *Financial Counseling and Planning* 10: 25–37.

DiCenso, Alba, Gordon Guyatt, Andrew Willan, and Lauren Griffith. 2002. Interventions to Reduce Unintended Pregnancies among Adolescents: Systematic Review of Randomised Controlled Trials. *British Medical Journal* 324: 1426–30.

Duflo, Esther, and Emmanuel Saez. 2003. The Role of Information and Social Interactions in Retirement Plan Decisions: Evidence from a Randomized Experiment. *Quarterly Journal of Economics* 118: 815–42.

Elliehausen, Gregory, E. Christopher Lundquist, and Michael E. Staten. 2007. The

Impact of Credit Counseling on Subsequent Borrower Behavior. *Journal of Consumer Affairs* 41: 1–28.

Garman, E. Thomas, Irene E. Leech, and John E. Grable. 1996. The Negative Impact of Employee Poor Personal Financial Behaviors on Employers. *Financial Counseling and Planning* 7: 157–68.

Greenspan, Alan. 2003. The Importance of Financial and Economic Education and Literacy. *Social Education* 67: 70–72.

———. 2005. The Importance of Financial Education. *Social Education* 69: 64–66.

Hilgert, Marianne A., Jeanne M. Hogarth, and Sondra G. Beverly. 2003. Household Financial Management: The Connection between Knowledge and Behavior. *Federal Reserve Bulletin* 89: 309–22.

Hirad, Abdighani, and Peter M. Zorn. 2001. A Little Knowledge Is a Good Thing: Empirical Evidence of Pre-Purchase Homeownership Counseling. McLean, VA: Freddie Mac.

Joo, So-Hyun, and John E. Grable. 2000. Improving Employee Productivity: The Role of Financial Counseling and Education. *Journal of Employment Counseling* 37: 2–15.

Lusardi, Annamaria, and Olivia Mitchell. 2006. Financial Literacy and Planning: Implications for Retirement Wellbeing. Pension Research Council Working Paper No. 1. The Wharton School, University of Pennsylvania, Philadelphia, PA.

———. 2007. Financial Literacy and Retirement Preparedness: Evidence and Implications for Financial Education. *Business Economics* 42: 35–44.

Madrian, Brigitte, and Dennis Shea. 2001. Preaching to the Converted and Converting Those Taught: Financial Education in the Workplace. Working paper. University of Chicago, Chicago, IL.

Mandell, Lewis. 2001. *Improving Financial Literacy: What Schools and Parents Can and Cannot Do.* Washington, DC: Jumpstart Coalition.

———. 2004. *Financial Literacy: Are We Improving? Results of the 2004 National Jump$tart Survey.* Washington, DC: Jumpstart Coalition.

———. 2006a. *Financial Literacy: Improving Education — Results of the 2006 National Jump$tart Survey.* Washington, DC: Jumpstart Coalition.

———. 2006b. The Impact of Financial Literacy Education on Subsequent Financial Behavior. Working paper. State University of New York at Buffalo.

———. 2007. Teaching New Dogs Old Tricks. *Savingteen* (supplement to the January issue of *Credit Union Magazine*).

Mandell, Lewis, and Linda S. Klein. 2007. Motivation and Financial Literacy. *Financial Services Review* 16: 105–16.

Morton, John S. 2005. The Interdependence of Economic and Personal Finance Education. *Social Education* 69: 66–70.

Murray, Dennis. 2000. How Much Do Your Kids Know about Credit? *Medical Economics* 77: 58–66.

National Association of State Boards of Education (NASBE). 2006. *Who Owns Our Children?* Alexandria, VA: NASBE.

National Council on Economic Education (NCEE). 2005. *Survey of the States: Economic and Personal Finance in Our Nation.* New York: NCEE.

Organisation for Economic Co-operation and Development (OECD). 2005. *Improving Financial Literacy: Analysis of Issues and Policies.* Paris: OECD.

van Rooij, Maarten, Annamaria Lusardi, and Rob Alessie. 2007. Financial Literacy and Stock Market Participation. NBER Working Paper No. 13565. National Bureau of Economic Research, Cambridge, MA.

Volpe, Ronald P., Haiyang Chen, and Sheen Liu. 2006. An Analysis of the Importance of Personal Finance Topics and the Level of Knowledge Possessed by Working Adults. *Financial Services Review* 15: 81–99.

CHAPTER TEN

Learning from Individual Development Accounts

Michael Sherraden and Ray Boshara

Introduction

In this chapter we examine saving, particularly in the context of low-income households, and the role of financial education and other institutional factors as they may relate to saving and asset accumulation. Our primary lens for viewing these issues is research on individual development accounts (IDAs), which are matched savings accounts. The goals of IDA savings have typically included homeownership, postsecondary education, and small business capitalization. In this chapter, data on IDA savings transactions, individual characteristics, and program characteristics enable us to identify variables associated with saving behavior. We summarize key findings related to program characteristics and then turn to the implications of those findings for public policy, with particular attention to policies relating to financial education. We also draw on insights from an experts' meeting on financial education.

Our goal in this work is to inform relevant public policy, which needs to be more inclusive in terms of saving and asset accumulation. In recent decades, more policies, including public subsidies, have been devoted to asset accumulation, but these subsidies are enormously regressive. For the most part, the poor benefit very little. If public policy is shifting toward asset building, there are good reasons to include the whole population

LEARNING FROM INDIVIDUAL DEVELOPMENT ACCOUNTS   281

(Sherraden 1991; Howard 1997; Seidman 2001; Corporation for Enterprise Development 2004).

IDAs and the American Dream Demonstration

IDAs were proposed as a tool to include the poor in saving and asset accumulation, as a concrete mechanism for an "asset-based policy" that covers the whole population (Sherraden 1988, 1991). Since being introduced in 1991, IDAs and similar matched savings programs have been implemented in demonstration projects in the United States and around the world, and the concept of an asset-based policy that includes the poor has moved from an innovation to a mainstream idea.

Typically, a community organization will work with a financial institution in providing IDAs. Early funding of IDAs was from philanthropic foundations, with the Ford Foundation playing a leading role. Today IDA funding comes mostly from government, both federal and state, with significant resources from the United Way of America and other nonprofit organizations. Results of IDA programs to date are promising in terms of saving and asset building, but no IDA program has yet reached the scale of serving millions of people. The original proposal for IDAs was that they be an element of lifelong, universal, and progressive policy, but instead IDAs have been implemented in a demonstration format as short-term savings targeted toward low-income adults. Financial education was proposed as a required feature of IDA programs.

Traditional theories of saving have not been very effective in explaining saving behavior, especially among the poor.[1] Promising recent developments are occurring in behavioral economics, suggesting that people may not always be fully informed and rational. For example, it is becoming clear that, contrary to the prediction of the theory, savings are not perfectly fungible. IDA participants, in thorough in-depth interviews, report separate mental accounts for short-term and long-term savings. Moreover, as indicated in the chapter by Lusardi, Keller, and Keller in this volume, people may prefer restrictions on their savings, which is again a departure from neoclassical assumptions. Aiming for a theoretical approach somewhat closer to the data on how people actually think and behave, and to serve as a guide for public policy, the perspective in this study is institutional—that saving and asset accumulation may occur in large part because of explicit access, rules, information, assistance, restrictions, and subsidies—for example, as in a 401(k) plan (Sherraden 1991; Beverly and Sherraden 1999; Sherraden, Schreiner, and Beverly 2003; Sherraden and Barr 2005).

The American Dream Demonstration (ADD) was the first large test of IDAs.[2] ADD operated at thirteen program sites across the United States from 1997 through 2001 with 2,364 participants. The average participant deposited $16.60 net per month into an IDA. About half of the participants (48 percent) were not "savers" (defined as someone having at least $100 in net IDA savings); "savers" had average monthly net deposits of $32.44. Match rates varied, with 2:1 being most typical. Regarding research, ADD produced the most thorough data set on savings by low-income people that we are aware of. Elsewhere we have described the ADD project, data, and these research results in considerable detail (Schreiner and Sherraden 2007).

To be clear about the meaning of the data and analyses reported in this chapter, all IDA participants in ADD are self-selected and program selected. All IDA savings reported are IDA savings alone and do not speak to potential shifting of assets (these issues are addressed in an experiment that was also part of ADD). The data and analyses reported here enable asking a different but no less important question: What individual traits and program features are associated with IDA savings? This question is critical for designing public policy—including financial education—to promote saving.

For purposes of this discussion, a two-step regression analysis first estimates the model to sort out the "savers" from the "low savers"—the latter being those with less than $100 (most had close to zero) net IDA savings and who can be considered not very successful. The analysis then estimates the model for savers—those with over $100 (most well over) net IDA savings and who can be considered successful. This strategy is an oversimplification, but it allows us first to ask what is associated with IDA success and then to ask what, among those who are successful, is associated with different saving outcomes. The regressions include many individual and program variables.

Interestingly, the observed individual variables as a whole are surprisingly weak predictors. For example, education, employment, and welfare receipt have modest or no statistical ties to saving outcomes, and—one of the most important findings—income (both recurrent and intermittent) is at best weakly associated with saving outcomes. The poorest participants, controlling for other variables, did not have saving outcomes statistically different from those who were not as poor, and the poorest saved a higher proportion of their income. In theoretical terms, this finding suggests that something other than observed individual characteristics may be linked to saving outcomes. In practical terms, this finding suggests that saving by the very poor should not be dismissed in public policy (Schreiner and Sherraden 2007).

In contrast to individual variables, program variables are often statistically related to saving outcomes in ADD, and effect sizes are sometimes surprisingly large. Selected program-related results in ADD are presented in table 10.1.[3]

As the reader can see in table 10.1, the matching rate is positively associated with being a saver, but among savers it is negatively associated with average monthly net deposits (AMND). This suggests that the matching rate may attract and keep people saving in the IDA program, but that once in, participants may find that higher matches "substitute" for their own effort in reaching asset accumulation goals. As a result, individuals may not save more in response to higher matches. In other words, matching of savings may have complex influences on saving behavior by IDA

TABLE 10.1 **Selected individual development account program characteristics and saving outcomes in the American Dream Demonstration: Direction of significant relationships (p-value)**

Independent variable	"Saver"	Among "savers," average monthly net deposits
Match rate:		
1:1		
2:1	+ (.07)	− (.01)
< 2:1	+ (.03)	
Match cap:		
Limit on matchable deposits ($/month)		+ (.01)
Use of automatic deposit:		
No		
Yes	+ (.01)	
Hours of financial education:		
1–10		+ (.01)
10–20		
20–30		

Note: Only the variables that are significant are reported. A plus sign indicates a positive association, and a minus sign indicates a negative association. The p-value indicates the probability that the reported result is a chance finding, with .05 and lower being the usual scientific standard for significance. Details of data and analysis are in Schreiner and Sherraden (2007).

participants. Interestingly, these results are similar to saving patterns in 401(k) plans, where (above a minimum level) increases in matching rate tend not to increase saving amounts.

While a match cap (the amount of savings that can be matched each month) is not associated with being a saver, among savers it is highly and strongly associated with AMND. This is, perhaps, the most striking finding in the study. Increasing the match cap by $1.00 results in an additional $0.57 in AMND: a huge effect. In other words, controlling for many other variables, if we compare two IDA programs, one matching $20 per month and another matching $30 per month ($10 difference in match cap), the latter program will generate an AMND that is $5.70 higher. Connecting these remarkable results with behavioral economics, we know from in-depth interviews with IDA participants in ADD that the match cap is, in the minds of many participants, transformed into a target or goal that they are striving for (Sherraden et al. 2005a; Sherraden and McBride forthcoming). This raises the interesting possibility that a savings target by itself, with no match, might have a pronounced effect on saving behavior.

Not surprisingly, use of automatic deposits is positively associated with being a saver, but among savers it is unrelated to AMND. The automatic feature, once in place, tends to keep people saving but does not promote higher saving amounts among the savers—perhaps precisely because they are on autopilot.

Turning to general financial education (which is required of all IDA participants), one to ten hours of education is positively associated with AMND, but there is no discernable relationship after ten hours. Among savers, each of the first ten hours of education is associated with an increase of $1.16 in AMND. This is a very meaningful effect. Ten hours of financial education would generate $11.60 in additional savings per month, or $139 per year. If matched at 2:1 (typical in ADD), increased asset accumulation would be $418 per year, and, over a period of four years, $1,670. For a low-income IDA participant who is saving for a home, this amount of money, combined with other IDA savings and homeownership assistance programs, can make a real difference (indeed, we find that homeownership is the most common use of IDAs). However, above ten hours of financial education, we find no significant relationship with AMND. This suggests that the payoff in financial education may be only in the first ten hours. Because financial education is quite expensive to deliver, this is important to know.

From Program Features to Institutional Constructs

The above findings are striking and generally important for policy design. However, the program variables discussed are particular to IDAs. It would be inefficient to build a general body of knowledge about saving based on particular program characteristics. Instead, our challenge is to seek constructs that are more general and more useful for knowledge building *across a range of circumstances.* In this regard, we have sought to identify "institutional" constructs that may be related to saving outcomes.

We offer seven constructs that we believe are important aspects of institutions designed to promote saving and asset accumulation. The constructs are (1) access, (2) information, (3) incentives, (4) facilitation, (5) expectations, (6) restrictions, and (7) security. These seven constructs have emerged from research on IDAs and other savings programs (Beverly and Sherraden 1999; Rutherford 2000; Sherraden, Schreiner, and Beverly 2003; Schreiner and Morduch 2003; Sherraden et al. 2005b; Sherraden and Barr 2005; Clancy, Cramer, and Parrish 2005; Schreiner and Sherraden 2007; Sherraden and McBride forthcoming). Based on our research on IDAs, saving plans, and considerable evidence in behavioral economics, we may eventually add another construct: (8) simplicity. To illustrate program variables representing institutional constructs, looking at the variables in table 10.1, we regard match rate as an incentive (a financial inducement), match cap as an expectation (an identified target), automatic deposit as facilitation (being helped), and financial education as information (learning more about it).

This may not be exactly the right list of constructs, and improvements are always welcome, but this list may be a step in the direction of building knowledge that can guide policy. To illustrate briefly from the IDA research results reported above, if the goal is increased saving by participants, we have considerable reason to believe that expectations (in the form of a match cap) provide greater policy leverage than incentives (in the form of a match rate). We have reason to believe that information (in the form of financial education) may plateau regarding effects on saving outcomes. We have reason to believe that facilitation (in the form of direct deposit) will keep people saving but not increase their savings. These findings have direct implications for policy design.

A key point in this discussion is that more than incentives are involved.[4] Indeed, incentives in an economic sense may not be the most important factor in increasing saving. Expectations and information may matter more.[5] In any saving policy or program, individuals are interacting with a complex pattern of institutional constructs that could be affecting outcomes. For example, access to a saving opportunity can be fundamental. If a 401(k) or similar retirement plan is not offered in the workplace, the odds of an individual saving for retirement are greatly reduced. From this perspective, it is too simplistic to focus only on one factor that may affect savings. For productive work in this area, knowledge should be built around multiple and sometimes interacting constructs.

Another way to look at this is that economics, both neoclassical and behavioral, addresses individuals (or other units) and how they make choices. Choices are made in the context of constraints, although constraints are often specified only in terms of lifetime resources, with little or no attention to the limitations resulting from lack of information and lack of financial literacy. One way of understanding the institutional context of saving is that it is a specification and testing of constraints to build systematic knowledge that can have both intellectual and policy relevance.

Getting Institutions Right

This discussion cuts across private and public sector initiatives. In our view, there is an important role for government in promoting asset accumulation—for example, in the same way that public policy has defined, regulates, and subsidizes 401(k) plans. A saving policy should include everyone, be lifelong and flexible, and provide at least equal public subsidies for the poor in dollar terms with a goal of achieving adequate levels of asset accumulation in line with the stated purpose of the policy or program (retirement security, homeownership, education, or other).

Creating inclusive saving and asset-based policy that can result in saving as a long-term national project will require visionary leadership. This project would be, in the most basic sense, the creation of a universal system of accounts, an infrastructure to promote saving and asset accumulation. This could be analogous to the creation of a national system of highways to promote transportation. Once the infrastructure is in place, development will occur.[6] Political leaders and planners would have to understand asset building in these terms. Once established, such a policy would likely generate strong political support; for example, note the exceptional impacts and popularity of the Central Provident Fund of Singapore (Sherraden et al. 1995; Vasoo and Lee 2001). And the same seems likely to happen with the Child Trust Fund in the United Kingdom, a universal and progressive policy giving all children an account at birth.[7]

Many applied scholars have made important contributions in understanding savings and financial services for the poor.[8] However, product and service innovations, no matter how well designed, are probably not enough. If saving and asset building are to be inclusive, the overarching policy should be in the form of a savings plan, such as a 401(k) or 403(b) plan, the Federal Thrift Savings Plan, or a college savings (529) plan. Such plans are in fact how most Americans are able to save. Savings plans (contractual savings) have important features that lend themselves to reaching a large portion of the population. These features include centralized and efficient accounting, outreach and education, a limited number of low-cost investment options, low initial and ongoing deposit requirements, automatic deposits, and opportunities to establish other practices and defaults that increase saving performance. These include automatic enrollment, savings match, match cap (amount of savings that can be matched), a default low-cost fund, and automatic increases in savings deposits with pay raises. During the payout period, an automatic minimum annuitization of savings may also be desirable for income protection. Of course, these plan features are expressions of institutional constructs for savings, as already discussed.

To illustrate, experience with automatic enrollment in 401(k) plans (which is about access) finds huge increases in participation when going from an opt-in to an opt-out format (opt-out means that everyone is automatically enrolled into the plan but people can choose to get out). For females, participation rose from 35 to 86 percent; for Hispanics, from 19 to 75 percent; and for those earning under $20,000 annually, from 13 to 80 percent (Beshears et al. 2006). Similarly, commitment to saving more later (restriction of future choices) in the *Save More Tomorrow* program has led to substantial increases in contribution rates over time (Thaler and Benartzi 2004). Overall, 401(k) plan features can have large influences on saving outcomes.[9]

In our view, there is potential in using college savings (529) plans as platforms for inclusion in asset building, especially for children's savings accounts. To be sure, some states' 529 plans have high fees and high investment costs, and such high costs are undesirable. But state 529 plans that keep costs low, have very low deposit requirements, provide outreach to state residents, and match savings for the poorest savers are the ones that have potential as platforms for inclusive children's savings accounts (Clancy and Sherraden 2003; Clancy, Orszag, and Sherraden 2004; Clancy, Cramer, and Parrish 2005). It is encouraging that the overall trend in 529 plans, as they mature, appears to be toward offering simple choices with lower annual fees.

Ultimately, saving outcomes result from the interaction of individual and institutional characteristics. But in our view the policy effort should be primarily toward creation of effective institutions for saving and to a lesser extent toward enticing individuals to save more effectively. As an example of institutional saving, most university faculty members save regularly and successfully in retirement plans, and this may have little to do with individual behavior. Once signed up, saving happens regularly and automatically month after month and year after year, regardless of what information faculty may have or how prudent their actions.

Policy Innovation and the Role of Financial Education

From an institutional perspective, financial education will be most effective if it is embedded in policies and programs rather than left to individuals to access in an unstructured "market" of information. Financial education should be built into programs and delivered efficiently, especially to those who may need it most. To do this comprehensively may require strategies such as segmenting consumers so as to better match education to needs, identifying and implementing the best financial education strategies for particular situations, improving the efficiency and effectiveness of delivery of financial education, and moving consumers beyond a narrow definition of financial knowledge to financial capability. There is not enough space in this chapter to detail these strategies, but lengthier discussion is available elsewhere.[10]

Financial education in isolation will not necessarily be effective in leading to positive financial decisions. The manner in which financial institutions interact with consumers can encourage or discourage good results. Currently, the playing field in financial services is uneven. Sophisticated marketers and sellers are promoting complex products to a weakly informed consumer base. Research, policy, and regulatory changes should encourage rethinking of the role of financial institutions in this regard. Embedding this philosophy into the services test of the Community Reinvestment Act is one approach that should be considered. Positive strategies might include eliminating consistently detrimental components of certain products, such as universal default and over-the-limit fees on credit cards; requiring consumers' consent before providing overdraft privileges on debit and prepaid cards; prohibiting certain especially hazardous products, such as credit life insurance; and providing all disclosures in clear, concise language written at a seventh-grade reading level.

Another institutional approach would be to train more and better providers of financial education to low-income or low-wealth households. There are many individuals providing financial counseling today for low-income or low-wealth Americans. However, they are concentrated in credit counseling, helping those already in serious difficulty; homeownership counseling; and working with IDAs. Not only are more dedicated counselors needed, but people who regularly interact with low-income or low-wealth consumers should be trained to provide good financial advice. Suggestions include creating a financial counseling corps of volunteers, establishing financial counseling accreditation and certification, and encouraging financial education at work.

Turning to policy, perhaps the most promising strategy is to prepare young people for financial life. Although most young people have access to money—from allowances, gifts, and earnings—they often lack the knowledge to manage it effectively. Specifically, it may be desirable to provide financial education in schools. Financial education could be integrated into core courses, K–12, and made part of each state's standardized testing. Given that existing high school programs do not seem very effective, as the chapter by Mandell in this volume well illustrates, policies could be pursued that link financial education to specific actions and tools, such as Kids Accounts, to make education more relevant.

Another strategy is to build a more effective financial education system for adults. Today's adults have much more responsibility for making financial decisions and managing their own personal finances than in the past. They must make investment decisions, select from a proliferation of financial products and services, and plan their own retirement. Although they are faced with many more complex financial decisions, adequate financial education is not widely available. How do we go about this? One direction would be to encourage financial education in the workplace by creating incentives for private employers to provide comprehensive financial education. In this regard, it may be possible to identify, evaluate, and disseminate best-practice models for businesses (including small businesses) to provide financial education in the workplace.[11]

Another promising direction is to change the way information is delivered to consumers. One policy idea is to provide point-of-sale education as consumers obtain products (accounts, credit cards, mortgages, and so on). Similarly, it may be possible to connect tax refund recipients to asset-building opportunities. One policy idea is to increase federal funding for outreach and education efforts to connect Earned Income Tax Credit (EITC) recipients and other low-income refund recipients to asset-building opportunities. Also, we should explore opportunities to provide education at teachable moments, such as when an individual is starting a new job. In all of this, policy should provide incentives for financial institutions and other companies to provide proactive advice to consumers before they get into trouble.

Another promising direction is to make existing public funding more efficient. One idea would be the integration of federal funds allocated to various low-income programs that include financial education to maximize outcomes. Strategies supported with federal dollars, such as IDAs, homeownership programs, and tax preparation programs, could be integrated to maximize impacts and streamline administration and management. In addition, government could use its convening power to make financial education more effective. Policy could establish a national public-private financial education partnership to galvanize national attention around the crisis on financial education.

Reflecting on financial education and savings policy overall, a deeper understanding will be helpful. The standard understanding is that people first learn more, and then they save and accumulate assets. An alternative (and not contradictory) view is that when people begin to accumulate assets, for example, in an IDA program, they may then learn more about financial life.[12] Both of these statements are undoubtedly correct to some extent, although the latter has been somewhat neglected in economic thinking and public policy for the poor.

Policy Progress

Since asset building and IDAs were proposed, there has been modest policy progress on IDAs in the United States. There were increases in welfare asset limits in nearly all states during the 1990s. IDAs were included as a state option in the 1996 Welfare Reform Act. The federal Assets for Independence Act, the first public IDA demonstration, became law in 1998. Other legislation to extend IDAs (and other asset ownership opportunities for the poor) is before the U.S. Congress (Boshara 2003; Boshara, Cramer, and O'Brien 2007). Over forty U.S. states have adopted some type of IDA policy (Edwards and Mason 2003). All of this signals a change in thinking but not a major change in policy as of yet. Most IDA programs in the United States are very small.

By putting savings and asset accumulation by the poor on the map, however, IDAs have made more significant policy changes possible. In 2006, split refunds, auto 401(k), and improvements to the federal Savers Credit were enacted, which together will generate billions in new savings by poor and low-income Americans. Split refunds allow taxpayers to automatically direct their refunds—which, thanks largely to the EITC, average about $2,000 per year for low-income families—into three types of accounts, including savings accounts. Auto 401(k) removes the legal concerns of employers of enrolling workers—including low-income workers—into a company's 401(k) (or equivalent) retirement plan. The Savers Credit—a tax credit to encourage low-income workers to save for retirement—while still not refundable, was made permanent and indexed for inflation.

However, perhaps the most important contribution to date is that saving and asset accumulation by the poor, which was seldom discussed fifteen years ago, is today a mainstream idea in the United States, and political support is usually bipartisan. Both Republicans and Democrats use the language of "increasing personal savings," "asset building," "asset-based policy," "stake holding," and "ownership society." The policy environment has been quite active with variations on this theme. In recent years, multibillion dollar proposals—from leading Democrats and Republicans alike—have been offered to enable poor children and adults to build savings and assets. Indeed, proposals to establish children's savings accounts at birth and a national system of IDAs are the only multibillion savings proposals that have brought left and right together in the last few years. Research on IDAs has had impacts on policy development elsewhere, including the Saving Gateway and Child Trust Fund in the United Kingdom (H. M. Treasury 2001, 2003; Sherraden 2002; Blair 2001; Paxton 2003; Kempson, McKay, and Collard 2003, 2005), Family Development Accounts in Taipei (Cheng 2003), IDAs and "Learn$ave" in Canada (Kingwell et al. 2004), and matched savings programs for the poor in Australia, Uganda, Peru, China, Korea, and elsewhere.

Interestingly, because IDAs have required financial education from the beginning, this emphasis has remained attached to saving and asset-building innovations in the United States and has accompanied almost all of the international policy examples mentioned above. As another part of this observation, when IDAs started in the United States, it was very difficult to locate a financial education curriculum, and very few people were thinking about it. IDA programs created a demand for financial education (because it was required), and this in turn stimulated the market. Today, dozens of examples of financial education curricula are in use. How good these curricula are, or what exactly makes financial education effective, is something we still know little about.

Reflection and Conclusion

As the reader may have gathered, we believe that saving and financial education cannot be left entirely to the private sector, especially if the poor are to be included. There is an important role for government. People do not always know how to save and invest, may not plan well for the future, and are often tempted to spend for short-term satisfactions. Given human nature in this regard, we all may need structure, information, expectations, facilitation, and restrictions if we are to become capable financial managers who can save and accumulate assets to achieve life goals. If this is how we are as humans and if this is what we need, why not create conditions that enable more of us to do better than we otherwise would?

Without doubt, there is an important role for financial education as part of an institutional structure for saving that a good government might put in place. But it might be best to think of financial education as one component of "financial capability," a broader idea that encompasses connections with saving institutions (Johnson and Sherraden 2007).[13] In this regard, three key points from this paper are as follows: financial education is one of multiple policy and service elements that should be considered in relationship to one another; positive effects of financial education may plateau at some point, while other factors—such as saving targets and restrictions—may continue to be influential, and this has implications for cost and effectiveness; and finally, regarding practical application, financial education should not be a stand-alone, but should be embedded in other systems and financial services that can enhance successful delivery, especially to those who may need it most.

Notes

The authors appreciate the comments of Shaun Mundy and anonymous reviewers and the editorial guidance of Annamaria Lusardi. Among the key funders of this body of work, we are especially grateful to the following foundations: Ford Foundation, Citi Foundation, Charles Stewart Mott Foundation, and F. B. Heron Foundation.

1. The traditional neoclassical models focus on preferences for consumption and lifetime income; see, especially, Friedman (1957) and Modigliani and Brumberg (1954). Overviews of saving theories and evidence are presented by Korczyk (1998), Beverly and Sherraden (1999), and Carney and Gale (2001).

2. The American Dream Demonstration (ADD) was implemented by the Corporation for Enterprise Development, with the Center for Social Development at Washington University in St. Louis designing the program and related research. The key funders for the research reported here are the Ford Foundation, Charles Stewart Mott Foundation, F. B. Heron Foundation, and MetLife Foundation.

3. Summary data in table 10.1 and discussion related to table 10.1 are based on Schreiner and Sherraden (2007).

4. Regarding incentives and savings pertinent to this discussion, see also Engen, Gale, and Scholz (1996) and Hubbard and Skinner (1996).

5. Similarly, see the chapter by Lusardi, Keller, and Keller in this volume, which reports that financial information and "seven easy steps" are effective in fostering contributions to pensions.

6. For this insight into a universal system of accounts as a large-scale public good, we are indebted to Fred Goldberg.

7. IDA research in the United States influenced the adoption of asset-based policy and the Child Trust Fund in the United Kingdom.

8. See especially the contributions of Caskey (1994, 2005) and Sherraden and Barr (2005).

9. For further discussion of the effects of 401(k)s on saving outcomes, see, among others, Joulfaian and Richardson (2001).

10. This section is based on an expert meeting and reports by the Financial Services and Education Project of the New America Foundation (2007a, 2007b).

11. For a recommendation on using new employee orientation, see again the chapter by Lusardi, Keller, and Keller in this volume.

12. The idea that assets may lead to greater financial knowledge is a key point of *Assets and the Poor* (Sherraden 1991). The reasoning is, in part, that having the savings and assets makes financial information more salient and therefore more likely to be taken in by an individual and retained. For more thorough inquiries into the relationship of accounts and financial education, see Johnson and Sherraden (2007) and New America Foundation (2007c).

13. The capability framing connects with a much larger discussion of individual

and household development initiated by Sen (1993, 1999). In discussions of savings
and asset building internationally, this framing is especially influential.

References

Beshears, J., J. J. Choi, D. Laibson, and B. C. Madrian. 2006. The Importance of De-
fault Options for Retirement Savings Outcomes: Evidence from the United
States. NBER Working Paper No. 12009. National Bureau of Economic Research, Cambridge, MA.
Beverly, S. G., and M. Sherraden. 1999. Institutional Determinants of Saving: Im-
plications for Low-income Households and Public Policy. *Journal of Socio-
economics* 28: 457–73.
Blair, T. 2001. Savings and Assets for All. Speech at 10 Downing Street, London,
April 26.
Boshara, R. 2003. Federal Policy and Asset Building. *Social Development Issues*
25: 130–41.
Boshara, R., R. Cramer, and R. O'Brien. 2007. The Assets Agenda 2007: Policy Op-
tions to Promote Savings and Asset Ownership by Low- and Moderate-income
Americans. New America Foundation, Washington, DC.
Carney, S., and W. Gale. 2001. Asset Accumulation among Low-income House-
holds. In *Asset for the Poor: The Benefits of Spreading Asset Ownership*, edited
by T. Shapiro and E. Wolff, 165–205. New York: Russell Sage Foundation.
Caskey, J. P. 1994. *Fringe Banking: Check Cashing Outlets, Pawn Shops, and the
Poor.* New York: Russell Sage Foundation.
———. 2005. Reaching Out to the Unbanked. In *Inclusion in the American Dream:
Assets, Poverty, and Public Policy,* edited by M. Sherraden, 149–66. New York:
Oxford University Press.
Cheng, L. C. 2003. Developing Family Development Accounts in Taipei: Policy In-
novation from Income to Assets. *Social Development Issues* 25: 106–17.
Clancy, M., R. Cramer, and L. Parrish. 2005. *Section 529 Savings Plans, Access to
Post-secondary Education, and Universal Asset Building.* Washington, DC: New
American Foundation.
Clancy, M., P. Orszag, and M. Sherraden. 2004. *College Savings Plans: A Platform
for Inclusive Savings Policy?* St. Louis: Center for Social Development, Wash-
ington University in St. Louis.
Clancy, M., and M. Sherraden. 2003. *The Potential for Inclusion in 529 Savings
Plans: Report of a Survey of States.* St. Louis, MO: Center for Social Develop-
ment, Washington University in St. Louis.
Corporation for Enterprise Development. 2004. *Hidden in Plain Sight: A Look at
the $335 Billion Federal Asset-building Budget.* Washington, DC: Corporation
for Enterprise Development.

Edwards, K., and L. M. Mason. 2003. State Policy Trends for Individual Development Accounts in the United States, 1993–2003. *Social Development Issues* 25: 118–29.

Engen, E. M., W. Gale, and J. Scholz. 1996. The Illusory Effects of Saving Incentives on Saving. *Journal of Economic Perspectives* 10: 113–38.

Friedman, M. 1957. *A Theory of the Consumption Function.* Princeton, NJ: Princeton University Press.

H. M. Treasury 2001. Saving and Assets for All. *The Modernisation of Britain's Tax and Benefit System, No. 8.* London: H. M. Treasury.

———. 2003. *Details of the Child Trust Fund.* London: H. M. Treasury.

Howard, C. 1997. *The Hidden Welfare State: Tax Expenditures and Social Policy in the United States.* Princeton, NJ: Princeton University Press.

Hubbard, R. G., and J. S. Skinner. 1996. Assessing the Effectiveness of Saving Incentives. *Journal of Economic Perspectives* 10: 73–90.

Johnson, E., and Margaret S. Sherraden. 2007. From Financial Literacy to Financial Capability among Youth. *Journal of Sociology and Social Welfare* 34: 119–42.

Joulfaian, D., and D. Richardson. 2001. Who Takes Advantage of Tax-deferred Savings Programs? Evidence from Federal Income Tax Data. *National Tax Journal* 54: 669–88.

Kempson, E., S. McKay, and S. Collard. 2003. *Evaluation of the CFLI and Saving Gateway Pilot Projects.* Bristol, United Kingdom: Personal Finance Research Centre, University of Bristol.

———. 2005. *Incentives to Save: Encouraging Saving Among Low-income Households.* Bristol, United Kingdom: Personal Finance Research Centre, University of Bristol.

Kingwell, P., M. Dowie, B. Holler, and L. Jimenez. 2004. *Helping People Help Themselves: An Early Look at Learn$ave.* Ottawa, Canada: Social Research and Demonstration Corporation.

Korczyk, S. M. 1998. *How Americans Save.* Washington, D.C.: American Association of Retired Persons.

Lusardi, A., P. Keller, and A. Keller. 2008. New Ways to Make People Save: A Social Marketing Approach. This volume.

Mandell, L. 2008. Financial Education in High School. This volume.

Modigliani, F., and R. Brumberg. 1954. Utility Analysis and the Consumption Function: An Interpretation of Cross-section Data. In *Post-Keynesian Economics,* edited by K. K. Kurihara, 388–436. New Brunswick, NJ: Rutgers University Press.

New America Foundation. 2007a. Helping Consumers Make Wise Financial Decisions. Report from a Roundtable Meeting on the State of Financial Education and Policy, March 21–22. Washington, DC: New America Foundation.

———. 2007b. *Policy Ideas to Help Consumers Make Wise Financial Decisions.* Washington, DC: New America Foundation.

———. 2007c. *Analyzing the Relationship between Account Ownership and Financial Education*. Washington, DC: New America Foundation.

Paxton, W., ed. 2003. *Equal Shares? Building a Progressive and Coherent Asset-based Welfare Policy*. London: Institute for Public Policy Research.

Rutherford, S. 2000. *The Poor and Their Money*. Delhi: Oxford University Press.

Schreiner, M., and J. Morduch, eds. 2003. *Replicating Micro Finance in the United States*. Washington, DC: Woodrow Wilson Center Press.

Schreiner, M., and M. Sherraden. 2007. *Can the Poor Save? Saving and Asset Accumulation in Individual Development Accounts*. New York: Transaction.

Seidman, L. 2001. Assets and the Tax Code. In *Assets for the Poor: Benefits and Mechanisms of Spreading Asset Ownership*, edited by T. Shapiro and E. N. Wolff, 324–56. New York: Russell Sage Foundation.

Sen, A. 1993. Capability and Well-Being. In *The Quality of Life*, edited by M. Nussbaum and A. Sen, 30–53. Oxford: Clarendon Press.

———. 1999. *Development as Freedom*. New York: Knopf.

Sherraden, M. 1988. Rethinking Social Welfare: Toward Assets. *Social Policy* 18: 37–43.

———. 1991. *Assets and the Poor: A New American Welfare Policy*. Armonk, NY: M. E. Sharpe.

———. 2002. Opportunity and Assets: The Role of the Child Trust Fund. Presentation at seminar organized by Prime Minister Tony Blair, 10 Downing, and dinner speech with Chancellor of the Exchequer Gordon Brown, 11 Downing, London, September 19.

Sherraden, M., and M. S. Barr. 2005. Institutions and Inclusion in Saving Policy. In *Building Assets, Building Credit: Bridges and Barriers to Financial Services in Low-income Communities*, edited by N. Retsinas and E. Belsky. Washington, DC: Brookings Institution Press.

Sherraden, M., S. Nair, S. Vasoo, T. L. Ngiam, and M. S. Sherraden. 1995. Social Policy Based on Assets: The Impact of Singapore's Central Provident Fund. *Asian Journal of Political Science* 3: 112–33.

Sherraden, M., M. Schreiner, and S. Beverly. 2003. Income, Institutions, and Saving Performance in Individual Development Accounts. *Economic Development Quarterly* 17: 95–112.

Sherraden, Margaret S., and A. M. McBride. Forthcoming. *Saving in Low Income Households: Building Assets amid Uncertainty* (working title). Ann Arbor: University of Michigan Press.

Sherraden, Margaret S., A. M. McBride, S. Hanson, and L. Johnson. 2005a. Short-Term and Long-Term Savings in Low-Income Households: Evidence from Individual Development Accounts. *Journal of Income Distribution* 13: 76–97.

Sherraden, Margaret S., A. M. McBride, E. Johnson, S. Hanson, F. Ssewamala, and T. Shanks. 2005b. Saving in Low-Income Households: Evidence from Interviews with Participants in the American Dream Demonstration. Research report. Center for Social Development, Washington University, St. Louis.

Thaler, R., and S. Benartzi. 2004. Save More Tomorrow: Using Behavioral Economics to Increase Employee Saving. *Journal of Political Economy* 112: 164–87.

Vasoo, S., and J. Lee. 2001. Singapore: Social Development, Housing, and the Central Provident Fund. *International Journal of Social Welfare* 10: 276–83.

PART IV

Learning from the United States and Other Countries

CHAPTER ELEVEN

Learning from the Chilean Experience: The Determinants of Pension Switching

Olivia S. Mitchell, Petra E. Todd, and David Bravo

Introduction

Analysts have long debated the pros and cons of Chile's personal accounts pension system, which was launched in 1981 as a replacement of a number of bankrupt pay-as-you-go defined benefit schemes.[1] The new system of Administradoras de Fondos de Pensiones (Afps) is a defined contribution (DC) personal account model, which today has assets equal to 60 percent of the national gross domestic product (GDP). Numerous other Latin American countries followed the Chilean model, and recent U.S. proposals for Social Security reform have also looked to Chile as a possible model for reform.[2]

Notwithstanding the system's success, politicians have recently proposed reforms in this decentralized, private structure, in response to relatively low coverage rates and commissions/fees that some say are excessive.[3] Low coverage rates are attributed to the existence of a large informal sector within which workers are not required to contribute to the system and to low labor force participation rates among women (see Arenas de Mesa et al. 2007). Regarding commissions and fees, the designers of the privatized pension system had believed that competition among fund administrators and free entry into the market would ensure that fees and commissions would be kept low.[4] Yet it has been argued that low rates of financial literacy and regulations governing the pension industry have kept consumers from becoming informed about and selecting wisely among plans (see Rodriguez 1998).

This chapter examines consumer knowledge about the pension system to determine whether financial illiteracy might account for the persistence of market frictions in the pension marketplace. Our particular focus is on the marketing of the Chilean pension system: how it has changed over the years and how the changes have influenced pension fund switching behavior. Until the early 1990s, there was a proliferation of sales agents accompanied by increases in marketing expenditures and the number of AFP firms in operation. During that time, it was not uncommon practice for sales agents to offer gifts such as small appliances to encourage people to switch pension plans. The Chilean pension regulatory agency grew concerned about such practices, particularly since all AFPs held virtually identical asset allocations because of stringent portfolio allocation rules and mandatory guarantees (Bravo and Vásquez 2004). While some pension switching could of course enhance competition, it was widely believed that pension turnover was "expensive for the system and may also be damaging for members, if they are carried out without due information" (Superintendencia de Administradoras de Fondos de Pensiones [SAFP] 2003).[5]

Accordingly, in 1997, regulations were imposed that greatly changed marketing practices. First, licensing requirements for AFP sales agents were instituted and pension firms were required to hire only licensed sales agents. Second, AFP participants wanting to switch money management firms had to appear in person to submit copies of their identity cards, and they also had to bring along copies of their annual pension plan statements. As we show below, these regulatory changes did dramatically curtail switching across pension money managers. What is not yet known is whether the new rules limiting switching patterns affected pension participants equally or whether pension turnover declined more for particular socioeconomic groups. For instance, it could be hypothesized that those with low levels of education and who are least financially literate would reduce their pension turnover most, if the "protective" rule changes were targeted at this subset of participants. Alternatively, making switching harder might discourage turnover patterns more among better-educated, more highly paid workers, with the highest opportunity costs of time.

This chapter examines these questions empirically with a unique new data set known as the Encuesta de Protección Social (EPS), which was gathered collaboratively among the University of Chile, the University of Pennsylvania, and the Subsecretaría de Previsión Social in Chile. The EPS links household demographic information gathered through a panel data survey with a longitudinal history of administrative pension records obtained from the pension regulatory agency. These data allow a detailed microeconomic analysis of how individuals make pension decisions, particularly exploring the key factors underlying workers' decisions to switch from one pension provider to another. To preview our findings, we show that participant pension switching patterns did change after the reform of the pension market in Chile. In particular, the decline in pension turnover was mainly concentrated among the better-educated participants, among whom prereform switching levels had been the highest.

The Chilean Pension Reform

Chile today is a relatively well-off nation compared with its Latin American sisters, with a per capita GDP of US$12,700, a life expectancy of seventy-seven years, and a literacy rate of 96 percent.[6] Yet some 11 percent of its 6.3 million employed population works in agriculture and 13.7 percent of the population lives in poverty, so there is still a substantial "informal" economy of self-employed microentrepreneurs (Tokman 2001; Mideplan 2007). Chile was a pioneer in social insurance schemes, establishing its first social security system in 1924. As explained in Arenas de Mesa et al. (2007), this system evolved from an occupationally based pension arrangement, to a national old-age pay-as-you-go system, to an unusual (for its time) funded DC plan launched in 1981, which was supplemented with a social safety net. At the time of the DC plan launch, the older system was facing collapse, with unfunded benefit promises eroding, erratic coverage, and interest-group politics impeding many from getting coverage.

The old system was replaced in 1981 with a new mandatory DC scheme wherein wage workers were required to pay 10 percent of their monthly earnings to one of the privately managed and licensed pension funds.[7] In addition workers had to pay 2–3 percent more to cover survivor/disability insurance as well as management fees on the deposits.[8] From the start, the government exerted strong control over the investment choices: initially workers' money could only be held in government bonds, but over time, the investment options have been expanded. Nevertheless, workers are still permitted to hold their money in only one AFP at a time, and they must move all their pension accruals to a new AFP if they wish to switch money managers. This restriction was intended to help participants keep track of their money and avoid the growth of many small and potentially orphan accounts, a phenomenon observed in some other Latin nations. Other rules of special note include the fact that participants who contribute for twenty years are guaranteed a minimum pension if the need arises, which is financed from general revenue; the standard retirement age is 60 for women and 65 for men; and early retirement is permitted for those with sufficient wealth amassed in the pension. As with all DC plans, retirement income depends on the workers' lifelong contributions, investment earnings (net of commissions), retirement age, and life expectancy at the retirement age.

The requirement that each worker's assets be held with a single money manager has, some say, provided workers with the incentive to switch from one pension plan to another in rapid succession, producing "churning" across AFPs over time. This is not perceived to be an economically sensible strategy, as all AFPs have invested in virtually the same portfolios over time (Valdes Prieto 2005).

Initially, the Chilean system did not regulate fund-to-fund switching; after a short time, however, participants were restricted to four switches per year (SAFP 2003). Between 1982 and 1987, the rules were tightened slightly more, limiting affiliates to three switches per year; furthermore, participants seeking to move their money from one AFP to another had to appear in person at an AFP office to make the request rather than do it by mail. This in-person appearance requirement was lifted in 1987, and with this change came a substantial surge in the sales force associated with the AFP system. Sales forces grew by 23 percent per annum over the ensuing decade, and switching patterns began to take off. Indeed, by 1996, turnover reached 50 percent, the highest rate recorded in Chile (see figure 11.1), a result which some suggested could diminish pension accumulations by one-fifth (James et al. 1998). Eventually the pension regulatory agency, the AFP superintendency, grew concerned that there was "too much" switching, so in 1997 it required that any affiliate who wished to switch fund managers would have to appear in person at the AFP bearing not only a copy of his or her identification card but also a copy of his or her annual AFP statement. This 1997 change is believed to have had a substantially dampening effect on switching and on the size of the AFP sales agent force. In fact, sales agent employment fell from almost 17,500 in 1997 to just over 2,000 by 2005, and fund manager expenses due to sales force dropped quickly.

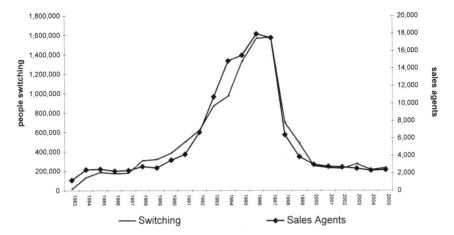

FIGURE 11.1 Participants in the Chilean pension system switching and number of sales agents by year, 1983–2005. (Source: Authors' calculations from data provided by the Chilean Superintendency of the AFP system.)

The Chilean pension system has also undergone other changes over time. For instance, the number of money managers peaked at twenty-one in 1994 but then fell steadily after that to its current all-time low of six managers.[9] During the first sixteen years of the system's existence, there appeared to be a negligible relationship between the number of AFPs and various indexes measuring concentration among the largest AFPs. But after 1997, market concentration rose steadily as the number of AFPs fell. This change was associated with a subsequent more than doubling in profitability (measured as the net return on equity), although the 2001 market shock took its toll, from which the AFPs are only slowly recovering.

Prior Studies

Only a few empirical studies to date have examined the factors that influence workers to switch from one pension money manager to another in Chile, and all but one of these focuses exclusively on aggregate flows of affiliates across plans. For instance, Berstein and Micco (2002) correlate net turnover patterns across AFPs to changes in the relative size of each firm's sales force, which the authors interpret as a measure of the probability of being contacted by a sales agent from that firm.[10] The study concludes that AFPs with more sales agents attracted greater relative net inflows.

When they estimate the model separately in the pre- and post-1997 reform periods, they find that the effects of sales agents are attenuated, although the direct positive effect remains significant. Berstein and Micco also suggest that having more sales agents can reduce workers' sensitivity to poor return performance and higher fees and suggest that "welfare might be improved by imposing restrictions [on] switching." A follow-up study (Berstein and Ruiz 2004) again asks how net turnover flows by AFP vary with the number of sales agents over the period 1995–2002. The analysis does not test for structural changes in coefficient estimates, but the authors infer that having more sales agents had a small positive effect on net AFP inflows prior to the 1997 reform with no significant effect afterward. Accordingly they argue that the regulatory change decreased competition over fees and commissions. A study by Marinovic and Valdes-Prieto (2005) evaluates separately models for the pre- and post-1997 periods, but it does not test whether there are structural shifts over time. Cerda (2005) concludes that a larger sales force and higher marketing expenditures raised exit rates, but here too, the empirical work does not statistically test whether adding sales agents had a differential effect before versus after the 1997 reform.

To our knowledge, only Berstein and Cabrita (2007) have explored pension switching using worker-level data, drawing on a file of 24,662 pension system affiliates from a 2005 database owned by the superintendency of the AFP system and containing information on individuals' account-switching patterns.[11] The authors link workers' pension switches to AFP characteristics and compare results during the prereform phase (1988–96), the postreform phase (1998–2005), and the entire period (1988–2005). For our purposes, the most important finding is that the probability of switching is positively associated with the probability of being contacted by a sales agent. Berstein and Cabrita do not, however, test whether there was a significant structural shift in the model around 1997, the time of the regulatory reform. In addition, they do not test whether the reform engendered differential switching behaviors across participants of different types.

Our Methodology

In what follows, we use the EPS to explore whether workers' pension-switching patterns vary in Chile according to socioeconomic factors, whether switchers are more or less financially literate, and whether pension-switching patterns changed after 1997 for workers of different types. The survey was first fielded by the Microdata Center of the Department of Economics of the Universidad de Chile in 2002; in 2004, a follow-up survey was administered to the same households as well as to a refresher sample. The data set includes information on respondent and household characteristics including educational status, marital status, and employment status, as well as some data on health, disability status, and utilization of medical services. Administrative data from the Chilean government have also been appended, permitting us to link worker-side with agency-side records on contributions, balances, switching patterns across AFPs, investment portfolios, and other important pension attributes.

Of substantial interest for the present analysis is the fact that the EPS incorporates several questions aimed at assessing respondents' financial literacy. In this chapter, we focus on 2004 survey affiliates age 18 to retirement (60 for women, 65 for men), where the wealth and literacy questions are particularly complete.[12] In particular, we test whether the 1997 regulatory reform had an effect on participant switching at all and, if so, whether the effect was more powerful for the more versus the less financially literate. One hypothesis is that workers who know little about their pension system will have only a weak interest in and willingness to contribute to their retirement accounts and will not be active traders. Studies from the U.S. labor marketplace suggest that many workers are woefully unaware of key aspects of their national and corporate defined benefit retirement plans (Mitchell 1988; Gustman and Steinmeier 1999; Gustman, Steinmeier and Tabatabai, this volume). As yet, however, less is known about whether similar problems arise for workers in DC plans,[13] and no one has linked Chilean pension plan behavior with financial literacy patterns. This is of value since financial ignorance has been shown to translate into failure to plan and save for retirement in the U.S. context (Lusardi and Mitchell 2006, 2007), and it may also be a factor in the Latin American context. To this end, it is important to see how financial knowledge, or lack thereof, may be linked to important economic behaviors such as pension turnover.

In the Chilean case, we use several different indicators of financial literacy. First, we incorporate the respondent's schooling, on the grounds that more exposure to education could enhance financial literacy. Second, we use a measure of length of experience with the AFP system, which varies across individuals primarily because of variation in the timing of the first formal sector job. Third, we exploit several specific questions testing respondents' knowledge of the Chilean pension system. Our earlier work demonstrated that questions about retirement system knowledge can be usefully grouped into the three phases of the pension lifecycle: contributions, investments/accumulations, and payouts (Arenas de Mesa et al. 2008).

Table 11.1 follows this natural grouping to summarize what 2004 EPS affiliates thought they knew about the Chilean pension system and how correct these answers proved to be. Overall, the findings suggest troublingly low levels of financial literacy. Panel A, for instance, shows that only 69 percent of the participants indicate that they receive an annual statement that summarizes past contributions and projects future benefit amounts, while, in fact, the documentation is sent out quarterly by each AFP. Fewer than half of the affiliates (46 percent) know how much they contribute to the AFP system—even though the contribution rate has been set at 10 percent of pay since the system's inception. Only one-third (34 percent) of the respondents state a contribution amount that matches at all closely (±20 percent) with what is reported in their individual (administrative) records. Few affiliates know what commissions/fees are charged on their accounts. The fact that so many system participants are unaware of key attributes of their retirement program, despite the program having been in operation for over twenty-five years, is discouraging. It suggests a need for investor education, particularly if workers are to be encouraged to save more and more effectively for retirement.

Information on what workers have accumulated and invested in their pension appears in table 11.1B, where we see that only about half (53 percent) of those surveyed claim they know how much they have accumulated in their accounts; furthermore, only about one-fifth (22 percent) actually report amounts that are correct to within ±20 percent of actual accruals (compared with administrative records). One-third (33 percent) of the respondents state that they know how their own money is invested, but only 16 percent are correct regarding which of the five funds they hold (compared with administrative records).[14] Only one-third (38 percent) knows that fund A is the riskiest portfolio, of the five permitted by the government: funds B–E hold increasingly higher fractions of safer assets and a lower equity share. Table 11.1C focuses on retirement benefits, and it shows that around 80 percent know the legal retirement age but that fewer than 10 percent know how the AFPs actually compute benefits (in fact, a sizeable group believes that the system is a defined benefit structure, instead of a DC plan!). The current system also provides a minimum pension guarantee from the federal government if twenty-year contributors

TABLE 11.1 **Knowledge of Chilean pension system attributes**

Variable	%
A. Contributions	
Received AFP statement within twelve months	69.2
Claims to know AFP amount contributed	38.0
Correct on AFP contributions	30.9
Says knows fixed AFP commission	1.7
Says knows variable AFP commission	2.1
Says knows both commissions	0.5
B. Accumulations/investments	
Says knows AFP accumulation	52.7
Correct on AFP accumulation (±20%)	21.6
Knows about multifunds	47.4
Knows how many multifunds	32.8
Correct on number of multifunds	20.2
Says knows own investment mix	32.8
Correct on fund type	15.8
Knows riskiest fund	38.1
C. Payouts	
Knows female legal retirement age	76.5
Knows male legal retirement age	80.0
Knows how AFP calculates pensions	9.3
Says knows minimum pension requirements	31.1
Correct on minimum pension requirements	0.2
Knows minimum pension exists	44.9
Says knows minimum pension amount	32.8
Correct on minimum pension amount	3.4

Note: AFP = Administradoras de Fondos de Pensiones.
Source: Derived from Arenas de Mesa et al. (2008); sample includes AFP affiliates surveyed in 2004, ages 18–60.

had insufficient funds to reach the promised threshold as of retirement. But here too participant information is meager: fewer than half (45 percent) are even aware of the guaranteed minimum benefit. Interestingly, of the one-third (33 percent) who claims to know the minimum benefit level, only a miniscule minority—3 percent—can accurately report this minimum benefit. It is worth noting that AFP participants in Chile seem similar to the majority of their U.S. counterparts covered by company pensions (Gustman, Steinmeier, and Tabatabai in this volume).

To more compactly summarize the responses to these three sets of pension knowledge questions, we implement a summary index or scoring system that was developed by Brockett et al. (2002) known as PRIDIT. This approach evaluates each respondent's answer to a financial literacy question by weighting a correct response more heavily when other respondents mostly get it wrong and less heavily if most others provide a correct answer. As an example, correctly answering a question that only 10 percent of respondents answer correctly is rewarded more than correctly answering a question that everyone gets right, but getting it wrong is not associated with much of a penalty if no one knows the answer. In this way, the PRIDIT score is sensitive to others' performance. The scoring is centered at zero, which refers to the mean score of all who respond to a given question. We then sum these scores across questions to generate a respondent's literacy index score by cluster of pension knowledge.[15] An advantage of this process is that the weights take into account what others know across questions. For instance, if two people tend to get two questions right, their answers on both will be less informative compared with the questions that distinguish between people. The PRIDIT weights for clusters A–C in table 11.1, referring to pension contributions, pension accumulations/investments, and pension outflows, respectively, appear at the top of table 11.2. Here we see that average scores are relatively higher on the accumulation than on the pay-in/pay-out questions, and those who switched pension managers have even higher pension literacy than the full sample.

Turning next to switching patterns, table 11.2 also indicates the number of times a worker switched from one AFP to another over the period 1981–2004. In particular, we seek to determine how often Chilean AFP members switch fund managers and whether switchers are similar to nonswitchers. In the U.S. 401(k) context, we have found that DC plan participants are fairly inactive on average, trading in their pension plan only about once every two years. Nevertheless, there is an important segment of active 401(k) plan traders, namely, more highly paid men. This has been interpreted as an "overconfidence" effect, in that active trading tends to reduce, rather than enhance, plan performance (Mitchell et al. 2006a, 2006b). Accordingly, one hypothesis we seek to test is whether pension switchers are among the least educated and least financially literate. An initial insight into this behavior in the Chilean context is facilitated by table 11.2, which shows that the mean number of pension switches per year, 0.2, was quite low in the population as a whole; only 15 percent ever switched over their work life. In other words, most people switch zero or one times, but some switch pension managers as many as eight times in a single year. It is important to note that a small but important fraction of people changed pension managers owing to cor-

TABLE 11.2 **Descriptive statistics for analysis sample**

Variable	All respondents	Respondents who switched Administradoras de Fondos de Pensiones at least once during the year
Pridit A: contributions score	10.7 (111.6)	19.07 (124.06)
Pridit B: accumulations score	20.5 (103.9)	43.32 (104.06)
Pridit C: payouts score	11.5 (99.0)	20.93 (98.94)
Mean number of voluntary switches	0.20 (0.52)	1.31 (0.57)
Proportion of people switching voluntarily	0.15 (0.36)	1.0 (0.0)
Mean number of merger-related switches	0.01 (0.11)	0.07 (0.27)
Average age	35.71 (10.12)	34.70 (9.24)
% With highest degree elementary	0.16 (0.37)	0.09 (0.29)
% With highest degree high school	0.60 (0.49)	0.56 (0.50)
% With highest degree college	0.24 (0.43)	0.34 (0.47)
% Married	0.70 (0.46)	0.72 (0.45)
% Divorced, widowed, or separated	0.11 (0.31)	0.11 (0.32)
% Male	0.64 (0.48)	0.64 (0.48)
Average monthly remuneration (in 1,000 pesos)	171.82 (186.24)	228.44 (214.00)
Years of participation in the AFP system	7.67 (6.05)	7.87 (5.30)
Number of sales agents	6,331 (5543)	
Sales agents/affiliates	0.001 (0.001)	
Number of AFP firms	11.8 (4.3)	
Number of affiliates	4,985,673 (1,648,032)	

Note: Data are mean (standard deviation). Observations represent an individual in a given year. There are 8,641 observations in all; 12,886 observations that switched Administradoras de Fondos de Pensiones firms at least once during the year.
Source: Authors' computations are from the 2004 Encuesta de Protección Social sample of affiliates and administration pension fund data.

porate mergers, and in what follows we subtract these from the voluntary switch analysis.[16] Other sample statistics are also summarized, with one salient difference being that active switchers tend to be more highly paid and better educated than those who never alter their pension holdings over time. About one-third (34 percent) of switchers have a college degree, in comparison with 24 percent for the whole AFP affiliate sample. There is no discernible difference by sex, with the same proportion male (64 percent) in both the more and less frequent switcher groups. There is a big difference in the level of contributions, with more frequent switchers making almost double the amount of contributions. They also have much higher financial literacy scores, by all three PRIDIT literacy measures (A, B, and C). The average age of the sample is 35.4, with the higher proportion of males reflecting the fact that the male labor supply is higher in Chile and that males are more likely to be in formal sector employment. With regard to education, 16 percent of the sample has six or fewer years of education (elementary), 60 percent has seven to twelve years (high school), and 24 percent has more than a high school degree. The majority of the sample (70 percent) is married. Chilean workers are required to pay 10 percent of their wages to their pension fund up to a maximum threshold. The average monthly remuneration is 171,000 pesos, or roughly $285 dollars. The last five lines of the table refer to average characteristics of the AFP industry over the 1981–2004 time period, including the average number of sales agents, the average number of total AFP affiliates, and the number of AFP firms in operation.

Results

Next we test whether switching patterns were significantly reduced after the regulatory reform that made switching more onerous and, if so, for whom. We also seek to determine whether making switching more difficult was more of a deterrent to switching among the low-paid, uneducated workers or among the more affluent and better educated. In the former case, making switching more difficult could be interpreted as enhancing consumer protection for the financially vulnerable, if sales agents use tactics that induce less-educated consumers to sign up for higher cost funds. On the other hand, since the regulatory change mainly increased the time costs of switching, the change may have increased transaction costs most for the well-to-do. The net effect of the regulatory change is ambiguous and must be determined empirically.

Our analysis of switching patterns and financial literacy uses 84,641 person-years of EPS data. We estimate a series of multivariate models linking the annual number of voluntary switches made by each individual to different sets of control variables. First, we include indicator variables for whether the person-year observation occurred before or after the 1997 reform, along with mandatory contribution levels. The estimates in table 11.3, column (1), indicate that the average number of switches declined after 1997 by 0.12 per annum. Column (2) adds a time trend for control for general changes over time in switching behavior, perhaps attributable to technological advances that facilitated switching, and also adds as a regressor the number of AFP firms in operation, as the latter could be expected to offer more opportunity for switching. The addition of these control variables only slightly lowers the estimated effect of the 1997 reform from 0.12 to 0.11 switches per year. Next, column (3) includes sociodemographic controls that will take into account possible differences in characteristics of pension affiliates over time. We find that higher numbers of switches are associated with being better educated, having higher mandatory contribution levels (and therefore higher wages), and being married. We also find that individuals with a longer experience with the AFP pension system (controlling for age) switch more. Switching patterns appear to be highly similar for men and women after controlling for the levels of contributions and other factors, a finding that differs from U.S. studies reporting that men switch funds more than women. To allow for flexibility, age is entered as a quadratic (we use age and age squared) and is found to have a positive but decreasing effect on switching up to age 44, after which it has a negative effect. Older people tend to have more accumulated in their pension funds, so switching would generally have greater implications for them in terms of potential cost savings.

People who are not working do more switching, which may be a reflection of the fact that the AFP fee structures may make it optimal to switch when an employed person becomes unemployed. That is, AFPs charge both a fixed fee and a variable fee that depends on the mandatory contribution amount, and different AFPs generally charge different combinations of fixed and variable fees. The fee structures have changed over time. Because of the fee structure, when people become unemployed, it might be optimal for them to choose a different AFP.[17] Interestingly, the socioeconomic factors prove to be useful controls in that they are statistically different from zero, but their inclusion does not materially alter our estimates of the 1997 reform effect. In other words, the estimated impact of the regulatory reform is robust to the inclusion of these socioeconomic factors as controls.

To examine which groups are most affected by the reform, additional models in columns (4) and (5) permit the 1997 regulatory reform to have a different impact depending on the respondent's education level. The results indicate that the number of switches is curtailed most among the better educated, who were also the most frequent switchers prior to the reform. Switching also dropped for the least educated, but by only half as much. In this sense, the reform may have had a greater impact on the better off—and more financially literate—rather than on the lesser informed, as might have been hoped. Controlling for the number of AFP firms in operation also shows that people switched more when there were many AFP firms from which to choose. Nevertheless, even given the number of firms in the market, it is clear that the 1997 reform is associated

Covariates	(1)	(2)	(3)	(4)	(5)
Constant term	0.12	−0.07	−0.13	−0.17	−0.22
	(0.003)	(0.01)	(0.03)	(0.028)	(0.03)
Age	...	...	0.005	0.006	0.008
			(0.001)	(0.001)	(0.001)
Age squared	...	...	−0.0001	−0.0001	−0.0001
			(0.00001)	(0.00002)	(0.00002)
Male	...	...	−0.003	−0.002	−0.002
			(0.004)	(0.004)	(0.004)
High school	...	...	0.04	0.06	0.07
			(0.005)	(0.006)	(0.007)
College	...	...	0.09	0.11	0.10
			(0.006)	(0.007)	(0.009)
Married	...	...	0.02	0.02	0.02
			(0.005)	(0.005)	(0.005)
Divorced/widowed/separated	...	...	0.06	0.06	0.07
			(0.007)	(0.007)	(0.007)
Working	...	...	−0.05	−0.05	−0.04
			(0.01)	(0.01)	(0.01)
Mandatory contribution	0.001	0.001	0.001	0.001	0.001
	(0.00003)	(0.00003)	(0.00003)	(0.00003)	(0.00003)
Mandatory contribution squared	−9.61E−7	−7.91E−7	−7.32E−7	−7.34E−7	−7.38E−7
	(3.47E−8)	(3.77E−8)	(3.83E−8)	(3.85E−8)	(4.06E−8)
Years experience in the AFP system	...	...	0.002	0.001	0.001
			(0.0005)	(0.0005)	(0.0005)
Post-1997	−0.20	...	−0.11	...	...
	(0.004)		(0.009)		
Post-1997 × elementary school	...	...	...	−0.04	−0.04
				(0.01)	(0.01)
Post-1997 × high school	...	...	...	−0.12	−0.13
				(0.005)	(0.01)
Post-1997 × college	...	...	...	−0.11	−0.12
				(0.008)	(0.01)
Time trend	...	0.001	0.002	0.002	0.003
		(0.0005)	(0.0006)	(0.0006)	(0.0006)
Number of AFPs	...	0.013	0.013	0.01	0.01
		(0.0007)	(0.0007)	(0.0007)	(0.0007)
PRIDIT A: contributions score	...	...	...	...	0.000004
					(0.00002)
PRIDIT B: accumulations score	...	...	...	...	0.0002
					(0.00002)
PRIDIT C: payouts score	...	...	...	...	0.00004
					(0.00002)
Number of observations, person-years	84,640	84,640	84,640	84,640	76,972
Adjusted R^2	0.0470	0.0512	0.0602	0.0560	0.0623

Note: Standard errors are in parentheses. AFP = Administradoras de Fondos de Pensiones.
Source: Authors' computations are from the 2004 Encuesta de Protección Social sample of affiliates and administration pension fund data.

with fewer pension plan switches. Column (5) augments the equation to include the three PRIDIT variables that we propose as measures of financial literacy as we have described. Only the PRIDIT B score proves to be positively and statistically associated with higher pension switching rates. In other words, those workers with more knowledge about their pension accumulations and investment patterns are also those who tend to switch more often.

We have also estimated all of the specifications separately for men and women, but results are not reported in detail for the sake of brevity. Most critically, all of the estimated patterns noted previously are consistent with the new results. The magnitudes of estimated coefficients are similar, with the exception of the coefficients on the pay, which are of the same sign but differ in magnitude for men and women. For both groups, the average number of switches declines by about 0.10 after the 1997 reform in specifications similar to columns (2)–(5), with the more educated exhibiting a greater decrease. Again, only the PRIDIT B variable is statistically significant: greater financial literacy according to this measure boosts the average number of switches by the same amount for men and women.

Table 11.4 presents estimates analogous to those in table 11.3, except that the specification includes individual-level fixed effects, which allow for any individual-level unobserved determinants of switching. Because we have repeated observations for each individual, we can account for individual-specific differences among individuals. In the fixed-effect specifications, the coefficients associated with regressors that are fixed over time or that vary in a deterministic way with age within individuals cannot be identified. For example, within individuals, the time trend and the exposure to the AFP system are collinear with age and therefore are not separately identified. Also, the PRIDIT variables cannot be included because they are measured only at a single point in time. The estimated coefficient associated with the 1997 reform is virtually unchanged by the inclusion of fixed effects; specifically, the average number of switches is 0.10 lower after the regulatory reform. Also, the switching pattern by work status and level of remuneration remains the same as in table 11.3. F-tests of the joint significance of the individual fixed effects reject the hypothesis of no fixed effects at conventional significance levels.[18]

For exploratory analysis, we also consider the relationship between the pension knowledge (PRIDIT) variables and individual characteristics in table 11.5. Here we see that education is highly statistically positive and significant for all of the financial knowledge measures. The coefficient on male is positive and statistically significant for the PRIDIT A measure, statistically insignificantly different from zero for the PRIDIT B measure, and negative and statistically significant for the PRIDIT C measure. This suggests that men are more knowledgeable than women about contributions but less knowledgeable on rules governing payouts and minimum pensions, which might be related to the fact that women can expect to receive their pension about three years earlier on average because the mandatory retirement age is lower for women. Workers who have higher contribution levels are more knowledgeable about their pension contribution amounts and about investments, but they are not differentially knowledgeable about payments and minimum pension rules. A longer experience with the AFP system is associated with a higher level of financial literacy according to all three measures. It is noticeable that the R^2

TABLE 11.4 **Estimates of multivariate fixed-effect model for number of voluntary switches**

Covariates	(1)	(2)	(3)	(4)
Constant term	0.12	−0.04	−0.24	−0.28
	(0.003)	(0.01)	(0.04)	(0.04)
Age	...	...	0.012	0.015
			(0.002)	(0.002)
Age squared	...	...	−0.0001	−0.0001
			(0.00002)	(0.00002)
Working	...	...	−0.04	−0.04
			(0.01)	(0.01)
Mandatory contribution	0.001	0.0008	0.0008	0.0008
	(0.00003)	(0.00004)	(0.00003)	(0.00003)
Mandatory contribution squared	−8.45E−7	−6.28E−07	−6.13E−7	−6.14E−7
	(3.84E−8)	(4.3E−08)	(4.37E−8)	(4.40E−8)
Post-1997	−0.19	−0.10	−0.10	...
	(0.005)	(0.009)	(0.009)	
Post-1997 × elementary school	...	...	...	−0.03
				(0.01)
Post-1997 × high school	...	...	...	−0.12
				(0.01)
Post-1997 × college	...	...	...	−0.10
				(0.01)
Time trend	...	0.002	...	...
		(0.0006)		
Number of Administradoras de Fondos de Pensiones	...	0.01	0.01	0.01
		(0.0007)	(0.0007)	(0.0007)
Number of observations, person-years	84,641	84,641	84,640	84,640
p-value from F-test of fixed effects equal to 0	< 0.0001	< 0.0001	< 0.0001	< 0.0001
Adjusted R^2	0.0457	0.0494	0.0602	0.0560

Note: Standard errors are in parentheses.
Source: Authors' computations are from the 2004 Encuesta de Protección Social sample of affiliates and administration pension fund data.

TABLE 11.5 **Estimated relationship between financial literacy and demographics**

Covariates	PRIDIT A	PRIDIT B	PRIDIT C
Constant term	−26.16	−56.83	−111.42
	(24.31)	(23.05)	(23.43)
Age	−0.87	−0.37	2.00
	(1.22)	(1.16)	(1.18)
Age squared	0.01	−0.004	−0.01
	(0.01)	(0.01)	(0.01)
Male	8.68	−1.08	−12.70
	(3.13)	(2.97)	(3.02)
High school	21.37	41.30	27.38
	(4.93)	(4.67)	(4.75)
College	39.80	92.03	45.56
	(5.71)	(5.41)	(5.50)
Married	1.52	−1.65	−3.17
	(3.56)	(3.38)	(3.43)
Divorced/widowed/separated	−0.52	−18.87	−12.47
	(5.70)	(5.41)	(5.50)
Working	−0.22	−15.77	8.95
	(10.70)	(10.15)	(10.32)
Mandatory contribution	0.07	0.21	0.03
	(0.03)	(0.02)	(0.02)
Mandatory contribution squared	−0.00006	−0.0001	0.000002
	(0.00003)	(0.00002)	(0.00003)
Years of experience with the Administradoras	0.46	1.73	1.18
de Fondos de Pensiones system	(0.32)	(0.30)	(0.30)
Adjusted R^2	0.02	0.15	0.06

Note: The number of observations, person-years (year 2004 only), is 4,928. Standard errors are in parentheses.
Source: Authors' computations are from the 2004 Encuesta de Protección Social sample of affiliates and administration pension fund data.

is much higher for the PRIDIT B measure than for the other measures, indicating that socioeconomic factors are a better predictor of knowledge about accumulations and investments. This is plausible, given that these demographic and economic factors are important predictors of earnings, which in large part determine investment levels through the minimum contribution rules.

Conclusions and Implications

Recent studies of financial decision making suggest that financially illiterate consumers tend to make poor financial decisions—saving inadequately, managing their money inefficiently, and even retiring too soon. This analysis of the Chilean pension system is the first to link education

and financial literacy with an interesting retirement saving outcome—
switching between pension money managers who are basically investing
in identical portfolios. We also test whether the least educated and financially literate appear to be most affected by regulation restricting such
pension turnover.

We show that the change in regulatory rules on the marketing of AFPs
substantially suppressed the overall number of participant switches. Nonetheless, although the number of voluntary switches declined, the drop was
concentrated mainly among a particular group—the better educated. Our
evidence implies that the policy did little to target those who might be
thought to be most in need of consumer protection; rather, it influenced
the switching behavior of the better educated and the most highly paid
who had previously been most likely to switch pension fund managers.

This analysis has implications for other countries contemplating pension reform. An oft-noted critique of those seeking to implement an individual account–style pension system is that consumers may be poorly
informed and therefore incapable of making sensible economic decisions
about their own retirement saving. While this is surely true, the Chilean
experience shows that regulations intended to reduce pension turnover
affected mainly those who were doing the most switching in the first
place—the better educated and higher earning members. To the extent
that lowering turnover reduces overall administrative expenses, overall
system performance can be enhanced. Whether it has a differential effect on investment returns for different types of workers is the subject of
future research.

Notes

The authors acknowledge research support from National Institute on Aging grant
no. AG023774-01 and funding from the Mellon Foundation to the Population
Studies Center on Latin American demographic issues. The research was also supported by an award from the Population Aging Research Center at the University
of Pennsylvania Population Studies Center and the Boettner Center for Pensions
and Retirement Security and Pension Research Council at the University of Pennsylvania. Research assistance was provided by José Luis Ruiz, Jeremy Skog, and
Javiera Vásquez. Useful suggestions from Solange Berstein, Gary Engelhart, and
Annamaria Lusardi are gratefully acknowledged. Opinions and errors are solely
those of the authors and do not reflect views of the institutions supporting the
research or of the institutions with which the authors are affiliated.

1. Many have written on the Chilean pension system (for example, Cheyre 1988; Iglesias and Acuña 1991; Baeza and Margozzini 1995; and SAFP 2003). Some of the literature is summarized by Arenas de Mesa et al. (2008).

2. Other Latin American countries that reformed their pension systems along similar lines include Peru (1993), Colombia (1994), Argentina (1994), Uruguay (1996), Bolivia (1997), Mexico (1997), El Salvador (1998), Costa Rica (2001), the Dominican Republic (2003), Nicaragua (2004), and Ecuador (2004). Cogan and Mitchell (2003) discuss prospects for funded individual defined contribution account pensions in the United States.

3. A recent critique citing the problem of low coverage rates is Holzmann et al. (2005). Chilean president Michele Bachelet has proposed several changes in the AFP system; for details, see Consejo Asesor Presidencial para la Reforma Previsional (2006) and Gobierno de Chile (2006).

4. The Chilean pension reform was implemented by General Pinochet's military government, which was advised by a team of University of Chicago economists.

5. Others arguing that pension switching in Chile has been costly include Berstein and Cabrita (2006); Berstein and Ruiz (2004); Cerda (2005); James, Smalhout, and Vittas (2001) and Valdes Prieto (1999, 2005); for additional citations, see Consejo Asesor Presidencial para la Reforma Previsional (2006).

6. For more detail, see http://www.cia.gov/cia/publications/factbook/print/ci .html.

7. In addition to the funded defined contribution accounts, the Chilean old-age system includes a welfare benefit for the destitutes, a minimum pension guarantee for long-time contributors, and the opportunity to make additional voluntary contributions. These other elements are not the central focus of this chapter; for more detail, see SAFP (2003).

8. Mandatory system contributions are capped at a ceiling earnings level of approximately US $2,200 a month; fewer than 8 percent of AFP contributors earn over that ceiling.

9. Barrientos and Boussofiane (2005) find that more efficient providers survived better than less efficient ones.

10. Their model also controls for AFP-specific changes in advertising expenditures, information technology expenditures, fund returns, and fund commissions and fees, all expressed in relative terms.

11. The authors note that the actual AFP identification codes had to be imputed, in some cases, as they found that old AFP codes had been overwritten when a new firm merged with or bought an old one. To correct this, the authors used published data on AFP-specific fixed commissions to reverse-engineer the codes for the actual AFPs covering the sample over time.

12. The sampling frame of the 2002 *Historia Laboral and Seguridad Social* survey consists of individuals enrolled in the social security system for at least one month during the 1981–2001 time period. The sample included individuals who

in 2002 were working, unemployed, out of the labor force, receiving pensions, or deceased (in this case, the information was collected from surviving relatives). The sample was drawn from a sampling frame of approximately 8.1 million current and former affiliates of the social security system that was compiled from official databases (obtained from the secretary of labor and social security). This sample covers around 75 percent of the population aged 15 and older in 2001. The sampling frame in 2004 was augmented to include a subsample of individuals not affiliated with the social security system, so that the sample is representative of the entire Chilean population over the age of 15. The proportion of individuals in the population who are affiliated or not affiliated with the social security system is known, so weights can be used to adjust for the choice-based sampling data design.

13. There is some very recent research on 401(k) plan switching patterns by Mitchell et al. (2006a, 2006b).

14. During the first twenty years, Chilean AFP affiliates could decide only which AFP they wanted to invest with but were not permitted to diversify their holdings across AFPs, nor could they choose asset allocations. In 2000, the government permitted the AFPs to open a more conservative account for retirees or those within ten years of legal retirement. In 2002, each fund administrator was permitted to expand the number of investment offerings from two to five in order to allow participants to diversify their asset allocations. Under this new "multifund" structure, each AFP must offer a so-called fund A, which invests 80 percent of the portfolio in equities; fund E, which holds 100 percent fixed income; and funds B–D, which hold intermediate fractions of equities. Workers may elect to hold up to two funds in a single AFP at a time (see Arenas de Mesa et al. 2008).

15. In practice, Skog (2006) notes that the PRIDIT model first measures what proportion of the population has an identifying trait, such as answering a question correctly. The difference of an individual's score from the mean is then calculated. These scores are then normalized, and the principle component of a group of questions is computed and used to calculate the final PRIDIT score. Skog (2006) uses these literacy scores as dependent variables and reports that older, healthier, more highly paid, and more educated men are more pension literate across the board. He also contends that people appear more likely to inform themselves as knowledge becomes more relevant, implying that they may respond to incentives when investing in self-education.

16. We measure switching using the administrative data, which provide monthly information on each affiliate's AFP. This information is merged with the socioeconomic and financial literacy information from the Encuesta de Protección Social, and the analysis uses the subset with data from both sources. It should be mentioned that we inferred that a person's *reported* AFP was incorrect in a case in which this AFP was not in existence during a given year. When this AFP had recently merged with another AFP, we imputed the new AFP value to the individual. In a few cases, less than 5 percent, the AFP could not be confirmed and the

observation was dropped. Similar data checks were conducted by Berstein and Cabrita (2006), who assisted this project in providing guidance on the AFP imputation algorithm.

17. We plan to examine this potential reason for nonworking individuals to switch in future work.

18. We also estimate random-effects models, which are not reported here for brevity; the results are quite similar to those reported in the text.

References

Arenas de Mesa, Alberto, David Bravo, Jere Behrman, Olivia S. Mitchell, and Petra Todd. 2008. The Chilean Pension Reform Turns 25: Lessons from the Social Protection Survey. In *Lessons from Pension Reform in the Americas*, edited by Stephen Kay and Tapen Sinha, 23–58. Oxford: Oxford University Press.

Baeza, Sergio, and Francisco Margozzini. 1995. *Quince Años Después. Una Mirada al Sistema Privado de Pensiones*. Santiago, Chile: Centro de Estudios Públicos.

Barrientos, Armando, and Aziz Boussofiane. 2005. How Efficient Are Pension Fund Managers in Chile? *Revista de Economia Contemporânea* 9: 289–311.

Berstein, Solange, and Carolina Cabrita. 2007. Los Determinantes de la Elección de AFP en Chile: Nueva Evidencia a Partir de Datos Individuales. *Estudios de Economía* 34: 53–72.

Berstein, Solange, and Alejandro Micco. 2002. Turnover and Regulation: The Chilean Pension Fund Industry. Working Paper No. 180. Central Bank of Chile, Santiago.

Berstein, Solange, and José Ruiz. 2004. Sensibilidad de la Demanda con Consumidores Desinformados: El Caso de las AFP en Chile. *Revista de Temas Financieros* 1 Superintendencia de Banca y Seguros, Perú.

Bravo, David, and Javiera Vásquez. 2004. Comportamiento Manada en las Administradoras de Fondos de Pensiones. Working paper. Department of Economics, University of Chile.

Brockett, Patrick L., Richard A. Derrig, Linda L. Golden, Albert Levine, and Mark Alpert. 2002. Fraud Classification Using Principal Component Analysis of RIDITs. *Journal of Risk and Insurance* 69: 341–73.

Cerda, Rodrigo. 2005. Movilidad en al Cartera de Cotizantes por AFP: La importancia de ser Primero en Rentabilidad. Documento de Trabajo 309, PUC.

Cheyre, Hernán. 1988. *La Previsión en Chile Ayer y Hoy*. Santiago, Chile: Centro de Estudios Públicos.

Cogan, John F., and Olivia S. Mitchell. 2003. Perspectives from the President's Commission on Social Security Reform. *Journal of Economic Perspectives* 17: 149–72.

Consejo Asesor Presidencial para la Reforma Previsional. 2006. *El derecho a una vida digna en la vejez. Hacia un contrato social con la previsión en Chile.* Diagnóstico y Propuestas de Reforma vol. 1. Santiago, Chile: Consejo Asesor Presidencial para la Reforma Previsional. Available at http://www.consejoreformaprevisional.cl.

Gobierno de Chile. 2006. Proyecto de Ley que Perfecciona el Sistema Previsional. Mensaje de la Presidenta de la República enviado a la Cámara de Diputados, December 15.

Gustman, Alan, and Thomas Steinmeier. 1999. What People Don't Know about Their Pensions and Social Security: An Analysis Using Linked Data from the Health and Retirement Study. NBER Working Paper No. 7368. National Bureau of Economic Research, Cambridge, MA.

Gustman, Alan, Thomas Steinmeier, and Nahid Tabatabai. 2007. Do Workers Know about Their Pension Plan Type? Comparing Workers' and Employers' Pension Information. This volume.

Holzmann, Robert, and Richard Hinz, together with Hermann von Gersdorff, Indermit Gill, Gregorio Impavido, Alberto R. Mussalem, Michal Rutkowski, Robert Palacios, Yvonne Sin, Kalanidhi Subbarao, and Anita Schwarz. 2005. *Old-Age Income Support in the Twenty-first Century: An International Perspective on Pension Systems and Reform.* Washington, DC: World Bank.

Iglesias, Augusto, and Rodrigo Acuña. 1991. *Chile: Experiencia con un Régimen de Capitalización 1981–1991.* Santiago: CEPAL/PNUD.

James, Estelle, Gustavo Ferrier, James Smalhout, and Dmitri Vittas. 1998. Mutual Funds and Institutional Investments. Paper presented at the World Bank, Washington, DC.

James, Estelle, James Smalhout, and Dmitri Vittas. 2001. Administrative Costs and the Organization of Individual Account Systems: A Comparative Perspective. In *New ideas about Old Age Security. Towards Sustainable Pension Systems in the 21st Century,* edited by R. Holzmann and J. E. Stiglitz, 254–307. Washington, DC: World Bank.

Lusardi, Annamaria, and Olivia S. Mitchell. 2006. Financial Literacy and Retirement Planning: Implications for Retirement Wellbeing. Pension Research Council working paper.

———. 2007. Baby Boomer Retirement Security: The Roles of Planning, Financial Literacy, and Housing Wealth. *Journal of Monetary Economics* 54: 205–24.

Marinovic, Ivan, and Salvador Valdes-Prieto. 2005. La Demanda de las AFP Chilenas: 1993–2002. Presented at the Society of Chilean Economists (SECHI), Santiago.

Ministerio de Planificación (Mideplan). 2007. La Situación de la Pobreza en Chile 2006. Serie Análisis de Resultados de la Encuesta de Caracterización Socioeconómica Nacional (CASEN 2006). Available at http://www.mideplan.cl.

Mitchell, Olivia S. 1988. Worker Knowledge of Pension Provisions. *Journal of Labor Economics* 6: 21–39.

Mitchell, Olivia S., Gary Mottola, Steve Utkus, and Takeshi Yamaguchi. 2006a. The Inattentive Participant: Trading Behavior in 401(k) Plans. Working paper. Pension Research Council, the Wharton School, University of Pennsylvania, Philadelphia, PA.

———. 2006b. Winners and Losers: 401(k) Trading and Portfolio Performance. Working paper. Pension Research Council, the Wharton School, University of Pennsylvania, Philadelphia, PA.

Rodriguez, Jacobo. 1998. El Sistema Chileno de Pensiones a los 18 Años: Su Estado Actual y sus Desafíos Futuros. CATO Institute Policy Analysis Report 340. Available at http://www.elcato.org/node/1358.

Skog, Jeremy. 2006. Who Knows What about Their Pension Plans? Financial Literacy in the Chilean Individual Account System. Working paper. Pension Research Council, the Wharton School, University of Pennsylvania, Philadelphia, PA.

Superintendencia de Administradoras de Fondos de Pensiones (SAFP). 2003. The Chilean Pension System. 4th ed. Santiago, Chile: SAFP.

Tokman, Victor E. 2001. Integrating the Informal Sector in the Modernization Process. SAIS Review 21: 45–60.

Valdés Prieto, Salvador. 1999. Las Comisiones de las AFPs: ¿Caras o Baratas? Estudios Públicos 73: 255–91.

———. 2005. Para Aumentar La Competencia Entre las AFP. Estudios Publicos 98: 87–142.

CHAPTER TWELVE

Learning from the Experience of Sweden: The Role of Information and Education in Pension Reform

Annika Sundén

Introduction

Public and occupational pensions are the major sources of income for most workers during retirement. How much income workers will have in retirement depends on a range of decisions—from how much to work and save to when to retire. Recent trends in pension reform around the world are likely to increase individuals' need for information about pension plans as well as the need for general financial literacy. Furthermore, because of the increased financial pressures caused by aging populations, pension reforms often result in a reduction in replacement rates, hence increasing the need for individuals to save for their own retirement.

Previous research has documented that individuals often have limited financial knowledge and know little about the characteristics of their public and occupational pension plans or how much to expect in retirement benefits (see, for example, Mitchell 1988; Gustman and Steinmeier 2004; Lusardi and Mitchell 2007b; Gustman, Steinmeier, and Tabatabai, this volume). As a consequence, workers run the risk of reaching retirement with inadequate resources and may have to postpone retirement or lower consumption in retirement. Several studies have confirmed that financial literacy and planning affect savings and retirement outcomes. Individuals who approach retirement without planning have lower savings. Similarly, individuals with little or no financial knowledge are less likely to be successful planners and savers (Ameriks, Caplin, and Leahy 2002; Lusardi and Mitchell 2006, 2007a). Studies have also shown that knowledge about pension benefits affects retirement behavior. For example, workers who underestimate their benefits are less likely to retire early than those who overestimate their benefits (Gustman and Steinmeier 2001; Chan and Huff Stevens 2008). The experience with 401(k) plans in the United States provides evidence that funded individual accounts introduce further difficulties for workers and that financial illiteracy can negatively affect outcomes (see, for example, Munnell and Sundén 2004; Beshears, Choi, Laibson, and Madrian 2006).

Possible reasons for the lack of knowledge are that pensions are complex entities and learning about pensions is difficult. The complexity involved makes the costs of collecting information appear greater than the benefits of understanding the plans. Furthermore, the retirement process is something individuals only go through once; participants do not have the benefit of learning by doing. In addition, old age is often viewed as something unpleasant and a cause for worry, so learning about pensions and retirement can involve psychological costs. Finally, participants may not appreciate the benefits of collecting information because they expect that the public pension system will provide adequate benefits.

The changing pension landscape and the widespread lack of knowledge about pensions have prompted policy makers and employers to provide more information about pension plans through information campaigns and financial education programs in the workplace.

Sweden is an interesting example of this development. Sweden introduced a comprehensive pension reform during the 1990s that transformed the public defined benefit plan to a defined contribution plan. The pension reform changed the provision of public pension benefits in a fundamental way and redefined the benefit promise. In the new system, benefits are closely linked to contributions, and lifetime earnings will determine benefits. The reform recognized the impact of increased life expectancy on the financial stability of the system and built in an automatic adjustment of benefits in response to changes in longevity. The design means that additional responsibility is put on participants. The new system also puts increased responsibility on individuals to plan for retirement through the introduction of a funded individual account component.

The purpose of this chapter is to discuss Swedish pension reform and the important role that information and education have played both in its implementation and on an ongoing basis. As part of the information effort, a new annual statement for the pension system has been developed: the Orange Envelope.

Information and education efforts have to some extent paid off. Most participants know about the annual pension statement and have also opened the Orange Envelope. However, fewer than half of participants view their own understanding of the new system as good, and many are still unaware of the key principles of how benefits are determined. For example, the notion that the individual account component is more important for retirement income than the pay-as-you-go portion of the system seems to be widespread.

The large supply of funds in the individual accounts has had an immobilizing effect, contrary to intentions. In the 2006 enrollment period, fewer than 10 percent of new participants chose how to invest their portfolios. Participants also report that they lack sufficient knowledge to manage their accounts. The Swedish experience makes clear that, in addition to financial education, carefully considering the number of funds in the system as well as the design of the default fund is important to participants' ability to manage their individual accounts.

The first section of this chapter describes the Swedish pension reform and the importance of information and education under the new system. This is followed by a discussion of the information and education efforts that have been implemented in connection with the pension reform. The final two sections examine the funded individual accounts and participants' investment behavior and provide concluding remarks.

The Swedish Pension Reform and the Need for Information

The Swedish Pension Reform

Pension reform discussions in Sweden started in the early 1990s prompted by large projected shortfalls in the earnings-related scheme. The defined benefit design was sensitive to changes in economic growth and the aging population, and further pressures were added owing to the maturity of the system. A government commission was appointed in 1991 and quickly worked out the principles of the reform. The reform proposal was passed "in principle" by parliament in 1994 with broad political support. The final legislation was passed in June 1998, and the new system went into effect in 1999.[1] The reform transformed the public pension system to a notional defined contribution plan—that is, a defined contribution plan financed on a pay-as-you-go basis. In addition, a second tier of funded individual accounts was introduced.

A guiding principle for the policy makers was that a majority of the political parties should stand behind the reform to ensure the pension system's future stability. The result was a compromise between the Social Democrats and the center-liberal parties and, thus, includes both pay-as-you-go elements and funded individual accounts. A defined contribution plan was favored because it made it possible to create a strong link between contributions and benefits and also ensured a contribution rate that would remain unchanged in the future.

The earnings-related scheme in the new public pension system consists of two components: a defined contribution plan funded on a pay-as-you-go basis, the notional defined contribution plan (NDC), and small funded individual accounts, the Premium Pension. The introduction of the individual account component was contentious but eventually became part of the compromise. The motivation was to allow participants to take advantage of the higher rate of return in the capital markets as well as to tailor part of their pension to their risk preferences. In connection with the public pension reform, three of the four main occupational plans replaced their defined benefit plans with funded individual accounts.

An important objective of the public pension scheme in Sweden has always been to provide adequate retirement income for all residents. The new pension system therefore includes a basic means-tested guaranteed benefit to ensure a minimum standard of living in retirement for individuals with no or low earnings–related benefits.[2]

The total mandatory contribution rate is 18.5 percent of earnings: 16 percent is credited to the notional account component, and 2.5 percent to the individual account component, the Premium Pension.[3] Individuals earn pension rights from labor income, benefits from unemployment insurance, and other social insurance programs, as well as from years spent at home taking care of children, time in military service, and in education.[4] Because all income counts toward benefits and women participate in the labor force almost to the same extent as men, the need for guaranteed benefits will decrease in the future.

In the NDC, contributions are recorded in workers' individual accounts, and the account values there represent individuals' claims on future pension benefits. The account balance grows with annual contributions and the rate of return on the account. Every year of earnings counts toward pension rights; the system has no lower or upper age limit for earning credits. The rate of return is set equal to per capita real wage growth in order to link earned pension rights to the earnings of the working population. Retirement ages are flexible, and benefits can be withdrawn starting at age 61. At retirement, annual benefits are calculated by dividing the balance in the notional account by an annuity divisor that is linked to the average life expectancy at retirement for a given cohort at age 65.

Because most of the system is still a pay-as-you-go system it remains sensitive to demographic change. To deal with possible financial instability, the system includes an automatic balancing mechanism. As soon as the system is in imbalance, the indexation of earned pension rights and current benefits is reduced to bring the system back into balance. The adjustment works automatically and does not require any explicit action by politicians.

The Premium Pension constitutes a relatively small portion of the new system, and participation is mandatory. Policy makers decided to offer investors a broad choice in the Premium Pension, so any fund company licensed to do business in Sweden is allowed to participate in the system.[5] When the system was launched in 2000, approximately 460 funds participated. Today, almost eight hundred funds are part of the system. The majority of funds (more than 70 percent) are equity funds, and about half of the funds invest primarily in international equities. A large number of funds specialize in one type of asset, such as information technology funds, while few funds are designed with retirement savings in mind; only 4 percent of the available funds are life-cycle funds. The mix of funds in the Swedish system is somewhat different from that of funds in the United States, where life-cycle funds are becoming common as an investment option in pension plans.[6]

The Swedish government has established a default fund for participants who do not choose to put together their own portfolios. In initial discussions, reformers had suggested that the default should be a low-risk fund mostly invested in interest-earning assets. Yet policy makers were concerned that such a strategy would have a negative effect on the distribution of benefits, because low-income workers would be more likely to invest in the default. Currently, the default fund seeks to achieve a high long-run rate of return at an overall low risk level.[7] The fund follows a fixed allocation of stocks and bonds in which equity holdings cannot exceed 90 percent of the total value and may not fall below 80 percent; of these, a maximum of 75 percent can be invested in foreign stocks. Currently, the default fund holds 65 percent of its assets in international equities and 17 percent in Swedish equities.

When individual pension rights have been determined, participants select how to invest their funds.[8] Participants may choose up to five funds.
Once a participant has chosen an allocation, all future contributions are
invested according to that allocation until the participant makes a change.
Individuals are allowed to change funds on a daily basis. A participant who
makes an active investment choice may not invest any share of the portfolio in the default fund or shift to the default at a later date.[9] At retirement,
annuitization is mandatory. In contrast, in defined contribution plans in
the United States, annuitization is voluntary and, although participants
in general are better off converting their wealth to an annuity at retirement, demand is low.[10] In Sweden, the government is the sole provider of
annuities, and participants can choose between a fixed or variable annuity.
The level of the annuity is based on standard insurance practices and uses
unisex life tables of persons in the age cohort from the year the calculation is made.[11]

The Need for Information

The new system puts additional demands on participants. In order to make
decisions about retirement age and how much to save, participants in the
system need information about how the level of benefits varies according
to labor supply and retirement age. In the prereform defined benefit plan,
benefits were determined by a combination of individual earnings and
years of service—benefits were 60 percent of the average of a worker's 15
years with the highest earnings, with thirty years of service required in order to receive full benefits. This formula made it relatively easy to express
benefits as a replacement rate. Because benefits in the new system are not
defined but will depend on contributions and the rate of return on those
contributions, it is difficult to express the expected benefit in terms of a
replacement rate. Projections that help participants estimate how their
retirement wealth will translate into monthly payments are therefore an
important component of the information that Swedish participants need.

Participants must also understand how benefits vary with retirement
age. In the prereform plan, full benefits were paid at age 65, the normal
retirement age, but benefits could be withdrawn from the age of 60 with
an actuarial reduction. In the new pension system, retirement is flexible
and benefits can be withdrawn from age 61. In converting the benefit to
an annuity, life expectancy matters. In the Swedish system, the automatic
adjustment of benefits in response to changes in life expectancy means

that younger cohorts of workers will need to postpone their retirement to achieve the same replacement rate as older cohorts. For example, with current projections, the annuity divisor for the cohort born in 1940 is 15.7, compared with 17.9 for the cohort born in 1980. Thus, those born in 1980 need to postpone retirement a full two years compared with those born in 1940 (who retire at age 65) to neutralize the effect of increased life expectancy. The crucial message is that successive cohorts have to work longer to maintain similar replacement rates.

An implication of the NDC design is that all adjustments to maintain financial stability take place on the benefit side. In addition to automatically adjusting benefits to life expectancy, the system includes an automatic balancing mechanism that will ensure that the NDC system's assets always cover its liability by adjusting the indexation of earned pension rights and benefits.[12] When the automatic balancing mechanism was introduced, it was described as "an emergency brake" that would only be used rarely and only in situations when the system was in crisis. If automatic balancing occurs, one risk is that it signals to the public that the system is in crisis. A challenge for the communication strategy is to convey that the automatic balancing is a regular component of the indexation of earned pension rights.

The lion's share of benefits in the Swedish pension system is determined by the NDC and thus by how much an individual works; only a relatively small share of retirement income depends on investment behavior and asset returns. On the other hand, the Premium Pension puts additional demands on workers. Participants are expected to put together a diversified portfolio suitable for retirement savings from a menu of almost eight hundred funds. The funds in the system allow workers to take on very large risks, so poor knowledge of how to balance risk and return could have dire consequences.

Information and Financial Education

The new system puts more of the risk and responsibility related to retirement planning on individuals, so providing information to participants has been a crucial component in the implementation of the Swedish reform and continues to be so.

A broad information campaign was launched to educate participants when the new system was introduced in 1998. The campaign included a detailed brochure that described the new pension system, public service announcements in the media, seminars that discussed the new pension system, and a Web site. During the campaign, participants also received their first account statement for the pension scheme, the so-called Orange Envelope.

The Orange Envelope is the cornerstone of communication to participants about the pension system. It is sent out annually and includes account information as well as a projection of benefits for the NDC and the Premium Pension. In addition to providing information about expected benefits, the Orange Envelope summarizes how the new pension system works and highlights for participants the fact that benefits are determined by lifetime earnings.

Occupational pension plans make up approximately 15 percent of retirement income, and in order to judge whether benefits will be adequate, participants need projections of total retirement income. Therefore, the Social Insurance Agency and the Premium Pension Authority (PPA) together with the insurance companies for the occupation plans have launched a Web site that presents forecasts of both the public pension and occupational pension benefits.

For the individual account component, the PPA—the government agency that administers the plan and acts as a clearinghouse for fund selections—provides information on fund choices, investment risk, and fees and has its own Web site where participants can review and manage their accounts. A catalog listing all the participating funds is distributed once a year.[13] The funds are listed by type (interest-earning, mixed, life-cycle, and equity funds), and for each fund the catalog provides information on the rate of return for the past five years, the risk (measured as the standard deviation of returns for the past three years), and the fee.

In connection with the mailing of the Orange Envelope, workplace seminars are organized to provide information about the pension system.

How does information work? In order to gauge the effectiveness of communication with participants, the Swedish Social Insurance Agency conducts an annual survey about the Orange Envelope to examine how participants use it and how well it communicates information about the pension system. The survey has been conducted annually since 1998. The sample is 1,000 individuals between the ages 18 and 62, and interviews are conducted by telephone. The survey asks respondents to rate their knowledge of the pension system and indicate to what extent they read the information provided in the Orange Envelope. It also includes questions

to test participants' knowledge of the system. The survey includes demographic and economic background variables such as age, gender, marital
status, education, and income. In 2006, the average age of respondents
was 41 and slightly more women than men answered the survey. About 30
percent of respondents have a college degree, and most respondents have
incomes in the range of 17,000–25,000 Swedish crowns.[14] Slightly more
than half have private pension savings.

Most people know about the Orange Envelope. Figure 12.1 shows that
the share of participants who know that they have received the envelope
has held steady at around 90 percent. But those who made use of it are
a much smaller percentage. Roughly three-fourths of all participants say
they have opened the envelope, and about half report reading at least
some of the content.

Not surprisingly, older participants read the contents of the Orange
Envelope to a greater extent than younger participants, but the differences
are quite small with the exception of those younger than 25 (not shown).
The data also show that low-income individuals are less likely to examine
the envelope's materials. Participants who have private pension savings,
for example, an individual retirement account, are more likely to open and
read the envelope. Only 20 percent of all participants had compared the

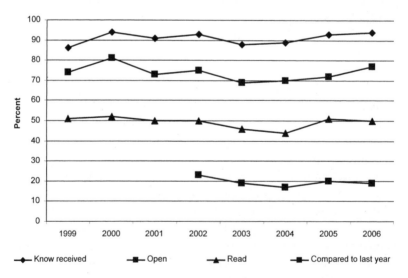

FIGURE 12.1 Share of participants who know about the Orange Envelope. (Source: Survey
of the Orange Envelope.)

information in the current Orange Envelope with the previous years' content. Thus, the group who is most likely to read and examine the materials corresponds to the group of participants who is most likely to already have some financial literacy. The pattern has changed little since the introduction of the envelope, so it is not clear whether the Orange Envelope has attracted less-interested participants.

To help participants translate their account balances into monthly benefits at retirement, the Orange Envelope includes a benefit projection. The benefit projection calculates the expected monthly benefit at three different retirement ages: 61, 65, and 70. Because it is difficult for participants to make these kinds of calculations on their own in a defined contribution plan, this information is clearly important in order to assess whether retirement benefits will be adequate. The results show that among those who *opened* the envelope, about 70 percent looked at the benefit projection during the first years the envelope was sent out. By 2005, the share had increased to almost 80 percent.

The Orange Envelope has been successful to the extent that almost everyone knows about it and also reads at least some of the contents. The question is whether the Orange Envelope has improved knowledge about the pension system. Because the survey is a cross section and no information is available on the level of knowledge about pensions before the envelope was introduced, it is not possible to link the use of the Orange Envelope to how knowledge about the pension system has evolved.[15] However, in addition to self-reported knowledge, the survey includes some questions that try to elicit participants' actual understanding and that can give an indication of how well participants understand the system and to what extent the Orange Envelope has contributed to that knowledge.

Self-reported knowledge about the pension system is fairly low, and more than half of participants view their knowledge as poor. Knowledge about the system peaked in 2002, when 48 percent reported that they had a good understanding of the system. By 2006 this share had decreased by 10 percentage points. The share of participants who report that they do not understand the new system at all is less than 10 percent, although the share has decreased somewhat in the last few years.

Men view themselves as being more knowledgeable than women, and formal education and income appear to be positively correlated with knowledge about the pension system. One measure of financial literacy could be previous experience with saving for retirement. About half of the respondents in the Swedish survey have private pension savings such as an individual retirement account, an indication that they have spent at least some time thinking about retirement. Having a private pension appears to be correlated with slightly higher self-reported knowledge about the public pension system—about 50 percent of respondents who have private pensions report that they have poor knowledge of the system, compared with 60 percent among those without such savings.

Among those who have read at least some parts of the Orange Envelope, the fraction that reports having good knowledge of the system is about 13 percentage points higher than among those who have not read the contents. In recent years, the share of those with poor knowledge or no knowledge at all has increased somewhat.

The survey also includes a set of questions to gauge actual knowledge of the pension system. Perhaps the most important piece of information about the pension system for participants is that benefits depend on lifetime labor supply. The share of participants who know that lifetime earnings determine benefits peaked in 2000, the year after the new pension system was introduced and an extensive information campaign was conducted, when slightly more than half of participants correctly answered a survey question to gauge this knowledge. Among those who read at least some of the Orange Envelope contents, the share is only slightly higher and follows a similar pattern over time. Overall, men are somewhat more likely than women to have knowledge about the basic principles of the pension system. Not surprisingly, income and education are also important determinants of actual knowledge—participants in the highest income class and with college degrees have better knowledge of the system than participants with low incomes and fewer years of education.

Knowledge of the pension system can also be measured by how well participants know the components of the system. Here the results indicate fairly little understanding of the system. Overall, 75 percent of participants cannot name any part of the pension system. Only about 10 percent of participants can accurately name the NDC benefit, the main component of the system. It is also surprising that so few participants know about the guaranteed benefit; a possible explanation is that few workers in the future will depend on guaranteed benefits.

Much of the public debate about the pension system has evolved around the Premium Pension and investment decisions. Anecdotal evidence indicates that participants have a skewed view of the importance of the Premium Pension and believe that investment decisions will determine most of benefits. The view is confirmed by the survey about the

Orange Envelope; participants are much more likely to know about the Premium Pension than about the NDC component. Again, participants who have read the contents of the Orange Envelope are slightly more likely to be aware of the different parts of the pension system. A possible explanation is, of course, that individuals who open and read the envelope are the ones that are interested in and have previous knowledge of the pension system.

To summarize, most people know about and read the contents of the Orange Envelope. Still, only about 40 percent understand that lifetime earnings determine benefits, one of the most important characteristics of the pension system. Even fewer know the different components of the system. But although self-rated and actual knowledge is somewhat low, participants have confidence in the system. More than one-third of participants are very confident about the system, and almost half have at least some confidence in the system. The share that has no confidence in the system has decreased from 20 percent at the time the new system was introduced to about 13 percent in 2006. The level of confidence could indicate that the overall information campaign has been successful in communicating that the pension reform has created a financially stable system.

Overall, the Swedish pension system offers a large amount of information. Even so, a majority of participants report that they would like additional information and help. Anecdotal evidence indicates that many participants feel uncertain and think that they should be more engaged in their pension decisions. Much of this uncertainty is likely to stem from the investment decisions connected to the Premium Pension. The fact that participants in general overestimate the role of the Premium Pension could contribute to the overall anxiety.

Investment Behavior

Although the individual account component—the Premium Pension—is relatively small in the overall pension system, it has been the focus of discussions about the need for information and education. The system offers participants broad choice, and they are expected to put together a portfolio from a selection of nearly eight hundred mutual funds. All types of mutual funds are allowed in the system, so participants are expected to know how to construct a portfolio suited for retirement savings. With the wide range of funds available, participants run the risk of taking on either

too much risk or too little; the extent to which the system has positive effects on retirement benefits will depend on participants' ability to make
rational investment decisions. The challenge for the information and education efforts is to guide participants in making such decisions.

The first investment election in the Premium Pension took place during the fall of 2000.[16] The objective was to induce as many participants as
possible to make an active choice, and the PPA launched a large campaign
to encourage participants to select their own portfolios. In addition to the
PPA, private fund managers also put significant resources into ad campaigns to attract investors.

About 68 percent of participants made an "active choice" and chose
their portfolios in 2000. Subsequently, the share has fallen precipitously:
today fewer than 10 percent of new participants make an active investment decision (figure 12.2). Women and men are equally (un)likely to
make active choices (not shown).

One explanation for the sharp decline in participants choosing their
portfolios could be that the new entrants after 2000 are mostly young
workers entering the labor market, far from retirement. However, close
to 60 percent of participants in the same age group chose their own portfolio in the first investment elections in 2000. A more likely explanation
for the downward trend is that participants paid much less attention to
the Premium Pension in later enrollment periods. The fund industry has

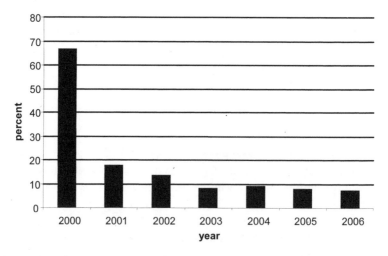

FIGURE 12.2 Share of new participants making an active choice, 2000–2006. (Source: Premium Pension Authority.)

continued their marketing campaigns, but the government no longer actively encourages participants to make an active choice and instead focuses on providing information about the funds' risks and fees. But maybe the most important explanation is that selecting a portfolio among almost eight hundred funds is just too difficult. The number of investment options in the Swedish plan vastly exceeds what is available in other countries that have introduced individual accounts or in 401(k) plans in the United States. Psychologists and economists in general believe that more choice is better, but recent research in both fields challenges this view by showing that a large number of options can, in fact, be demotivating (see, for example, Lowenstein 1999; Iyengar and Lepper 2000).[17]

Another possible explanation is that the default fund has performed better than the average portfolio. Overall, the rate of return for the period 2000–2005 for participants who made an active choice has been below that for a randomly picked portfolio. The initial investment selections in 2000 coincided with the peak of the run-up in the stock market, and in the year following the first investments the stock market tumbled. The default fund is also considerably cheaper than other funds—the fee for the default fund is 0.16 percent, while the average fund fee for participants who made an active choice was 0.55 percent.

Participants in general report that they lack knowledge to manage their accounts: half of participants report that they have poor knowledge, while about one-third report having some knowledge (table 12.1).[18] Not surprisingly, self-reported knowledge increases with age, income, and education. Participants who reported having poor knowledge were asked whether they would like additional help in making investment decisions; 60 percent answered that they would like additional support, primarily information about how to think about investments, such as the trade-off between risk and return.

Among participants who have made active investment decisions in the Premium Pension, experience to date indicates that workers are making mistakes similar to those that have been documented in, for example, 401(k) plans in the United States. For example, recent evidence suggests that only about 40 percent of 401(k) participants' portfolios have balanced exposure to diversified equities (see the chapter by Mottola and Utkus in this volume).

Participants' portfolios are heavily weighted toward equities—in 2006, 89 percent of assets in the Premium Pension were invested in equities. The high equity share is not necessarily an indication of an undiversified

TABLE 12.1 **Share of participants with poor, some, and good knowledge of managing premium pension**

	Poor knowledge	Some knowledge	Good knowledge
All	50.4	30.4	15.2
Age:			
18–24	72.4	17.9	9.7
25–34	56.0	27.3	16.7
35–44	51.7	29.4	18.8
45–54	47.6	33.6	18.8
55–62	36.4	37.0	26.6
Monthly earnings (SEK):			
< 17,000 (very low)	57.3	29.8	12.9
17,000–25,000 (low)	50.2	31.3	18.5
25,000–33,000 (middle)	37.9	34.1	28.0
33,000+ (high)	27.4	29.8	42.8
Education:			
Less than high school	48.8	35.3	15.9
High school	53.3	31.4	15.4
College	46.7	26.7	26.6

Source: Survey of the Orange Envelope.

portfolio for the average investor because most of retirement income comes from the pay-as-you-go portion of the public pension system that depends on the participants' human capital and can be thought of as a bond.

However, we would expect workers with high risk in their human capital to diversify their overall portfolio and invest their Premium Pension in less risky assets. Low lifetime earnings can serve as a proxy for high risk in human capital, so a positive relationship between risk in the Premium Pension portfolio and income would signal rational investment behavior. When investment behavior is related to income, the results show a U-shaped relationship: participants at the bottom of the income distribution take on as much risk as those at the top, indicating that they are not diversifying their overall portfolio (see Palme, Sundén, and Söderlind 2007). Variability in income or high risk for disability or unemployment does not appear to affect the investment decision. This could indicate that workers with high risk in their human capital ignore these risks and thus take on too much risk in their Premium Pension. On the other hand, participants who expect to receive the guaranteed benefit have little to lose by taking on additional risk in their pension investments because the level of the guarantee provides a minimum secure benefit.

A common mistake among participants in individual accounts is to concentrate too much of their assets in their own country, sector, or company.

Such a strategy means that a participant's financial assets are concentrated in the same country or sector as their human capital. In the Swedish case, participants employed in the manufacturing sector—the sector that is probably most correlated with the Swedish stock market—are the least likely to invest in foreign assets. This indicates that participants do not diversify their portfolios to offset the risks that arise from the concentration of human capital in Sweden. Instead, portfolio choice appears to reflect home bias.[19] Participants in banking and the insurance industry are more likely to invest in foreign assets, possibly reflecting more financial knowledge. Finally, participants do not appear to rebalance their portfolios over time. Since the initial investment selections in 2000, only 20 percent of participants have changed allocations.

Participants' investment behavior in the Premium Pension is largely consistent with the results found for nonpension investment behavior of Swedish households (see Calvet, Campbell, and Sodini 2006). Looking at nonpension assets, households in general have diversified portfolios. However, investing in equities and mutual funds is correlated with income and education; households with nondiversified portfolios tend to have lower education and lower wealth. The results indicate that when these households enter equity markets they run the risk of investing poorly, maybe as exemplified by the high risk taken on by participants in the Premium Pension who have low earnings.

As a result, groups of workers may experience systematically poor outcomes in the Premium Pension, and for many participants the default fund may have been a better alternative than an active investment strategy. In later enrollment periods, the PPA has taken a more passive role and to a large extent limited its provision of information about the funds' risks and fees. The objective is to improve the public's financial knowledge so that participants can make good investment decisions. To this end, the agency introduced an interactive investment tool on its Web site in 2005. The tool guides participants through a set of questions to determine their tolerance for risk. Based on the resulting risk-tolerance level, a portfolio allocation is suggested, and the participant is presented with a selection of funds to achieve that portfolio allocation. To encourage active participants to review their allocations, all participants who had not changed allocations since 2000 were encouraged through a letter to visit the Web site and use the investment tool. So far, it is mostly participants who already take an active interest in their Premium Pension who have used the tool (Premium Pension Annual Report 2006).

Should active participation in the Premium Pension be encouraged? The question is whether this strategy will be successful. Experience with financial education programs from the United States shows some positive effects, but overall, the results indicate that it is difficult to improve financial knowledge.[20] Information and education are clearly important components of the Premium Pension, but the experience with encouraging active choice illustrates how imperfect consumer information can lead to inefficient outcomes.

Conclusion

Swedish pension reform replaced the public defined benefit plan with a defined contribution plan. Most of the scheme is still pay-as-you-go, but it also includes a small component of funded individual accounts. One of the most important objectives of the Swedish pension reform was to design a pension system that would be financially stable over time, even when faced with adverse demographic and economic developments. The defined contribution design was chosen to provide increased work incentives and to give participants an opportunity to control some of their pension funds.

The new defined contribution plan redefines the benefit promise and puts more risk and responsibility on participants to plan for retirement. The automatic adjustment of benefits to life expectancy means that individuals will have to either work longer or save more to maintain replacement rates. Reliable projections of expected benefits and an understanding of how benefits vary with retirement age are crucial for participants. Furthermore, the broad investment choice in the funded individual account requires that participants be familiar with general principles of investing. Therefore, an instrumental component of the reform has been information and education. In particular, a large effort has been put into the development of the annual account statement, the Orange Envelope.

The information and education efforts have to some extent paid off. Almost everyone knows about the Orange Envelope, and most individuals have at least opened it. When the envelope is mailed out in the spring, news media regularly report about the pension system and expected benefits. On the other hand, results from surveys regarding the information and education initiative in Sweden indicate only limited success in increasing knowledge about the new system so far. For example, fewer than 40 percent of respondents indicate that they have a good understanding of the new system. Many participants are still unaware of the key principles regarding how benefits are determined, and the notion that the individual account component is more important for retirement income than the NDC benefit seems to be widespread.

In the Premium Pension, the large number of funds to choose from has had a paralyzing effect, contrary to intentions. Moreover, participants' interest in choosing their portfolios in the Premium Pension has decreased considerably since its inception. In the 2006 enrollment period, fewer than 10 percent of new participants chose how to invest their portfolios. The experience with the Swedish Premium Pension makes clear that, in addition to financial education, carefully considering the number of funds in the system as well as the design of the default fund is important to participants' abilities to manage their individual accounts.

The outcome of the Swedish pension educational efforts should be viewed in light of the fact that the new Swedish pension system has been in effect for less than ten years and that most people who will depend fully on the new system are still far from retirement. On the other hand, participants report that they would like more information and, in particular, would like more help choosing funds in the Premium Pension. Given the amount of information available, the demand for more information sends a signal that something is missing in the current communication with participants. Thus, the challenge for the National Social Insurance Agency is to consider alternative ways of communicating with participants so that they have the tools they need to plan for retirement.

Notes

I would like to thank Maarten van Rooij for suggestions and comments.

1. For a discussion of the pension reform and a detailed description of the new pension system see Sundén (2006).

2. The guaranteed benefit is payable from age 65 and is currently about 40 percent of the average wage of a blue-collar worker. The guaranteed benefit is indexed to prices, and its importance in the pension system is therefore likely to decline over time. The benefit is financed by general tax revenues and is conceptually separated from the earnings-related scheme.

3. Contributions are split equally between employees and employers; employee contributions are limited by a ceiling, while the employer's share is levied on all earnings. The ceiling is approximately 1.5 times the average wage.

4. Credits for child rearing are earned until a child is 4 years old.

5. Fund companies seeking to participate must sign a contract with the PPA, which governs reporting requirements and fee structure. The total fee in the Premium Pension consists of two parts: a money management fee and a fixed administrative fee charged by the PPA. Fund managers charge the same fee for participants in the pension system as for participants in private savings markets. Because administration of the accounts is handled by the PPA, a share of the fee must be rebated to participants. The average money management fee is 0.56 percent of assets for active participants and 0.16 percent for those in the default fund. In addition, the PPA charges a fixed administrative fee of 0.16 percent of assets.

6. For a discussion of life-cycle funds as an investment option in retirement plans see the chapter by Viceira in this volume.

7. The five-year return should be in the top quartile of returns for all funds.

8. Individual pension rights are established once workers' income tax reports have been consolidated with employers' reports, a process that takes an average of 18 months.

9. This rule was a result of the center-right parties' desire to limit the government's involvement in money management.

10. See the chapter by Brown in this volume for a discussion of the role of annuities in retirement planning.

11. The Premium Pension provides a voluntary survivor benefit. If a survivor benefit is elected and the individual dies before retirement (during the accumulation phase), the survivor benefit pays a fixed amount for five years. If the individual dies after retirement, the survivor benefit will be paid as a lifelong annuity to the surviving spouse.

12. The assets in the notional defined contribution (NDC) are equal to the capitalized value of contributions.

13. Only new participants receive the catalog automatically. The information is also available on the PPA's Web site.

14. USD = 7 Swedish crowns. The income distribution of the sample is very similar to Sweden's overall income distribution.

15. A study of the introduction of an annual benefit statement in the United States showed positive effects on workers' knowledge of their benefits (Mastrobuoni 2006). In the Netherlands, workers also receive statements, and two out of three workers report that they are adequately or well informed; however, surveys of financial knowledge indicate that knowledge is fairly low. Workers in the Netherlands also indicate that they would be willing to take additional control of their pensions if they received additional financial education (van Rooij, Kool, and Prast 2007).

16. In preparation for the new system, the government began collecting contributions for the funded individual accounts in 1995 and held the money in an interest-bearing government account at the National Debt Office until the year

2000. According to the original timetable for the reform, the elections should have taken place in 1999 but were delayed because of implementation problems with the computer systems handling the administration.

17. Furthermore, making investment decisions is complicated, and many individuals have limited financial experience. As a result, they are likely to make mistakes, as shown by the experiences with 401(k) plans in the United States (Munnell and Sundén 2004).

18. The question about participants' abilities to manage their individual accounts was added to the survey in 2003, and the results are similar across years.

19. Karlsson, Massa, and Simonov (2006) show that menu choice may be an explanation for home bias in the Swedish case; that is, the bias is embedded in the menu of funds offered to participants.

20. For an overview of the effects of financial education, see Lusardi and Mitchell (2007b).

References

Ameriks, John, Andrew Caplin, and John Leahy. 2002. Wealth Accumulation and the Propensity to Plan. *Quarterly Journal of Economics* 68: 1007–47.

Beshears, John, James J. Choi, David Laibson, and Brigitte Madrian. 2006. Simplification and Saving. NBER Working Paper No. 12659. National Bureau of Economic Research, Cambridge, MA.

Brown, Jeffrey R. 2008. Understanding the Role of Annuities in Retirement Planning. This volume.

Calvet, Laurent E., John Y. Campbell, and Paolo Sodini. 2006. Down or Out: Assessing the Welfare Costs of Household Investment Mistakes. NBER Working Paper No. 12030. National Bureau of Economic Research, Cambridge, MA.

Chan, Sewin, and Ann Huff Stevens. 2008. What You Don't Know Can't Help You: Pension Knowledge and Retirement Decision Making. *Review of Economics and Statistics* 90: 253–66.

Gustman, Alan L., and Thomas L. Steinmeier. 2001. Imperfect Knowledge, Retirement, and Saving. NBER Working Paper No. 8406. National Bureau of Economic Research, Cambridge, MA.

———. 2004. What People Don't Know about Their Pensions and Social Security: An Analysis Using Linked Data from the Health and Retirement Study. In *Public Policies and Private Pensions,* edited by W. Gale, J. Shoven, and M. Warshawsky, 57–119. Washington, DC: Brookings Institution.

Gustman, Alan L., Thomas L. Steinmeier, and Nahid Tabatabai. 2008. Do Workers Know about Their Pension Plan Type? Comparing Workers' and Employers' Pension Information. This volume.

Iygengar, Sheena, and Mark Lepper. 2000. When Choice Is Demotivating: Can One Desire Too Much of a Good Thing? *Journal of Personality and Social Psychology* 76: 995–1006.

Karlsson, Anders, Massimo Massa, and Andrei Simonov. 2006. Portfolio Choice and Menu Exposure. Paper presented at the European Finance Association 2006 annual meeting, Zürich, Switzerland.

Lowenstein, George. 1999. Is More Choice Always Better? Social Security Brief. National Academy of Social Insurance, Washington, DC.

Lusardi, Annamaria, and Olivia S. Mitchell. 2006. Financial Literacy and Planning: Implications for Retirement Well-Being. Pension Research Council Working Paper No. 2006-01. The Wharton School, University of Pennsylvania, Philadelphia.

———. 2007a. Baby Boomer Retirement Security: The Roles of Planning, Financial Literacy, and Housing Wealth. *Journal of Monetary Economics* 54: 205–24.

———. 2007b. Financial Literacy and Retirement Preparedness: Evidence and Implications for Financial Education Programs. *Business Economics* 42: 34–44.

Mastrobuoni, Giovanni. 2006. Do Better-Informed Workers Make Better Retirement Choices? A Test Based on the Social Security Statement. Working paper. Collegio Carlo Alberto, Turin, Italy.

Mitchell, Olivia. 1988. Worker Knowledge of Pension Provisions. *Journal of Labor Economics* 6: 28–39.

Mottola, Gary R., and Stephen P. Utkus. 2008. Red, Yellow, and Green: Measuring the Quality of 401(k) Portfolio Choices. This volume.

Munnell, Alicia H., and Annika Sunden. 2004. *Coming up Short: The Challenge of 401(k) Plans.* Washington, DC: Brookings Institution Press.

Palme, Mårten, Annika Sundén, and Paul Söderlind. 2007. How Do Individual Accounts Work in the Swedish Pension System. *Journal of the European Economic Association* 5: 636–46.

Premium Pension Agency. 2006. Annual Report. Stockholm.

Sundén, Annika. 2006. The Swedish Experience with Pension Reform. *Oxford Review of Economic Policy* 22: 133–48.

van Rooij, Maarten, Clemens Kool, and Henriette Prast. 2007. Risk-return Preferences in the Pension Domain: Are People Able to Choose? *Journal of Public Economics* 91: 701–22.

Viceira, Luis M. 2008. Life-Cycle Funds. This volume.

CHAPTER THIRTEEN

Learning from the Experience of Organisation for Economic Co-operation and Development Countries: Lessons for Policy, Programs, and Evaluations

Barbara A. Smith and Fiona Stewart

Introduction

In the four years since the establishment of the Financial Education Project at the Organisation for Economic Co-operation and Development (OECD),[1] there has been a noticeable increase in awareness in the OECD countries of the importance of financial education. Many of these countries have not only implemented financial education programs but have also conducted financial literacy surveys to determine the level of financial understanding of their populations. In addition, policy makers in an increasing number of OECD countries are concerned about the effectiveness of financial education programs and are interested in developing ways to evaluate them.

There is much that can be learned from the experience of OECD countries. In this chapter, we discuss the findings of financial literacy surveys in selected OECD countries and relevant studies in behavioral economics, examining their implications for the design and implementation of financial education programs. In addition, we provide brief descriptions of selected financial education programs currently offered in the OECD area.

We also highlight the evaluations of financial education programs, with
an emphasis on those programs related to retirement saving, and discuss
their implications for the design and implementation of financial education programs. We conclude with some suggestions for future directions
for program evaluations.[2]

We find that financial education is increasingly necessary as consumers
take on more responsibility for their financial decisions, especially with
respect to retirement saving. At the same time, surveys across OECD
countries show low levels of financial literacy across the board and of
pension-related financial literacy specifically. The OECD countries are offering a wide variety of financial education programs on such topics as
credit, investment, and saving for retirement, which are provided through
a range of delivery channels, including the Internet, brochures, classes,
and individual counseling. The findings of financial literacy surveys on
consumers' views on financial issues, as well as the insights of behavioral
economics research into how consumers make financial decisions, provide
useful information for improving the effectiveness of financial education
programs. Although little evaluation has yet been undertaken, some initial
lessons can be drawn, including that seminars and personalized programs
and counseling can have a significant effect on saving levels and behavior.
We conclude that evaluation methodology will need to be improved and
that evaluation needs to be incorporated into the design of financial education programs.

Financial Literacy Surveys and Lessons

The Importance of Financial Literacy

Financial education has always been important for consumers in helping
them budget and manage their income, save and invest efficiently, and
avoid becoming victims of fraud. However, the topic is becoming ever
more important as financial markets and products become more sophisticated and as more risk and responsibility for financial decisions are passed
to households.

Financial education is important for consumers in general but particularly in relation to pensions and retirement saving. Pensions are exception-
ally long-term contracts with wide social coverage, involving individuals
with low levels of education and income who, therefore, often display a
low tolerance for risk. At the same time, private pensions, an increasingly

important source of retirement income, are particularly complex products involving tax issues, assumptions over future salaries, longevity, interest rates, and so on. In addition, various demographic and social factors—including increasing life expectancies and the rise of defined contribution pensions that rely on individual choice—are making the risks individuals face in relation to private pensions more severe.

Financial Literacy Surveys

Financial literacy surveys conducted in recent years in OECD countries show that consumers have low levels of financial literacy and lack awareness of the need to be financially educated in general and in relation to retirement saving specifically.[3]

A survey conducted for the National Council on Economic Education in 2005 shows that financial knowledge is sorely deficient for working-age adults and high school students; the finding for high school students is confirmed by the Jump$tart Coalition for Personal Financial Literacy, as reported by Mandell in chapter 9 of this volume. Similarly, a survey by John Hancock Financial Services found that less than one-quarter of Americans of working age consider themselves to be "knowledgeable investors," and even among this group there is considerable confusion about financial matters (Francis 2004).

Americans' lack of financial knowledge has been confirmed by Hilgert, Hogarth, and Beverly (2003), who examined the responses to a twenty-eight-question true/false financial literacy quiz, with questions examining knowledge about credit, saving patterns, mortgages, and general financial management. Overall, this study found that respondents could answer only two-thirds of the questions correctly. Respondents were least knowledgeable about mutual funds and the stock market: only half knew that mutual funds do not pay a guaranteed rate of return, and 56 percent knew that "over the long term, stocks have the highest rate of return on money invested." These findings are confirmed by other studies on smaller and more specific samples, such as Moore (2003), who also documents low levels of literacy among mortgage borrowers in Washington State. Lusardi and Mitchell (2006) examined financial literacy among a sample of older respondents (50 and older) and found that only one-third of respondents could do basic calculations, had a grasp of the effects of inflation, and understood risk diversification. In another study on the early baby boomers (those age 51–56 in 2004), they found that many respondents did not know about the working of interest compounding (see Lusardi and Mitchell 2007b). Other studies, such as Agnew and Szykman (2005), compare level of actual and self-reported knowledge and report that many respondents are not aware of or overestimate their level of financial knowledge.

In Japan, the Consumer Survey on Finance found that 71 percent of adult respondents have no knowledge about investment in equities and bonds, 57 percent have no knowledge of financial products in general, and 29 percent have no knowledge about insurance, pensions, and tax. Yet defined contribution plans, introduced in Japan in 2001, require workers to make decisions about investments in equities, bonds, and other financial products (Central Council for Financial Services Information 2002).

In the United Kingdom, the Financial Services Agency ranks as one of its main concerns the fact that consumers are making financial decisions based on inadequate understanding (Wheatcroft 2004). An Australian survey of adults notes that 21 percent of those who received and read their superannuation statement did not understand it. In fact, 29 percent of respondents cannot identify asset allocation from a superannuation statement, and 38 percent cannot identify the five-year investment performance from the same statement. Only 37 percent of Australian respondents have determined how much they will actually need to save for retirement. Only 19 percent have used an Internet calculator to compare the effects of interest rates and fees on investments. Finally, 32 percent of respondents think that saving money in a bank account is an appropriate retirement investment vehicle (ANZ Banking Group 2003).

These findings about low levels of financial literacy are of concern because there is evidence from surveys in a number of countries that individuals are not saving enough for retirement. For example, a report from New Zealand concluded that many individuals are either unwilling or not able to save enough for retirement, adding that about 30 percent of households spend more than they earn (Weir 2004). A survey from the Bank of Ireland Life revealed concerns that even those who are saving are not saving enough, adding that only about 52 percent of workers age 20–69 are investing in a pension at all (*Business World* 2004). According to a survey by the Employee Benefit Research Institute, four out of ten American workers state that they are not putting aside any money for retirement (see Helman and Paladino 2004).

A survey by the Royal Bank of Canada found that respondents consider choosing the right investments for a retirement saving plan to be more stressful than going to the dentist (*Canadian Press* 2005). That individuals find making financial decisions difficult and stressful is due not only to a lack of financial knowledge but also to the fact that many consumers feel either that financial information is difficult to find and understand or that there is so much information that they are overwhelmed, a finding confirmed in the survey by Lusardi, Keller, and Keller, discussed in this volume.

Financial Literacy Surveys and Implications for Financial Education Programs

Responses to financial literacy surveys indicate that many consumers have little knowledge about common financial products and lack information on such financial concepts as basic as interest compounding, risk diversification, and the relationship between risk and return. Thus, providers will need to focus on providing financial education programs through a variety of channels to reach as many consumers as possible and on ensuring that this information is easy for consumers to understand. Further, although financial literacy levels are low in general for consumers, they are especially low for certain groups of consumers, such as the less educated, those at the lower end of the income distribution, and minorities. Thus, policy makers should consider targeting financial education programs to the groups of consumers who are most in need of it. Policy makers will also need to decide the best way to convey this information to target audiences.

The fact that consumers feel more confident than their actual financial knowledge warrants suggests that an important focus of financial education programs needs to be increasing consumers' awareness of their need for financial information. If consumers are not aware that they need financial information, they will not seek it out. Thus policy makers need to think about the best ways to reach these consumers and convince them that they need financial education. As an example, policy makers might consider conducting national campaigns to raise awareness about the importance of understanding financial issues.

Consumers receive financial information through a variety of sources, and these sources tend to differ according to demographic characteristics. Many consumers, notably those with lower incomes, receive financial information through television programs. A large number of consumers prefer to receive financial information through personal contact, such as consumer help lines or personal advisors. Policy makers will need to think about the most effective delivery channel for the consumers they are targeting.

Behavioral Economics and Implications for
Financial Education Programs

FINDINGS FROM THE LITERATURE ON BEHAVIORAL ECONOMICS. Comple-
menting these financial literacy surveys, there have been an increasing
number of studies in behavioral economics that relate financial and saving behavior to psychological factors. For example, several studies find that
while a certain percentage of consumers are dedicated savers who think
that individuals should take responsibility for their retirement, a much
larger percentage have a "live for today" attitude and prefer spending
money to saving it. Other studies find that many households would like to
save more but lack the willpower or are overwhelmed by too much choice.
The findings of these studies and the existence of heterogeneous saving
behavior across consumers have important implications for the design and
implementation of effective financial education programs.

MacFarland, Marconi, and Utkus (2004) studied the link between psychological attitudes toward money and retirement planning using the results of a survey of 1,141 randomly selected individuals in Vanguard record-
keeping plans. The authors found that slightly more than 50 percent of
participants in their sample have no strong retirement goals and lack the
discipline to set and adhere to goals; consider financial matters to be a
source of stress, anxiety, and confusion; or are uninterested in the future.
For individuals such as these, retirement plans that rely on the voluntary
decisions of participants will have only a limited ability to assure retirement security. These findings suggest that in order to meet the needs of
those consumers who are nonplanners, financial education programs will
need to emphasize simpler decisions, less information, reduced complexity,
fewer choices, and tangible present-day (as opposed to some future day)
benefits. The authors conclude that what might be best for this nonplanner
group is automatic enrollment in a 401(k) plan with appropriate contribution rates and investment allocation defaults so that even if they do nothing they will approach an adequate level of saving for retirement.

Choi et al. (2002) studied the impact of automatic enrollment in 401(k)
plans using both a survey of individual saving and an analysis of administrative data on the 401(k) saving behavior of employees in several large
corporations that had implemented changes in their defined contribution
plans. The authors determined that almost none of the employees who reported that they intended to increase their saving rate actually did so. One
explanation for this behavior is that rather than take action to increase

their saving or enroll in a retirement saving plan, employees will often do what is easiest, which might be nothing, a phenomenon that the authors refer to as a "passive decision" or following the "path of least resistance." However, by changing the design of 401(k) plans so that the default is automatic enrollment when the employee becomes eligible, employers can use this employee inertia to greatly increase participation rates with few employees ever taking action to disenroll. With automatic enrollment, participation rates after six months of tenure rose from between 26 and 43 percent to between 86 and 96 percent. The authors conclude that plan design can significantly affect the saving behavior of individuals. The caveat here is that because few employees opt out of default options, employers' choices of default saving rates and default investment funds have significant effects on the saving levels of employees and have to be chosen with great care. For example, setting the default to a low percentage rate may still result in insufficient retirement saving.

Thaler and Benartzi (2004) address the issue of low saving rates in 401(k) plans and suggest an approach for increasing those rates. They base their approach on research showing that individuals prefer future opportunities to save over current ones, that because of inertia and procrastination individuals tend to stay in a program once enrolled, and that because of loss aversion individuals are reluctant to increase their retirement saving if this means a reduction in take-home pay. This research on individuals' behavior was used to design the Save More Tomorrow (SMarT) program, which gives workers the option to commit themselves now to increase their saving rate later, for example, each time they get a raise. This program has been introduced in several firms. Where it was used in conjunction with an investment consultant who met with the employees and discussed saving options, the workers who joined the SMarT plan more than tripled their saving rates in 28 months from 3.5 to 13.6 percent.

Research also shows that the number of funds offered by a 401(k) plan has an effect on participation.[4] Recent research on consumer choice has found that too many options lead to "choice overload," with the result that consumers are less motivated to choose and less motivated to commit to that choice (Iyengar, Huberman, and Jiang 2004). Too many options increase the likelihood of not choosing optimally and thus increase the burden on consumers. This burden is likely to be even higher if there are costs associated with making a nonoptimal choice or if consumers would need to commit significant time and effort in order to make informed comparisons among available options. This research finds that participation rates peak when only two funds are offered. As the number of funds increases, participation rates decline. Each time the number of funds is increased by ten there is a corresponding decrease of 1.5–2 percent in the participation rate. So, while participation stood at 75 percent when only two funds were offered, it went to a low of approximately 60 percent when fifty-nine funds were offered. For plan providers dealing simultaneously with workers who have very little knowledge and who need simple explanations and limited choices and with workers who are quite sophisticated and want detailed information and more choices, one solution is the use of a "tiered" approach. In such an approach, the simplest explanations and most limited number of choices are offered in the lowest tier. However, one of the available choices in this lowest tier is an option called "more funds" or "more information." By selecting this option, a worker would be able to access a second tier where additional, more sophisticated investment opportunities would be offered.

FINANCIAL EDUCATION AND OTHER APPROACHES TO RETIREMENT SAVING. Behavioral economics shows that there are some population groups that cannot or will not save for retirement. Financial education should therefore be combined with other mechanisms—such as improved disclosure, automatic enrollment, limited investment options, and well-structured defaults—in order to increase the adequacy and security of retirement saving. At the Financial Education Project, we developed a diagram (figure 13.1) that explains the relationship of financial education to other approaches, with the common goal being the attainment of adequate retirement income.

OECD Recommendations on the Design and Implementation of Financial Education Programs

In 2005, the OECD Council approved its *Recommendation on Principles and Good Practices for Financial Education and Awareness* (OECD 2005b). The recommendation included a definition of financial education as "the process by which financial consumers/investors improve their understanding of financial products, concepts and risks and, through information, instruction and/or objective advice, develop the skills and confidence to become more aware of financial risks and opportunities, to make informed choices, to know where to go for help, and to take other effective actions to improve their financial well-being" (Annex, first principle).

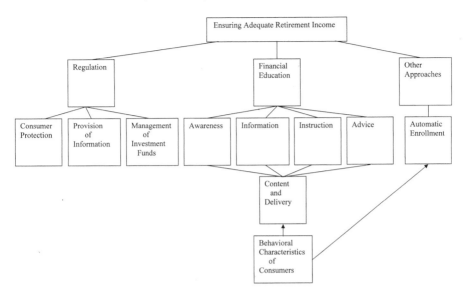

FIGURE 13.1 Tools for achieving adequate retirement incomes.

Thus, financial education goes beyond the simple provision of financial information and advice.

The principles and good practices were designed to provide guidance on improving financial education and awareness in OECD and non-OECD countries. They were drawn from the financial literacy studies and behavioral finance research outlined here as well as surveys of financial education programs and experience in OECD member countries. Several examples of these principles and good practices are presented here:

- Financial education programs should focus on high-priority issues, which, depending on national circumstances, may include important aspects of financial life planning, such as basic saving, private debt management, or insurance as well as prerequisites for financial awareness, such as elementary financial mathematics and economics. The awareness of future retirees about the need to assess the financial adequacy of their current public or private pension schemes and to take appropriate action when needed should be encouraged.
- National campaigns should be encouraged to raise awareness of the population about the need to improve their understanding of financial risks and ways to protect against financial risks through adequate saving, insurance, and financial education. Specific Web sites should be promoted to provide relevant,

user-friendly financial information to the public. Warning systems by consumer, professional, or other organizations on high-risk issues that may be detrimental to the interests of the financial consumers (including cases of fraud) should be promoted. Financial education should be provided in a fair and unbiased manner. Programs should be coordinated and developed with efficiency.

- Financial education should start at school. People should be educated about financial matters as early as possible in their lives (see the chapter by Mandell in this volume).[5] Financial education should be regarded as a lifelong, ongoing, and continuous process.

- Financial institutions' accountability and responsibility should be encouraged not only in providing information and advice on financial issues but also in promoting financial awareness in their clients, especially for long-term commitments and commitments that represent a substantial proportion of current and future income. Financial institutions should be encouraged to provide information at several different levels in order to best meet the needs of consumers. Financial institutions should be encouraged to train their staff on financial education and develop codes of conduct for the provision of general advice about investment and borrowing. Financial institutions should be encouraged to clearly distinguish among financial education, financial information, and commercial financial advice.

- International cooperation on financial education should be promoted, including the use of the OECD as an international forum to exchange information on recent national experiences in financial education.

Current Financial Education Programs

The OECD's survey of financial education programs in member countries identified nineteen countries that already provide, or are planning to provide, workers with information about pensions and how to invest their savings for retirement: Australia, Austria, Canada, Czech Republic, Finland, Germany, Hungary, Ireland, Italy, Japan, Mexico, the Netherlands, New Zealand, Poland, Portugal, Sweden, Turkey, the United Kingdom, and the United States.[6]

The most common way of providing retirement saving information is through publications. These come in a variety of forms including brochures, magazines, booklets, guidance papers, newsletters, annual reports, direct mail documents, letters, and disclosure documents. The majority of providers of these publications are from the public (or semipublic) sector: government agencies, ministries (of finance and social affairs), central banks, and regulatory and supervisory authorities. Consumers' and employees' associations as well as pension fund organizations are also important providers of these publications. Most publications are intended for a broad selection of investor population groups, but a few target specific groups, including employees and members of specific pension funds.

The next most frequently used method of providing retirement saving information is through Web sites. The topics covered in these Web sites are similar to those of publications. Most sites are intended for all investor population groups. An example of such a site is that of the Investor Education Fund in Canada, which contains several investment calculators and a variety of resources to help investors determine their risk level. In contrast, one initiative in Poland is targeted particularly to insurance and pension fund clients. Another project, in Sweden, is a Web portal grouping together the numerous information pages and Web sites already in existence that provide information and advice on the many different pension systems available to future Swedish retirees (see the chapter by Sundén in this volume on Swedish pensions).

Training courses, such as retirement seminars, are also often used to deliver financial information on pensions. Providers range from employers (United States) to pension fund organizations (the Netherlands) and an independent retirement investment information service (Australia). Courses also tend to be targeted at a specific population group—employees or company board members and/or policy makers, for example.

A number of countries have undertaken public education campaigns for the promotion of financial education on investment and saving. Providers of these campaigns span the public, semipublic, private, and independent nonprofit sectors and include regulatory and supervisory bodies, government agencies, and consumer associations. They also include a variety of provision methods—brochures, Web sites, radio, television, and so on.

For some countries, it is governments and regulators that provide information and education on general issues, while financial institutions provide more specific product information. In others, regulations exist on the types of information employers can provide. It is important to have some coordination on the provision of information because, although information about pensions is widely available, people do not know which sources of information to trust, how to access this information, or how the information relates to their circumstances. Successful programs have been shown to be ones with strong leaders but involving many different partners (for example, the Pensions Awareness Campaign in Ireland). See the appendix for examples of the different roles various parties play in financial education and awareness campaigns.

Improving Financial Education Programs

The experience of the OECD's Financial Education Project has shown that insights into improving financial education programs can be found in the responses to financial literacy surveys and in the research based on behavioral economics. Evaluations of financial education programs are another avenue for analyzing the effectiveness of financial education programs and assessing which approaches have worked well.

Evaluations and Implications of Employer-provided
Financial Education Programs

Several studies have evaluated the effect of retirement seminars. For example, one study found that participation in and contributions to voluntary saving plans (401[k] plans) are greater when employers offer frequent retirement seminars (Bayer, Bernheim, and Scholz 1996). The authors found that non–highly compensated workers experience the largest effects, with a 12-percentage-point increase in participation rates and a 1-percentage-point increase in the contribution rate.[7] Highly compensated workers experience an increase in participation of 6 percentage points but no increase in contribution rate. Lusardi (2004) also found that attending a retirement seminar increases workers' saving. The effect of the seminars is especially strong for those with low levels of education and those with low levels of saving. Using data from the Health and Retirement Study, she found that attending retirement seminars increases financial wealth by 18 percent. For those at the bottom of the distribution, the increase in financial wealth is 70 percent. Another study, by Clark and d'Ambrosio, discussed in this volume, finds that 40 percent of the participants changed either their retirement income goal or their retirement age goal after attending a financial education seminar. However, there was limited follow-through on the part of participants on plans to increase retirement saving.

The evidence on the effectiveness of brochures and other written material is also mixed. Bayer, Bernheim, and Scholz (1996) found that written materials, such as newsletters and summary plan descriptions, have no effect on participation and contribution rates. However, Clark and Schieber (1998), using employment records gathered by Watson Wyatt Worldwide from nineteen firms covering 40,000 employees, found that certain types of written material do have an effect. They compared three levels of plan communications: distribution of plan enrollment forms and required periodic statements of account balances, provision of generic newsletters related to participation in 401(k) plans, and provision of materials specifically tailored to the 401(k) plan sponsored by the individual company. The authors found that relative to only having the required information, the provision of generic newsletters increases participation by 15 percentage points, while the provision of information specific to the individual company's 401(k) plan increases participation by 21 percentage points; thus, providing both generic and tailored information can increase participation rates by 36 percentage points.

A survey by Ernst & Young (2004) of human resources and employee benefits professionals in a cross section of large employers found that personalized counseling programs are most important in changing participant behavior and that financial information alone is not sufficient. In most of the firms surveyed there is little response to traditionally provided financial education such as brochures upon enrollment and quarterly statements thereafter. When employers use more personalized programs such as telephone or in-person counseling, there is a substantial increase in the percentage of workers who raise their contributions to their 401(k) plans. The study concluded that one-on-one counseling is better able to help employees understand the importance of saving and to equip them to determine the best course of action to meet their financial needs. However, such counseling can be expensive for employers to provide.

There are several caveats about the evaluations of financial education programs. The evaluation of financial education programs is in its early stages. As the OECD (2005a) report on financial education noted, there have been relatively few evaluations conducted of employer-provided financial education programs. Many of these evaluations are subjective in that they asked participants in the program to assess how much they had learned and whether their behavior would change as a result of what they had learned. There was no follow-up to determine whether the behavior of these participants had actually changed. There can be a big difference between what individuals plan to do and what they actually do, as the studies mentioned previously in the text have shown. Further, evaluations of those who attended workplace seminars might suffer from a bias in that workers who attend such seminars might be more disposed to change their behavior than those who do not attend. In other words, their behavior might not be representative of the average worker. This latter limitation also affects objective evaluations of financial education programs. Objective evaluations identify some goal, such as an increase in participation rates or in contribution rates to a defined contribution plan, and then use data and statistical techniques to determine whether there is a significant relationship between attendance at a financial education program and a change in the goal variable.

Providers of financial education programs often lack the expertise and experience to conduct effective evaluations. As a result, there might not be a clear idea of what the goal of the program should be or how it should be measured. Measures of success vary by type of program; what defines success will differ depending upon whether the program targets workers, consumers in debt, or individuals without a bank account. Even when the goal is identifiable and measurable, it might still be costly to gather and analyze the necessary data.

There is also disagreement in the literature about whether the evaluation should take place at the program level or whether there should be an evaluation of the impact on the larger community or on policy. Some researchers argue that evaluations should not be summative—that is, they should not attempt to measure whether the programs had an impact— but rather formative; in other words, they should help organizations and programs to improve (Snibbe 2006). In addition, some of the behavioral change that these financial education programs are trying to foster will come slowly, so that progress might be best measured over years rather than weeks or months. Finally, the only way to demonstrate that a particular program is having an effect beyond what individuals could have done for themselves is to conduct studies that have both a treatment group and a control group and follow individuals over a long period of time. However, such studies often involve large costs in terms of time, staff, and funding to gather and evaluate the necessary data. For all of these reasons, evaluation is rarely built into the program from the beginning, but this is starting to change, as we describe below.

Improving Evaluation of Financial Education Programs

Despite the issues mentioned above, there are a number of organizations that are looking at program evaluation to see whether measures can be de-

vised that will improve programs and assess impact.[8] Some have called for
the development of national standards for the evaluation of financial education programs. The one thing all of these approaches have in common is
an emphasis on the importance of including program evaluation in the initial design of the program. We highlight a few of these approaches here.

- The Urban Institute and the Center for What Works,[9] through the Outcome Indicators Project, have collaborated on an approach that measures program performance, developing what they refer to as a "common framework"—a set of
  common outcomes and outcome indicators—that nonprofit organizations can
  use to measure performance. The Web site for the Outcome Indicators Project
  contains outcomes and performance indicators for fourteen specific program
  areas, including adult education and family literacy.
- The Financial Education Evaluation Toolkit, produced by the National Endowment for Financial Education, provides program-specific evaluation.[10] Making
  use of an online database and companion manual, the toolkit provides information on writing program objectives, identifying program impact indicators,
  determining the type of evaluation for each program (one-time, short programs;
  long programs; multisession programs), designing evaluation instruments, and
  reporting program impact. Separate sections of the toolkit are devoted to describing the evaluation planning process, taking readers step-by-step through
  the online evaluation database and analyzing and summarizing the evaluation
  data to most effectively improve financial education programs.
- A study by the New Zealand Retirement Commission looks at measuring
  program impact in the broadest sense.[11] This study proposes a comprehensive
  framework that could be used to evaluate a specific program or a series of initiatives. The framework addresses five different aspects of measurement that
  are involved in program evaluation, such as objectives, costs, program improvements, and effectiveness at both a program and a wider level. Although not
  all five aspects of the framework would necessarily be applicable to each program, the framework would provide structure for program providers in thinking
  about evaluation. These five aspects are listed below:
  - Need: What objectives does the program address?
  - Accountability: How much is the program used and how much does it
    cost?
  - Fine-tuning: How could the program be improved?
  - Micro Impact: How effective is the program against its objectives?
  - Macro Impact: What impact is the program having relative to the big policy
    picture and compared with other policy initiatives?

Conclusions

Financial education is increasingly needed not only because consumers are taking on more responsibility for their financial decisions, especially with respect to retirement saving, but also because surveys across OECD countries indicate low levels of financial literacy, both generally and specifically with respect to pensions and retirement saving.

The provision of financial education can benefit from the findings of both financial literacy surveys and behavioral economics research. Lessons can be drawn from financial literacy surveys in relation to the design and implementation of financial education programs (for example, use a variety of channels to reach consumers, promote easy access and simple language, and target the most vulnerable groups). Such lessons are highlighted in the OECD's *Recommendation on Principles and Good Practices for Financial Education and Awareness.* Behavioral economics studies show that some individuals cannot or will not save, and, therefore, other complementary methods (such as consumer protection or automatic enrollment into retirement saving schemes) might need to be used in parallel with financial education programs to improve the level and efficiency of saving.

More countries are offering financial education programs and are thus increasingly concerned with the effectiveness of these programs. Although little evaluation has yet been undertaken, some initial lessons can be drawn, including that seminars and personalized programs and counseling can have a significant effect on saving levels and behavior. Evaluation methodology will need to be improved (most likely through learning from experience in other fields), and evaluation will need to be applied more widely, ideally being incorporated into the design of the financial education program.

Appendix

This appendix reports the experience of selected OECD countries.[12]

Government Awareness Campaigns

AUSTRALIA: This education campaign, implemented by the Financial Literacy Foundation in coordination with the Australian Securities and Investment Commission and the Australian Tax Office, includes four main activities that aim to raise awareness: a call center to reply to questions regarding fund choice; the Super Choice Internet site; written publications targeted at employees and employers informing them of their obligations and rights; and an advertising initiative informing employers and employees of their obligations and rights provided by the choice law. A recent evaluation of the campaign's first phase concluded that consumers and employers rated the initiative highly. The campaign was further developed, particularly among employer groups, in 2006.

ITALY: This campaign, designed by the Ministry of Labor in cooperation with the pensions supervisor, will provide workers with information on all aspects of reform of the Italian pensions scheme, on the characteristics of different pension plans, and on the different choices available to workers. The campaign will likely include a dedicated Internet site with links to appropriate pension-related sites, a telephone call center with operators knowledgeable about the reform, a brochure describing the reform and the choices that workers need to make (to be sent to all private sector employees), and announcements and advertising in the media (newspapers, magazines, radio, and television).

NEW ZEALAND: As part of the KiwiSaver initiative, a new voluntary work-based retirement saving scheme, the government has developed a national financial education campaign. The purpose of this educational campaign is to provide workers with the basic tools required to make simple financial decisions. Initially, the campaign will provide workers with information that will enable them to decide whether KiwiSaver is appropriate for them, if it will help them achieve their saving goals, and if they can afford to participate. Officials are hoping that the KiwiSaver educational campaign will be able to build on and complement financial education work already being conducted by a number of government and nongovernment departments and agencies.

UNITED STATES: A public information campaign, Choose to Save, promotes saving today in order to ensure a secure financial future. The program, sponsored by the nonprofit Employee Benefit Research Institute, is delivered nationally using a wide range of media including newspapers, radio, television, and the Internet; train and bus advertisements; and conferences. Partners such as the United States Department of Labor cooperate on producing written materials including booklets (*The Power to Choose)* and brochures (*Top Ten Ways to Save for Retirement)*. Public service announcements originally developed for radio and television stations in just one metropolitan area are now broadcast in forty-nine states. Internet tools are also provided, including the *Ballpark Estimate Retirement Planning Worksheet* (available at http://www.choosetosave.org/ballpark/), which helps consumers estimate how much they need for retirement saving, and over one hundred online financial calculators, which assist investors with a wide range of financial-planning issues including credit, budgeting, home mortgages, and all aspects of their future financial security.

Pension Regulators and Securities Market Supervisors — Information Provision

MEXICO: The pension reform of 1997, which replaced the country's pay-as-you-go system with a defined contribution system, generated a need to provide more information for workers and to introduce them to a basic financial education scheme related to the pension system. The Mexican government agency Consar is responsible for disseminating information on the new pension system, which it does through a permanent information campaign that is organized in partnership with unions, employer associations, and the financial entities managing the individual accounts in the new pension system. The campaign's main goal is to generate interest and concern among employees about preparing effectively for their retirement. The campaign uses the Internet and all media channels (television, radio, newspapers, magazines, billboards) for its principal delivery methods.

SPAIN: The supervision of pension funds is carried out by the General Directorate of Insurance and Pension Funds. On the Web site of this directorate, members of pension funds can find information about balance sheets and profit and loss accounts of pension funds, registration, regulation on courses, sectorial statistics, consultations to clarify regulations, frequently asked questions, and the process for making a complaint against the managing entity.

ITALY: The Web site of the securities markets' supervisory authority, Consob, features an Investors' Corner to draw investors' attention to relevant information. Consob's Investors' Corner provides information on frauds or abusive activities, signing an investment contract, the risks of investments in financial instruments, and the educational campaigns sponsored by Consob as well as other helpful information pages. These pages include information in plain language about mutual funds as well as calculators to make it easier for investors to compare financial products.

POLAND: The Polish Securities and Exchange Commission, a central government authority, produced an Investor's Guide in 2003, which included basic information on investing in the Polish capital market. Updated and reissued in 2004, this guide initiated a series of brochures targeted at beginner investors (that is, those with no dealings in the capital markets as yet who want to learn about investment possibilities or those who have just begun investing in the capital markets). Three Investor's Guides, entitled Investment Funds, What to Invest in—Investments ABC, and Sources of Information on the Capital Market, were published in 2004.

Social Partners and Others — Instruction

AUSTRIA: A wide variety of investment publications are offered by private, nonprofit entities such as the employees' association, the Austrian Chamber of Labour

(BAK). BAK publishes and distributes brochures targeted at employees (such as The Savings Book, Financial Investment and Financial Advisor, Building Loan Agreement, 10 Steps to Employee Assessment). These brochures cover issues specific to employees and include information on all kinds of investment products in which they could potentially be interested, including stocks, securities, and funds. For each particular investment product discussed, the publications also point out the associated advantages, disadvantages, and risks. Published in October 2003, these brochures are also available on the Internet.

CZECH REPUBLIC: Fit for Investment, a program targeting private investors that was initiated in 2002, is provided by ČEKIA (an information agency). The main aims of the program are to enhance the knowledge of public investors about investment principles and to reinforce trust in the capital market. The program does this through a series of training courses and annual conferences. They attract more than three hundred individual investors every year in most major cities, but mainly in Prague.

UNITED KINGDOM: The Trade Union Congress (TUC) in the United Kingdom is a good example of the role that trade unions can play in financial education relating to pensions. In addition to keeping members informed and knowledgeable regarding the pension environment and reforms (via detailed briefings and reports on pension policy), the organization also provides specific information and training relating to pensions. Publications provide members with detailed information on pensions, and leaflets have been targeted specifically at young members to highlight the need to save early in life. The TUC also provides training for pension fund trustees.

Employers — Financial Advice

JAPAN: In the defined contribution plans introduced in Japan beginning in 2001, participants make their own investment decisions and bear the investment risk. However, the new Defined Contribution Pension Law (DCPL) requires sponsoring employers to provide "investment education" to participants so that they can make investments based on their own responsibility (DCPL, Art. 22). Investment education includes information on defined contribution plans, other corporate plans, and public pensions; characteristics of financial products such as bank deposits, investment trusts, bonds, stocks, and insurance; and basics of investment such as types and characteristics of risk and return. An employer can entrust the investment education duty to an operation management institution. In this case, the employer is under the duty of care in designating and supervising the operational management institution (see Morito 2006).

UNITED STATES: Employer-provided financial education programs include those operated by companies such as United Parcel Service (UPS; since 2000) and Weyerhaeuser Ltd. (since 1984) on long-term planning for saving and retirement.

Both initiatives include classes of one or two days in length and are offered at regular intervals, with keen support from management. They are targeted at specific age groups and provide employee participants with a good range of resources and written materials (such as course book manuals that include explanations as to how company benefits fit into broader financial-planning strategies). The UPS program offers a Web-based service assisting employees with the development of a personal financial action plan as well as computer software providing advice on debt management, budgeting, insurance, and retirement and personal saving. The Weyerhaeuser program covers nonfinancial advice for employees, such as how to improve their quality of life and maintain good health (Braunstein and Welch 2002).

Notes

The analysis, comments, and conclusions set forth in this paper represent the work of the authors and do not represent the views of the OECD or of the Board of Governors of the Federal Reserve System, the Federal Reserve Banks, or their staff. The authors would like to thank Maarten van Rooij for suggestions and comments on an earlier draft of this paper.

1. The OECD is an international organization made up of thirty member countries working together to compare policy experiences, seek answers to common problems, identify good practice, and coordinate domestic and international policies. The OECD member countries are Australia, Austria, Belgium, Canada, the Czech Republic, Denmark, Finland, France, Germany, Greece, Hungary, Iceland, Ireland, Italy, Japan, Korea, Luxembourg, Mexico, the Netherlands, New Zealand, Norway, Poland, Portugal, the Slovak Republic, Spain, Sweden, Switzerland, Turkey, the United Kingdom, and the United States.

2. The information presented in this chapter is largely based on the OECD's recent report on financial education (OECD 2005a).

3. For additional information on financial literacy in the United States and selected foreign countries, see Lusardi and Mitchell (2007a).

4. See the chapter by Sundén in this volume that shows that Sweden has offered its citizens many funds (about eight hundred) to choose from, with Swedes increasingly selecting the default option.

5. Because evidence on the effectiveness of financial education offered in high school is limited, it might be important to start financial education as early as possible and to look for ways to increase its effectiveness.

6. A thorough review of financial education programs in the United States can be found in Hogarth (2006).

7. Given that the average contribution rate is 3 percent, an increase of 1 percentage point represents an increase of 33 percent in the contribution rate.

8. For an overview of the current state of financial education and program evaluation in the United States and an assessment of critical gaps in program evaluation see Lyons et al. (2006).

9. For additional information on the Outcome Indicators Project, see http://www.urban.org/center/cnp/Projects/outcomeindicators.cfm.

10. For additional information on the Financial Education Evaluation Toolkit, see http://www.nefe.org/eval/.

11. For additional information on this study, see http://www.retirement.org.nz/files/Alison_OConnell_Pres_1Dec06.pdf.

12. Unless otherwise indicated, the sources for the example financial education programs illustrated in this section come from responses to OECD questionnaires on financial education, sent either to delegates of the OECD's Committee on Financial Markets in 2004 or to delegates of the OECD's Working Party on Private Pensions in 2005.

References

Agnew, J., and L. Szykman. 2005. Asset Allocation and Information Overload: The Influence of Information Display, Asset Choice and Investor Experience. *Journal of Behavioral Finance* 6: 57–70.

ANZ Banking Group. 2003. *ANZ Survey of Adult Financial Literacy in Australia.* Melbourne, Australia: ANZ Banking Group.

Bayer, P., D. Bernheim, and K. Scholz. 1996. The Effects of Financial Education in the Workplace: Evidence from a Survey of Employers. NBER Working Paper No. 5655. National Bureau of Economic Research, Cambridge, MA.

Braunstein, S., and C. Welch. 2002. Financial Literacy: An Overview of Practice, Research and Policy. *Federal Reserve Bulletin* 88: 445–57.

Business World. 2004. BoI Warns—1 M Have No Pension Plan. September 27.

Canadian Press. 2005. Retirement Saving, Financial Planning More Stressful Than Seeing the Dentist. February 21.

Central Council for Financial Services Information. 2002. *Public Opinion Survey on Household Financial Assets and Liabilities.* Tokyo, Japan: Central Council for Financial Services Information.

Choi, J., D. Laibson, B. Madrian, and A. Metrick. 2002. Defined Contribution Plans: Plan Rules, Participant Decisions, and the Path of Least Resistance. In *Tax Policy and the Economy,* vol. 16 edited by J. Poterba, 67–113. Cambridge, MA: MIT Press.

Clark, R., and M. d'Ambrosio. 2008. Adjusting Retirement Goals and Saving Behavior: The Role of Financial Education. This volume.

Clark, R., and S. Schieber. 1998. Factors Affecting Participation Rates and Contribution Levels in 401(k) Plans. In *Living with Defined Contribution Plans,* edited by O. Mitchell and S. Schieber, 69–96. Philadelphia: University of Pennsylvania Press.

Ernst & Young LLP Human Capital Practice. 2004. *The Role That Financial Education Programs Play in Influencing Participant Behavior in 401(k) Plans.* New York: Ernst & Young LLP.

Francis, D. 2004. Ownership Society: Why the U.S. Can't Buy In. *The Christian Science Monitor.* September 27.

Helman, R., and V. Paladino. 2004. Will Americans Ever Become Savers? The 14th Retirement Confidence Survey, 2004. EBRI Issue Brief 268. Washington, DC: Employee Benefit Research Institute.

Hilgert, M., J. Hogarth, and S. Beverly. 2003. Household Financial Management: The Connection between Knowledge and Behavior. *Federal Reserve Bulletin* 89: 309–22.

Hogarth, J. 2006. Financial Education and Economic Development. Paper prepared for Improving Financial Literacy, an international conference hosted by the Russian G8 presidency in cooperation with the OECD, November 29–30.

Iyengar S., G. Huberman, and W. Jiang. 2004. How Much Choice Is Too Much? Contributions to 401(k) Retirement Plans. In *Pension Design and Structure: New Lessons from Behavioral Finance,* edited by Olivia Mitchell and Stephen Utkus, 83–95. New York: Oxford University Press.

Lusardi A. 2004. Saving and the Effectiveness of Financial Education. In *Pension Design and Structure: New Lessons from Behavioral Finance,* edited by Olivia Mitchell and Stephen Utkus, 157–84. New York: Oxford University Press.

Lusardi, A., and O. Mitchell. 2006. Financial Literacy and Planning: Implications for Retirement Wellbeing. Pension Research Council working paper. The Wharton School, University of Pennsylvania, Philadelphia.

———. 2007a. Baby Boomer Retirement Security: The Role of Planning, Financial Literacy, and Housing Wealth. *Journal of Monetary Economics* 54: 205–24.

———. 2007b. Financial Literacy and Retirement Preparedness: Evidence and Implications for Financial Education. *Business Economics* 42: 35–44.

Lyons, A., L. Palmer, K. Jayaratne, and E. Scherpf. 2006. Are We Making the Grade? A National Overview of Financial Education and Program Evaluation. *Journal of Consumer Affairs* 40: 208–35.

MacFarland, D., C. Marconi, and S. Utkus. 2004. "Money Attitudes" and Retirement Plan Design: One Size Does Not Fit All. In *Pension Design and Structure: New Lessons from Behavioral Finance,* edited by Olivia Mitchell and Stephen Utkus, 97–120. New York: Oxford University Press.

Mandell, L. 2008. Financial Education in High School. This volume.

Moore, D. 2003. Survey of Financial Literacy in Washington State: Knowledge, Behavior, Attitudes, and Experiences. Technical Report No. 03-39. Washington State University, Social and Economic Sciences Research Center.

Morito, Hideyuki. 2006. Reconsidering Japanese Corporate and Personal Pensions: From a Legal Point of View. OECD/INPRS Korea Conference on Private Pensions in Asia, Seoul.

National Council on Economic Education. 2005. What American Teens and Adults
    Know about Economics. Washington, DC: National Council on Economic
    Education.

Organisation for Economic Co-operation and Development (OECD). 2005a. *Im-
    proving Financial Literacy: Analysis of Issues and Policies.* Paris: OECD.

———. 2005b. *Recommendation on Principles and Good Practices for Financial
    Education and Awareness.* Paris: OECD.

Snibbe, A. C. 2006. Drowning in Data. *Stanford Social Innovation Review* Fall:
    39–45.

Sundén, A. 2008. Learning from the Experience of Sweden: The Role of Informa-
    tion and Education in Pension Reform. This volume.

Thaler, R., and S. Benartzi. 2004. Save More Tomorrow: Using Behavioral Econom-
    ics to Increase Employee Saving. *Journal of Political Economy* 112: 164–87.

Weir, J. 2004. The Push to Save for Retirement. *Fairfax New Zealand Limited,*
    August 31.

Wheatcroft, P. 2004. "Lender, Beware" Is FSA's Advice. *The Times,* January 21.

Contributors

RAY BOSHARA is vice president and director of the Asset Building Program at the New America Foundation. The program aims to significantly broaden the owner-ship of assets in the United States and around the world. Previously, he served in the U.S. Congress as a senior legislative assistant to Representative Tony P. Hall and as a professional staff member of the House Select Committee on Hunger. He has also worked for the United Nations and in the private sector for the Corporation for Enterprise Development (CFED), the Aspen Institute, and Ernst & Young. Mr. Boshara has testified before the House Ways and Means Committee and the Senate Finance Committee and has advised the Bush and Clinton administrations, as well as leaders in Europe and elsewhere, on asset-building policies. In 2002, he was selected by *Esquire* magazine as one of America's Best and Brightest. A graduate of the John F. Kennedy School of Government at Harvard, Yale Divinity School, and Ohio State University, Mr. Boshara is the recipient of several leadership awards, including a Littauer Fellowship at Harvard and CFED's Asset Building Innovation Award.

DAVID BRAVO is professor of economics and director of the Center of Microdata at the University of Chile. His research interests are labor economics, empirical microeconomics, program evaluation, education, income inequality, and Social Se-curity. He has been the principal investigator on research projects financed by the Chilean Council of Science, the secretaries of labor, education, and finance, and the Research Network of the Inter-American Development Bank. He was advisor to the minister of labor and social security in Chile between 1990 and 1993. He has also worked on several projects involving education and labor markets in Chile and has published several papers and four books on these topics. He is the principal investigator of the First Social Security Survey in Chile. Dr. Bravo has an MA and a PhD from Harvard University.

JEFFREY R. BROWN is the William G. Karnes Professor of Finance at the College of Business at the University of Illinois at Urbana-Champaign and associate director of the National Bureau of Economic Research Retirement Research Center. Prior to joining the Illinois faculty, Dr. Brown was an assistant professor of public policy at Harvard University's John F. Kennedy School of Government. In 2001–2002, he served as senior economist at the White House Council of Economic Advisers, where he focused primarily on Social Security, pension reform, and terrorism risk insurance. He also served on the staff of the President's Commission to Strengthen Social Security. In January 2005, President George W. Bush nominated Dr. Brown to become a member of the Social Security Advisory Board. He is a research fellow with the Employee Benefits Research Institute and a senior fellow of the China Center for Insurance and Social Security Research. Professor Brown is coauthor of the book *The Role of Annuities in Financing Retirement* from MIT Press, and is cofounder and coeditor of the *Journal of Pension Economics and Finance*, published by Cambridge University Press. Dr. Brown has a PhD in economics from the Massachusetts Institute of Technology, an MA in public policy from Harvard University, and a BA from Miami University.

ROBERT L. CLARK is professor of business management and economics at the North Carolina State University College of Management. Dr. Clark has conducted research examining retirement decisions, the choice between defined benefit and defined contribution plans, the impact of pension conversions to defined contribution and cash balance plans, the role of information and education on retirement planning, government regulation of pensions, and Social Security. He has examined the economic responses to population aging in developed countries and has written widely on international retirement plans, especially the Social Security and employer pension systems in Japan. Dr. Clark has also been engaged in a variety of projects assessing the key issues in the economics of higher education and the future of higher education in North Carolina. Dr. Clark has a PhD from Duke University.

MADELEINE D'AMBROSIO is vice president and executive director of the Teachers Insurance and Annuity Association–College Retirement Equities Fund (TIAA-CREF) Institute. The institute's mission is to initiate and support strategic research and educational programs on issues related to pensions and retirement, insurance, investments, corporate governance, higher education, and financial literacy. Ms. d'Ambrosio is a member of the National Academy of Social Insurance, the Cornell Higher Education Research Institute Advisory Board, the American Association of Community Colleges Corporate Council, and the Financial Women's Association. She is also a trustee of the Employee Benefit Research Institute. Ms. d'Ambrosio is the coauthor with Robert L. Clark, North Carolina State University, of *Financial Education and Retirement Savings, Saving for Retirement: The Role of Financial Education,* and *Managing Retirement Accounts: Gender Differences in Response to Financial Education.* Ms. d'Ambrosio has a BA from Manhattanville College.

ALAN L. GUSTMAN is the Lauren M. Berry Professor of Economics at Dartmouth College and a research associate at the National Bureau of Economic Research. He also serves as a co–principal investigator of the Health and Retirement Study and is a member of the Executive Committee of the University of Michigan Retirement Research Center. Dr. Gustman's research has focused on four central issues in labor economics and the economics of aging: retirement, pensions, Social Security, and saving. Together with Thomas Steinmeier, he has examined how retirement is defined and has contributed explanations for the wide differences in retirement behavior among individuals. Moreover, he has investigated the variety of incentives observed in pension plans and the sharp trends in these incentives over time. He has also analyzed how pensions and Social Security affect retirement and saving behavior and has considered related public policy questions pertaining to Social Security, pension regulation, and labor market and retirement income policies. Dr. Gustman has a BA from the City University of New York and a PhD in economics from the University of Michigan.

HOWELL E. JACKSON is vice-dean for budget and the James S. Reid Jr. Professor of Law at Harvard Law School, where he teaches courses on the regulation of financial institutions, securities regulation, pension law, international finance, and analytical methods for lawyers. His research currently deals with the regulation of the international securities market, reform of the Social Security system, problems in consumer finance, and comparative cost-benefit analyses of financial regulation. He is coeditor of *Fiscal Challenges: An Interdisciplinary Approach to Budget Policy,* published by Cambridge University Press; coauthor of the *Regulation of Financial Institutions,* published by West, and of *Analytical Methods for Lawyers,* published by Foundation Press; and author of numerous scholarly articles. Dr. Jackson has served as a consultant to the United States Treasury Department in connection with the Gramm-Leach-Bliley Act and also as an adviser to the United Nations Development Programme, the World Bank/International Monetary Fund, and the Harvard Institute for International Development in connection with various projects involving the reform of financial systems in other countries. He is a trustee of CREF and affiliated TIAA-CREF mutual funds. He has a JD-MBA degree from Harvard University and a BA from Brown University.

ADAM M. KELLER is executive vice president for finance and administration at Dartmouth College. Mr. Keller has been at Dartmouth since 1978, when he joined the Department of Community Medicine. His accomplishments in the department include participation in the creation of the Center for the Evaluative Clinical Sciences, the growth of the New Hampshire–Dartmouth Psychiatric Research Center, the development of Family Medicine, and the construction of a family practice center in Lebanon. For several years, he served as the director of the Dartmouth Primary Care COOP Project, a research network of over one hundred primary care practices in northern New England. In 1991, Mr. Keller joined the dean's office at Dartmouth Medical School as the chief financial officer. From 1995 until June 2003, he served as the associate dean and chief operating officer. Mr. Keller also taught about the economics of primary care practice in the required family medicine clerkship. He has a BA from Harvard University and an MA in public health from the University of Minnesota.

PUNAM ANAND KELLER is the Charles Henry Jones Third Century Professor of Management at the Tuck School of Business at Dartmouth College. Her research field is social marketing, and she is currently the president-elect of the Association for Consumer Research. Her research is based on the marketing principle that social marketing programs need to be customized for different target segments. Her findings demonstrate that risk perceptions and choices are determined by individual differences, including stage in the decision process, mood, prior attitudes, regulatory goals, age, and gender and that it is possible to predict which program will best fit each segment. In addition, her research sheds light on the effectiveness of several message factors used to communicate risk. Dr. Keller publishes her research in marketing, psychology, and health journals. At Dartmouth, Dr. Keller holds joint appointments in the schools of business and medicine. Dr. Keller has a BA in economics and statistics from Elphinston College, Bombay University, an MBA in marketing from the Bajaj Institute of Management, Bombay University, and a PhD in marketing from Northwestern University.

ANNAMARIA LUSARDI is professor of economics at Dartmouth College and a research associate at the National Bureau of Economic Research. She has taught at Dartmouth College, Princeton University, the University of Chicago Harris School of Public Policy, and the University of Chicago Graduate School of Business. From January to June 2008, she was a visiting scholar at Harvard Business School. She is a member of the Technical Review Committee for the Bureau of Labor Statistics National Longitudinal Surveys Program and a member of the Scientific Committee of the Center for Research on Pensions and Welfare Policies (CeRP), Turin, Italy. She has advised the U.S. Treasury, the U.S. Social Security Administration, the Dutch Central Bank, and the Dartmouth-Hitchcock Medical Center on issues related to financial literacy and saving. Dr. Lusardi has won numerous research awards. Among them are a research fellowship from the Irving B. Harris Graduate School of Public Policy Studies at the University of Chicago, a faculty fellowship from the John M. Olin Foundation, and a junior and senior faculty fellowship from Dartmouth College. She is the recipient of the Fidelity Pyramid Prize, awarded to authors of published applied research that best helps address the goal of improving lifelong financial well-being for Americans. Dr. Lusardi has a PhD in economics from Princeton University and a BA in economics from Bocconi University, Milan, Italy.

LEWIS MANDELL is professor of economics and former dean of the School of Management, State University of New York (SUNY) at Buffalo. He is also the principal researcher for the Jump$tart Coalition for Personal Financial Literacy, where he has run the large-scale, biennial, national surveys of the financial literacy of high school seniors since 1997. He began his career at the University of Michigan where he directed the Surveys of Consumer Finances. In addition to his academic positions, he served as the director of economic research for the U.S. Comptroller of the Currency. He is the author of twenty-one books relating to the finances of consumers. In 2004, he received the William E. Odem Visionary Leadership Award in financial literacy, the highest award in the field, and was given the SUNY Chancellor's Award for Outstanding Teaching. Currently, he is a member of the Standing Committee for the new national examination in economics, which was administered by the Department of Education in 2006 as part of the No Child Left Behind Act. Dr. Mandell has a BA from the City College of New York, an MA from Northwestern University, and a PhD from the University of Texas.

OLIVIA S. MITCHELL is the International Foundation of Employee Benefit Plans Professor of Insurance and Risk Management and the executive director of the Pension Research Council at the Wharton School of Business at the University of Pennsylvania. At the University of Pennsylvania, Dr. Mitchell is also the director of the Boettner Center on Pensions and Retirement Research. She is a research associate at the National Bureau of Economic Research and a co-investigator for the AHEAD/Health and Retirement Studies at the University of Michigan. Dr. Mitchell's main areas of research and teaching are private and public insurance, risk management, public finance and labor markets, and compensation and pensions, with a U.S. and an international focus. Dr. Mitchell recently served on President George W. Bush's Commission to Strengthen Social Security. Dr. Mitchell has published extensively in the area of saving, pension, and retirement. Her coauthored study on Social Security reform won the Paul Samuelson Award for outstanding writing on lifelong financial security from TIAA-CREF. Together with Annamaria Lusardi, she is the recipient of the Fidelity Pyramid Prize, awarded to authors of published applied research that best helps address the goal of improving lifelong financial well-being for Americans. Dr. Mitchell has an MA and a PhD in economics from the University of Wisconsin-Madison and a BA in economics from Harvard University.

GARY R. MOTTOLA is a researcher at the Vanguard Center for Retirement Research, where he supports the center's goal of conducting primary research on the saving and investing behavior of Americans. In this role, Dr. Mottola also collaborates with leading academics and other industry researchers on various retirement-related research projects. Dr. Mottola's current research interests include the antecedents and effects of investment menu design in 401(k) plans, trading and investment behavior among retirement plan participants, the impact of workforce diversity on participant behavior within retirement plans, and efficient portfolio decision making by 401(k) participants. Dr. Mottola is a social psychologist who has coauthored several academic publications on intergroup behavior, and he is a visiting scholar at the Wharton School of Business. Dr. Mottola has an undergraduate degree from SUNY Albany, an MA from the City University of New York at Brooklyn, and a PhD from the University of Delaware.

JAMES M. POTERBA is the Mitsui Professor of Economics and the head of the Massachusetts Institute of Technology Economics Department. He is also the director of the Public Economics Research Program at and president and chief executive officer of the National Bureau of Economic Research and a trustee of CREF. His research focuses on how taxation affects the economic decisions of households and firms. His recent work has emphasized the effect of taxation on the financial behavior of households, particularly their saving and portfolio decisions. He has been especially interested in the analysis of tax-deferred retirement saving programs, such as 401(k) plans, and in the role of annuities in financing retirement consumption. In 2005, Dr. Poterba served as a member of the President's Advisory Panel on Federal Tax Reform. He studied economics as an undergraduate at Harvard and has a PhD in economics from Oxford University, where he was a Marshall Scholar.

MICHAEL SHERRADEN is Benjamin E. Youngdahl Professor of Social Development at Washington University in St. Louis. He is also the director of the Center for Social Development and past chair of the PhD program in social work. His work has received widespread recognition for its impact on public policy. He is the creator of the widely praised individual development accounts, a matched savings program designed to help working poor people accumulate assets. Dr. Sherraden's work on assets has influenced policy development in the United Kingdom, Taiwan, Canada, and other countries around the world. He is also engaged in research and policy on civic engagement and productive aging. Dr. Sherraden has served as an adviser and consultant to the White House, the Department of Treasury, the Department of Housing and Urban Development, the Department of Health and Human Services, the Carnegie Council, and many other organizations. He has an MSW and a PhD from the University of Michigan and an AB from Harvard.

BARBARA A. SMITH is a senior supervisory policy analyst in the Consumer and Community Affairs Division of the Board of Governors of the Federal Reserve System. Prior to taking that position, she established and directed the Organisation for Economic Co-operation and Development's (OECD's) Financial Education Project, which produced the first major international study of financial education programs.

She has also worked as a senior economist at the U.S. Government Accountability Office in Washington, D.C., where she was responsible for leading projects on Social Security and pension issues. Dr. Smith has taught economics at Old Dominion University in Norfolk, Virginia, and worked as a research associate at Mathematica Policy Research and as a junior economist at the Council of Economic Advisers. She has a PhD from the University of Michigan.

FIONA STEWART is an administrator in the Financial Affairs Division of the OECD. She coordinates the Working Party on Private Pensions, a group that brings together policy makers and the private sector from the OECD's thirty member countries in addition to nonmembers with observer status (such as Brazil, Chile, India, and Russia). She also works with the International Organization of Pension Supervisors, an international body dedicated to cooperation and research on pension supervisory issues. Prior to joining the OECD, she worked in the investment industry for ten years. As head of American Express Asset Management in Japan, she was responsible for investment in the Asian equity market. She was also part of an international team that invested globally. Ms. Stewart has degrees from Oxford and Johns Hopkins University and a chartered financial analyst qualification.

THOMAS L. STEINMEIER is professor of economics at Texas Tech University, a research economist at the National Bureau of Economic Research, and a co–principal investigator of the Health and Retirement Study. He previously taught at Dartmouth College and Oberlin College. For the last twenty-five years, Steinmeier's research has focused on four central issues in labor economics and the economics of aging: retirement, pensions, Social Security, and savings. Together with Alan Gustman, he has examined how retirement is defined and reasons for the wide differences in retirement behavior among individuals, investigated incentives observed in pension plans and sharp trends in these incentives over time, analyzed how pensions and Social Security affect saving behavior, and considered related public policy questions pertaining to Social Security, pension regulation, and retirement income policies. Dr. Steinmeier has a PhD from Yale University.

ANNIKA SUNDÉN is a research associate at the Swedish Institute for Social Research at Stockholm University and head of the Research Unit at the Swedish Social Insurance Agency. Previously, she was the associate director of research at the Center for Retirement Research at Boston College and an economist at the Federal Reserve Board in Washington, D.C., where she was involved in the design and implementation of the Survey of Consumer Finances. Her research interests include the economics of retirement, pensions and Social Security, and household saving behavior. Her recent publications include *The Swedish Experience with Pension Reform, Coming Up Short: The Challenge of 401(k) Plans,* and *Portfolio Choice, Trading and Returns in a Large 401(k) Plan.* Dr. Sundén has a BS from the Stockholm School of Economics and an MS and PhD in labor economics from Cornell University.

NAHID TABATABAI is a research associate in economics at Dartmouth College. Dr. Tabatabai is the staff person responsible for the labor and pension sections of the Health and Retirement Study (HRS), which is a panel study funded by the National Institute on Aging with over 22,000 participants who represent all persons over 50 in the United States and which permits longitudinal analysis over all interview years. Dr. Tabatabai's responsibilities include ensuring the smooth functioning of the complex HRS panel study design as it affects the labor section, designing research tools for users of the survey, creating measures of pension wealth and incentives from matched employer-provided pension plan descriptions, and facilitating the modernization of question design to capture the changing economic and pension environment affecting the work and saving decisions of older persons. She has a PhD in resource economics from the University of Massachusetts.

PETRA E. TODD is professor of economics at the University of Pennsylvania and a research associate at the National Bureau of Economic Research. Her research focuses on labor economics, econometrics, population and demography, law and economics, and program evaluation. Recently, she has done research on pensions in Chile and evaluated government programs in Mexico. She has won numerous awards, and her research has been supported by the National Institutes of Health, the National Science Foundation, and TIAA-CREF. Dr. Todd has a PhD in economics from the University of Chicago and a BA in economics and English from the University of Virginia.

STEPHEN P. UTKUS is the director of the Vanguard Center for Retirement Research. The center conducts and sponsors research on retirement savings and retirement benefits in the United States. Its work is designed to assist employers, consultants, policy makers, and the media in understanding developments in the U.S. retirement system. Mr. Utkus's current research interests include attitudes and expectations regarding retirement, financial markets, and employer-sponsored retirement plans; the psychological and behavioral aspects of participant decision making; trading and investment behavior among retirement plan participants; fiduciary and governance aspects of retirement programs; and global developments in public and private pension plans. Mr. Utkus is a member of the advisory board of the Wharton Pension Research Council and is a visiting scholar at the Wharton School. He has an undergraduate degree in computer science from the Massachusetts Institute of Technology and an MBA in finance from the Wharton School.

STEVEN F. VENTI is the DeWalt H. Ankeny Professor of Economic Policy and professor of economics at Dartmouth College. He is also a research associate at the

National Bureau of Economic Research. Dr. Venti's research focuses on the relationship between tax policy and saving, the effectiveness of saving incentives, housing policy, and the process of wealth accumulation. He is the recipient of numerous research awards, among them the Paul Samuelson Certificate of Excellence Award from TIAA-CREF. His research has been supported by several institutions, including the National Institute on Aging and the Social Security Administration. He has a PhD and an MA in economics from Harvard University and a BA in economics from Boston College.

LUIS M. VICEIRA is professor of business administration at the Harvard Business School, a faculty research fellow for the National Bureau of Economic Research, a research affiliate at the Centre for Economic Policy Research in London, and a member of the Scientific Council of NETSPAR, which is the network for research on the economics of pensions, aging, and retirement at Tilburg University (The Netherlands). His research focuses on the analysis of asset allocation strategies for long-term investors, both individuals and institutions, in the face of changing interest rates, risk premia, and risk. This research is the subject of his book *Strategic Asset Allocation,* coauthored with John Y. Campbell of Harvard University and published by Oxford University Press in 2002. In 2003, this book received the TIAA-CREF Paul Samuelson Award for outstanding scholarly writing on lifelong financial security. He has also received the 2005 Graham and Dodd Award; the 2004 Prize for Financial Innovation of the Q-Group, Inquire Europe, and Inquire U.K.; the second 2003 Fama/DFA Prize for Capital Markets and Asset Pricing; the second 2000 Inquire Europe Prize; and the 1999 Fame Award for his contributions to the theory and practice of asset management and quantitative investment research. Professor Viceira has an MA and a PhD in economics from Harvard University.

DAVID A. WISE is the John F. Stambaugh Professor of Political Economy at the John F. Kennedy School of Government, Harvard University, and is the director of the Program on the Economics of Aging at the National Bureau of Economic Research. His work focuses on issues related to saving and population aging. His recent books and papers include *Social Security and Retirement around the World, Frontiers in the Economics of Aging, Facing the Age Wave, Inquiries in the Economics of Aging, Social Security and Retirement around the World: Micro-Estimation, The Transition to Personal Accounts and Increasing Retirement Wealth: Macro and Micro Evidence, Aging and Housing Equity: Another Look, Implications of Rising Personal Retirement Saving, The Taxation of Pensions: A Shelter Can Become a Trap, Utility Evaluation of Risk in Retirement Saving Accounts,* and *Analyses in the Economics of Aging.* Dr. Wise has a PhD in economics from the University of California–Berkeley.

Author Index

Page numbers with t indicate table legends, and those with f indicate figure captions. Authors whose names are concealed by the use of et al. *in the text are not reported here; only the first author is included.*

Subject Index

Page numbers with t indicate tables, and those with f indicate figures.

of sales of confidential financial information, 98–99, 101*t*
Securities Exchange Act, section 28e, 93–94
of trilateral dilemmas, 83–100, 101*t*, 107–10, 110n1
Welfare Reform Act, 290
life annuities. *See* annuities
life-cycle funds, 6–7, 35, 127, 140–73
buy-and-hold investment strategy, 154–60
default enrollment, 252
design of, 165–70
human capital considerations, 160–69, 171, 174nn9–10
individualized approaches, 167–69, 172
industry-specific funds, 142
Markowitz's mean-variance analysis framework, 148–49
mean reversion in stock returns, 155–60, 171–72, 174nn6–8
portfolio allocation, 142–48, 153, 154–55, 157–59, 164–67
risk tolerance, 166, 167–68
role-down schedules, 143–48
in Sweden's pension system, 328
wealth and tax considerations, 169–70
life insurance, 195
life-style (risk-based) funds, 141–48, 150–53, 167, 170–71, 173, 173n4
long-term bonds, 150–51, 170–71, 174n9
long-term care insurance, 191

males. *See* gender factors
managed account services, 6, 119–20, 122–23, 133
default plans, 12, 34–35, 119–20, 133, 138n14, 252
efficacy of, 129–32
portfolio allocation actions, 128–30, 135–36
Markowitz, Harry, 148–49
matched savings accounts. *See* individual development accounts
mean returns on U.S. stocks, bonds, and treasury bills, 156–57*f*
mean reversion in stock returns, 155–60, 171–72, 174nn6–8
mean-variance analysis of asset allocations, 148–49

Medicaid, 191
medical expenditure shock, 191, 196
men. *See* gender factors
Merton, Robert, 149
Mexico's financial education and literacy levels, 362
military retirement benefits, 25
Modigliani, Franco, 200
money market funds, 153, 172
money's worth (MW) concept, 186–87
mortality premiums, 180–81
mortality risk, 165, 167
cumulative prospect theory, 194
socioeconomic factors, 186
mortgage brokers
consumer education, 259
trilateral dilemmas of, 102–4, 108, 113nn24–26, 113n29
yield spread premiums, 86–88, 101*t*
Murphy, Paul, 250–51
mutual funds, 140–41
age-based (life-cycle) funds, 141–73
automatic rebalancing, 143
life-style (risk-based) funds, 141–48
transfer agent service contract fees, 96–97, 112nn15–16
12b-1 rule, 93–94, 101*t*
See also life-cycle funds
mutual fund theorem of portfolio choice, 148–49

National Association of Securities Dealers, 94
National Association of State Boards of Education (NASBE), 258
National Council on Economic Education (NCEE), 258, 347
National Endowment for Financial Education, 359
National Income and Product Account (NIPA) wage and salary earnings, 17, 20–21
neoclassical models of savings, 281, 293n1
new pension products, 2, 6–7
New Zealand's financial education and literacy levels, 348, 359, 361
Nyce, Steve, 66
NYSE fixed commissions, 91–93, 101*t*, 102, 112n21